WEST OF 98

WEST OF 98

LIVING AND WRITING THE NEW AMERICAN WEST

Edited by Lynn Stegner and Russell Rowland

With an Introduction by Lynn Stegner

University of Texas Press ⟨⟩ AUSTIN

Parts of "The Conceit of Girls" first appeared in *Jo's Girls: Tomboy Tales of High Adventure, True Grit, and Real Life*, ed. Christian McEwen (Boston: Beacon Press, 1997).

Parts of "Cowboy Up, Cupcake? No Thanks" originally appeared in the magazine *5280*.

"Places Names" from *Dancing on the Edge of the World*, © 1989 by Ursula K. Le Guin, is used by permission of Grove/Atlantic, Inc.

"East to the West" was originally published in *High Country News* (March 2010).

"A Dark Light in the West: Racism and Reconciliation" originally appeared in the Fall 2010 issue of the *Georgia Review* [64(3)], pp. 365–386.

"Covers the Ground" and "The Black-tailed Hare" are © 1996 by Gary Snyder from *Mountains and Rivers Without End*. Reprinted by permission of Counterpoint.

Requests for permission to reproduce material from this work should be sent to:
Permissions
University of Texas Press
P.O. Box 7819
Austin, TX 78713-7819
www.utexas.edu/utpress/about/bpermission.html

♾ The paper used in this book meets the minimum requirements of ANSI/NISO Z39.48-1992 (R1997) (Permanence of Paper).

LIBRARY OF CONGRESS CATALOGING-IN-PUBLICATION DATA

West of 98 : living and writing the new American West / edited by Lynn Stegner and Russell Rowland ; with an introduction by Lynn Stegner. — 1st ed.
   p.   cm.
ISBN 978-0-292-72343-6 (cloth : alk. paper)
ISBN 978-0-292-72686-4 (pbk. : alk. paper)
ISBN 978-0-292-73585-9 (e-book)
   1. American literature—West (U.S.)   2. West (U.S.)—Literary collections.   I. Stegner, Lynn.   II. Rowland, Russell.   III. Title: West of Ninety-eight.
PS561.W35   2011
814'.6080978—dc22

2011014034

The manner of the country makes the usage of life there,
and the land will not be lived in except in its own fashion.

MARY AUSTIN, *LAND OF LITTLE RAIN*

CONTENTS

Space, as anyone with an empty closet or an abandoned heart knows, has a tendency to fill itself up as quickly as possible, often without much conscious awareness of means or consequences. So it was with the western regions of America, once a wilderness frontier that was in effect a line drawn existentially in the sand that tempted, goaded, and by subterranean signals and heraldic entrapments, electrified dreams that had lain numb, and threw open the doors on lives that had become claustrophobic. To talk about the West, how and why it was settled—in truth, colonized—and how it is now after our first full century of widespread settlement, may be a little like dissecting a creature still alive, still moving: parts of it dying or already dead, while others are developing compensatory muscles, adapting, and one hopes, surviving.

Russell Rowland and I crossed paths several years ago in Montana and out of that meeting, and that landscape, (which at the time, I recall, was on fire, as much of the West is each year), grew the idea of a book. It was a solid, if modest, idea—a handful of writers talking about what it means to be a Westerner. Could we open it up and examine the parts, and the sum of the parts, and arrive at some sort of composite that would let us see more or less honestly who we are become, to invoke an arcane syntactical truism? Russell and I kept working our way up the cliff until we found ourselves on top of a mesa where the view was big—very big indeed. Letters of invitation had gone out to members of the literary tribe, the numbers mounting as those who accepted then suggested others, and one day we realized that we had ourselves an old-fashioned fence-painting in the best Tom Sawyer tradition. Sixty-seven writers, each of whom could talk credibly about living west of the 98th meridian, and when and in what form that sensibility of being Western was born in upon them. Among other things, the initiating letter suggested that what we were after was a kind of Greek chorus that might define, remark upon, and otherwise characterize the West as each of us grew to know it, and, equally important, the West that is still becoming. A declaration not of our independence this time, but of our interdependence. In one of the pieces contained in this volume,

Gretel Ehrlich quotes the poet Joseph Brodsky—"that the sole purpose of evolution is beauty." If that is the case, then we have lost a great deal of the West's native or given beauty as we evolve toward another order of beauty, perhaps simply the beauty inherent in a mutually sustainable relationship with landscape and the obduracy of its own rules, and a bond of justice with the peoples who were either displaced or used or abused, or inveigled to serve the purpose of plundering another field of oil, another slope of timber, another vein of mineral wealth.

Let me back up and ask a question that may seem obvious: Why writers? Why not geologists, biologists, historians, or cultural anthropologists? Or, in view of that definitively defining condition of the West, the underscoring beneath the Bottom Line, aridity, why not hydrologists?

Because *how* a thing is conveyed may end up being of greater value than *what* is conveyed. We might have given you the West in what scientists call its general life parameters, its rainfall totals and populations, its geophysical anatomy; we could have exhumed historical facts and factoids, what Kris Saknussemm calls the "theme park" of history; we might have invoked the megafaunal extinctions of the short-faced bear, the giant ground sloth, the mastodon, *Bison antiquus*, the Dire wolf, as lessons in halting the extinctions occurring right now, this very day, like the pika or the sage grouse, the Guadalupe fur seal, or the brown bear, which is disappearing across its entire range largely because our species has been picking them off with guns. We could have talked about water and the preemptive definition that is aridity, and then gone on to the fluid dynamics of the Great Basin, and the collateral water/power wars; or, in a more lyrical mood, conjured the visual blatancy of the West that draws tourists from around the world, the literal dirt in all its colored layers, clinal lifts and folds, mountain ranges thrusting up and toppling monumentally down, plateaus and buttes like stepping-stones across eternity. Or we could have invoked, by a form of synecdoche, the ecology of a lodgepole pine forest infected with pine beetles to illuminate the dying West, as Beth Loffreda does in her piece, "Pinus Contorta." We could have done all of this, but about the *experience* of how it was, the pages might have ended up patched and half blank. *How it was, how it is,* here, in the West—just that.

It is the difference between drinking the glass of water and *knowing* the thirst. And it may be that knowing the thirst, imperfect or misguided as it can be, carries more truth finally than what's in the glass.

This collection of essays, poems, and meditations is about the thirst; about the West grown up in, and loved—or hated—and found and lost and found again. And it's about the old thirsts, too, the vestigial destinies manifest in each of us who experiences the enormous exhalation and exaltation that is space. Room to breathe, room to dream, room to exercise the right to make your own mistakes, and not someone else's, especially not someone who happened on the scene before you did. To fail on one's own terms in one's own time. To have a chance equal to those around you. And it's about the cultural atavisms from that brief period in the West's history—I'm speaking, of course, of the rise and fall of the cowboy kingdom and the Olympian myths it spun out, and out of control—that yet express themselves in language, in clothing, in the intransigent transience, in regional personalities that demand stoicism, or in the stubborn insistence on doing for oneself even while that same stubborn insistence says that you help your neighbor, all of you together, because the land will do you in without community.

Part of my youth was spent in the San Juan Archipelago, 450 islands at high tide, an additional 300 at low. It was an easy place to get lost in, especially at tide's turn. Recently I spent a week hiking in the Chisos Mountains of West Texas, another place easy to get lost in. The West may be the place where it is still possible to get lost—and die of it. That's one definition. And not so strangely, a comforting one, too. Against the hard, mostly invisible abrasion that is the proximity of death, lives are shaped and polished and even glittering. But then, it has always been close: we are losing species and ecosystems by legions. Looking away does not stop these ends from arriving.

Ezra Pound, that great democrat, once said, "Literature is news that *stays* news." However the West and its general life parameters may change for better or for worse this century, writers on being Western is news that will stay news.

That being said, it is still my charge to brush in a base coat on the larger canvas in order that the *how* of the West, its fits and starts, its cultural colors and textures, might rise impressionistically from the underlying *whats*.

Let's return to space and the equalizing pull it seemed to exert on the eastern states of the late eighteenth century: because that space was not exactly empty. It was in fact already broadly, though by no means densely, occupied by indigenous peoples, or "Indians," not yet graduated to the appellative status of Native Americans, well over a half million of them, in fact, from approximately 450 different tribes, not to mention Spanish outposts and mission settlements across the Southwest, Texas, and Southern California. Lewis and Clark's expedition of 1804–1806, reporting on the flora and fauna of the West, catalyzed a relatively scattered fur trade; the thirty-year "era" of the Mountain Man commenced and, in the slap of a tail, summarily collapsed. North American beaver would feed the fires of European millinery fashion until by 1840 the populations were so exhausted they *couldn't* feed that dragon, and in any case, the winds had shifted eastward by then, away from aquatic rodents to Oriental silk-worms as the material source for top hats. Out-of-work trappers turned their attention to immigrants seeking guides. Others piled into this new profession, and in short order, westering was a national occupation bordering on the compulsive.

It was a habit that found some of its deepest roots in European rights of primogeniture that left everything to the firstborn and nothing to subsequent offspring. This was not confined to Europeans, for as David Mas Masumoto remarks in his piece, Japanese second sons were also driven to emigrate, knowing that property would not pass to them either. Our earliest citizens, then, were self-selected venturers and gamblers willing to take radical steps toward a better life on no less than an entirely *other* continent.

But a certain, shall we say, unhealthy puissance obtained throughout the opening of the West. Americans, swarming across the Plains, bullied their dreams into being, appropriating, stealing, or indifferently squatting upon lands that seemed to be theirs by virtue of desire alone, and desire many times over. Thirst. Alas, blood-thirst as well. Having been denied elsewhere, disaffiliated, or simply last in line, immigrants seemed to feel that that space meant there was no line, not one that had to be officially recognized. Indians were, regrettably, more welcoming than wary. In California, genocide was a Sunday afternoon pastime, a pre-Anglo population of 250,000 nose-diving to 20,000 within a half century. "Civilization or extinction, has been the fate of all people who have found themselves in the trace of the advancing Whites, and civilization, always the preference of the Whites, has been pressed as an object, while extinction has followed as a consequence of its resistance." So said that old windbag, Senator Thomas Hart Benton, the firebrand behind Manifest Destiny and ravening western expansion. "The West wasn't settled by nice people," Jim Harrison says, referring to Anglo-American incursions "as a rag-tag invading army of soldiers and settlers." It wasn't enough that Indian populations were suppressed, cheated, removed, and often massacred (mostly by the us Army in defense of citizen settlers), the treaties the federal government established with them were nothing more than tricked-up ultimatums that were themselves only unilaterally binding—on the Indians. The federal government broke those treaties, every single one of them. In view of the record, it's difficult to regard this last, deeply cynical backhander as the White Man's original sin, as Jim Hepworth calls it, because there were just so many sins originating willy-nilly across the region. Our

native populations have been badly dealt, and many of this book's con-
tributors call for some manner of recognition or reparation, if only (once
again, cynically) to shore our sagging credibility in a global environment
where we are often critical of behavior indistinguishable from that embedded (or enshrouded) in our own historical record.

Along with the certainty that territorial expansion had been somehow ordained, that "Progress is God," land was conflated with the pursuit of happiness as the American desideratum. There were no reins or
even brakes on this juggernaut of dreams, and once the railroads crossed
the contiguous United States, immigration rates leapt to warp speed.
Who had time to develop a symbiotic relationship with the land, as the
Indians had over many centuries of semi-nomadic ways? Who could take
seriously endless variations on a theme of brown? A little water would
fetch up a garden as green and as giving as any self-respecting Yankee's
back forty in the East—right? But among the many things the West was
about, as my co-editor points out, was bad information. Except for John
Wesley Powell's report that few wanted to believe: "Nobody told the pioneers that 160 acres of this land, the amount available through the original Homestead Act [of 1862], couldn't possibly support a family because
there just wasn't enough water [to irrigate it]." That was the so-called free
land available to settlers, which had to be "proved up" in five years. The
railroads were also offering land at four to fifteen dollars an acre. Because
in exchange for building the railroads (with 6 percent public bonds and
thirty-year loans), the federal government had ceded every other section
for every mile along the line to the railroad companies, which quite logically then became de facto real estate developers as they made haste to
unload that land to pay off their debts. It ought to be noted that the value
of those railroad land grants represented four times the cost of transcon-
tinental line construction. The sirenic flyers of the railroads along with
the Immigration Bureau's tall-tale posters and handbills sown across the
Atlantic states and Europe lured immigrants into the Western wilderness.
Bad information? How about *dis*information?

But the human heart is a lonely hunter, and it will believe what it seeks,
it will latch onto the smallest threads of truth in an eye-dazzling fabric
of lies. For social and religious freedom, for better prospects, for land and
wealth, for the past to be mercifully expunged and a new day to dawn, the
siren song needed be hardly more than a jingle—which is exactly what it
was.

What did those future Jeffersonian yeomen find? How much land did
the stockman think he would need to feed his fifteen hundred head of
English cattle on the Central Plains?

What the farmer found was soil without rain enough to quench it, and when successively plowed, not enough even to hold it in place; the cattleman discovered that in many parts of the West it could take as many as forty or fifty acres to feed just one of his ill-suited steers. West of the isohyetal line, which fairly closely follows the 98th meridian, rainfall drops below the twenty inches a year required to farm without irrigation. This is where the hard-and-fast West begins. No wonder pioneers made a beeline across the Great Plains to Oregon Territory and California, where something of what they knew about crops and farming might find useful purchase. The prairies were said to be good for grazing animals, not growing food. But free land is free, after all, and the "era" (again, that oversized word) of open-range cattle ranching, of cattle drives and cowboys with all their Byronic romance, lasted little more than a couple of decades before the settlers began patching together settlements, and, with the help of newly invented barbed wire fencing, protecting their homesteads from range cattle. If anyone had bothered to read, or take seriously, Powell's 1878 *Report on the Lands of the Arid Region of the United States*, they would have met both the gatekeeper and the rulemaker of the West—aridity. Except for the swath of country west of the Cascades in Oregon and Washington, an area equal to no more than one-third the land in both states, and a few intermontane areas of the Rockies, the remainder of the West is arid. I have heard educated Westerners exclude California from this equation, but they are simply wrong, as any vineyardist during the 1976 drought found out soon enough. True, it rains in California, but nary a drop during the growing season. For the cattle business, the proximate end came on the hooves of overstocking and overgrazing the land, what John Daniel refers to as "cow-burnt rangeland," together with exacerbating calamities like the 1886 drought, which was dogged by a horrific winter and what became known as "The Big Die-up," and finally, a collapsing beef economy. The cattle and the cattle economy were both dying. But by then, the soddies were in town and they too would soon fail—in their own fashion, to be sure—the core curriculum of the West.

It may seem as though I'm pounding this little nail awfully hard and that the concept and condition of aridity have been driven home and countersunk well below the clear grain of comprehension. Because surely anyone who lives here in the West must know it as *the* proviso that directs matters from behind the green curtain. But beyond the knowledge that it is the Ur dynamic of the West, the source of everything from soil content and stability to the spacing between juniper and piñon, between Albuquerque and Phoenix (what Walter Prescott Webb called an "oasis civilization" and what Mary Austin admired about the Shoshone: "The Shoshones live like their trees, with great spaces between them, and in pairs and in family groups, they set up wattled huts by the infrequent springs. More wickiups than two make a very great number"); that the vastly and deceptively simple *look* of the West where space, as Wallace Stegner observed, "acts as a preservative" of the stereotypical western landscape, life, and character—beyond and despite this nearly two hundred-year, applied education, the West more often than not behaves like someplace east where water is abundant, where the land recovers quickly from the sins of its stewards, and where anyway, the American can-do mentality will serve to put right whatever wrongs it finds, those that came with the land as well as those committed by human occupation.

A couple of broad swipes with the paintbrush are in order: The waddies, or cowboys, along with their cattle, were fenced in—and out—by the settlers, which to a certain extent forced more adaptive ranching practices that included interbreeding with cattle native to the arid ecosystem, like the Mexican longhorn, who could eat just about anything the parched land grudgingly relinquished. Much of the rangeland had been trod up and grazed down to sagebrush, greasewood, shadscale, salt grass, etc., or even to bare rock, the soil, without its binding of grassroots, simply blowing away. Like some kind of occupation-wide experiment in behavioral modification, ranching gradually shunted northward to Montana and Wyoming, where the number of cattle found sustainable balance with available resources and where the country at least *wants* to be grass, even while there are unmistakable limits on how many cows it can support.

And the sodbusters, after decades of disastrous farming practices and cyclic drought, with the occasional dust bowl thrown in, either abandoned their homesteads or stuck, renegotiating, with respect this time, the terms of their contract with the land. In the midst of all this sorting out, there came the California gold rush of 1849. Whatever the West stood for in terms of promise, opportunity, milk and honey, or at minimum, the reprieve of amnesia, the past erased in the blinding sun of a fresh start, nothing could be as elemental, as culturally primitive across the globe, as just plain *old*—and so, as utterly galvanizing—as gold. In the history of human civilizations, this appetite comes turbo-charged straight up from the cerebellum. If gold gave off a scent, our blood could smell it. In less than a year and from all compass points, eighty thousand would-be miners flooded the gold fields. The network of westering trails deepened and branched. And the boomtown in all its inglorious details was born, dashed, born again. Not much, really, has changed. Here is Douglas Unger writing about Las Vegas and its own veins of ore: "It's simple casino logic and the very essence of gaming, that, with each new bet placed, the past ceases to exist; it's the future that counts, and Las Vegas is a city that keeps re-inventing itself by its own improbable vision of the future."

Co-evolving with westering and its indisputable wonders was an unparalleled raid on natural resources, beginning with the obvious, like timber, fur, and fish; then the less obvious hiding beneath the surface—gold, silver, copper, coal, and the not-so flashy minerals like molybdenum or uranium that may end up having greater value; followed by the surface itself, the literal dirt either worked until the life was worked from it or driven away by drought and the ceaseless, often violent weather of the Plains; and lastly, resources like water, found above and below the ground. This was what David Guterson calls "the era when I was king." When we were all putative kings who, just as Charlemagne, so crowned ourselves. Entities like the Bureau of Reclamation were created to expand and extend the pattern of plundering that mere mortals had already set in motion. The appellation itself is almost childishly inspired, as if all things in the playground of the western world belonged perforce to the us id, and suggesting that a federal agency would *reclaim* water that had somehow been *taken* from us. The process of damming rivers and ground-pumping aquifers, sending the water places where water was not and people and crops were, had the effect of killing those rivers and of degrading the soil and subsoil to the extent that not even native species could survive, and, furthermore, of despoiling what was fast becoming a commodity—the scenery itself. (Our first—and the world's first—national park, Yellowstone, was established in 1872 in response to the natural beauty early Americans found in the West.) In the Owens Valley during the late twentieth century ground-pumping was finally curtailed, in part because, besides the imported fruit trees and crops, even the native cottonwoods that lined every creek and traced in shimmering green every seasonal wash, were dying, one after another, for lack of the water that was being channeled down to Los Angeles. My husband was working on a piece in 1979 for *Harper's Magazine*, about western water and power wars, and we were in the Owens Valley as those great cottonwoods were dying. Just outside Lone Pine on our first afternoon, we stopped to talk to a woman gardening in her front yard. At one point during the conversation, she walked funereally over to the faucet from which the garden hose emerged, turned the handle, and the three of us watched the hose snake about, hissing and spewing nothing but air.

Today, the implausibly vast Ogallala Aquifer that underlies the Great Plains has been so aggressively tapped and depleted, far outstripping the rate of recharge, that even optimistic calculations predict that it will dry up within the first quarter of this century. These are not the crimes of technologically advanced, hard-hearted latecomers either, people with no appreciation of what used to be. As Greg Sarris, writing of his native Sonoma, points out, "By 1903 most of the landscape was transformed. Gone were the vast wetlands. The water table throughout the region had dropped an average of two hundred feet: creeks went dry in summer. The big trees were gone. Many of the great animals were extinct in the region, not just the grizzly bears, but the herds of elk and pronghorn, and the mighty condors gliding the thermals with their fourteen-foot wingspans." Quantitative differences eventually do lead to qualitative differences, and the subtractions from our paradise have begun to add up. To borrow from Patricia Nelson Limerick, "a river of melancholy runs through Western experience."

The concept of *use* in this region arrived fully formed and with no call for amelioration—no whitewashing, soft selling, or apology. "Creating" wealth was what we Americans instinctively did—and perhaps do—with our land and its resources. It was what we did too often with its native citizens as well, and with immigrant minorities, like the Chinese, who built our railroads and—quietly, with great dignity—enriched our culture. There is an area of psycholinguistic study that looks at how our language, our syntax, shapes our actions, and it may be that this habit of *use*, of greed dressed up in the finer raiments of ingenuity or resourcefulness, can begin to change by changing the language. If the word "resource" were replaced with something like attribute, or quality, we might begin to perceive what is here in the West not as invincible givens that can never be used up, or as things given *to* us, but as the fragile characteristics of a living entity, to be understood and appreciated, and to whom we must first do no harm. As the saying goes, habits are often only the antiquity of error. And habits can be broken.

Both the riches as well as the obstacles to those riches that our early citizens encountered in the West were nevertheless essential to the Western experience, and by extension, to the development of the Western character and culture. A theology of landscape, of place-specific practices and beliefs, cannot be avoided here. To a certain extent we are all converts simply by virtue of the dirt under our feet. Several years ago I was asked to come up with characteristics that might help define Western literature, and the first determinant I mentioned was that they are narratives that could not have taken place anywhere else. Place acts as character, as friend and foil, as parent and progeny, as legacy and legatee. Place is never a movable backdrop; it is actor.

The second significant feature of both Western literature and of the region's personality involves motion. Whether because it informed our coming here as a people, or because, once having arrived, many settlers had to keep moving on for one reason or another, transience and social fluidity are located (an ironic usage) somewhere in the DNA of a Westerner. The frontier was once a physical reality correlating to the land itself, and as that line between the civilized and the wild was pushed clear to the Pacific, it left a psychological residue, a ghostly presence of the frontier mind and myth that drifts past the window and seduces or haunts us just as surely. Across a landscape that is universally thought to be epic, peopled by characters who have become, at least in the telling and retelling, proportionately heroic, the frontier myth has been supercharged practically beyond recovery. *Our* recovery. If we can't stop thinking that there is something just around the bend that needs conquering or that might be fractionally better, we'll never learn how to save what is now ours to actually treasure. "The Real West will finally begin when both the name and the habits we now cherish in our films and other fictions are erased," Charles Bowden writes. "Maybe it will be called something unthinkable now. Say, something like Home."

And even if some of us may no longer believe our myths, as Larry Watson suggests, our characters still do. Here is Page Lambert writing similarly: "In what ways do our stories defend who we believe ourselves to be?" The history, however brief, of this region has us roped, thrown, and piggin' strung, ready for branding.

The light of many of these truths may expose without yet providing final illumination. What more is there to say, for instance, about the ethos of the cowboy? He still rides among us! It's time we evolved away from that whole collection of what are now, for all intents and purposes, maladaptive traits. As Wallace Stegner once said, "our principal folk hero, in all his shapes good and bad, is essentially antisocial." Competence, courage, independence—all certainly attractive qualities. But lace these with notions of unbridled freedom, of the absence of commitment that that freedom can imply, and of cooperative ventures questioned only because they represent some form of authority, and you end up with a country of wayfarer rats. Louis B. Jones observes that "we're all immigrants, or come from emigrants, and somewhere back there somebody had to gnaw off something essential in order to free himself. Immigrants are immigrants for a reason." Back to self-selection. During the fifteen years when my husband and I were running a lot of Western rivers, we used to say, as the rule against which we measured the character of people we met, "He'd be a good man to go down the river with." That meant not that he was competent or self-reliant or particularly fit; it meant that he struck us as a co-operator, as someone who was not emotionally booming and busting, but who was steady, reliable, responsible. In other words, not a cowboy.

The American West is still a metaphor mill serviced and maintained not only obviously by the entertainment industry, by literature, clothing companies, makers of gallery art and roadside kitsch, by regional architects featuring the Western "style," but also by insiders and outsiders worldwide. Recently I heard an interview with a Russian plutocrat who had been asked what it was like in his country after the collapse of communism and the Soviet Union: "It was a Wild West," he said. "It was a territory with no sheriff, no rules." As critical as this was intended to be, it is also part and parcel of what makes the idea of the American West still attractive to many of us, the wildness in human nature, the semblance of freedom in a world that demands relentless adjudication between personal desire and social responsibility. No one of us strives to be "domesticated" because such a state of affairs would rob us of our basic creaturely dignity. And the West, with its actual and metaphoric wilderness, has always kept us in contact with that defining essentiality. Tom Miller, writing of la frontera, says, "I need the border for its anarchic sense of reality." Will any of us ever not need some expression of anarchy or, in a scaled-down format, at least weekend emancipation? Even the freest among us feels bound by old wounds, or choices that have gone stale, or even the tyranny of too much freedom, too many choices. As myth, the American West still conjures a great mainspring of hope, and our dreams, our thirsts, may be, by their very nature, impossible to slake. The legend of the West is integral to who we are; as Larry McMurtry says, "lies about the West are more important to [readers] than truths." Or perhaps the lies are truer than truths. They tell us not what we have, but what we want; not who we are, but who we wish we were. Leaning this way, into the wind, is a known factor in the human equation. And more often than one might imagine, the wind will hold us up, even if the ground beneath our feet is falling away. "The real West," says Kris Saknussemm, "is somewhere you never actually get to, it's always where you're going."

The myths *are* important, so long as we know that they are myths, that they play only a bit part in the modern West and had only a marginal reality in the Old West, where human lives were crushingly lonely, hard to the bone, damaging of heart and habitat, and dependent not upon self-reliance but upon the not-nearly-as-romantic act of cooperation. If we know this, then Western myths may have their value just as any set of founding myths does, and the parables that those myths spawn may be educative of right living.

Unavoidably, many of the pieces in this volume talk about change, about newness, which, after all, is nothing new. What *is* new is the rate of change. The American West was opened and settled in a single century. Another century saw the region stippled in, with 80 percent living in urban centers and the rest dotting the empty geography between. Two hundred years of industrialization and exponential population growth can't be ignored and, beat for beat, simply can't be adapted to fast enough. And I don't mean just ecological adaptation, I mean emotional, psychological. "How do you capture the heart and soul of a place, not to mention *your own place* in that place, when it transforms itself every couple of years and becomes somewhere else?" Page Stegner asks in his piece, "The Sense of No Place." And we are learning now that even human evolution has been speeding up since Homo sapiens started planting crops about ten thousand years ago. We are not only subject to the forces of Nature, we have become one of its phenomena, like volcanic activity or climate warming, which is actively, measurably, changing the planet, but with the added element of consciousness. The West is our home field, and each of us has a dog in this fight.

We must know enough, learn enough, in order to have hope of not becoming an indicator species, like the canaries in the coal mines, who signal not that they are dying their individual deaths—though they are—but that the whole ecosystem has been irrevocably compromised.

With each successive crop of stewards, the West does gain a little. It was never intelligence we lacked, it was information—or perhaps more honestly—belief in that information. There are still those, for instance, who will not accept the data that establishes the reality of climate warming, or *climate disruption*, as Paul Ehrlich insists we call it so that it doesn't sound so cozy. But we have not yet drawn even with our environmental consequences; we're like a man running uncontrollably downhill, trying to catch up with his own momentum. Falling is likely; surviving is in question. Because of history and a shattering evidentiary record, we know now, truly, that the West is arid. And on the human, sensory level, we can feel that knowledge of aridity in the sear wind against our skin and taste it in the alkali water and, to steal a line from Ursula Le Guin, smell it in "the holy sage, that purifies." We can hear it in the windy silence of a seasonal wash or in the roar of a spring flash flood, chocolate colored and bristling with debris, as it barrels down a slickrock side canyon into the San Juan or the Yampa or the Colorado River. Mostly, though, as a vision-based species, we *see* aridity. Of all the senses that the West stimulates, it is sight that enlarges even while it falters and loses itself across the landscape, loses as it gathers up the bigness and the mystery of the space that aridity defines. Even in its seeming cure, you can see the aridity in the rain that doesn't reach the ground, those sooty veils of virga that tatter down from skies boiling with late summer weather. The space itself suggests a kind of primordial virginality, as though here, across these limit-less plains, in these improbably high mountains, through those rolling yellow hills that fall softly to the sea, anything can happen. The trouble is, anything *has* happened. Now, something needs to be done. Something responsible and responsive. Something that begins to approach a sustainable Western economy, together with a trend Barry Lopez invokes, "the movement toward a civil society."

What I haven't mentioned is beauty. The West is so beautiful in so many places that sometimes you can feel the seams of your heart straining and tearing against it. Beauty is restorative. Much of this beauty resides in the fragility of the West, which makes it as contingent as the noble land itself. Part of that fragility, one of its parents at least, is wildness. And as a region with a broader regional personality that supersedes our individual place personalities, the West with its frontier past and frontier subconscious continues to whittle out our character and ineluctably cathect it.

Perhaps we are due for a prayer: May we keep the wild and beautiful places and keep them healthy; may we enter what Charles Wilkinson calls the Fourth West during which we realize fully "the importance of land to our humanity"; and may we let the manner of the country determine our usage of life here.

Russell Rowland and I have let these pieces settle the way the West was settled, east to west, beginning with Louise Erdrich's "lowly assertion of grass" and crossing the Great Plains, some drifting southward, others heading due west across the Rockies toward the coastal states. Like the tracks and traces of western expansion, the arrangement may seem to have a hither-and-yon quality, though in view of the remarkable variety of content and tone that seemed to defy grouping and analysis, as well as group analysis, this plan made the best sense in the end. If some of the pieces sound elegiac, and some do, others have that clear-eyed alertness that a brush-up with loss can inspire. This place is worth saving, worth cherishing, because this place is now home.

Louise Erdrich | BIG GRASS

My father and I love the small and receding wild places of the agribusiness moonscape of Red River Valley cropland. Throughout my childhood in North Dakota, we hunted and gathered in the sloughs, the sandhills, the brushy shelterbelts, and unmowed ditches, on the oxbows and along the banks of the mudded rivers. On the west road that now leads past the Walmart to the Carmelite monastery just outside of Wahpeton, we picked prairie rose hips in fall and dried them for Vitamin C-rich teas in the winter. There was always, in the margins of the cornfield just beyond our yard, in the brushy scraps of abandoned pasture, right-of-ways along the railroad tracks, along the river itself and in the corners and unseeded lots of the town, a lowly assertion of grass.

It was big grass. Original prairie grass—bluestem and Indian grass, side-oats grama. The green fringe gave me the comforting assurance that all else planted and tended and set down by humans was somehow temporary. Only grass is eternal. Grass is always waiting in the wings.

Back when the few hunters in the woods were thoughtful people, my father wore dull green and never blaze orange. He carried a green fiberglass bow with a waxed string and, strapped to his back, a quiver of razor-tipped arrows. Pre-dawn on a Saturday in fall he'd take a child or two into the woods near Hankinson, Stack Slough, or the cornfields and box elder and cottonwood scruff along the Wild Rice or Bois de Sioux rivers. Once, on a slim path surrounded by heavy scrub, my father and I heard a distant crack of a rifle shot and soon, crashing toward us, two does and a great gray buck floated. Their bounds carried them so swiftly that they nearly ran us over.

The deer huffed and changed direction mid-air. They were so close I felt the tang of their panic. My father didn't shoot—perhaps he fumbled for his bow but there wasn't time to aim—more likely, he decided not to kill an animal in front of me. Hunting was an excuse to become intimate with the woods and fields, and on that day, as on most, we came home with bags of wild plums, elmcap mushrooms, more rose hips.

Since my father began visiting the wild places in the Red River Valley, he has seen many of them destroyed. Tree cover of the margins of rivers, essential to slow spring runoff and the erosion of topsoil—cut and leveled for planting. Wetlands—drained for planting. Virgin prairie (five thousand acres in a neighboring Minnesota county)—plowed and planted. From the air, the Great Plains is now a vast earth-toned Mondrian painting, all strict right angles of fields bounded by thin and careful shelterbelts. Only tiny remnants of the tall grass remain. These pieces in odd cuts and lengths are like the hems of long and sweeping old-fashioned skirts. Taken up, the fabric is torn away, forgotten. And yet when you come across the original cloth of grass, it is an unfaded and startling experience. Here is a reminder that before this land was a measured product tended by Steiger tractors with air-cooled cabs and hot-red combines, before this valley was wheat and sugar beet and sunflower country, before the drill seeders and the windbreaks, the section measures and the homesteads, this was the northern tallgrass prairie.

It was a region mysterious for its apparent simplicity.

Grass and sky were two canvasses into which rich details painted and destroyed themselves with joyous intensity. As sunlight erases cloud, so fire ate grass and restored grass in a cycle of unrelenting power. A prairie burned over one year blazes out the next, redeemed in the absolving mist of green. On a warm late-winter day, snow slipping down the sides of soft prairie rises, I can feel the grass underfoot collecting its bashful energy. Big bluestem, female and green sage, snakeweed, blue grama, ground cherry, Indian grass, wild onion, purple coneflower, purple aster spring to life on a prairie burned the previous year.

To appreciate grass, you must lie down in grass. It's not much from a distance and it doesn't translate well into most photographs or even paint, unless you count Albrecht Dürer's *Das grosse Rasenstück*, 1503. He painted grass while lying on his stomach, with a wondering eye trained into the seed tassels. Just after the snow has melted each spring, it is good to throw oneself on grass. The stems have packed down all winter, in swirls like a sleeper's hair. The grass sighs and crackles faintly, a weighted mat, releasing fine winter dust.

It is that smell of winter dust I love best, rising from the cracked stalk. Tenacious in its cycle, stubborn in its modest refusal to die, the grass embodies the philosopher's myth of eternal return. *All flesh is grass* is not a depressing conceit to me. To see ourselves within our span as creatures capable of quiet and continual renewal gets me through paralysis, bewilderment, loss. Snow melts. Grass springs back. Here we are on a quiet rise, finding the first uncanny shoots of green.

My daughter's hair has a scent as undefinable as grass—made up of mood and weather, of curiosity and water. Just to be, just to exist—that is the talent of grass. Fire will pass over. The growth tips are safe underground. The bluestem's still the scorched bronze of late summer deer pelts. Formaldehyde ants swarm from a warmed nest of black dirt. The ants seem electrified, driven, ridiculous in tiny self-importance. Watching the ants, we can delight in our lucky indolence. They'll follow one another and climb a stem of grass threaded into their nest to the end, until their weight bows it to the earth. There's a clump of Crested Wheatgrass, a foreigner, invading. The breast feather of a grouse. A low hunker of dried ground cherries. Sage. Still silver, its leaves specks and spindrels, sage is a generous plant, releasing its penetrating scent of freedom long after it is dried and dead. And here, the first green of the year rises, showing at the base in the tiny budded lips.

Horned larks spring across the breeze and there, off the rent ice, the first returning flock of Canada geese search out the open water of a local power plant on the Missouri River. In order to recreate as closely as possible the mixture of forces that groomed the subtle prairie, buffalo are included, at Cross Ranch Preserve, for grazing purposes. Along with fire, buffalo were the keepers of the grass, and they are coming back now, perhaps because they always made sense. They are easier to raise than cattle, they calve on their own, and find winter shelter in brush and buffalo berry gullies.

From my own experience of buffalo—a tiny herd lives in Wahpeton and I saw them growing up and still visit them now—I know that they'll eat most anything that grows on the ground. In captivity, though, they relish the rinds of watermelon. The buffalo waited for and seemed to know my parents who came by every few days in summer with bicycle baskets full of watermelon rinds. The tongue of the buffalo is long, gray, and muscular, a passionate scoop. While they eat watermelon, the buffalo will consent to have their great boulder foreheads scratched but will occasionally, over nothing at all, or perhaps everything, ram themselves into their wire fences. I have been on the other side of a fence charged by a buffalo and I was stunned to a sudden blank-out at the violence.

One winter, in the middle of a great snow, the buffalo walked up and over their fence and wandered from their pen by the river. They took a route through the town. There were reports of people stepping from their trailers into the presence of shaggy monoliths. The buffalo walked through backyards, around garages, took the main thoroughfares at last into the swept-bare scrim of stubble in the vast fields—into their old range, after all.

Grass sings, grass whispers. Ashes to ashes, dust to grass. But real grass, not the stuff that we trim and poison to an acid green mat, not clipped grass never allowed to go to seed, not this humanly engineered lawn substance as synthetic as a carpet. Every city should have a grass park, devoted to grass, long grass, for city children haven't the sense of grass as anything but scarp on a boulevard. To come into the house with needlegrass sewing new seams in your clothes, the awns sharp and clever, is to understand botanical intelligence. Weaving through the toughest boots, through the densest coat, into skin of sheep, needlegrass will seed itself deep in the eardrums of dogs and badgers. And there are other seeds, sharp and eager, diving through my socks, shorter barbs sewn forever into the laces and tongues of my walking boots.

Grass stems out in August, full-grown to a hypnotizing silk. The ground begins to run beside the road in waves of green water. A motorist, distracted, pulls over and begins to weep. Grass is emotional, its messages a visual music with rills and pauses so profound it is almost dangerous to watch. Tallgrass in motion is a world of legato. Returning from a powwow, my daughter and I are slowed and then stopped by the spectacle and we drive side roads, walk old pasture, until we find real grass turned back silver, moving, running before the wind. Our eyes fill with it and on a swale of grass we sink down, chewing the ends of juicy stems.

Soon, so soon.

Your arms reach, dropping across the strings of an air harp. Before long, you want your lover's body in your hands. You don't mind dying quite so much. You don't fear turning into grass. You almost believe that you could continue, from below, to express in its motion your own mesmeric yearning, and yet find cheerful comfort. For grass is a plant of homey endurance, pure fodder after all.

I would be converted to a religion of grass. *Sleep the winter away and rise headlong each spring. Sink deep roots. Conserve water. Respect and nourish your neighbors and never let trees gain the upper hand.* Such are the tenets and dogmas. As for the practice—*grow lush in order to be devoured or caressed, stiffen in sweet elegance, invent startling seeds*—those also make sense. *Bow beneath the arm of fire. Connect underground. Provide. Provide. Be lovely and do no harm.*

I've had it with TV pontificators and weatherpersons and newsfolk refer-ring to the stretch of US from Pennsylvania to Las Vegas as the Midwest. It's the reason I don't watch TV, or one of them. But TV's tedious mastery of generalizations and genius for homogenizing keep slipping, like Orwell-ian proofs, into print. Soon all but California and New York (excluding *up*state New York and *down*state California) will be part of the Midwest. I lived in the Midwest for a decade, in central Illinois to be exact, and the Midwest is not Kansas or the Oklahoma outback or the mountains and hills and buttes of North and South Dakota or Wyoming.

My local landscape, across the wide Missouri into the southwestern corner of North Dakota, has the appearance of northeast New Mexico, the white area of few roads. T. Roosevelt, John Steinbeck, and others note that when you cross the Missouri you enter the West. The other side of the Mississippi may render a taste of the West but once over the Missouri, you're in it, in mountain time. The Dakotas and Montana and Wyoming, states that made up most of the original Dakota Territory, were referred to when I was in school as the Northwest, to distinguish them from the *Pacific* Northwest, and Roosevelt, the first writer to set in type the topog-raphy of western North Dakota in *Hunting Trips of a Ranchman*, the first volume in a nature trilogy, called the area the Northern Plains and, alter-nately, the Northwest.

Let me add, too, that those who refer to most of the US as the Midwest are often the same who allude to the earth and its shifts in weather, espe-cially when calamitous, as *Mother Nature*, as though a mean old lady is up to her shenanigans. It isn't prudent to call a kangaroo an elephant, I assume, and that's the effect on me of referring to a variety of regions as the Midwest, along with *Mother Nature*'s dubious effrontery across it.

Here are a few distinctions of the place where I live. Yucca blooms in the ditches, coyotes and antelope prowl the countryside, buffalo and elk are usually fenced in, especially the buffalo, so although they don't really roam, the deer—mule and white-tail, too—do, I guess, play. Occasionally a moose drifts through. The average annual precipitation is twelve inches, counting snow, less than half of most of the Midwest. The countryside is rugged, with scoria and lignite lying below or erupting through the surface, and scoria's red-pink tinge is visible on backcountry roads and in formations that bulk through the soil and stand bare at the summit of a hogback or teepee or mesa-top butte. We have buttes of every variety.

The Little Badlands surrounding Medora, where Roosevelt lived, extend north all the way to Watford City and south to Bowman and are pictorially more colorful than the monumental formations in the better-known badlands of South Dakota. *South* Dakota is where you find four faces of presidents sculpted by the Dane Gutzon Borglum into the summit of a granite cliff in the Black Hills—black as seen from a distance due to indigenous spruce blanketing them. The Black Hills were *Paha Sapa*, holy ground, to the Sioux, deeded to them in perpetuity until gold was discovered there and the US employed Colonel Custer and others to protect the miners and, in effect, drive the natives out. The abuse of natives is not restricted to the West of course but using gold, once the monetary standard, as a reason seems so.

In the Midwest you will not see acres of the sky-blue blossoms of flax, an azure that only these plants produce, because nearly all the flaxseed, a recent health find, in the US is raised in North Dakota—94 percent to be exact. And the chrome-yellow blossoming crop across so many miles of landscape it can cause hard-hearted me to gasp is also all but exclusive to the state—canola, for canola oil, 91 percent of the US supply raised here. The state ranks first in the nation in the organic production of oil seeds, oats, buckwheat, flax, and sunflowers, and raises 50 percent of the hard red spring wheat ground fine for bread, so that a consumer could say that one half of every loaf of bread from any store, even in the Midwest or the East, originates in North Dakota.

Our cash crops aren't only aboveground. It is now known that North Dakota hovers over one of the largest oil reserves in the nation, the Bakken Reservoir, which likely has a second reservoir beneath, as recent studies have projected. The potential of the Bakken has barely been plumbed, but taxes reaped by the state from oil and gas production is one of the reasons why North Dakota, in the hell-in-a-handbasket economy of 2008–2009, emerged as the wealthiest state in the lower forty-eight.

As our legislature gathered for its every-other-year 2008–2009 session (citizens can't be convinced there's enough business to employ politicians full time), it was revealed that North Dakota had over two billion dollars in cash reserve. State politicians are fiscally conservative, if they want to stick around, and the problem they faced with this bounty—other than what proportion to save—was where to direct it.

This excess of liquidity was met head-on by another that answered many questions of the reserve's direction right off: an overabundance of water as 2008 passed into 2009 and the spring melt. Snows had been heavy across the state and a season of flooding began from south to north and east to west. A potential flood of the Red River threatened Fargo and would have spread wide if high school and university students hadn't joined residents and the National Guard, a unit of over two hundred troops, in a massive sandbagging effort. Fargo was on flood watch for weeks but ended mostly safe, although Fargo seemed to receive most mention on national news, perhaps because it's the largest, shall we say, city in the state, with a population of a hundred thousand. Or perhaps because of that movie—which, by the way, is set in Minnesota. People here don't talk like that.

A weatherperson-newsfolk was arrested in Fargo, along with his camerapeople, for climbing a sandbagged dike, highly illegal, so he could get better shots of the swift current Mother Nature presented, I suspect.

The Red is a watercourse as contrary (and at times unruly) as outliers suspect North Dakotans are. It's the only river in the US to flow north, to a terminus in Hudson Bay. Try that in the Midwest. The Red is hardly wider than a car-length or two during its normal run and, narrow and oddly northerly though it is, it has, during a severe cresting in 1997, expanded to a breadth of sixty-five miles. This year it was expected to crest at forty-three feet but only reached forty-one. Normal is about nine.

Meanwhile, real floods were occurring across the state, and perhaps the worst visitation was on Valley City, where the university had to be evacuated and the sewage system started backing into houses. The river serving as culprit there, the Sheyenne, crested at twenty-two feet, its highest since the 1880s, the decade North Dakota became a state. The Cannonball, a river Custer followed out of Mandan on his fateful visit to the Little Big Horn, flooded West Mott, in southwest North Dakota, two weeks before any other flooding, or fear of floods, was perceived anywhere else. I live a dozen miles from Mott and didn't hear about this except from residents.

One resident told me somebody called him on the phone and said he had five minutes to get out—don't try to save anything, he was told. Two weeks later, after clean-up started, the Cannonball flooded again—West Mott's fifth flood in thirty years (Custer's curse?) and after the last, in 1997,

FEMA offered to buy all the houses in this parklike region of the city, over-spread by huge cottonwoods. A few contrary Dakotans, however, wouldn't sell out. I doubt that they will now.

Back east, the town of Lisbon, where the Sheyenne River swings south, was evacuated, residents piling out in goose-hunting boats and canoes. Outlying areas of Jamestown, where the James and Pipestem rivers meet, flooded, and the James so threatened one sector of town that the live-in patients at the Anne Carlsen Center for disabled children were evacuated for six weeks to a variety of houses and motels, even other towns. The two hundred Guardsmen moved to Jamestown, where the sewer system was about to back up, but didn't quite, and barracked at the college until they got the all clear, which wasn't until June 2009.

The mighty Missouri, which winds through the western half of the state and curves around Bismarck, where the nineteen-story state capitol stands, has been tamed since the 1950s by a series of dams, including the world's largest earthen dam, Garrison, located in western North Dakota. Garrison holds in abeyance the nation's largest freshwater lake—not counting the Great Lakes shared with Canada—as our legislature in its every-other-year session held in abeyance the two billion dollar reserve until they figured how much they needed to spend on the floods. Then the Missouri grew clogged with ice during a false-spring melt and houses in the vicinity of Bismarck, built too close to the river, not only flooded but were broken into by thieves in boats—rare for a state with the lowest crime rate in America. And I for one among other perhaps nervous Dakotans, since no budget had appeared, imagined a similar false-spring seep or sneaking away of the billions, but was saved from serious consideration by the Dakotan's inherited hearty disbelieving dry humor handed down by the first residents, the Sioux.

Meanwhile, houses along the shores of Lake Tschida, formed by a dam on the Heart River between Elgin and Glen Ullin, flooded when the lake filled with such a surge of melt the dam couldn't release water fast enough to counter the rise. Rural families in the area, near Carson and New Leipzig, had to be airlifted out in Blackhawks, and most of that spring you could hear helicopters overhead, no matter where you traveled (if you could) as further floodwaters rose toward farmhouses. None of those moments of course made the news.

Our neighbor's basement flooded for the first time from the melt of snow in his yard, as I learned when he came to borrow a sump pump and wet vac. And when photos of roads I used to travel, overlaid with water, appeared on the Internet—even the interstates, 94 running east and west and 29 north and south, were covered in places, closed—I couldn't help making the metaphorical connection that keeps rising as I attempt to reconstruct that time, the link between North Dakota's monetary reserve, which set it apart not only from the Midwest but from the rest of the nation, and its abounding floods.

Could one claim an objective correlative, as T. S. Eliot might? Or a curse of abundance, in the tone of a Milton or a Dante or a Blake?

Perhaps an excess of liquidity of any sort, including monetary reserves in multiple digits, can overflow otherwise containing boundaries. Perhaps it was an excess of liquidity, the unleashed profusion of dollars poured toward sub-prime mortgages and the excess spending couples became enmeshed in if they bought a new house, as we did, that brought this down. My wife found a place in Jamestown, where I took a teaching job in 2006, and I said, "They'll never give us a mortgage when they find out we owe"—you needn't know the amount—"on our little farm"—a quarter, as is said here, meaning a quarter section, or 160 acres—a garden plot in the area. But with barely a background check we got the place, and I suspect it was a series of two billion such acts that washed away the financial stability of the rest of the world—a speculation as valid as others I've heard. See it as Hardy's or Hopkins's convergence of the twain: abundance meets green-eyed greed.

Certainly plenty of non-Dakotans discovered how to dredge diversions to their own redoubts or cellars bricked by Poe. By a magical sleight-of-hand, Mr. Madoff made off with lots, siphoning, in comparable quantity, one of the Great Lakes into his Eastern swimming pool. Perhaps Woody Allen will make a movie, in a comedic vein, of course, to explain the mechanics of the maneuver. And since it was an overabundance of dollars and spending that brought down the pillar of the East and signpost to nations, Wall Street, should trillions more be printed to sandbag the expanding, muddy, muddled mess?

Our legislature, composed of a majority of canny farmers, some of whose fields remained under water up to the most recent unloading of 2010 snow, didn't disappoint the voters. They allocated funds for infrastructure repairs and rebuilding. They started the process of planning a dike for Fargo and the city across the street of the Red, Moorhead (Minnesota, where they talk funny) with perhaps a diversionary system carrying the Red's water inland, as at Winnipeg. Fargo may soon gain a system comparable to the complex berm and floodgate arrangement installed at Grand Forks after seven thousand houses flooded out there in 1997, when the Red broadened to sixty-five miles. Roads and highways have been spiffed up and new walk-through culverts and bridges installed.

A healthy amount of money went into the Heritage Center in Bismarck, to expand its present impressive building and displays, and a good extra also went into education (though not enough for some), including eight million for a new library at Dickinson State, the university that serves those of us west of the Missouri. A few felt our legislators didn't have to save quite as much of the two billion as they did but in the present financial crisis across the Midwest and out East, everybody wants to look like a fiscal conservative.

Old-timers in North Dakota warned about throwing good money after bad, and if there's yet another bailout or stimulus or surge of billions, I wonder if it might better be seen as throwing bad after what was once good. As a Westerner who happens to be a Dakotan, I wonder at the wisdom of pumping doubly indebted money into further proliferation when every measure meant to guarantee financial stability, whether hastily or carefully constructed, all those levees, dikes, and dams of global bureaucracy and their watchdogs, have failed.

These thoughts bore down on me with special pressure today when I got my pickup stuck in a yard as deep in snow as last year. Where are the snows of yesteryear? Underfoot and piled high.

I had to call the neighbor, who, last spring, borrowed my sump pump and wet vac, to come and dig me out with his huge loader tractor. The rock and wallow of the pickup reminded me of driving my aging car, in the midst of the floods last spring, through a stretch of the Cedar that had risen seventy feet above its banks to flow across the blacktop and how the current of the river, nearly to the bumper, tugged at the tires and undercarriage as if to draw the car seventy feet down the other side. At least I didn't float away or haven't flooded out since. Wait a minute. What did I say about the Midwest? Hold in place this mental sandbag for me for a while, would you, while I check on that and my bank account.

Larry Watson

WHOSE WEST?
WHICH WEST?
WEST OF WHAT?

You tell me—is this story a Western? A man and a woman are in love, but each is married to another. They live in Rattlesnake Springs, Wyoming, and they meet in the Frontier Saloon to talk over their dilemma. And how about this narrative, set even farther west: Once again, a couple is in love, and again committed to others. They live in Seattle, and they get together in a coffeehouse to discuss their situation. . . . These are not trick questions or "real" fictions in disguise. Hold onto your answers for the time being . . .

I was once on a panel whose purpose was to discuss "Problems Facing the American West," and while I feared it was a mistake for me to be included in the proceedings, I thought that if I kept my mouth shut, I could keep that from being generally known. But a panelist who says nothing is even more antithetical to the enterprise than one who says stupid or banal things, so I knew that eventually I would have to venture an idea or two. I cautiously suggested that defining the West can be a difficult proposition, and I ended my brief remarks with a question: Which West are we talking about today?

To say that my question was regarded as unhelpful would be an understatement. My remarks were immediately attacked—and by a fellow panelist. The American West can be easily and exactly defined, he said, his voice full of scorn. He proceeded to offer a definition sure to please meteorologists and cartographers, since it referred to annual rainfall totals and a meridian line. I don't think he gave credit to Wallace Stegner in his remarks, but by then my ears were burning from the scolding, so I might not have heard everything.

Had I been given an opportunity to explain why I believed the West is difficult to locate and define, I'd have done what chastened children and people in therapy so often do: Blame my upbringing.

I grew up, you see, in a city on a border, though no map would identify it as such. In fact, maps show Bismarck, North Dakota, lies not only in the middle of the state but in the middle of the continent. (Rugby, North Dakota, the town I was born in, has the official title "Geographical Center of North America.") But maps, no matter how general or specialized, can only reveal so much about a place. And as Alfred Korzybski famously said, "The map is not the territory."

Bismarck is on the east side of the Missouri River, and right across the river is Mandan, the town where, John Steinbeck says in *Travels With Charley*, the West begins. If we accept Steinbeck's judgment (and there's no compelling reason why we should) that would mean Bismarck is right on the edge, the borderline, dividing the West from—what? The East? Hardly. The Midwest? Plausibly. For the cartographic record: Bismarck is slightly west of the hundredth meridian. And Rand McNally once solved the problem of where North Dakota belongs by leaving the state out of its atlas altogether.

During my years in Bismarck I saw plenty of evidence to complicate the issue of where we belonged, regionally. Both ranches and farms surrounded the city, and growing up I heard so many references to "family farms" and "family ranches" I thought for a time the terms were synonymous. In the 1950s it was possible to see cars, motorcycles, or horses on the city streets. Plenty of Bismarck men wore wingtips and fedoras, but just as many wore boots and Stetsons. And my lawyer father wore cowboy boots with his three-piece suits.

The family itself furnished further confusion. Our relatives in Fargo lived in the Midwest, didn't they? They were right on a map's border, the division between North Dakota and Minnesota. And the aunts, uncles, and cousins in Bozeman and Butte—surely they lived in the West. Yet all those lives seemed similar—houses in middle-class neighborhoods, trips to the grocery store, coffee klatsches in the kitchen, barbecues in the backyard. . . . And not at all different from our life in Bismarck in between them. Both my grandfathers filed homestead claims on the Dakota prairie, but before he settled down as a homesteader, my paternal grandfather had been Bronco Gus, a horseman of some distinction in western North Dakota and eastern Montana. But my grandfather bore no resemblance to the Marlboro man, and while his cowboy credentials were all in order, he was proudest of the later life he led as a farmer and a man who helped establish a town with a church and school. (Fortunately, he didn't live to see them all vanish.)

Incidentally, my cowboy grandfather emigrated from Sweden. Cowboys continue to run in the family, but in versions even more unlikely than my grandfather; my cousin—born in Fargo—has her own ranch in Montana and has only recently given up competing in rodeo competitions.

But any difficulty that one might have in determining whether one lives in the West (and many—millions—never experience a moment's doubt, a consequence of their nature as much as their geography) is nothing compared to the trouble that can come from trying to define the literary West. Now you may bring out your answers to the questions posed in the opening paragraph. Anyone looking for evidence of how wide open is the category "Western fiction" could be referred to a list compiled in 1999 by the *San Francisco Chronicle*. The newspaper conducted a survey of its readers in order to come up with the titles of the hundred greatest works of Western fiction. It's a list that is, as the saying goes, all over the map, without regard for meridian lines or annual rainfall totals. For every *Angle of Repose* or *A River Runs Through It* is an *L. A. Confidential* or a *Dune*. For every A. B. Guthrie is an Amy Tan; for every Zane Grey is a Thomas Pynchon.

But why shouldn't readers have felt unconstrained when it came to making their nominations? Anyone who has paid attention to Western Literature in recent decades has noticed that it is divided and subdivided into almost as many categories as there are works themselves. A cursory survey of recent articles in journals specializing in Western American literature reveals discussions of Westerns both "revisionary" and "divisionary" (I have no idea what that term means). There are articles on emigrant literature and native literature, on space Westerns and noir Westerns, on graphic novels and verse novels. There are analyses of Western realists, surrealists, and rhapsodists, of writers who write historical fiction and writers who write hallucinatory Westerns. There is the literature of the Old West and the New West, and novels that fit those categories can be published in the same year and can be set in years separated not by centuries but by a decade. A prominent Western writer recently received an award from a prestigious center of Western Studies, and in the award citation the writer was praised for writing about the "true west." Which implies, doesn't it, that many other writers are producing fiction and poetry of a false West?

If that category exists, wouldn't we like to see Louis L'Amour slotted there? Author of over a hundred books, with sales in the hundreds of millions, and many of those books made into movies, Mr. L'Amour was as responsible as anyone for perpetuating, if not creating, the straight-shooting, lonesome stranger brand of Western myth. Yet years ago, when CBS interviewed Mr. L'Amour, he devoted part of the interview to *correcting* misconceptions about the West. It was a curious moment—Louis L'Amour, mythmaker *and* debunker.

But the myths of the American West and the ruggedly independent, fiercely self-reliant Westerner have long had a curious relationship to the literature of the region. There seems to be no end to the fictions praised for revealing the truth behind the myths. Wouldn't you think that once they have been revealed as false, the job would be done? But as Larry McMurtry and others have noted, these myths refuse to die, no matter how often they're exposed to the sunlight.

Isn't the problem, however, with these zombie myths as with the *San Francisco Chronicle*'s list and its wildly disparate collection of names and titles, a confusion between writers and the people they write about? A writer might know that the West and Westerners have often been idealized and romanticized, depicted inaccurately and falsely, but that doesn't mean the inhabitants of the region know it. East and west of the 100th meridian are millions of Americans (both fictional and real) who have never read Tom McGuane or N. Scott Momaday, much less Patricia Limerick or Jane Tompkins. In other words, a writer might not believe any of the myths of the American West, but that doesn't mean his characters don't believe. The stories and poems of atheists can be populated with Christians, Hindus, Muslims, or Jews, devout believers all. Countless articles have been written, anthologies gathered, and conferences convened under the rubric of "a writer's sense of place" when it might make more sense to consider "a writer's *characters'* sense of place." And it would also do well to note that even the men and women who know that much of what is written and said about the American West is myth might still labor under the burden of those myths, knowing as they do that others believe something about them, true or not. And what was once believed changes over time. Much of the action of *The Great Gatsby* takes place on Long Island, on an easternmost tip of the United States, yet Nick Carraway (a native Minnesotan) refers to himself, Tom and Daisy Buchanan (from Chicago and Louisville, Kentucky, respectively), and Gatsby (born in North Dakota) as Westerners and their story as "one of the West." Borders and frontiers—we can count on them to shift and be shifty.

For my part, when I was working on the manuscript that would eventually be *Montana 1948*, I didn't think I was writing a Western, much less constructing or deconstructing any myth. I thought I was writing a story about a conflicted family whose troubles were more likely to be dramatized in kitchens, bedrooms, and parlors than under the wide-open skies of Montana. If someone would have asked me, in the midst of writing that or any other novel, what I thought I was producing, vis-à-vis, a region, I might have said, "A Northern." Except I know there is no such literary category. . . . I've never thought, with respect to annual rainfall, that I was setting a story in the Great American Desert; my settings owe more to Robert Frost's "desert places."

Of course, analyzing, classifying, dividing, and subdividing are activities that critics and scholars are more likely to engage in than artists. Indeed, an artist's relation to a border or boundary is problematical at best since artists are notorious for rejecting, violating, or drawing their own boundaries. Marsden Hartley's painting, *The End of New England, the Beginning of New Mexico*, could serve as the emblem for this principle. It's a landscape without any feature identifying a specific place and suggesting not only that the regions border one another but also merge—as they might in Hartley's memory or imagination. And isn't a writer's reluctance or outright refusal to be confined what accounts for all those categories of Western Literature? What writers and other artists thrive on is freedom and empty space—the unmarked canvas, the unchiseled stone, the blank page—unclaimed territories that offer so much possibility. Drive across Nevada or fly over Wyoming and tell me you don't think of space where discouraging words are in fact seldom heard.

The West . . . an "amnesiac culture" poet David Mason has called it. A "museum culture" is William Kittredge's term. But both use the term "culture," thus situating the West not in geography but in belief, attitude, knowledge, the arts. The West is a state all right, but not one that can be found on a map. It's a state of mind.

Dan O'Brien | VIEWED FROM GROUND LEVEL

It is early in the morning of November 5, 2008. Yesterday at this time I was driving to my polling place to vote in what the entire world has called a historic election. The trip took me about an hour each way and cost me about fifteen bucks. Most of the road is gravel and I had to be careful not to hit a deer because the nights have begun to freeze, the pastures have turned brown, and the only green grass is in the road ditches where moisture has collected over the summer. The deer pile into those ditches this time of year, trying their best to lay on an extra layer of fat before the really cold days begin.

Barack Obama won big. The press says it all has to do with world finance, which I do not understand, and wars in distant lands. I might be able to figure out what a derivative or a sub-prime loan is if I had a dog in the fight. But I don't own any stocks and my loan at the bank is the same one I have had for forty years. I know enough about wars in distant lands to know that I don't like them and that's a big reason I voted for Obama.

I was not alone. I actually voted for a winner this year. It's great to be part of history and I really am feeling a lot better about being an American. But I'm not sure that actually makes me a winner. For tomorrow they are predicting snow and enough wind to close the road. Today might be the last really gorgeous day we have for a while. Jill is working in Florida and I watched the celebration in Chicago's Grant Park on TV last night by myself. I guess I'm feeling a little bit lonely.

Obama seems like a nice guy and, even though he is probably real busy this afternoon, I wish he were here so I could grill him a buffalo steak out on our deck that overlooks the Cheyenne River. He would probably be pretty interesting to talk to even though John McCain might feel more at home. I believe that if Barack Obama were to be transported to our deck he might think he had been drafted and shipped off to one of those distant lands. I'm glad he's our president, but I wonder how much he knows about my life. I wonder what he knows about the public lands in the West, the Endangered Species Act, the effects of global warming in an already dry land, livestock prices, grazing strategies, the relationship between prairie

species. I even wonder how much he really knows about the destructive-
ness of farm subsidies, the devastating effects of industrial farming, or the
inability of our current capital markets to honestly account for the complete cost of agricultural production. I wonder if he has any idea how little
I care about Wall Street—how unimportant I know it is in the long view.

But it would still be good to have him to dinner. Sit him down, turn
off the phones, look out across the heart of America, eat a little buffalo,
and just not say much for a while. I'd tell him we were out of wine and
that Black Velvet would have to do. I'd watch his eyes and see if he even
noticed the antelope moving on the bottom of the valley, see if he rubbed
his chin as the light changed on the distant bluffs. I'd set it up as a sort
of test; if he could actually be quiet and pensive and notice a few things
without me calling them to his attention. I'd get a hold of the whiskey
bottle when I went in to get a couple pieces of Jill's apple pie made from
the apples off the tree right there beside the deck. I'd freshen his glass and
sit back down and whistle to Henry, my English setter.

Barack wouldn't know that Henry and I had gone grouse hunting on our
way home from voting. He was playing basketball when Henry and I were
hunting. I picture him pounding up and down an asphalt urban court,
while I walked a couple miles through fenceless pastures and Henry ran
twenty or thirty miles—up and down rolling hills, through hundreds of
native species of grass, sedges, and forbs. When Henry bounded up on the
deck and over to check out the president, I'd talk about all those miles of
grasses that Henry had run through, the birds and animals he'd run into,
smelled, barely escaped. I wouldn't tell Barack that I believe his urban
basketball court is a poor and temporary substitute for the real thing or
that I believe that encouraging a vision of the future world as necessarily
urban and crowded is a mistake. Like I said, he seems like a nice guy and
I'd like him to figure that out for himself. I'd just introduce him to Henry.
It would be good to see a little dog hair and slobber on Barack's slacks.
Henry is a non-hypoallergenic dog so there is no chance Barack would
want to take him to the White House, but Henry knows a lot that the
president needs to know. He has seen it from ground level.

When Henry puts his paws into the president's lap I would do one
small, weird thing: I'd ask the president to smell his paws. I wouldn't tell
him that what he smelled was a primal trace of those miles and miles of
grasslands. I wouldn't even try to tell him what it was like when Henry
and I went grouse hunting after I voted for him. I wouldn't press the fact
that he had landed in a place where animals and humans conversed. That
would be a little too much for a first meeting.

But maybe I could get Barack Obama to lay his elegant hands on

Henry's sweet, silky head, look into the soft brown eyes, and consider something he might never have thought of before. Maybe he'd come away knowing a little more about my life and a little more about the real bedrock of America and indeed the world. Maybe it would make him curious and a year or so into his presidency, when he found himself bored stiff in a meeting of powerful people, he'd suddenly look at them as they prattled on about GNP, subsidy caps, bailouts, and balancing world trade and feel something unexpected. Maybe he'd have to repress a smile as a stray thought came to him, "These silly bastards have never seen the Cheyenne River," he might think.

I really don't think Barack Obama knows much about what's important in my life. But he's a smart guy and capable of sorting the real stuff from sound and fury. If I had a couple hours with him on our deck that overlooks the Cheyenne River it would not surprise me if some evening, a couple years into his first term, I got a call from Washington. I'd answer the phone and it would not be the president's secretary because Barack would not want anyone to know what he'd been thinking, that his curiosity had finally gotten the best of him. It would be the man himself, and in his beautiful baritone voice he would say,

"Dan?"

"Yes, Mr. President."

"Let me speak to Henry."

Kent Meyers   NAKED TIME

In South Dakota, the Missouri River marks the boundary between two different worlds. The eastern approach is over flat land, the black soil supporting corn and soybeans, and the valley is a long, smooth drop to the water. The west side of the valley, called the Missouri Breaks, is gullied and corrugated, barely knitted together by a thin skein of grass. West of the Breaks the land rolls, ranchland rather than farmland, dotted with Hereford and Angus cattle and with pronghorn antelope, casual survivors of the extinction that took the passenger pigeon and nearly the buffalo, and survivors, too, of the so-called Clovis extinction, the pronghorn's ridiculous speed an adaptation to the assaults of the Dire wolf and short-faced bear, its farseeing eye retaining, one can suppose, images of the continent when mammoth and mastodon roamed, and *Bison bison* had not yet even arrived.

Glacier touched the land east of the Missouri, missed the land to the west. Twenty thousand years ago ice rose as high as two miles into the eastern sky, so much weight it deformed the earth's crust like a hand pressing down on a water balloon. I grew up in Minnesota and spent many summer days picking up from our fields rocks that had been dropped by the Laurentide ice sheet. I felt the glacier's presence on the land as palpable and immense. Breezily riding a bicycle down the long slope of our driveway through a green corridor of corn, I could shut my eyes momentarily and imagine the weight and complete darkness that once existed where I rode, the ice wild with shrieks and groans.

One would expect glaciers to phase out, to scatter islands and shards of ice so that, approaching, you'd be uncertain when you had arrived. But the glaciers I've seen, in Alaska, end abruptly. They drop straight down to bare ground dampened by their own melting. The ice devours all light but a cool aquamarine, a light so pure and distant and coming from so deeply *within* that you feel it in your chest like a cough. The ice tumbles up, ice-stacked-on-ice, in something resembling translucent buildings hurled randomly upon each other—rooms and corridors, offices and libraries and cathedrals of ice space. Staring at it, you can feel *indifference* as a force. You feel the meaning of *crush*. The earth under your soles becomes acutely familiar, because you can reach out your hand and touch an alien planet.

As the Laurentide retreated, fierce winds powered by the extremes of temperature over the ice sheet picked up pulverized rock and ground it into fine dust. Settled, this dust became a loess soil. In parts of the Midwest it is fifteen feet thick, and so rich it's as if the winds that laid it are still energized within. The plants of the long-grass prairie, watered by Caribbean moisture, kept it from eroding, so that for twenty thousand years it has blanketed the Midwest.

This soil doesn't exist west of the Missouri River. Geologists think that the Missouri once flowed straight east to join the Mississippi somewhere in present-day Minnesota, but as the ice sheet descended the continent, the Missouri was forced southward. Every year the glacier grew, pushing the river south, until the glacier stopped growing and left the Missouri with its present-day bend to St. Louis. Thus, the Missouri traces the final shape of the ice sheet. There must have been a time when the Laurentide was calving into the Missouri's gray plain, museums of aquamarine releasing and serenely falling and smacking the river with explosive force, startling the tusked and long-toothed and farseeing animals on the western banks.

So much has been written about the American West as a place where vision enlarges. The pronghorn's eye, reputedly as good as a man's with eight-power binoculars, is a kind of biological metaphor for this. On a short-grass prairie, good eyesight and straightforward speed are the simplest ways to survive. Deer, adapted to more various environments and more hidden predators, cut right and left with every jump; the mountain lion is already upon them. Pronghorn antelope simply run, straight-ahead and full tilt. Catch me if you can. They saw the Dire wolf a quarter-mile away, or the eight-foot-tall short-faced bear, which surely didn't even try to slink. Antelope are so adapted to all-out running over a landscape without obstacles that they have never acquired the ability to jump, not even enough to clear a three-foot-high barbed wire fence. They duck under this strange thing introduced into their ancient environment. It's eerie to see a pronghorn, at full speed, melt into the ground, take that long-legged body low enough to get between the strands of wire, then pop back up, full-stride, on the other side.

Early explorers to the West were awed by how far they could see and how small that seeing made them feel. But time, too, is visibly vast on the land here. The surface of the continent is literally older. There is no new, thick topsoil to cover the evidence of former years, nor is there enough rainfall to support plant life abundant enough to prevent the erosion that year after year reveals ancient burials. Time is always being stumbled upon here. It has no clothing. You come upon it naked everywhere. It can almost be too intimate, too near.

Growing up, I imagined *ancient* through a lens of ice. But in the Midwest the truly ancient lies inaccessible beneath ten feet of topsoil. The door to imagining it is blocked by glacial ice. But cross the Missouri River—a single step, the glacier's abrupt, tumbling terminus—and that door stands unhinged. Time yaws, drops away. Twenty thousand years lurch into a hundred million. It's the difference between a borrow pit and the Grand Canyon. The epochs begin their march through the periods, lining up to form the eras, stretching back and back, the names an incantation: Pliocene, Miocene, Oligocene, Eocene, Paleocene, which form the Quaternary and Tertiary periods, which form the Cenozoic era, and then the Upper and Lower Cretaceous (note the metaphor of depth), which, with the Jurassic and Triassic periods, form the Mesozoic era, then they stretch away so sudden and breathtaking that the epochs disappear entirely in the far perspective of it, the periods like immense peaks stretching across the mountain ranges of time: Permian, Pennsylvanian, Mississippian, Devonian, Silurian, Ordovician, Cambrian, pinned by the great ridge of the Paleozoic, barely visible over a half-billion years away.

One's vision in the American West is time-inflected in ways not possible elsewhere. One fall day I picked an East Coast friend up in Laramie, Wyoming, and drove her to Spearfish, South Dakota. She couldn't see right, she told me. She knew those were cattle grazing against the hills, but she couldn't gain purchase on their distance. A quarter-mile? A half? A mile? The size of the mountains and cut of the land baffled her depth perception. She could recognize what she was seeing but, like the moon you can almost touch, couldn't make sense of its distance or account for its size.

In the same way you can almost grasp the twenty thousand years marked by glacial time. You can imagine it textured by human births and deaths, can believe ceremonies and traditions might be passed through the sieve of its sunsets and risings. But with a million years the sieve in its layers turns solid, leaving us, when we try to understand its immensity, only a gaspy, vertiginous sense of *beyond*. Everywhere in the American West events are placed within this timescape. The land is not only a geography but a geochrony of fossilized rock and the striated, muscular upheavals of mountains, the naked ages layered in the monoclines and anticlines.

In the South Dakota Badlands, dinosaur and ancient turtle bones, the beings of the ancient Bearpaw Sea, drip up from the ground as eroding rains drip down: another world as surely as those we might travel to through space. Walking in the Badlands there is always the possibility you will stumble upon time drowsing naked, floating up from the slow liquid of soil as if from green, algaeic waters.

        A few years ago I went to the auto salvage yard in Belle Fourche, South Dakota, to find a radiator for my old pickup. In the camaraderie of rust and junk, the linkage of old things, and the hide-and-seek of finding workable parts, the yard worker and I talked. He was happy. For newer cars the parts are labeled and placed on shelves, but my pickup is a '59 Chevy, my father's old farm truck, and to find a radiator we had to go out to the yard.

So we're riding, this young man and I, in a clanging pickup, over the rutted lanes between the strewn vehicles, weed-and-grass-grown, apartments for voles and mice—and oh what fun it is to ride in the junkman's junkheap, sleighing over the washouts, schussing down the ravines, head hitting the ceiling, bones disarticulating. We don't know what we're looking for. We know we won't find the radiator that fits. We're looking for a radiator that *might work*, and only when we reach the end of our quest will we know what we set out seeking.

We're prepared, we archeologists of the Detroitian epoch, with tape measures hooked to our belts, and both of us quickdraws, though he, I have to admit, quicker than I, so he does most of the measuring. But my ego's bruising is soothed by the pleasant taste of dust and dry grass, and the musty smell of small skeletons mummified in owl pellets. We're stopping at cars, finding hood latches where there are hoods, bending into the caves of the hibernating engines, measuring the radiators snuggled there.

And we're finally successful. We find one that will do—a radiator from a car, not a pickup, and not a GM vehicle, and two decades newer, different in every single measurement from the one I need to replace. But it has the same overall volume and will fit between frame and fan. I'll have to make a bracket from flat iron, drill new holes *there* and *there*, but sure enough, it'll do.

There is no phrase more pleasing to a fixer than *it'll do*, nothing more pleasant than making something that shouldn't work, work. Together the junkman and I have discovered a part that'll do, and we feel the solidarity and intimacy of the brotherhood of fixers, for whom imperfection is perfect, and finding the part that'll do is better than finding the right one. The right part simply fits. The it'll-do part requires vision and imagination and a re-defining of the possible. When you operate any machine that contains a part you've *made work*, it is your mind keeping the machine going. You're in constant relationship with it.

Quickly the ratchet glints, and the socket snicks onto it, and it chuckles and clicks, and rust squeals into a small red dust, and we pull the radiator up and bear it to the junkman's pickup and lay it in the bed. Then we relax. He's in no hurry. Once he returns to the shop, he'll be back to walls and fluorescent lighting and stacked and labeled parts. How long before someone else seeking something he can't identify happens by again? How often does this young man get to look for the thing known only when it's found? His boss knows these journeys to the promised wasteland of the forgotten, the unmapped geography of discard, have no allotted time for their taking. No efficiency expert with a stopwatch and clipboard has ever ridden with the junkman in his pickup to this place where time stretches and expands.

My companion leans against his pickup, having holstered his tape measure and toolboxed his tools. For all anyone knows, he's still tacking back and forth from metal reef to metal reef. I lean too. We stare at a hill a half-mile away. He nods at it, sensing that this seeking for remnants in the confines of the salvage yard is part of a larger understanding. He begins to speak of stone spear points that can be found on that hill. He names their age and type, describes their particular, identifying fluting. Then he turns and nods his head in another direction, and I turn with him as if we're cogged. He tells me how, several hills that way, a teepee ring might be found on the land of a rancher he knows, and stone spear points there, too—if you know how to look.

People march out of the past on his words, set up camp, go about their stone-strewing lives. With a PhD's depth of knowledge, he unfolds the entire landscape for me, maps it out through layers of time, geography and geochrony, hill-behind-hill and century-behind-century.

If you scratch the earth in the West, time oozes almost bloodily forth. Some *one* knapped this spear point, and right *here* lost it. *Here* a particular T. rex collapsed, and *here* a mammoth fell into a sinkhole. Strange and alien beings and yet so particular, so one, so once. Not just breathing, but breaths. Not just alive, but heartbeats, and between heartbeats, this event. That mammothy, tiptoey step over the bank, a great bellyflop splash, some unruffled swimming around, an attempt to climb out, and another attempt, and again, and the bank's steep defeat of each attempt, and the sun circling, and darkness, and the herd moving off, their many and familiar padded feet on the grass, and then silence and the water in the dark strangely less buoyant, and then its closing like a very low sky, and a single last breath.

Time flashes like that in the West, these still shots of remarkable clarity. And sometimes it can seem that time has ceased passing: this teeming town at Chaco Canyon is preserved in the dry air as bright as the day its mysterious builders wetted and formed the bricks. When you walk the stone steps on the mountain pathway at Mesa Verde, where so many feet have been placed that the stone is indented, your foot, in Nikes or Merrells or Crocs or what-have-yous, is placed in exactly *that* spot, the narrow pathway disallowing another, and you become a force of erosion like all those before you, without seeming to erode or have force.

The moments are so clear and so individual and so imaginable—within a time so vast, abstract, and beyond comprehension.

And that scratch in the earth can itself become an artifact. The tracks of Custer's expedition remain cut into the red clay of the Black Hills as if, around a bend, one might catch the wagons. There is so little topsoil to cure the wound, to close it over or encourage the roots that could bind it. The tracks of off-road vehicles in the deserts of Utah will be here centuries from now, epochs—resistant to curing.

Plow a loess soil, turn it upside-down with a moldboard plow every year for decades, and you hardly see a change. In winter you'll notice black snow but will think little of it. It will take farmers in the Midwest a century of such plowing to abandon the moldboard plow and recognize soil as a resource that can dwindle. But west of the Missouri, on that more ancient soil not-enough rained upon and lying more lightly upon itself, farmers learned that such plowing calls forth the dust cloud that blocks the sun and seeps like liquid through the cracks in your sashes though it grinds against your teeth when you eat. West of the river, discovery takes this form of knowing: soil, like ice, can sublime into vapor.

The geochrony of the West reveals a time that surpasses human attempts to encompass, and yet it holds and impresses and preserves such precise, individual moments—including our own: our boot tracks, our wheel tracks, our plow tracks. All is vast, and all is tenuous. Or all is vast and each is tenuous. In any case, in the American West we feel them both and feel more naked ourselves, present as we know we are to time's long, incomprehensible dream but also to its bright, breathing moments. In the Missouri Breaks, how barely held-together is the soil, how individual and separate the spears of grass in their tight bunches, how disarticulate our bones.

Ron Hansen | WHY THE WEST?

Why does big sky country lift my spirits?

Why is it that the British automobile manufacturer Rover named its high-end model a Range Rover? And why are the GMC SUVs named after Alaskan wilderness?

Why were Rob and I given cowboy boots for our third birthday? And why did we refuse to take them off?

Why is it that more people jump off the Golden Gate Bridge in San Francisco than the Brooklyn Bridge that spans the East River?

Why is it that a cigarette named after the Duke of Marlborough, an English lord, was famously advertised by a cowboy?

Why is the American director John Ford, born in Cape Elizabeth, Maine, principally known for Westerns, though they constitute less than one third of his films?

Why did my grandfather, who grew up in Spain, work as a hired hand in Iowa and finally ranch in Colorado?

Why was the bunkhouse that could house twelve hands still there some thirty years after it was last needed?

Why does Fort Huachuca, Arizona, have the greatest horse population in the Army?

Why does English artist David Hockney consider a major influence on his work the Laurel & Hardy films shot in Los Angeles?

Why are seven of the ten most populated cities in the United States located west of the Mississippi? And why can so few name all of them?

Why do so many Americans feel their country is overpopulated when 96 percent is parkland and open range?

Why do interstate truckers so often wear Western hats and boots?

Why are there still rodeos when so few of the skills on example are still practiced?

Why do I grin when my car radio can find no signals somewhere west of Ogallala, Nebraska?

Why are the riveted blue jeans that Levi Strauss began manufacturing in California in 1873 still, after all these years, in fashion?

Why are the Western comics starring Lucky Luke and the Dalton gang still a hit in France?

Why are Karl May's books about the American West still huge best-sellers in Germany more than ninety years after his death? And why did he never visit the region he wrote about?

Why do movie characters on the run almost always head west?

Why is prostitution legal in Nevada and nowhere else?

Why do cowboy poetry festivals attract greater audiences than the other kind?

Why did that Italian soldier in Rome insist on reciting the names of thirty-two Indian tribes?

Why did so many nineteenth-century artists who visited the West end up painting imaginary landscapes?

Why did John Wayne inherit his nickname, Duke, from a horse?

Why, in college, did I go out into the Omaha countryside at night and just stand in the fall fields, inhaling the healing air?

THE FENCE

One thing I noticed right away when I moved to rural Nebraska—people around here don't keep up their fences anymore. Along the dirt road that runs by my farm, the barbed wire fences around fields sag and collapse. Often only one strand is left, the wire gate dragged open and left in a tangle of weeds on the ground, the fence posts tilted and rotting. When cattle are present, the fence is a patchwork of mending—no one along this road has bought new wire in twenty-five years. The place at the top of the second hill is using orange plastic-mesh snow fence for the corner of their pasture. It's a glaring announcement that fencing, and perhaps even life, has gone temporary. Only the next place down from me, a horse facility, maintains its fencing—a high pipe-and-wood corral to keep the stallion safe and a board fence for the others. That place was built in the last ten years on a pioneer farmstead—no evidence of the farm anymore. Like mine, with eighty acres cut off and subdivided, there's barely a farm at all. And now my sixty-five acres need fencing too. The sagging barbed wire that breaks in my hands when I try to lift it from its weedy prison is all that keeps four-wheelers and snowmobiles from entering my land off the dirt road by the mailbox. To the east, my property is guarded by a deep ravine, creek, and woods—though I imagine the day is coming when children will risk the six-foot-deep beaver pools and find a way across to my farm. I need fencing everywhere I turn, and the cost plagues my sleep. I hate the idea of the steel posts and wire that will soon cut across the western horizon, dividing me forever from the unhampered sky and suburban neighbors, but it has to be done. They're going to build their tract houses on their twenty acres, and they've already shown that the concept of property for them is a sliding notion—what's theirs is theirs, what's anyone else's is theirs too. I caught the man on Lot B hitting golf balls across my land one afternoon last fall. When he noticed me, he stopped, turned without apology, and started hitting his balls across his own land. Later I noticed that he'd planted a small evergreen at the property marker, as if I were the intruder. The farmer sharecropping the land now has to drive his huge tractor delicately around the tree when he plants the winter wheat.

Then the man on Lot C drove over the soybeans last summer to get to his land, which isn't planted. He had no trouble doing this, even though drought had already significantly reduced the crop. I had to tell him to be careful with another man's living. He smiled in a goofy way and continued to drive over the soybeans until they were harvested. In the spring, my neighbor's cousin snowmobiled up my driveway and into my field over the late spring snow, gouging trenches into the fragile winter wheat just beneath that had begun to show green. I visited these neighbors to remind them what being neighborly means—staying off other people's land. Later someone would drive a truck up our drive and try to enter the field again, recognize the planting, and turn around, grooving the shoulders on either side of the drive so deeply that the tracks remained all summer. *It's the country*, those grooves say. *We can do anything we want here.*

I like to think that there was a time when fencing was done to keep livestock from wandering, keep them safe from theft, preserve the planted fields—and that everyone understood what it meant to enter another person's land. This spring I noticed that someone had cut down one of the beautifully straight walnut trees bordering my creek on the far side. Out of sight, out of mind, they must have thought. Now I listen for every sound of a chain saw and investigate. There's something about woods and water that makes other people feel as if the land must be free. I find shells from hunters, trash, evidence everywhere of people using the land as if it were a county park.

All fall long, hunters stop to ask permission to hunt the area, as if my house, my animals were not right along the edge. What about stray bullets, what about the horses in the next pasture? I devise stories of small children visiting, of birders walking the property, of any number of potential murder victims to hold them off. What about your deer, your turkeys, pheasants, ducks, quail, squirrels, rabbits—what about all that isn't yours? they ask with their raised eyebrows when I won't give permission. In their hearts they doubt that I have any rights at all; open land must be public.

I don't want the fences, you understand. When I bought the land, it was to see the sky, the rolling hills, the trees—to feel the space open my soul again. I did not want a repeat of my life in town, where every property is carefully marked into city lots uniform for the neighborhood. There is something in me that becomes, what, greedy?—no, more like *possessive* when I'm confined. I remember once owning a house in a St. Paul, Minnesota, neighborhood next door to a family with three kids. When an exceptionally dry summer came, they began to play across the front yards of the houses on either side of them, although I asked them not to since they were killing what little grass was left. Then one evening the father came out and tossed the football from his lawn to his son standing in front of my house. He glanced at me and smiled when he saw me at the window, staring while his son chased the ball into my roses. The next day I went out and bought a bunch of Alpine Current bushes and planted them in a line between our houses. The entire family looked anguished when they realized that their playing field was gone. I felt small and mean, the way you do when you lock the dog up for barking. I saw that part of myself then and knew I had to do battle with it.

Later, when I owned land in the Sand Hills of Nebraska for several years, it worried me sick to think of other people crossing it, using it to enter the Niobrara River, camping or hiking. It got so I couldn't stand to go out and look at it for fear of the tracks of vehicles and people I might encounter. Then my neighbor to the west, who owned a store in Valentine and had dealt with ranchers his whole life and should have known better, told the power company I wouldn't mind having the power poles march across my land so he could get cheap electricity. I drove out unexpectedly that time, to discover eight poles in a straight line cutting across everything I loved. The power company, of course, had to pull them out since they had trespassed, and the cable went underground for ten thousand dollars. I didn't feel one bit sorry that time—even when my neighbor said he couldn't send his kids to college if the poles got pulled. Start saving, I told him.

You can't trust a person's word out here anymore, the power man said.

It was a big relief to sell that land. I'm not a good person when it comes to property. I don't open my arms and say, take what you want. I think it's a feeling left over from my pioneer stock—I feel that I have worked too hard to get here, to own this piece of land, and now I have to protect it.

I'm not Thoreau. And come to think of it, neither was he. He camped in someone else's backyard, and his mother brought him all his meals. No, I'm what came after Lewis and Clark got done drawing maps and being awestruck.

In north central Kansas early fence posts were originally made from native limestone cut in five- to six-foot lengths, nine inches to a square side, and weighed 250 to 450 pounds each. In the 1880s and 90s, you could get them delivered for twenty-five cents apiece. Some forty thousand miles of post-rock fence were used in this area. There are still remnants standing as testaments to those days when a treeless plain had to be fenced, the fossil shells embedded in the visible surface between the grooves for the barbed wire. Imagine how great the urge for enclosure had to be to move three- and four-hundred-pound fence posts.

In La Crosse, Kansas, the Barbed Wire Museum is the only one in the world devoted exclusively to the "Devil's Rope." Out front is a ball of barbed wire, five feet in diameter, while inside is a large room whose walls are covered with more than seven hundred varieties of barbed wire, each catalogued with the name of the designer and the date—plus fencing tools, splicing techniques, dioramas of early wire use, and other information about "how the prairie was transformed into America's breadbasket." I bought six eighteen-inch samples during my visit and am still trying to figure out a good use for them. There's "Arrow Plate," patented 1878 by Hiram B. Scutt, with a four-pronged, blunt barb resembling an arrow in a twisted wire strand; "Hunts Link," patented 1877, whose interlocking strands resemble long paper clips with the ends twisted into sharp barbs; "Union Pacific Railroad Wire," patented 1874 by Joseph Glidden, with two four-sided wires twisted together and a single thin wire barb twisted in every three inches; "Loose Barb," patented 1868 by M. Kelly, with a long, sharp diamond-shaped wedge strung through a strand every five inches; and "Lazy Plate," designed by William Watkins in 1876, going back to the Arrow Plate with the widest part inserted between the wire strands so the prongs catch going across. And finally, there's a braided wire of four strands with no barb at all. Apparently, J. B. Cleaveland didn't hold with the ripping barbs when he created the elegant "Flemish Four Braid" in 1894.

You have to wonder if the strands of wire say something about their designers. Hunts Links, for instance, is very flexible, jointed every four inches. It would be easy to handle and string, and just as easy to cut and release. The Lazy Plate must have made it easier to insert the barbs than the Arrow Plate, whose designer had probably fought Indians for the land and meant never to be moved again. The Union Pacific wire looks the most common, probably the one most of us would recognize since the railroad cut its way across the country. Its form is simple, efficient, and the thin wire barb would cut the quickest and most painfully through hide or skin. The twisted wire is the heaviest gauge, as if the railroad always knew what its business was. They all did then, didn't they? There was less soul-searching about the meaning of property ownership, about the significance of putting up a fence to keep what was yours in, and what you didn't want as yours out. People could sight-read the land, the geography, tell you where their boundaries were just by looking. Now I have to hire the surveyor again and again to come out and drive me around to show me the exact places his survey stakes are set. If I forget so easily, how will my neighbors remember?

Picking up my wire samples always involves the barbs digging into my hands, catching on clothing. It makes it hard to imagine fencing the entire plains region. In truth, I've never fenced in my life. I've written about it, I've talked to people who have done it, including the men in my family. I know that old-time fencers were known by their signatures—the way they finished the ends off was highly individualized so a downed fence could be repaired by the person who strung it. I know that there's a fencing law for rural Nebraska, saying that people on both sides of the fence must split the cost of putting it up. I know that if it were left up to me, I'd probably go for the plastic snow fence too, but that's not what's going to happen. Still, I'm torn.

In *The Act of Creation*, Arthur Koestler wrote that "boundaries of self are fluid or blurred in the dream." All my life I have dreamed of this farm, of the absolute freedom from other people, their noise, and their buildings. I have never loved cities, never marveled at pavement, never thought a park a good substitute for what was gone. My geographical psyche has always been out here, without boundaries, where I live in fluidity, not having to check myself constantly to see if I exist as I should with others. At least, that was my dream of my dream.

Now I find the truth—fences, the opposite of being without boundaries and borders. Koestler speaks of "discovery by misadventure," the moment when things shift from plus to minus in science—the intersection where discoveries are often made. In other words, the unconscious mind working through reversals. Is it my own misadventure, then, to confront my ego on this dream plain and to discover the truth about my desires? Perhaps what I've always wanted hasn't been the unbounded space I told myself to imagine—maybe, instead, it's been a large space that is bounded by me, and me alone. Maybe I'm more like the Union Pacific Railroad and the early settlers than I ever imagined. After all, they quickly marked off their territories, erased the original peoples, and dug in. Fencing just made it official. Now we dig in with mortgages and get surveyors to measure to the inch by bouncing signals off satellites. But the desire is the same—to enclose oneself. "Don't fence me in," the anthem of the American West says, but maybe what it really means is "don't fence me out."

Therefore, the fence I want to build is a four-strand barbed wire strung tight enough to metal posts to bounce a steer or a four-wheeler off of. I want the neighborhood thoroughfare to stop here. I want my new suburban neighbors to shrink in fear at the glittering teeth across their backyards. I want them to warn their children to avoid the crazy woman in the farmhouse who keeps hogs right up against their lots. I want the hunters to understand I mean POSTED! KEEP THE HELL AWAY! I want a metal gate across the foot of the driveway, with a secret camera to spy on anyone trying to get in. I want something I'm never going to have now. But see, there I go again, ranting. I know why my neighbors have stopped keeping up their fences. They've given up.

I have always lived in at least two places. Literal places (never mind the myriad intangible ones, those in books or dreams or other fantastical locales). At first, I couldn't understand why other Wichitans didn't leave town over the summer; were they crazy? The atmosphere was like that of a Laundromat, alternately humid or arid, inescapably, miserably hot. My calendar was the school year calendar; I thought it applied universally.

In fact, I've never served under any other calendar, the one that vaguely trumps natural seasons and names them, instead, Fall Semester, Spring Semester, and Summer Break.

In the 1960s, our family owned a single car. A station wagon in which we all fit, five children, two parents, sometimes a pair of grandparents, at least one dog, and, later, against my father's wishes, a cat in a box (Ink, Francis, Grey Cat, Peter Rabbit). Across western Kansas and eastern Colorado we drove, nobody ever anywhere but in his assigned seat, my father at the wheel, often with a beer in hand. Damp cloth diapers, rinsed out at the last filling station, fluttered from windows. The younger children rode in the way-back, backwards, making faces and gestures at the cars behind. The baby was passed around the middle seat, where the women and older children sat; my grandfather smoked cigars, narrating and navigating in the front passenger position, and the dog rode panting at my father's ear. The dog was called Moe, a name that was either shortened from Geronimo (so claimed my brainiac brother Billy) or was in honor of a Stooge (according to my brother James, who was kind of a bully). My father arrived everywhere with a damp spot on his right shoulder.

We took a longer than necessary route because my father preferred empty Highway 96, a road upon which so little traffic passed that grass and weeds grew from its cracks. It meandered through a series of Kansas towns, each punctuated by a looming grain elevator on which its name was writ large. Ness, Leoti, Selkirk, Sugar City. These towers were markers in our annual pilgrimage, each a piece of the ritual. In Great Bend we indulged my grandmother's love of a certain banana crème pie (where also the dog had to be tied to a newspaper box outside the restaurant, served a bowl of water, attended to grudgingly by one of us when he began to howl). My father delighted in wildlife—deer, antelope, coyote, any number of raptors—and we were rewarded by spying these for him. There would also be car sickness and complaint; the cat would be let loose and always end up under the brake pedal, my father cursing. By sunset, we would arrive, finally, at our beloved Sands Motel in Pueblo, where we piled from the car into, always, the same two blessedly air-conditioned rooms. My father reserved these rooms using a postcard from the Sands he'd taken the summer before. Why was he amused by the thought of the proprietor receiving his own postcards?

From Pueblo, looking west, we could see the purple outline of the Rockies like a faint promise. Their existence never failed to send a zing of expectation through the sternum. I think we all shared this sensation; the mood was invariably optimistic. A dip in the small motel pool and the (very rare) dinner at a restaurant (The Top of the Town, where my younger brother always ordered the same thing, always made the same joke, he'd have the halibut, "just for the halibut," a food he didn't even enjoy) erased all of the hot and close ten-plus hours in the car. It was thrilling to delay our gratification, to break the trip into halves. One life, in Kansas, at school, traded for the other, in Colorado, utterly free. And here, for a moment, between the two.

In our small summer town we stored a Jeep. A 1961 model, the same year my parents purchased their little Telluride house, the same year I was born. When my brothers were old enough to drive, we took the Jeep back to Kansas with us. Whoever was the teenage driver, naturally, was the one who had to handle the Jeep, the vehicle without air conditioning or automatic anything (steering, brakes, transmission). It went no faster than forty-five miles an hour. It had a radio, but why? You couldn't hear anything except the straining engine or the shouting of sibling companions. Thus began a modified version of the same annual journey, except that the Jeep was sent ahead, hours before the station wagon, driven by whichever child was newly licensed, accompanied by the next in line.

Add, then, to the pilgrimage the inevitable overheated engine in western Kansas, steaming Jeep pulled off the weedy highway to await the station wagon. A late-morning sultry heat, the sunflowers and the crickets and the vast flatness of my native state, an understanding that our father was coming, eventually, to solve our problem. We would wait, me as passenger with Billy, or me, driver, with my younger brother. At least we could relish the relative silence, the absence of jarring vibration. There was a grain elevator in the distance, as usual, and perhaps railroad tracks. Everyone complains about Kansas, complains or derides or dismisses, its

monotony, its huge nothingness. But stranded in the center of it, in a disabled Jeep, en route to Colorado, the sense of both space and specialness
was overwhelming and somehow glorious. The only car for many miles.
The only feature on the landscape. The singularity. The solitude. The
space between.

My grandfather would die. My older brothers would outgrow family
summers. The Sands Motel would be plowed under to make room for a
Holiday Inn Express. My father would grow disenchanted with Telluride's
transformation from funky mining town to trendy ski town. The fishing,
he claimed, had gone to hell. He might have thought he invented the word
Californication.

But I never stopped thinking of that place, the one that occupied the
time between the end of Spring Semester and the beginning of Fall Semester, as one where I belonged. Every early June I head there still, now from
New Mexico or Texas. I know the way by markers on the highways, the
small highways I prefer, the little dumpy motels where I like to stay,
those places that are friendly to the dogs with whom I travel, those air-
conditioned rooms where my children have often jumped on the beds,
swum in the pools, come back to after a meal on the town.

At the end of this current summer, the not-quite-but-almost fiftieth
anniversary of my family's ownership of its little unchanged shack in
Telluride, I will drive to Kansas. The occasion is my daughter's wedding,
which will be held at my mother's house, that same place where I grew up.
I'll be driving there just before Labor Day, and I'll take the same route my
father would, if he were alive, if he were able to drive, if he were still fond
of Telluride and of returning home from there. Those grain elevators continue to announce loudly the names of the remote and bedraggled towns
that persist in their shadows. The sound of cicadas in late August, in late
afternoon, has always been the sound of the end of summer. Coming
home to Kansas always felt melancholy, always emphasized the sense of
something acquired thrillingly (say, a summer romance) that had to be left
behind for something less frivolous (say, sophomore year in high school).
The heat lightning on the horizon merely echoed the sensation. Time was
passing. Years were going by. Death was coming.

Living in a few places affords me a sense of multiple lives. Perhaps it
accounts for my insane fantasy of owning one of those farmhouses just
outside the Kansas town, the ones with the large porches overlooking the
vacant highway, surrounded by cottonwood trees planted as windbreaks
long, long ago by the first travelers expanding westward. Overhead, jets
carry the latest travelers coast to coast with far more efficiency, people
whose apprehension of my state, the whole enormous windblown region,

in fact, is summed up by the way they describe surmounting it: *flyover*. You only get the one life, but how nice it is to consider the others you might reasonably live. Sitting there on a dusk-lit porch, for instance, in the slight lull between destinations, at neither end nor beginning, watching the occasional car go by.

Rick Bass

THE LIGHT AT THE
BOTTOM OF THE MIND

I'm more of a place person than a people person. Pretty intensely so. Though my great luck in the West has had at least as much to do with people as with places. People like Tom Lyon and Moyle Rice in college (the former who introduced me to Peter Matthiessen's *The Snow Leopard*, the latter who explained to me with utter kindness the correct spelling of the French novelist he kept raving about—that it was not some mythic Native American chieftain of the Utes, perhaps, Flow-Bear, but instead, Gustav, author of *Madame Bovary*). A newspaper editor, Nancy Williams, who even in college thought I would be a writer long before I figured it out; friends like Doug Peacock and Terry Tempest Williams, who remain for me the ethical benchmark and gold standard for environmental activism. Pen pals like David James Duncan, Kittredge and Annick, Harrison, McGuane, Chatham, Lopez, Kingsolver, Stegner. The journalism of Dick Manning, back during the Plum Creek days. Postcards from Abbey, datelined Oracle: there is no end to the assistance and support I've gotten, making a home in the West. I've been lucky. I was born a Westerner—Texas being the edge of West, just as it is also the last of the South—but I've been lucky to be welcomed by deeper, further, farther Westerners.

You'd think then that I'd be a people person, through and through—that for better or worse, my life has been cobbled together through the attentions and kindness and efforts of others—and I don't mean to take any of them for granted. But when I think of how I came to be a writer, I think more about the specifics of place than about the talent and focus of individuals who chose to share their time—their energy—with me. Who chose to invest in me.

I don't know if it's this way for people in other professions, and in other places, but I think that here in the West, it might be: that we are led to our lives by others, but then anchored—and shaped—by place.

Part of me feels a little guilty about that greater allegiance to place than to people. Again, I don't mean to discount my friends, and I could never have become a writer, or more fully a Westerner—whatever that is—without their assistance—but in my soul, my allegiance, or rather, primary passion, is to place. That's the wellspring from which a story comes, and for me, the place where a life comes from.

When I think about how I came to be a writer, I think about only a handful of places, microsites, really, insignificant in terms of size, but possessing immense importance in that path. And whether I was drawn toward those places like some migrating salmon or turtle, to a place I had never seen or been before, but where I needed to be, at the time I needed to be there, or whether I was just lucky, I cannot say. The answer to such a question might be *both*.

For me, some places—and often they are the kinds of places we find in wilderness—are like super-cells in the bloodstream, a hundred- or even a thousandfold more vital to operations of the larger organism of self than are the other regular cells. Acting as catalysts for the production of stories and perhaps even the summoning of what we tend to call magic— the powerfully coincident—these microsites influence all the other processes and subsequent events in a writer's, or a Westerner's, life, disproportionately huge in the way they determine the nature of all else in their immediate vicinity, as in the manner with which one tiny watchspring, placed in the correct position, can control the gearworks of an enormous timepiece.

Microsites for me, long before I was pulled to and ultimately anchored in the Yaak Valley of extreme northwestern Montana—perched on the borders where Montana, Idaho, and British Columbia come together— were an independent bookstore in Mississippi—Lemuria—and a school, the improbable good fortune of going to that school in northern Utah, at the mouth of Logan Canyon, where each morning and evening the locomotive-rush of the cooling, sinking winds came roaring out of the beautiful canyon, tumbling out into the small town tongues of gold and orange aspen leaves on those invisible rip currents. Another was my white writing table situated out in the center of a hot green weedy field, in the backyard of my rented farmhouse in Mississippi, at the edge of the deep green woods. Every story I have ever written has been about people, but it has been generated by the power and specificity of place, and by the influence, the relationship, of that place to and upon the people in the story.

I am remembering now another microsite, a small but intensely powerful node in my subconscious. I'd like to say it was in the Yaak—and for me there are many such places in the Yaak—but the first microsite I remember, the first node, occurred long before I even knew there was a Yaak. It was in Texas, of all places, and it was both a time and a place, an event— though perhaps *event* is too freighted a word—that, though understated, seemed to sear and etch itself onto my mind in a way that the witnessing of other images had never done before.

It was New Year's Eve, and I was camping up in the hill country with my father, grandfather, uncles, and cousins, in the place where our family has gone to hunt deer each year for seventy-five years now. I was maybe ten years old and had been sent down to the creek with the metal pail to get a bucket of water with which to prime the old pump.

Our home-built camphouse was up the stony hill a short distance, and the men were inside playing dominoes. It was deliciously cold—there had been an ice storm, a novelty for Texas—and I remember the sounds being extraordinarily clear and crisp in that cold air: the snap of dominoes on the Formica tabletop in the dining area and the little *squeak* and *squeal* of the metal pail as I carried it down to the creek.

Why did my senses choose to register the world, to absorb and begin to interpret the world—to *notice* the world—so much more intensely that one night, as opposed to all the days and nights that had preceded? The more I think about it, or about my own life, at least, the more it seems to me that maybe not all of us are born upon first entering the bright light of the world, but that instead sometimes we are delivered as if still sleeping, or encased in some sort of protective caul, unknown even to ourselves.

It is a cliché perhaps to consider such moments of luminous aware-ness as a second birthing, but I have heard so many others speak of such moments, particularly writers, and more particularly, the writers we tend to think of as "nature writers," that it occurs to me I might not be the only one who spent many years in a kind of curious slumber before being called or summoned to awaken and notice the world. And in that notic-ing, learning to love the world more deeply. As if—unlike the wild ani-mals that have already existed in the world for so long—such a skill set did not arrive ready-made within all of us, but in some of us had to be elicited, developed, by some perhaps irreplicable mix of landscape, ex-perience, and family. And maybe it was or is not so much an awakening as a transcendence. A larger path or current carries you along for however many years—call it ten, call it twenty; call it forty or fifty—and then one day, in some certain hour, you find yourself beached on the gravelly shores of an island, a sandbar, with your senses more radiant, more connected to further and farther things.

At the creek, I crouched beside the water-gathering place and listened to the sounds of the domino game. A heavy fog shrouded the hill coun-try and I could see my breath as I exhaled—again, to a South Texas boy, a rarity, if not a novelty—and though the cabin was not far away at all—

thirty, forty yards?—in my memory, it was a much greater distance: as if in the sharpening of the primary senses of sound, sight, and touch, the other entanglements, other combinations of the senses, such as depth and distance, were looser. As if a reordering was occurring. Again, the word is *transcendence*.

The little creek was frozen in the eddy where I usually dipped the bucket. The center of the creek—barely wider than a boy's running jump—was still unfrozen, and in the darkness I could hear the quick gurgling. The clarity of the sound seemed somehow sharper than any I had ever heard before. I could discern slipstreams of the hastening water, individual ropes and river braids, one sliding over and around the other as that water hurried past. And without meaning to make too much of the moment—though it *was* a moment, calm and assuring, but also bright with the electricity of some kind of newness—I felt connected to the creek, closer to it, simply through that strangely enhanced hearing, which was doubtless due in part to the clearer, drier, colder night air, but due also, I think, to that burning away—finally!—of the silvery caul.

In that new state, I felt as if the water was passing through me—through my mind. I would not have said so back then, but in my memory of that time, what it seems like to me now—how I remember it—is that the sound of the water, rushing past, over and around center-stream stones, might as well have been the same sound it would make running through the folds and crenulations of my brain. It was that electrifying—I keep using that word, *electricity*, but what other phrase can there be for the sensation of current running in parallel all through your mind, silver currents shimmering with light?—and yet it was not a frenetic sort of energy, but instead, becalming, inspiriting. Perhaps there by the creek that night I was the equivalent of a ground wire, the negative terminal that allows the electricity to pass through a vessel without damage, for I felt no surge or jolt, only a keen and calm attentiveness. A stillness, there beside the rushing water.

I turned my flashlight on, shone it out at the trembling little current that was so alluring to my ears, and then played the light upon the little eddy, a space no larger than a big washbasin. There was only the thinnest sheet of ice over the eddy, the ice latticed and striated with the intricate fault lines of its fragility. It would require no effort to tap through it, to shatter it and dip my bucket into the frigid water—the ten-year-old boy of me anticipated such minor mayhem—but I paused just before breaking the ice, noticing some small movement beneath the ice, some tender evidence of life.

It took me a moment to realize what I was seeing. The movements I had noticed were really only the shadows of life; suspended halfway down in the cold water beneath the ice was a school of tiny perch, so young and slender as to be translucent—almost invisible in that clear water—and strangely, it was their shadows I had noticed, cast by my flashlight beam passing through their delicate bodies, not the fish themselves, which were gathered close together as if for warmth, finning slowly, and staring at me with gold-rimmed eyes that appeared to bulge ever-so-slightly, unaccustomed as they were to finding themselves beneath a shelf of ice.

In the play of my flashlight beam, as the light strafed down through the translucent ice, and into and through the nearly translucent fish, I could see their internal organs—their feathery red gills, their dark little hearts and livers, the leaf-veins of their cartilaginous bones.

A thousand different sensations passed through me, a thousand different recognitions. How alien and isolate the fish were, as suspended in the world as is a ten-year old boy between childhood and adolescence, much less the metamorphosis of adulthood. Who among us, either as child or adult, has not felt at odd times a random disconnect or even estrangement from the rest of our humankind—set apart, isolate, ice-bound?

Gills flapping, laboring to breathe, and laboring simply to keep from becoming as frozen as the ice above them, and which threatened to surround them, the fish were things of utter beauty—like underwater jewelry, but so much more beautiful for their brief living.

And for the first time, I think, I felt the responsibility of my own species—of the little gods we are, here on earth. I might as well have been Zeus-with-a-thunderbolt to those fish, looking down from on high, peering down through one world and into a netherworld, all-knowing and all-seeing. There was another universe beneath the ice, and it was strange and beautiful.

Perhaps in that moment the first tricklings of a certain current coursed through my mind, the first rivulets, that would eventually form the neural pathways of how I looked at writing stories, and, later, how I would consider the telling of them. But perhaps, as well, that was the first moment in which I truly saw beyond myself, or saw, for the first time, some new distance of quantum magnitude beyond myself. And if so, what sweet irony, that such immense new distance beyond self should be played out across a measurement of only a foot or two—though across that short distance, another world, other worlds.

And in seeing beyond myself, in observing with such a shock of familiarity and yet also surprise the improbable concept, to a Texan at least, of fish living beneath the ice, and of the collapse and compression, the *strata*, of all these different worlds, and layers of worlds—cold night sky,

ice, water, gravel—and in feeling empathy for the beautiful little fish, re-
splendent in their natural medium but trapped between earth below and
ice above—I think I was able also, paradoxically, to look back at myself
and observe the boy who crouched there with his light and therefore to
some small degree understanding the nature and condition of those fish.

The sound of the silver creek, still rushing past, still gurgling, still re-
assuring. A silver light shimmering in my brain is how I remember it
when I think about it now, though back then the only light was the miniature spotlight of my flashlight directed in a vertical column down into
the depths of that other world. But what I know now is that the creek *was*
coursing through my brain, washing away unnecessary plaque, or protective, fatty plaque left over from birth. Rivulets carving and eroding small
gullies, like creek beds, down which stories would tend to flow, following
for the most part the shapes and boundaries of those first-cuttings. As if
my mind had been waiting for that, had been needing that. I'm talking
about stories here, but I could just as easily be talking about a love for wilderness—a delight in seeking, imagining, and then exploring, unknown,
even unmapped, territory.

Was it a spiritual awakening, a moment of divine transcendence, or
merely an electrochemical stirring, a galvanic hypnosis, a chance encounter? Perhaps another than myself can better say or decide.

Carefully, I tapped at the ice with my bucket, knocking a small irregu-
lar fracture in the glassine surface, and gently filled the bucket, being careful not to dip too deep. I could imagine the consternation this sudden
swirling caused the fish, but still they remained in the eddy, and I imagined that they might even have been grateful for the increased clarity of
vision that was now returned to them; that once again, if only through the
spyhole of that opening, they were able to regard with their tiny fish eyes
the bright gold stars above, or, that night, the silvery cloudbank of fog and
rhime.

I studied the fish a few moments longer, still mesmerized by their presence, and then—as if it was time for me to return to my world—I heard
a different, wilder sound, further and farther—the honking of geese overhead. They were passing through, heading for the rice fields out on the
Katy prairie, but they must have been disoriented by the storm or separated somehow from their larger flock because they kept circling directly
overhead, honking and braying as if looking for a place to land—and with
my new ability to perceive the world vertically, I understood suddenly
how it must have looked to that small band of lost or straggling geese:
that just as I was hunkered over the fish, peering at them with a glow of
light through the ice, so too were the geese, far above, circling and peer-

ing down through the thin sheet of fog, to the glow of our camphouse, the only light for miles around, there in the hill country. That they might even have been looking for a place to land, a refuge and sanctuary from the strange storm that had coated the world with ice.

Two discoveries, then, in that river-rivulet carving, that night: that if there can be secret layers below, so too then must there be the opportunity for similar layers above. That we are not so much in the center of everything as instead in the middle: connected, briefly and tenuously, to some things smaller, and other things larger.

I knew all of this, that night, and for the first time, without knowing yet that I knew it. The knowledge had entered me, but it had done so as emotion and empathy, certainly not as explication or goal, ambition or desire. It had entered me as landscape enters us: possessing us, one day. The geese continued to circle and bray, as if calling down to the world over which they flew, and from up on the hill I heard the laughs and shouts of my family. I turned my light off so that I was in the darkness again and went back up the hill to the cabin, the creek water spilling from my bucket and splashing against my leg with every step, my breath clouds rising in the silver bursts of my own incandescent and improbable living, breath by breath and step by step and second by second, there in the darkness but moving back toward that light, tiny in the world, but with something—call it spirit—that seemed to fill up, inhabit, all the space available to it.

Again, we could be talking not about a life, but about the character and quality, the nature, of story, or of the wilderness itself.

It took a while after that—almost twenty years of drifting, wrong turns and dead-end paths or side-routes—but I got up to the Yaak, arrived there without even knowing where or what it was. My girlfriend and I drove up and over the high unpeopled pass of Dodge Summit late one summer and looked down upon the North Fork and the sleeping little blue-green valley, and I thought, *This is familiar.*

We stepped forward, into the valley. I wouldn't call what passed through me—the current between me and the landscape—a kind of electricity, as instead simply a kind of rightness: a path, an opportunity, crafted by my chance experiences in nature as a child, and by the recession of the deep ice, in the Yaak, creating the Yaak, fewer than ten thousand years ago.

It was that same feeling of awakening—that for twenty-nine years, I had slept. And that landscape—this time in the form of wild country, and wilderness—had roused me once more, in ways that needed doing. As if, without wild landscape, there is a tendency among some of us to grow numb, to become heavy-lidded; to lie down and quit.

I didn't know yet who all had been active on the valley's behalf before me—who the *people* were, some of them in distant cities and others of them hidden back in the woods, warring over its future.

I was still a place person, not a people person. But it occurs to me now, even if it didn't then, that in this day and age more than ever, people and wilderness are paradoxically linked: that wilderness needs people, just as people need wilderness. I'm grateful to the people who worked for the Yaak long before I ever knew there was such a place, and to those who have yet to begin work, but soon shall. Like a healthy wilderness itself, it is all a continuum, and all an intricate connectivity of parts: more than can ever be known. I don't especially like being around people—it's one of the reasons the wet, buggy, cold, rainy, snowy, nasty Yaak is so attractive to me—but more than ever, I must acknowledge that they—we—have some say in the matter of what will be swept under and erased from the face of the earth, or protected forever, for people who will never know us, and who will arrive one day at the edge of such wilderness and benefit from it, in ways we cannot begin to imagine, but can somehow sense: and that it is on their behalf, as well as our own clamant needs, that we labor.

Pumpkins pitched over dog-ear fence tops by a mother maddened, vexed by voices in her head, splattering pulp, seed every which way wind woed, dust, our woes a necessary thing. This was afternoon hot in August rush. This was yester. Those days we radioed our way into dusk, clowning out misery, rolling in rhythms Detroit laid out in tracks that crossed country catching us abandoned on crisscross Plain, narrowing rows through summer, into deep later fall. This was the heat of it, the indiscriminate weather chalked up and marked all over our brows, chasing baseball sleeves with black-browning outside, skin mauled in summer wear. These were the salted, skip through summer days. Days tablets touching tongue allowed us to torch ourselves in swelter avoiding inside stay thick with swamp coolers and crazy blaring louder than the AM band transistor dial, analog life we wondered. This was the half of it. That side we'd tell you.

What were we doing here? Winding past horizons meant for Eastern rims. Far past conceptual sunrise, into sundown territory where older cousins strayed and Dad took work. What were we without water and ridges to run? We were skimming Plains and scattered days either in refugee mode or fostered habit. We were moving.

Morning was story about due sunrise of here. Where we'd lay our ears toward wave echoing sound, from past temporal limitation, while milking the mile of while—West. Here, the lack of comfort, stray shrug like a lame pup near highway lip, snarling away any chance to be cared for, fostered. We were without urge to be held tight as young, least we be rejected, or smothered in it. Morning was full of urge. Full of what is up over here and how can I simply be invisible. Morning was urgent possibility and getting out of the hold without catching a quick pinch, or slap, was bringing up nothing worth arguing for and nothing more said than need be. It was glimpse forward and lament sleep long due and now gone to differ. Morning was catch the light before it shines through thin. Catch it clean and wide, hovering over a wood-pinned wash in yellow-white gleam. It was opportunity or measure of forgotten, your choice when it came down to it, despite the covey. Morning was Mom so spent from warring all night, her coffee shuffle barely got her around to scoop sugar over anything that didn't move on the table and call it breakfast. Morning was anything but sweet. Morning was move—fast—move—out of here with as little interaction as possible. Morning was clean, hair still wet hit the dirt running in wind so strong it would flip you if you weighed less than fifty pounds, like all of us then. Morning was books flying up when you flipped, covers torn off, fines due and more issued. Morning was glue when that came on. Morning was something make you forget about tomorrow. Morning unglued.

Unraveled we were. Gangly, glowering or glee-stricken, mostly not knowing how to feel, what approach to muster. Invisible, clown, fist to cuffs—all of it a scramble. These days cleared out ant piles with kill concoctions, like there was no muster to it at all. These days morning took to afternoon like luna moths to flickers.

Days rolled by in such haste their hems wore on edges called dusk and dawn. It was here we inhabited, in the turning. Each day brought something tragic and beautiful. The glory skipped its way beyond our reach and the tragic often stayed awhile. Sometimes he became our pal, sometimes showed his cousinness. It was a strange day when our cousin Richard had his face blown off by his own wife, right in front of the kids, and the state did not find her in offense. It was West that way. Must have hurt her to see him so riddled with malaria after surviving pungi sticks and shrapnel, after coming home. Must have been so much for her to see she just had to end him, so the state said. I don't know about her hurt, but I know we were all thrilled to see him alive and then he was taken. Days were like that. Days had their wearing.

Nights were june bugs, staying out till lights were out and sneaking back in, pre-school. Some nights staying with the neighbor kids watching how one would blow a trumpet, 1961, he maybe ten, and a hero for us. Watching him blow the trumpet, tell his own heroes, steal toys for us from neighbor kids he didn't like much and hand them over like we were something. Nights were runs through Black Cat Alley and over 11th Street caliche then, into some weird sense of what was this world about anyway, then we'd remember stories placing us elsewhere and know why the fit never snugged us. Nights were hearing how Mom was tortured and ghost come clambering alongside windows' edges. Nights were horses we rode at full run and then saddled. Nights were something free. We were loose in them and never tucked up. Nights were uneasy.

Dreams carried more than any day and dreams gave everything anyone needed know. Nights only delivered them. Night gave them up and gave us over to dreaming. Night delivered us. Still it was uneasy. Who knew what torturers would come from that closet and get Mom all uproared into the late of it. Who knew what it held in the rustle, tumble, fall of it and the long wait for reprieve in dawning. Night was truth and dreams were reality, the two inseparable colts always playing those bite and run tag games. Dreams had my bet and night was necessary to watch it play out. When else could we rest for an hour? If you could say we did.

Strangest thing about the fostering, the abandonment for asylum stays Mom would be committed to, strangest thing about it was the coolness existing in triple digit summers, taboo tabs and masks we wore to every single thing we approached. Still they linger and it has been decades now. Strangest thing about Seibert, Leoti, and small places they placed us to, was the alienation, the courage it took to simply walk in front of the towns-people there. The avoidance of us except to question. The toppling of days into dawns without the typical patterns during the high stress times. The gunning for no tomorrow while perched on the edge of a wooden chair in badly done neckties meant to strangle. Strangest thing was wondering what world this was and when would we enter the one meant to hold us. Would it take dying to be home, like that?

When you ask me what the West most impressed me with, it was that. It was full before we came into it and little place open for anyone like us. No matter you're born here, you belong back there and no one will ever let you forget that, no, Sir, no one will ever let that go. Still, you make a go of it. Your relatives are caught in the crosshairs along with you. To keep anything from taking them unnecessarily, you hang in there and do your duty, and sometimes that's simply breathing, sometimes clutching the disfigured postcard your dad gave you, other times it's figuring out no one lives in the walls your mom yells at all through night, then catching dreams to challenge whatever Underwood and the Pavilion dole out in the wired caps they apply to your mom's head, jolting her elsewhere one more time, before they change their ways. Remember those little yarn octopi they had her make? Tooled leather purses, belts. They had quite a craft factory going there with all those blacked-out patients, didn't they? Windows so high, well, you get the picture.

BETWEEN THE SANS BOIS
AND THE KIAMICHI

How dull to say I was born in the Great Depression, the fifth child, the third son, of Austin Oscar and Bessie Vernon Adams Barnes, near the town of Summerfield, in LeFlore County, Oklahoma. Yet these facts set me firmly in time and place. My family was a poor man's mixture of everything everybody else was who had invaded Indian Territory at the time of my father's birth in 1895 at Kullychaha. According to his telling, he was "some Indian and lots of Scots-Irish and other stuff." My earliest memories are of house and vista: from a porch facing a lane, I look up and down a road that stretches to the majestic mountains in the south and to the river north, beyond which I am told there are still more mountains. It was an infinitely long road, veering and disappearing into the blues of Winding Stair Mountain and the Kiamichi still farther south or in the opposite direction dropping into the river I had yet to see.

Only a few moments and images remain of the two or three years we lived across the field from a clump of trees that protected an ancient burial mound. But the image of the house is as clear in my mind as if I had left there only yesterday: two rooms, with a breezeway between them. One room had a fireplace and a space for sitting and a bed, where my mother and father slept. The other contained two beds and sundry items and boxes I no longer see with any clarity. I do not recall where I slept, nor where we ate. The image of the house as viewed from outside through a child's eyes is an immense one, the structure towering gray and hollow against a clouded autumn sky.

And the image begins to fuse with another: the house on Mountain Creek Road north of Wister. And again the image of house is clear. Now a larger, more expansive dwelling, with a long front porch and no breezeway, an enormous fireplace that I could walk into when the fire was out, a kitchen as large as a bedroom. But still the color of gray persists: many houses during that time were made from green lumber fresh from local sawmills and could not be painted with any success. Even after the lumber had aged, the rough-cut boards were usually not painted. Strange that

I have no memory of sunlight for the first six years of my life. Only the gray days and the deep, black nights.

The house on Mountain Creek Road seemed as large as a castle. I remember standing underneath the edge of the front porch to get out of the rain, with Colonel, my collie, sitting beside me. We were both looking across the road to a grassy prairie pasture that swept down a sloping hill to the creek beyond, where, had it not been raining, my sisters had promised to take me swimming. Conversely, I remember standing on the high bank of the swimming hole eating pawpaws my sisters had picked from the low limbs of a tree, looking back up the prairie and across the road to our house that stood, gray on gray, immense in its place on the hill.

The distance from the house on Mountain Creek to Wister, where two railroads crossed in a perfect X, was five or perhaps six miles. More than once, when my father—called *Ought* by family and friends—was freighting lumber from a sawmill he worked for during the winter months, I would get to ride atop a wagonload of fresh-cut pine lumber all the way into town. My father and his helper would sing rowdy songs as the iron-tired wheels popped gravel along the way. They would unload the resin-oozing boards into boxcars on the Rock Island or Frisco railroad sidings and then take me to the soda fountain for a double-dip ice cream cone at the only drugstore in town, tethering the team of horses between Model A Fords and Chevrolet roadsters to the hitching rail before the boardwalks and false-front buildings, remaining visages of a time that was rapidly disappearing without my even knowing that another age had been.

Strange, what you recall of days that seem to gray each into the other in a time when time seems hardly to have existed at all except now as in some long dream you see from a distant sleep. Images appear, vanish, appear again in such a fashion or frequency that these are themselves the history of the place where you were and, consequently, of what you were.

Our neighbor down the road, whom I now remember only as the Baldwin boy, had an ugly, jagged scar on his stomach. He never wore a shirt all summer, and the pink deep-scarred tissue above his navel gaped wide. He had two years before been run over by a mowing machine. He had fallen from the seat above the doubled crosscutting blade as the horses bolted out of the way of a striking copperhead. In his misfortune, he was lucky to escape decapitation or amputation. Accidents of that sort were common. In a land of alternating forests and prairies, ranches and farms, sawmilling and farming accidents were frequent. Eastern Oklahoma of that era, hardly thirty years after statehood, might well be referred to as the country of nine-fingered men.

I think the Baldwin boy may not have survived the war in Europe or the Far East. He was about the same age as my sister Marveda, several years older than I. He was so strong he could lift me with one hand and put me on his shoulder. That image comes readily enough with the gray houses, and at times during hay-cutting season I still see his shadow in the distance. I was terribly afraid to look at the scar, which he insisted made him strong. It must have been the first realization I had that we—man, woman, and child—were mortal, for I remember that each time I saw his scar I began to think of what it might be like to be dead.

HEARTLAND

The houses die, and will not die.
The force of walls remains. Take
the family portrait hanging oval
on the wall and, underneath it
on the chifforobe, a dish of mints.

There are houses that fall, but their
shadows stay, gray against summer's
dusk. And there are photographs that
show ghosts of mothers walking halls,
of fathers fiddling in moonlight.

Even in disrepair, there's a life
to the houses. The rush of wind stirs
a soul: footfalls on wood and stone,
the creak of kitchen door, the last
words of a son gone away to war.

The houses die, and do not die.
There is something that will not let
a space be given solely to grass.
The aura holds, the center will
not fold, forever framed against
the graying sky, the coming night.

I was five years old the last time I heard the mountain lion scream. We were living in another gray house some three miles or so northwest of Summerfield, up the hill from a wagon crossing on the Fourche Maline. It was near the ford that we heard the panther. My sisters, my mother, and I had been looking for pokeweed late one day across the river. I could navigate blackberry vines and scoot through brush without much effort and break off shoots of poke for supper, tasty and nutritious when cooked the Choctaw way with scrambled eggs. My sisters had swung me over a fence where I was to break off several shoots beyond their reach when we heard it, a low growl at first, then rising into a frantic scream. They yelled for me to come to the fence fast. I remember their jerking me straight up over the fence and then all of us running down the hill to the ford of the river. The intermittent screams of the cat continued for several minutes. We had heard the sounds in the night at other times, but never thought that a panther would ever be so close to us in broad daylight. We did not see the cat: we were too intent on leaving that domain as fast as our legs would go. Later, that night, we heard it again. One long cry, then silence. A neighbor had told us that the cat had been passing through the bottoms each spring for the last five or six years—to where, he could not say.

That was the way things were in eastern Oklahoma, 1938, when times were hard and life was good—and sacred. But a year later the WPA had done its work: roads were cut, burial mounds were dug into, small concrete dams were blocking nearly every stream. Sacred contours were annihilated. But the government was caring for its people. Many were the make-work jobs. A man could eat again, while all about him the land suffered. The annual spring migration of that lone panther was no more. The riverbanks that had been his roads and way stations bore the scars of the times, the scars of loss.

In my mind the rivers must always run free. But in truth today I do not recognize them. They are alien bodies on a flattening land where everything has been made safe, civilized into near extinction. Sounds of speedboats drown out the call of the remaining jays and crows. The din of highway traffic carries for miles now that the timber has fallen to chain saw or chemical rot. Green silence in the heavy heat of summer afternoons is no more.

The Fourche Maline River and Holson Creek flow through much of what I have written. I suspect they were always there, even back in the mid-1950s when I wrote my first bad short story and my first bad verse. My sense of place is inexorably linked to these two streams and to the prairies and woods between them.

I was born within spitting distance of the Fourche Maline, on a meadow in a house that no longer stands. A lone clump of gnarled sassafras and oak rises out of the meadow a short mile northeast of Summerfield, in the hill country of eastern Oklahoma, where the land was once heavy with wood and game. Nobody knows why the clump of trees was not cut down when the land was first cleared for the plow. Once there was a house a few feet east of the trees. The broken tile of a well long since filled still rises a few inches above the earth. But you have to look long, for the tall grass hides it like the night. I cannot remember a time when the house stood there. My mother said that the Adams family lived there for a short while at the turn of the century when she was only a few months of age. (Her parents, dissatisfied with their treatment in Mississippi, had headed west into Arkansas, then into east Texas, and from there into Colorado by oxcart, and finally back into Indian Territory, the new *Chahta* country, to claim what was theirs by treaty and blood.) But she could not recall the house, nor why it was no more.

Maybe the maker of the house knew why the trees were left in the middle of the field. At any rate, the trees are still there and are not threatened. Local legend has it that they once guarded a rich burial mound, but now no mound swells among the trees. Instead, a musky sink in the middle of the slump shows the scars of many a shovel and many a fire-lit night. The story of one night in particular sticks in my mind, though I was much too young at the time to know of the night at all. But like bedtime ghost stories, some things told again and again when you are young and lying with your brothers and sisters on a pallet before the hearth of the fireplace later illuminate the dim, unremembered years. It is the story of how my brother outran a horse.

Before I could stand alone, we lived on the lane that borders the east edge of the field where the trees still stand. My brother was nearing manhood and owned a horse and was a night rider. He learned that three men, neighbors and good-for-nothings, planned to dig in the trees. He asked to join them. He longed to prove himself a man. They had visions of gold and told him there was money buried there.

So when the October moon was dark, they gathered in the clump of trees and hung a lantern over the chosen spot. There was frost on the limbs of the sassafras and oaks. My brother broke first ground, and a hushed moan moved through the still trees. He dropped the shovel; later, strange pieces of bone-red matter began to show up in the dirt at the edge of the pit. While all were gathered about, another moan, much louder than the first, moved through the night—and my brother leaped out of the dark pit. But the good-for-nothings held him fast and howled with laughter as one of their cronies strode into the circle of the lantern's light, drunk on erupting mirth and bootleg whisky. Everyone had a good laugh at my brother's expense. And he laughed too.

But the laughter was short-lived. A deep, low moan—ghostly but unmistakably human—rolled up from the bowels of the black earth. For a moment, my brother recalls, a stillness like doom hung upon all of them. Then everybody was running, running: the good-for-nothings were running, the original moaner was running, my brother was running, and all the beasts of the field. A great shadow passed beside my brother. It was a horse. The moan persisted, even over the sound of thumping boots and racing hoofs. Now my brother passed the horse and burst through the barbed wire fence at the edge of the field with one wild bound. He flung himself down the lane and plunged through the doorway of our house and, stiff with fear, hugged himself close to the dying coals in the fireplace. An hour passed before he began to cry.

Several days later my father filled in the pit and brought home the lantern, dry of kerosene, the wick burned to a crisp.

The clump of trees in the middle of the field was the hub of the universe of my childhood and my adolescence. We always lived within sight of the field. And after the field became a great meadow, I found several days of bone-breaking work each summer, helping a cousin bale the tall and fragrant lespedeza that had been urged to grow there. But never did I seek the shade of those trees for my noonday rest. For me, they were too ghostly, foreboding, sacred. In the small knowledge of my mind's eye, I could see beyond all doubt that here was the final resting place of the broken bones of some great Choctaw chief. He had made it just this far west. He had come within sight of the blue Kiamichi range to the south, which was to become the last home for his dispossessed people, and had fallen dead on the spot from a homesickness of the soul. Among the sassafras and oaks he had been buried with all the pomp and honor that was left to his migrating children. I was wrong, of course: the burial mound is far older than any of the forced Choctaw migrations. Still, for me the spot was inviolate.

And thus it has remained. Only recently have I had the courage, and the reverence, to penetrate the gnarled clump of trees in the middle of the meadow. I went there in midafternoon and sat as motionless as I could while the sun dropped well below a long low line of trees far to the west. Sitting there, I tried to grasp something I could not name, something I knew as gone forever. I could not invoke it. I did not know its name. Once, just as the sun went down, I heard a hawk cry out high above the clump of leafless trees. Perhaps there was a moan. But I did not hear it.

THE EXACT CENTER OF THE WORLD

The owl among the trees wailing
like a mad mother's ghost is gone.
The mound of the guarding owl has sunk,

its skull nearly level with the ground.
The stones move in. A new forest
in twisted form crawls to the place
you found hard midnight at fifteen:
heard the screech owl moan, the moon fall,
and the breaking of ancestral bones.

Here you knew a first real fear and ran
past the second wind you never felt.
Dark times. But now the moon is back
and your eyes clear in the chalk of night.
Now you know all the ghosts are dead,
except the one never laid to rest:
this mound in this clearing is the exact
center of the world. All things move round
it. And here sundown explains nothing.

Named by the French, who early in the 1700s explored eastern Oklahoma, the Fourche Maline is by literal definition and personal observation a dirty stream, though one that once teemed with all the life that water could possibly bear. It was home to some of the world's largest catfish. I have seen mudcat and shovelbill taken from the river, on bank hooks and trotlines, mammoth fish that ran to more than a hundred pounds each. Their hides so scarred and tough you had to skin them with wire pliers or Vise-Grips. Bullfrogs loud enough to drown a rebel yell, turtles big as washtubs, and treacherous, rusty cottonmouths all called it home, dared you to enter their domain. I can remember big cat tracks on the shoals, mussel shells bitten in half.

The Fourche Maline was always a sluggish river, at least for the last twenty-five miles of its course. Though its source is in the western end of the Sans Bois mountain range, where the ridges are still thick with privately owned scrub pine and savannah sandstone, and where the water begins pure and clear, it is soon fed by farms and ranches with runoff from soybean fields and feedlots and by worked-out coal mines as it snakes its way eastward to join Holson Creek. I can recall a time when the Fourche Maline cleared in early summer even as far as its mouth after heavy cleansing rains, and the water of the deep pools tasted of springs. Now the river runs ever more slowly, if at all. Its life grows stagnant out of season.

ON THE BRIDGE AT FOURCHE MALINE RIVER

Forty feet below, the water stands as dull
as dog days. No movement toward the lake
ten snaking miles away. You stand here full
of hope you have always been told to have,
with no regard for the ruined years, those rabid
foxes at your heels.
              You stop here whenever
you have the time. The river's pull is strong.
The dark water, too thick and slow to reflect
anything outside itself, sends a constant song.
Worlds away you always know the river
is your home. You've never seen the river
run toward its sea. Yet it moves at the touch
when you take time to go down, lay your hands
on the warm river, and speak to the current
that flows into and through your blood.
                      It has
been years since you swam this muddy stream
and, bearing a rock for ballast, walked the bottom
straight across, bank to bank, in the longest breath
you ever held. Time and time again, as now,
you dream that walk. This time it's real. You leave
your clothes flapping on the rail and jump, wide,
into the warm water and feel the river
bottom wrap a gentle skin about your feet.
As you break upward for breath, you taste
the sweet meat of earth the river is made of,
and you remember the earth and that you are home.

On the other hand, Holson Creek—named for Holson Valley, from which it flows northward—was in the past a clear, fast-running stream. It flowed through the tall pines of Winding Stair and Blue Mountains, through pastureland thick with native grasses, among stones that seem still today old as the sky. When I remember Holson Creek as it was in my youth, I can still smell the sweet gum trees, the native cedar, the water willows, sharp in the summer, and hear the fussy barking squirrels, hear the rapids and small falls, see the banks littered with flint chips at places where the ancient ones stopped to make arrowheads and rest awhile by the clear water.

But now both rivers are slow, dammed. Where they meet, mouth to mouth, a lake begins. And for miles back up both streams it is difficult for the eye to discern movements of water, except in flood time, and then there is no guarantee which way they may run.

The land and streams are changing. Even what is protected pollutes: in the wildlife refuge, near the confluence of the Fourche Maline and the Holson, there are so many deer now that tick fever has thinned even the equalizing coyotes and has put salt fear into the veins of poachers, who once knew—who once were, right along with the coyote and vanished timber wolf—the true balancing force in nature.

Though fishing is sometimes fair, gone are the days of the scream of the mountain lion, the days of the big catfish. No one has seen a panther's track in the last sixty years, though the fish and game commission has recently introduced black bear into Kiamichi country. I doubt you could get snake bitten unless you worked at it. But I am a child of the past. I live it in my waking dreams. The gray clay banks along the Fourche Maline still hold their lure and the lore I assigned to them. I dug caves there. I danced the old songs. I attacked wagon trains, or, on the other side, killed Indians. And once in a rare sundown, I realized that here in the bottomland stood the only native holly tree I knew of anywhere in the great wooded valleys between the Sans Bois Mountains to the north and the blue Kiamichi to the south. The holly tree is gone, victim of the backwater of the Corps of Engineers. When backwater rises, is held like a cesspool for weeks on end, all flora and fauna rooted to place die. Even a simple child knows this.

What's more, and the hell of it all: I see but little hope, rather mainly dissolution of river, of land, and thus of spirit. You can see it plain on the faces of those who have witnessed, have lived, these civilizing years. Their faces are not lined without cause: there is something in the blood that needs rivers free, forests and prairies green with promise. Maybe lack of fuel and the death of automobiles will help, but I doubt it: I know people who will hike ten miles or more carrying a six-pack just to be able to throw the emptied cans into a stream to see how long they will stay afloat while they are pumped full of lead.

We have been called a nation of tourists. But I suspect, deep down, that some of us somehow know where home is—and what it has become.

EXCERPT FROM
*WALTER BENJAMIN AT
THE DAIRY QUEEN*

Well before I came of age, or even to articulate consciousness, that romantic nomad the American cowboy had been fenced and confined. Highways, fences, farms, and roads large and small made a patchwork of the once spacious prairies. Only in a few large ranches in Montana, Wyoming, Nevada, and New Mexico are cattle still moved from summer to winter pastures in the old, nomadic way. The seasonal movement of animals, such as still practiced with reindeer in Lapland, horses in Mongolia, camels in some places, sheep and goats in many places, is no longer necessary in America; as a means of tribal survival it has rarely been necessary. The long cattle drives that took place for about twenty years after the Civil War were large commercial ventures, initiated by cattle barons (or in many cases, would-be cattle barons); they were not tribal efforts and, once the longhorns passed, did not even involve native cattle—or cattle like the Mexican longhorns, which had come to seem native from having been herded for over three hundred years.

The myth of the American cowboy was born of a brief twenty years' activity just before railroads crisscrossed the continent north-south and east-west, making the slow movement of livestock impractical. The romantic phase of cowboying ended well before my father was born, and yet its legacy of habit, costume, assumption, and to a reduced extent, practice formed the whole of the world I was born into in 1936. Oil production was, and for some time had been, the dominant factor in the country economically, but oil drilling was not to acquire much social or stylistic weight for another forty years. Oil didn't arrive at full respectability until oilmen were secure enough financially that they began to buy ranches: before long oilmen, along with doctors, lawyers, and a few insurance men, seemed to own all the ranches.

I had no notion, as a boy—not the faintest—that I would end up a writer. It was not until my cousin went to war and left me those nineteen books that I even had a book to read; but I *did* know, early on, that I would have to deal with cowboying, either successfully or unsuccessfully, because there was nothing else in sight. I was given a horse at age three, and didn't take leave of cowboying until I was twenty-three. For twenty years I worked with my father and with the eight or nine ranchers with whom we swapped work. I realized early on that it would be unsuccess that awaited me because of my profound disinterest in cows. As soon as I got those nineteen books I began a subversive, deeply engrossing secret life as a reader. I very soon knew that reading would be the central and stable activity of my life, and that making a living would have to be made to fit in somehow, but if I could help it, it would not involve cows.

I mainly liked the cowboys I worked with when I was young, but I sensed early on that we were only nominally of the same species. I didn't pop books into my saddlebags or my chaps pocket to read at lunchtime or when there were breaks in the work. There weren't many such breaks anyway—my father was a firm believer in putting in a full day's work. Even though I never read while working cattle, I was soon thought to be a bookish boy anyway, and neither my father nor anyone else invested much hope in my future as a cowboy. They were possessed of enough savvy, those cowboys, to figure out immediately that I wasn't going to be doing what they did for a living—not for long.

The cowboys didn't care whether I stayed with their way of life or not, but for my father it was a trickier call. He knew early on that the ranching tradition to which he and his brothers had devoted their lives was doomed. He survived in it through hard work and great skill, but even so, had been in debt for fifty-five consecutive years and, at his death, still owned only four sections of land—not enough, in an arid region, to make any rancher much of a living. He knew that ranching had ceased to be a viable profession for smallholders or, really, for large holders either. (Although he knew that many cattlemen even in the days of the open range had gone broke, I'm not sure he understood that the range cattle business had never really been a secure profession, at least not on the central plains, mainly because the cattlemen had brought the wrong animal—English cattle—to an arid grassland to which they were not well suited. South Texas cattlemen, raising Mexican longhorns that *were* well adapted to their environment, did, on the whole, much better.)

Still, ranching was the only craft my father knew and his devotion to it was deep. It was not easy for him to live out a working life knowing that what he was working at would not survive him. It was, for him, tragic that the work he loved most—the outdoor work with men and horses—was not going to last beyond his time; the traditions it had bred would soon die with the work. It had only really lasted two generations, his father's and his own.

He had read a bit about the American West, but other than that had not much history. The history that mattered to him was the history his own family had lived, from the day William Jefferson and Louisa Francis unloaded their wagon on that hill. Of the larger and much longer history of men and ruminants, the droving, herding, pastoral nomadism that lay behind cowboying—centuries behind it—he knew little. Yet the movement of men and animals over the earth is an old and powerful thing; its hold on my father and all the cowboys I have known was deep. At a second remove, through the movies, it has held millions who weren't cowboys. The seeming freedom of nomadism, the movement of men and herds over the plains of the world, under spacious skies, retains a strong attraction even now, for people who will never know it at close hand as my father and his companions knew it.

There was no way and no reason for my father to escape the power of this tradition, since he was skilled enough even as a smallholder to survive within it. In an increasingly suburban world it was gratifying to him to feel that he could do his work with men and horses and answer to no man directly. But the fact of debt was always there: he escaped offices and time clocks, but not economics. An instructive text in this regard is Wilfred Thesiger's great *Arabian Sands*, the book about his travels with the Bedouin, by foot and camel, across the Empty Quarter of Arabia. Here were nomads who had to contend every day with the power of a great desert, a force far more threatening than a bank in Wichita Falls. At stake for them was life itself, not next year's loan. Yet they thought of themselves as the freest of the free—as long as they had camels they could go where they pleased, just as the cowboy once could on his horse. They considered themselves blessed and so did most of the cowboys I have known. Like the Bedouin, they owned very little, but they always had the freedom of the skies.

My own fate, in relation to the cowboy, has been more complicated than my father's. Some years ago, in a piece in *Esquire*, as I was attempting to explain why I liked to drive back and forth across America on the interstates, I suddenly realized that I hadn't escaped cowboying at all. What was I doing, proceeding north on I-35, but driving the trucks and cars ahead of me up to their northern pastures? My driving was a form of nomadism, and the vehicles ahead of me were my great herds.

Suddenly I saw how much my Cadillac cowboying explained. Unfit for ranch work because of my indifference to cattle—if sent to fetch a particular animal I usually came back with the wrong one—I went instead into the antiquarian book trade, becoming, in effect, a book rancher, herding books into larger and larger ranches (I now have filled a whole town with them, my equivalent of the King Ranch). I couldn't find the right cow, but I *could* find the right books, extricating them from the once dense thickets of America's antiquarian bookshops.

But the metaphor of herding can be pushed even further, to writing itself: what is it but a way of herding words? First I try to herd a few desirable words into a sentence, and then I corral them into small pastures called paragraphs, before spreading them across the spacious ranges of a novel.

Even the fact that I've now spent most of a working life herding words in the morning and secondhand books in the afternoon still doesn't encompass the full range of my involvement with the American cowboy and his Eden, the unfenced, unsettled nineteenth-century West. I began to write fiction and resisted dipping (or slipping) back into the nineteenth century for almost thirty years. Even when I was writing *Lonesome Dove* I didn't feel that I was writing about the Old West, in capital letters—I was merely writing about my grandfather's time, and my uncles', none of whom seemed like men of another time to me.

Since then, though, I've written six novels, many screenplays, and two miniseries set in the nineteenth-century West. This may have been due, in part, to the human tendency to look farther back as one gets older; it may also be because I had exhausted the contemporary themes I felt most interested in.

My experience with *Lonesome Dove* and its various sequels and prequels convinced me that the core of the Western myth—that cowboys are brave and cowboys are free—is essentially unassailable. I thought of *Lonesome Dove* as demythicizing, but instead it became a kind of American Arthuriad, overflowing the bounds of genre in many curious ways. In two lesser novels, *Anything for Billy* and *Buffalo Girls*, about Billy the Kid and Calamity Jane, respectively, I tried to subvert the Western myth with irony and parody, with no better results. Readers don't want to know and can't be made to see how difficult and destructive life in the Old West really was. Lies about the West are more important to them than truths, which is why the popularity of the pulpers—Louis L'Amour particularly—has never dimmed.

In the end my father's career and my own were not as different as I had once thought. He cattle ranched in a time he didn't like much, and I word ranched, describing the time he longed to have lived in and the kind of cowboys he would have liked to know. He died about a decade before *Lonesome Dove* and never knew that one of his central desires—to be a trail driver—had found its way into one of my books.

I find it a little painful to be among cowboys now—of course, there are not very many of them to be among. Those who survive are anachronisms, and they know it. Most of them live in suburban hells, and yet are stuck with a style that lost its pith more than one hundred years ago. Many of the men who survive as cowboys now spend their lives being nostalgic for an experience—the trail drives—that even their grandfathers missed. Rodeo, the only part of that experience that is accessible to the public, is a kind of caricature of cowboying.

The fact is, the American West was settled in one long lifetime. From Lewis and Clark to Wounded Knee is less than ninety years; the pioneer cattleman Charles Goodnight lived longer, and so did the plains historian Angie Debo. Well before the Custer battle, that shrewd entrepreneur William F. Cody (Buffalo Bill) was already putting on Wild West Shows for people who had never been, and would never be, west of New Jersey. What Buffalo Bill did to the Western experience was not unlike what television did to the Vietnam protests: he synopsized it. An Indian here, a stagecoach there, the Pony Express, a little trick riding, a few buffalo, Annie Oakley. It sold and it still sells—the stagecoaches still race at the Calgary Stampede.

What rodeos, movies, Western art, and pulp fiction all miss is the overwhelming loneliness of the westering experience. When my uncles (and even my father, for a year or two) were cowboying in the Panhandle they would eagerly ride horseback as much as thirty-five miles to a dance or a social, and then ride back and be ready to work at dawn. In Montana, Nebraska, Wyoming, the distances were even greater. Many Westerners were alone so much that loneliness was just in them, to a degree that finally made domestic and social relations difficult, if not secondary. The old joke that cowboys get along better with horses than they do with women is not a joke, it's a tragedy. The kinds of demands that the unfenced, unplowed, unwatered West made on human attention and human energy seemed to me to solitarize rather than socialize. Somehow the outlaw came to stand for this solitary Westerner—the man who has no ties because he kills. More common was the man who had no ties because he would rather work and keep working.

[. . .]

The problem of the American cowboy perfectly illustrates the classic problem of the field anthropologist: as soon as you find an unstudied tribe and introduce yourself to it, it ceases to be the tribe you found. The purest cowboys were those fourteen- and fifteen-year-old drovers who went up the trail with the first major herds in 1866 and the years just following, when the practice of trail driving flourished. A decade later Wild West Shows were going concerns and a voluminous pulp literature had developed: dime novels, the literature parodied in *Anything for Billy*. Teddy Blue reports that cowboys read pulp cowboy stories as avidly as any Eastern dude. Thus almost at the outset cowboys began to try to cultivate an image that the media told them was theirs—they began to play to the camera as soon as the camera was there, and the camera, for a long time, has been ubiquitous. In one year I was asked to write forewords or introductions to no less than nine books of photographs about cowboys or Western ranch life. One of these got introduced by Tom McGuane, another by Louis L'Amour, the industrious pulper who spent a good part of his life hoping that people would mistake him for a realist. The people who asked for the introductions were mostly shocked to discover that I didn't love cowboys and didn't want to wax poetical about them. (There can be few cowboys left in the West who have not been photographed for one or more of these books. The ranch women have also been photographed, as has much of the livestock.) The one book of photographs I *did* decide to write about was Richard Avedon's *In the American West*, a book I liked at once because it was so brutally antipastoral, so true to the gritty West of drifters and pig farmers, of truck stop girls and truckers; it was the book that put a period to the long tradition, begun by Alexander Gardner and William H. Jackson, John Hillers, Timothy O'Sullivan, and in this century, particularly by Ansel Adams, of seeing the West as one vast glorious pastoral landscape. Though those pictures may be wonderful they are in most cases empty of the often sad, more or less mute, inglorious humans who actually inhabit the great landscapes.

Susanna Sonnenberg

SLURRY, DRAINAGE, FRONTAGE ROAD

Before I came to Montana, I'd never heard *frontage road*. Or, if I had, its meaning was so thoroughly irrelevant I didn't bother to ask for it. In my early teens, my mother moved us from New York City to New Mexico, over-the-top in love with the reddening hills at sunset, the lavender twilights over the Rio Grande. I didn't care. Taos could have been the moon, and I wouldn't have noticed. I cared about boys, records, rides, and privacy. I learned *gorge* when someone was holding a party there and I needed a lift. The West did not speak to me.

Then, fifteen years later, long after my mother had departed for other landscapes, after my time in college and Paris, then London, Los Angeles, and more of New York, I moved to Montana for a really good guy and found myself in a city of fifty thousand residents, again on the moon. This time I paid attention and saw . . . *strangeness*. I succumbed to the prickle of culture shock. My landmarks were gone, my habits and skills useless. I'd never car-camped, had never pulled off at a fishing access, or seen a game license, or measured anywhere by a mile marker. I had never seen a deer up close, in the bed of a pickup. I didn't even know how to look and kept expecting its tongue to move.

My husband (as he was to become) was a Westerner, a descendent of Mormon settlers, a grandson of a sheep rancher. Andrew knew his way around, and he knew the ways. A line of trees or brush running low through a field meant water. The unobtrusive brown roadside signs numbered forest service roads. As we drove, he'd point at a scattering of antelope, or the bald eagle at the peak of a dead tree, or the brown rabbit vanishing into the bramble, and I always looked too late, after we'd passed, spotting nothing. I didn't know what could be seen. My eye, arrested by a billboard promoting salvation or a discount motel, sought the filler and landmarks and, finding none, informed my brain this was a nothingness, a non-place, a place where nothing happened. Andrew gave me Wallace Stegner to read, Ivan Doig, William Kittredge, Gretel Ehrlich, James Welch. It felt like pressure. "Place," he said. "It's about place." But not a place that interests me, I thought. Not the place where something is happening. He stopped the car during storms, and we'd roll down the windows. We'd sit in the spattering hail or rains, smell the dust gone damp and the drenched sage, and he was relaxed, complete. I liked it, but then it was time to go home. I wished he wouldn't say, "We'll take the frontage road," or "Let's see what's up this drainage." What about place for me? I had place: paved squares and glass panes, the neat box of a gilded elevator, the hushed, carpeted lobby of a midtown movie theater.

My New York friends assumed I'd be back. A few visited, always joking first thing about the size of the plane, or the quiet, empty airport, or the taxidermied grizzly on display there. News of Montana did not reach them on NPR, which told them stories about themselves. "New York," my stepmother said during one of her rare visits, "is the center of everything. You can't argue with that. It just is." My husband and I did not argue because we appreciated that arguing with a New Yorker who felt she was at the center of everything was wasted effort. Besides, I still sort of believed she was right. Sort of still believed in restaurant reviews, opera outings, Olmstead's crafted design of the landscape. I still failed to hear *center* and *everything* as the natural world was trying to make known to me: This is where snowberry grows, then is when the run-off is high, here is where the burn was the worst.

When my husband took me to Fairview, Utah, for the first time, he dropped me off at his grandparents' house and went fishing alone. I was intimidated by the potential boredom and my inexperience and had opted to stay at the house, which was maintained by absent aunts and uncles, his grandparents long dead. I wanted him to have whatever it was fishing afforded him, solitude and clarity, checking in on the banks and waters, the rhythms of dirt roads—these were meaningless to me, and I had no language of my own to give them meaning, which made me resent them. I had Willa Cather: "The air and the earth are curiously mated and intermingled, as if the one were the breath of the other. You feel in the atmosphere the same tonic, puissant quality that is in the tilth, the same strength and resoluteness." (I'd looked up *tilth* before I tucked the passage from *O Pioneers!* into my date book—"land that is tilled and cultivated.")

I stepped through the screen door into the sun, out of the kitchen with its wallpaper decades out of fashion, away from the high-backed formal furniture in the front room covered in sheets. I craved action and scanned for it as I stood on the edge of the slim lawn, mowed once a week by a neighbor. A car or two passed. One road ran straight through the silent town, connecting it to Mt. Pleasant, tall dry grasses waving and scratching, separating black top from pasture, where sleepy cows went about their sleepy business. Across the street, a door opened in a brick house, and a woman with a scarf over a white hairdo took her time down her steps and off the curb, until she reached me.

"Now who are you?" she said. "Visiting the Petersons?"

"I'm Andrew's friend. Lewis's oldest boy," I said, because that's how I'd heard him identify himself. "We're just here for a couple of days." She peered past me, checking on the Petersons' house. "I'm from New York. City," I added.

We watched as another few cars drove through. "Well, it's getting to be like New York City around here," she said. "So busy." I was about to crack a joke, join her sarcasm, when I realized she meant what she'd said. With her whole history she regarded the landscape and gave the changes this name, a label of extreme foreignness. I stood there, an emblem of busyness in her Fairview.

It occurred to me that I wasn't a temporary player in an overwrought romance, I wasn't a reader of Cather and Stegner. I was having an impact. I couldn't begin to imagine what it was, or how she'd talk about it, to whom. She probably used to read the weekly newspaper, which listed the bridge parties, listed who was traveling out of town, and who had just returned. Clista Peterson, it would say of Andrew's grandmother, served deviled eggs, Jell-O salad, ham roll-ups, and punch when she entertained her husband's cousins and their children two Sundays ago. The woman with me wasn't prying or competing for gossip (as I had been brought up to understand the gathering of information, from the perspective of an ego fulfilled) but feeling her town, what it was up to, how it surrounded her. She knew the covenant and I did not.

But that's Fairview, I thought. No stoplight, one gas station, one store for Andrew to pick up his fishing license and tippet; the Mormon ward house, an old tiny library, a new tiny post office; a couple of roads splitting away from the main passage, leading up to the ranches or the cemetery or someone's alfalfa fields. Emptiness beyond that, surrounding everything. "I'm in the middle of nowhere," I whispered on the phone to one of my city friends, who agreed and said, *Come back.*

In Montana, early on, I had this friend, not a great friend, but a girl I liked very much. She had lovely skin and lovely copper hair, and she laughed softly when she was a little drunk, so endearing. Mostly, we saw them as a couple. Her husband was our closer friend, an editor at the paper where we freelanced, the one who did the talking.

I loved bumping into her, easy in such a small city, and loved neither of us having much to do. We'd sit on the grass or walk the bike trail along the river, and the conversation would laze along, for its own sake of filling the pleasant hour and working up another link in the town. I liked that. I liked that when I went into the bakery, she was in the back in an apron, a yellow bandana holding back her red hair and, hearing my voice, she'd look up and wave, that brief click of affirming our respective places in the town. I liked to look at her smudged toes in flip-flops as we walked below the maple canopies on her street, and her dirty ankles and floured skirt. She made lemon squares each time we invited them for dinner. I'd never eaten food like that from the hand of a person I knew, who could write out the recipe from memory. She brought them because I loved them. I knew the person who had this baking talent, this sewing talent, this greenhouse talent, part of our town. Everyone in my New York life *thought*, so for potted plants and lemon bars and upholstery they relied on service, money the tidy contract.

One day she and I went to a thrift shop. After browsing, she came over and said, "Look at this dress! It was ten dollars but I jewed them down to five." I froze, and she saw this, and then she connected *jewed* to my expression, and then to me. It was a slow process.

She lowered her chin, and her hand that held the dress, and said, "Whoops, I guess I shouldn't say that."

"No," I said, too startled to talk more, too awake and stunned and reminded that I was not at home, and I was spooked.

"I'm sorry," she said in her softest voice, the slightly drunk, sweet one.

"It's okay," I said. No, it wasn't okay. How could I live here?

"It's just a phrase, just an expression."

We didn't speak during the drive back to our neighborhood, and the next time the two couples got together, I couldn't look at her, made sure not to be alone with her. I didn't want to put her lemon bar in my mouth.

In Montana I met other people who used the word *jewed*, which I'd never heard spoken aloud. In Montana I drove behind cars with stickers that read "This family supported by timber dollars," and joked, without a clue to the political histories, the fights, the fragile economy I'd eventually understand. I met people in the army for the first time, and people with sons and daughters in Iraq. One friend worked every summer in Alaska on a fishing boat. *Alaska*, wow, I said, Jack London as close as I'd come, a voice of another age and enterprise, a century-old conjuring of something so remote that for all I knew, it no longer existed. Eventually, I knew so many people who'd lived there or went there that Alaska ceased to be the punch line of extremity and distance it had always been before Montana. It grew real, it mattered. Eventually, I'd go there myself.

One winter morning someone I liked from work dropped off hot cinnamon rolls on our porch, and we found the pan with the paper. No note. Just the offering, the gesture itself complete and what mattered, not the giver, not the thanks, not the potential reciprocity or even the relationship itself, but I knew who'd done it because I knew her this way, understood her deeply as the sort of person who would like doing that. A friend called me one midnight, and I went to the ER and fetched her newborn, while she tended to her other child, who'd broken an arm. I brought the baby back to the hospital six hours later for his feeding, not only because I was doing it for my friend, but because the town needed this, and I was beginning to know.

In the parking lot outside Sportsman's Surplus one afternoon, I struggled to fasten inflated inner tubes to the roof of my car with a rope the man in the store had kindly given to me. A man watched from his truck, then he stepped down and walked over. His leather belt holstered several sheathed objects. "Need a hand?" he said, and I accepted. In the city I would have been on guard, would have defiantly proved I did not need a hand, or his hand. His interest would have felt predatory or smug, everything in the language of the personal triumph. But in a Missoula parking lot I understood, at last, that his genuine interest lay in securing the tubes to the rack. This wasn't about me, it was about the right way. He inspected the rope, running it through his fingers, and we talked a minute about the best sorts of rope for the job (this wasn't one of them). Then he lashed the cord over and under, swung it around the other side, stepped onto the ledge of my driver-side door ("Excuse me," he'd said), tugged a few good tugs to check. I had my son run into the hardware store and get him a bottle of water, for the day was high and hot. "Ought to do it," he said, and we shook hands. He accepted the water and walked back to his truck.

Everything in my former cities existed for *what's in it for me?*, even if that was never voiced so crudely. Lightning, for instance. A spectacle, a natural firework, then over; but now I knew people who spent summer months in wilderness lookout towers, and I heeded which direction the lightning strikes moved and supposed the very drainage where they touched down, how flammable that might be because of low run-off. From our porch, we watched the slurry planes over Mt. Sentinel. Our neighbor was a smoke jumper.

I see differently now, and smell and hear. The pine beetle has discolored the treescape, the arable fields around the city have been pushed under formaldehyde houses and garages. I read the articles about the scarcity of wolves and owls, and I wait for the geese to call in late November, before

I even realize it's late November. I know why people have cords of wood in the beds of their trucks or hay balanced to toppling; that morel mushrooms grow in the burnt forest; that the windy howl of a cookstove is part of camping. I see the snouts and flanks visible behind the tin bars of a trailer passed on the freeway. *Black ice* is no longer a term, a mystery, a footnote to a *London Review of Books* article, it's real, right here. It paves my winters. It's pulled my two dear friends into a ravine off a mountain highway and totaled their light truck. Black ice, they said over and over, as they told the story. It was black ice.

My two dear friends left Missoula and moved to Alaska. I missed them, my town and life smaller without them. We'd named them godparents, watched them get married. They'd been gone five years when we drove our two sons up through British Columbia and the Yukon, crossing the Yukon River to the Top of the World Highway. I often spotted the pale deer, the gray coyote, the motionless Dall sheep pressed against cliffsides before Andrew did, and we made our children look, and see.

We came to the mining town of Healy, where our friends lived. Andrew staked our tent in front of their cabin, the bottom layer billowy over the unruly tundra. We all prepared for our three-day trip into Denali National Park. Our friends told us what to do, how to pack. The boys carried their sleeping bags and mats, a few pairs of socks. We'd broken in our boots. In unexpected sunshine a bus left us on Denali's one road, and we scrambled down a small rise into the open, I Scream Gulch before us.

I had a hair tie, a blister kit, Carmex, tools of immediacy, ways to press into the surroundings. We knew what to do if we saw wolves, bears, or moose. We made our random way, unguided by trail because there was none. We stepped where we could step, edging along the river bars, avoiding wet if we could, tiring and resting and beginning again. The next morning, after the food had been secured in the bear-proof canisters and propped among rocks downwind of camp, we headed up. The slope defined the view ahead of us, but when we turned around to sit and rest, Mt. McKinley showed over the distant saddle. Its scope and scale rendered the forty miles between us ridiculous. Bigness absorbed me; there was no longing, no needing, no having. The voices of people I loved best traveled up and down the slope, and when the wind calmed around my ears I could hear them. As we ascended, the earth turned silkier, slippery, rocks smooth and jagged. I used my fingers, leaning in, grabbing at the rocks. It was difficult work for me, though not for my experienced friends and young boys. In the wedge of the steep valley, I decided to stay while the others moved up. "It's a hard climb," my friend said. "The scree like this."

"Scree?"

"This, all this, the small sharp rocks that make up the side of the slope. It's hard to get a grip, dig in."

There was a name. And there was a name for this, for this, for this. She knew them, she would use them, then I would say them. Scree, talus, shale. They left me, and I regarded the surroundings, feeling how fertile and agile and fragrant and ancient and necessary the land was. From pavement I'd had no idea what was at stake. I used to call this nowhere. *Nowhere*—left to be itself, what it had always been. *Nowhere*—explosions of species, unfolding of insect hatch, water carving against shallow banks, stripes and whorled patterns in the rocks, places filled up but with space, sky, transparent, yes, but not nothing, not an absence. I understood the honor of being this guest, making my few hatches against an incomprehensible canvas. I was the nowhere, the finite atom, the mortal, irrelevant molecule.

Jim Harrison   GEOPIETY

If the mountains were actually ennobling I would have noticed it by now. Everyone who can read comics is aware of the truly indigenous people of the West. We came much later, led by the US Cavalry and the railroads. As the cranky old lady at the grocer's said, "The West wasn't settled by nice people."

A lowest common denominator definition of geopiety is the famed truism, "Pigs love their own shit." At the highest level it is those who have a sacramental devotion to the land and take care of it accordingly, whether they are ranchers, hikers, or sportsmen.

Fungoid self-congratulations about where we live blind us to the disparities in land use. Places that locals call *God's Country* are spread rather evenly throughout the United States. The universal demon of theocracy was evenhanded in land rape in both east and west, the attitude that God gave us the land and we may do with it as we wish. There is no more otiose line in the history of American poetry than Frost's "The land was ours before we were the land's."

Coming from the lonesome eyrie of the upper Midwest, I could look both ways. I'm old now and age can bring on an air of desperate crankiness. My mom used to unpleasantly ask, "What if everyone was like you?" No thanks.

Writers are their own peculiar line-bred dog. In terms of geopiety, writers note that anyone who practices their art outside of New York City is considered regional. Reputation tends to depend on social contiguity. However, of late, regional and university presses have burgeoned to the point that New York is losing the potency of its authority. Of course everyone needs to be reminded that the standards are universal and aren't likely to be learned reading each other's MFA program work, whether in Wyoming or Vermont.

The grandest aspect of the West for me is the solution offered to my acute claustrophobia. My first trip was in 1955 and then from 1968 onward I came to Montana every year to fish, finally settling here seven years ago mostly because both our daughters lived here. Claustrophobia is unpleasant and it is a consolation indeed to see no other dwellings from our front window, though it is somewhat heretical for an environmentalist like myself to admit that coming from an ag background I have an extraordinary fondness for cattle.

With we white folks it is a hoax to cast ourselves in the role of the indigenous. A census in 1886 in Texas noted that of two hundred *cattle drovers* (what cowboys were called in the area back then) only twenty-two came from Texas, and there were many more from New York State. We are a nation of transients and history has accelerated our movement. My own Swede grandfather was in Wyoming and South Dakota before Wounded Knee. I would comfortably say that more than protecting its interests from venal developers, whether in real estate, logging, and mining, the dominant responsibility of the West would be to finally totally admit what we did to our first citizens as a rag-tag invading army of soldiers and settlers. This is the true ghost in our immense closet. Honest reparations are in order to honor the long nightmare of millions who did not ask to be born on the routes of our conquest. Only then may we have a more justifiable sense of belonging where we are.

Jim Harrison | RIVER SEQUENCE I–VII

RIVER I

I was there in a room in a village
by the river when the moon fell into the window
frame and was trapped there too long.
I was fearful but I was upside down
and my prayers fell off the ceiling.
Our small dog Jacques jumped on the sofa
near the window, perched on the sofa's back
and released the moon to head south.
Just after dawn standing in the green yard
I watched a girl ride down the far side
of the railroad tracks on a beauteous white horse
whose lower legs were wrapped in red tape.
Above her head were mountains covered with snow.
I decided we were born to be moving water not ice.

(MAY 18, 2009)

RIVER II

Another dawn in the village by the river
and I'm jealous of the sixty-three moons of Jupiter.
Out in the yard inspecting a lush lilac bush
followed by five dogs who have chosen
me as their temporary leader. I look up
through the vodka jangle of the night before,
straight up at least thirty thousand feet where the mountains
are tipping over on me. Dizzy I grab the lilacs
for support. Of course it's the deceitful clouds
playing the game of becoming mountains.
Once on our nighttime farm on a moonlit walk

the clouds pushed by a big western wind
became a school of whales swimming hard
across the cold heavens and I finally knew
that we walk the bottom of an ocean we call sky.

(JUNE 15, 2009)

RIVER III

Saw a poem float by just beneath
the surface, another corpse of the spirit
we weren't available to retrieve.
It isn't comforting to admit that our days
are fatal, that the corpse of the spirit
gradually becomes the water and waits
for another, or perhaps you to return
to where you belong, not in the acting
of a shaker sprinkling its salt
everywhere. You have to hold your old
heart lightly as the female river holds
the clouds and trees, its fish
and the moon so lightly but firmly
enough so that nothing gets away.

(JUNE 21, 2009)

RIVER IV

The river seems confused today because it has
swallowed the thunderstorm above us. At my age
death stalks me but I don't mind. This is to be
expected but how can I deal with the unpardonable
crime of loneliness? The girl I taught to swim
so long ago has gone to heaven, the kind of thing
that happens while we're on the river fishing and
seeing the wildly colored western tanagers and the
profusion of nighthawks that some call bullbats,
nightjars, and down on the border they call them
goatsuckers for stealing precious milk. I love
this misfiring of neurons in which I properly
understand nothing, not the wild high current

or the thunderstorm on which it chokes. Did the
girl swim to heaven through the ocean of sky?
Maybe. I can deny nothing. Two friends are mortally
ill. Were it not for the new moon my sky
would collapse tonight so fed by the waters of memory.

(JUNE 25, 2009)

RIVER V

Resting in an eddy against dense greenery
so thick you can't see into it but can pace
its depth by waning bird calls, hum of insects.
This morning I learned that we live and die
as children to the core only carrying
as a protective shell, a fleshy costume
made up mostly of old scar tissue
from before we learned how to protect ourselves.
It's hard to imagine that this powerful
river had to begin with a single drop
far into the mountains, a seep or trickle
from rocks and then the runoff from snow melt.
Of course watershed means the shedding
of water, rain, a hundred creeks, a thousand
small springs. My mind can't quite
contain this any more than my own inception
in a single sperm joining a single egg
utterly invisible, hidden in mother's moist
dark. Out of almost nothing, for *practical*
purposes nothing, then back as ancient
children to the great nothing again,
the song of man and water moving to the ocean.

(JUNE 28, 2009)

RIVER VI

I thought years ago that old Heraclitus was wrong.
You can't step into the same river even once.
The water slips around your foot like liquid time
and you can't dry it off after its passage.
Don't bother taking your watch to the river,

the moving water is a glorious second hand.
Properly understood the memory loses nothing
and we humans are never allowed to let our minds
sit on the still bank and have a simple picnic.
I had an unimaginable dream when young
of being a river horse that could easily plunge upstream.
Perhaps it came from our huge black mare June
who I rode bareback as she swam the lake
in big circles, always getting out where she got in.
Meanwhile this river is surrounded by mountains
covered with lodgepole pines that are mortally diseased,
browning in the summer sun. Everyone knows
that lightning will strike and Montana burn.
We all stay quiet about it, this blessed oxygen
that makes the world a crematory. Only the water is safe.

(JULY 6, 2009)

RIVER VII

The last trip to the river this year. Tonight I think
of the trout swimming in a perfect, moonless
dark, navigating in the current by the tiny pinpoint
of stars, night wind rippling the eddies
and always if you stick your head under
the surface, the slight sound of the pebbles
rubbing against pebbles. Today I saw two dead
pelicans. I heard they are shot because they eat
trout, crows shot because they eat duck eggs,
wolves shot for eating elk or for chasing
a bicyclist in Yellowstone. Should we be shot
for eating the world and giving back our puke?
Way down in Notch Bottom, ancient winter camp
for long gone Indians I am sweetly consoled
by our absolute absence except for a stretch
of fence on the bank, half washed away
by the current, a sequence of No Trespassing signs
to warn us away from a pricey though miasmic swamp.
The river can't heal everything. You have to do your part.
We've even bruised the moon. Still the birds are a chorus
with the moving flow, clearly relatives of Mozart,

the brown trout so lovely the heart flutters. Back home
something has eaten the unfledged swallows. It wasn't us.
I'm on another river now, swollen and turbulent.
The spirit is here. Are you? I ask myself.

(AUGUST 17, 2009)

Gary Ferguson   # WOLF AND COYOTE
AND KUMBAYA

Twenty miles this side of dawn, rolling west through Wyoming on Interstate 80 in a '64 Pontiac Tempest with the same name as John Muir's dog. Beside the highway I can just make out sagebrush and pronghorn and sagging lines of barbed wire, the pieces sharpening then blurring, a final smear of doubt before the world flares again in the June sun. In the distance, on the south horizon, is a faint line of dark, pillowy shapes; I stare hard out the driver's window, desperate to know if they're mountains or clouds. Just ahead of me a semi weaves back and forth across the lanes, drifts to the shoulder and then corrects, the driver shaking himself against sleep. Despite twenty-two straight hours of driving I've got no such problem. The dawn, the road, the sliver of moon in the rearview mirror has the feel of life breaking open, a purging of a childhood too tightly wound to the corn and the rust.

I've been waiting for this for a long, long time. Back in the fourth grade, in South Bend, Indiana, I recall one Sunday morning walking with my parents from our house three blocks to Redeemer Lutheran Church on Wall Street, wondering why God had plunked me down in such a place, bereft of even a good hill to scream down on a bike or skateboard. Poster child for the topographically challenged. As usual, I'd been hanging out that summer in the one shred of vertical I could find—giant oaks, maples, and sycamores, climbing them at every whipstitch for nothing more than the chance at a decent view. One blistering afternoon in July I scrambled down from the trees to tell my parents I needed a job of some sort, a way to fund this brilliant plan to take a big cardboard washing machine box and fasten to it a hundred helium balloons, a buck each at the Farmers Market, thereby flying out of our postage-stamp backyard to points unknown. Lying in bed at night, reviewing the mission in my mind's eye, I was forever looking down not on smoke and steel, but on an imaginary *pouf* of ragged wood lots and abandoned fields, on a loose rumple of hills with blue-green lakes puddled in their bellies.

About this same time, the season of my pending ascension, sentenced one morning for one crime or another to an hour of sitting in the big stuffed chair in our living room, bored senseless, leafing through a stack of magazines, I stumbled across an ad for a "Montana Vacation Kit." Two weeks later came a big white envelope stuffed with maps and postcards and photos of scrubbed families in flannel shirts smiling from atop horses and, in almost every background, lines of snow-covered peaks, scary and thrilling and vertical beyond my wildest dreams. If novelist Lawrence Durrell was right, that we are in fact "children of the landscape," then in my young mind Indiana would've been the pasty mother—scrunched brow, fingers forever squeezing worry from her hands. The Rockies, on the other hand, were beautiful cousin, rich aunt, and lunatic uncle all rolled into one. I was going to move west, I announced, to the Rocky Mountains and, in a new round of manic behavior, set about planning an escape to Colorado for the following year—a three-thousand-mile round-trip journey to be made on my metallic purple Sears Sting-Ray bike.

Now, nine years later, I'm making it. Making it for good. Pulling off at a nameless ranch exit to piss out the last of my truck stop coffee, I crawl out from behind the wheel and all but stagger at the smell of the place—this bright, bitter tang of alkali and sage. Gone are the old smells of home: the lemony grease of furniture polish, baked meat-loaf with ketchup glaze, chicken casseroles floating in mushroom soup. Gone is the scent of ripe garbage and bags of grass clippings waiting in the alley for pickup on Tuesday mornings; the sour whiffs of rubber drifting through the neighborhood from the Uniroyal factory some thirty blocks away. Here in this empty reach of Wyoming smells are no longer in the service of unlocking the past, as Proust would have it, but for kicking the past out the door and speeding away.

For all my enthusiasm, in the great tradition of westbound migrants I've brought with me a pocketful of spectacularly ill-conceived notions. Some grew out of the Kodachrome buzz I've had on since 1964, having inhaled one too many vacation brochures. Others came by way of Holly-wood, delivered on horseback by Ben and Hoss and Little Joe, and on occasion, by a twin-engine Cessna piloted by Sky King. But at the same time I'm also carrying deeper tales, native tales, first plucked from a corner of my grade school library on a ten-foot run of frayed, broken-spined books about Indians. One story I lean on a lot. From the Paiute, who for a thousand years roamed the wind-blasted canyons of Nevada and Southwest Utah, hunting deer and mountain sheep; weaving twined and coiled baskets from willow, yucca, devil's claw; and year after year, in the weak light of winter, huddling hip to hip on cliffrose mats in their fire-lit wickiups, re-imagining the world.

A long time ago, the Paiute say, the earth was danced by two brothers— Coyote and Wolf. Wolf with his perfect, wholesome vision for the world, a creator who never wanted anything more for the people than beauty and harmony, an abundant life—free of anguish, free even of death. Never far from his side, though, was his younger brother, Coyote. A creator of another sort—spoiled, mischievous, a glib talker who time and again pulled the people away from Wolf's lofty visions. As time went by the humans lost touch with those ideas of perfection—spilling them and forgetting, leaving them to wither on the stony ground. Finally Wolf went away, leaving the world to unfold according to the imaginings of Coyote. We cast our fate with Coyote, said the Paiute. And so our lives are driven by this strange mix of urge and shadow, by schemes going out into the world meaning to be clever, coming back full of pain.

The problem is, I don't buy the ending. At twenty it's inconceivable that anyone lucky enough to rub elbows with the landscapes of the West wouldn't be at least mildly inclined toward Wolf's way of looking at the world. True, back in Indiana people thought nothing of trading rich fields of foxtail and aster for shopping centers, cattail marshes for Waffle Houses and Putt-Putt golf. But surely something better must be at play out here beyond the 98th meridian—in these wide runs of Douglas fir, in meadows lit with paintbrush and prairie smoke and cinquefoil. Something akin to what author Sherwood Anderson talked about in the 1920s, noting how it took nothing more than an evening spent on an empty plain to drain the shrillness out of old men. Most people think such notions quaint, naïve. Yet I'll be clinging to them for years: working as a naturalist for the Forest Service in central Idaho; through the summer of 1980, when Jane and I will marry in a field of camas lilies at the foot of the Sawtooth Mountains; at the cowboy line camp we'll caretake in 1981, deep in the aspen woods of northern Arizona.

But by the time we land in Colorado the following year, even a full-blown Pollyanna like me will be hard pressed to keep the Kumbaya from unraveling. Coyote is everywhere—in town, on the trails, at night along the highway, eyes flashing in the headlights. President Reagan, having apparently been AWOL for junior high science class, on two separate occasions claims that living trees actually cause more pollution than humans—giving off not oxygen, but carbon dioxide. Self-proclaimed sagebrush rebels—the front guard of the burgeoning Wise Use movement—swell with indignation, insisting that federal lands in the West be given back to the states for development, no matter that the states didn't own them in the first place. Soon will come their much-publicized manifesto, calling for mining and oil development in all national parks and wilderness areas, for logging old growth forests and replanting them with species better suited to commercial harvest, for eliminating protection under the Endangered Species Act for any plant or animal "lacking vigor to spread in range."

Not that Coyote isn't also working the other side of the street. By the end of the 1980s, a lot of conservationists have become devoted business types, arguing for nature mostly on economic terms. Preserve wilderness today, we say, and the private property surrounding it will tomorrow be worth a whole lot more. Which proves horribly true. In the end it won't be ranchers and farmers who spark the furious slicing and dicing of critical riparian zones and wildlife migration corridors across the West, but men and women happy to stir their evening martinis and stare out the picture window at whatever nature might be left beyond the last fence of the subdivision.

In true Coyote fashion, what Americans glean from the West in the final decades of the twentieth century turns out to be that which seems most missing from our lives. Troubled by having grown up on too much asphalt and too much foul air, by mind-boggling events like the Calumet and Cuyahoga Rivers catching fire, preservationists like me seek a mythic paradise, giving little thought to integrating humans. On the other side are those undone by social change, shifting economies—people for whom the West has become a last chance for rugged individualism. One group seeks paradise, fails to find it, and grows cynical. The other struggles for stability, comes up short, and turns mean. By 1990, in bars from Nevada to Montana, I hear red-faced men grousing about how somebody should dynamite the nearest Forest Service or Bureau of Land Management office. And in a few places, somebody does. Environmentalists are hanged in effigy. On public lands along the southern border of Yellowstone I meet an outfitter so incensed by out-of-state hunters invading his "territory" that he resorts to shoving pieces of elk carcass under their tents while they're out hunting, hoping grizzlies will come in the night and rip the interlopers to shreds.

Ironically, around no topic does their rage burn hotter than the wolf, reintroduced into Montana, Wyoming, and Idaho in 1995 and 1996. I watch protestors at public hearings hefting signs declaring wolves to be the "Saddam Hussein" of the animal world. Death threats are made—against the animals, against the biologists. Senator Conrad Burns predicts a dead child within a year. Near my home in Montana people stop letting their children wait for the school bus, lest the wolves come and carry them away.

Twenty years ago I wrote about the end of nomadic life half a world away, in the outback of Israel, as the government prompted the Arab Bedouins to trade their drifting lifestyle for permanent homes in cinder block towns. "The hills I looked out on as a child had the rounded shapes of tents and camels," explained the principal of a Bedouin secondary school. "Now the soft contours have given way to the stark cubes of the block houses. It reflects a new mind-set. Now we're thinking in cubes; we're thinking in frames that have already been made." So too, I wrote, did the American West seem to be framed less and less by wild, rugged patches of stone and timber than by clear-cuts and mine tailings. By housing developments. By oil derricks blazing in what only yesterday had been dark and secret skies. Yet I couldn't fathom the coming of even tighter, harder frames—ones that would rob us of the chance to know wildlands not as a source of inspiration or braggadocio, but of both. Beauty and craziness stand together, said the Paiute. As do calm and terror. Thrill and sublimity. Life and death. Coyote and Wolf.

Wallace Stegner often expressed his own good hope for humans, wishing we might one day come to see ourselves as "part of the environment of trees and rocks and soil, brother to the other animals, part of the natural world and competent to belong in it." Of course such vision takes breath in realms far beyond the obsession to commodify. Beyond shaggy dog photos of wolves tossed into people's mailboxes to hustle money; beyond notions of the outback as stages for tough guys looking for the next game of survivor. Truly belonging to this place would mean embracing it as vastly layered and infinitely complex. Wilderness as primal blessing, forever being born and forever dying. Wilderness as the catch in our throat, the heat in our groin, the blood in our veins.

Now and then I still think of that trip at twenty, rolling across Interstate 80 in a '64 Tempest, looking south through the thin light of dawn for the sight of mountains. And yet time hasn't been kind to the memory, much of its color having leached away from too many years spent lamenting the passing of things. Not long ago, though, in that very same stretch of southern Wyoming, I stumbled on, if not a remedy, then at least a freshening. It happened on a clear day in early summer when on impulse I ditched the interstate for a certain southbound highway, from there to a potholed county road, then a two-track, and finally to an old trail bobbing and weaving along a lonely reach of the Colorado border. A place where wildness still held. Positively wordless. Wide-eyed with sun and creek water and bear shit and June snow. A world not so different, really, from the way Wolf said it would be.

Judy Blunt WHAT WE LEAVE

In June of 1997, I made the long drive to south Phillips County, Montana, accompanied by a tinge of sadness. Second Creek School had been without students for years, and with no children waiting in the wings, the decision had been made to close it permanently. All its contents were to be sold at auction. In addition to its own thirty-year accumulation of books and materials, it held all the books, desks, and materials we'd moved over from South First Creek School in 1965, as well as collections from the long-defunct Robinson, Rock Creek, and Fourchette schools. The sale would mark the end of an era. The First Creek Community Hall was falling into disuse and disrepair. The 4-H Clubs had folded. With the rural schools closed, the Regina and Sun Prairie communities had little to offer young families.

I turned south onto the Midale Road, rolling my eyes at the latest road improvement project. Some land-managing arm of government had thought to string wooden signs south like a trail of bread crumbs, every reservoir and creek, every branch and fork in the road posted with place names, arrows, mileage. Public lands were suddenly popular, and in an effort to accommodate visitors, the boggy gumbo grade had been fortified with gravel in a few places, too. Our end of the county had made a name for itself with big game hunters, some miracle of water, forage, and isolation combining to produce a number of trophy mule deer and elk. Varmint hunters had been welcomed, too, as a means of slowing down the prairie dogs in the absence of enough natural predators. South Phillips County, alone, supported twenty-six thousand *acres* of prairie dog towns, occupied by around a half a million prairie dogs. By the early nineties, the combined efforts of state and federal agencies had succeeded in planting a small, fragile population of black-footed ferrets among the prairie dogs on the CMR Wildlife Refuge south of my ex-husband's ranch. From my home in Missoula, I'd kept an idle ear to the ongoing soap opera of the endangered species experiment, the chest-thumping among local/state/federal officials over who was in charge, the tiny ferret radio collars tracked to mounds of coyote crap as the big predators ate the little predators, the official intervention when the plague began decimating the prairie dog population—once considered nature's way of controlling overpopulation. Now, with the ferret project at risk, officials set about dusting prairie dog towns with insecticide to kill the fleas that carried the plague that killed the dogs that fed the ferrets . . . and on and on.

The prairie rolled along as it always had. On an unfenced stretch of road we called the Veseth Pasture, a small band of antelope crossed in front of the car, and I pulled over and stopped for a moment to watch. Overhead, a pair of red-tailed hawks coasted on a lazy round of air, the dip and glide of pronghorns chasing the shadow of their wings on a landscape largely unchanged since the day I left. But I knew better. The changes had occurred over the rise, back from the road a ways, where the people lived. Fewer than half the families I grew up knowing still lived in the Regina and Sun Prairie communities, and fewer still had another generation beginning on the land. Although still locally owned, many of the ranch buildings I'd passed on my way south from Malta stood vacant, their secret given away by the stripe of tall weeds that grew down the center of the lanes leading in from the county road. Some, nearer to the highway, had strands of wire stretched across the cattle guards, a deterrent to hunters and joy-riding high school kids, but no real defense against thieves and vandals in four-wheel drives—the sort of outsiders ranchers worried about now.

Sale day began with a cool rain shower that cleared the air and stopped before the roads became too slick to get around. My sisters, Margaret and Gail, drove with me to Second Creek School in the morning to thumb through the amassed boxes and make up auction lots of our own choosing. Midway through disassembly, the schoolroom and teacherage were chaotic. Larger items were already moved to the auction site, while supplies and materials with mostly sentimental value had been pulled from shelves and piled in heaps. The offerings ran the gamut from worn, turn-of-the-century primers to the little Apple II computer the community had helped acquire in the eighties by collecting and redeeming Campbell's Soup labels. The old brass handbell our teachers had rung to call us in from recess had disappeared from the school one hunting season years before, but some obvious plums—like the old Red Wing drinking crock—were expected to draw spirited bidding. I searched for the alphabet story cards we'd used in first grade, but they were missing, perhaps buried under tons of books and materials, but more likely discarded in favor of the more modern, cartoon-style ABCs in primary colors that circled the schoolroom.

All the boxed lots accumulated by neighborhood volunteers in the morning were numbered and moved to the auction site at First Creek

Community Hall that afternoon. Margaret and I drove over together and in the end, bid ten dollars for a box we'd handpicked that included a dented tin globe, a couple of sets of Winston readers, and a dozen storybooks from the thirties and forties that I read as a child.

Driving back to the ranch from the Hall, we paused at the site of our first school. Only a jog in the barbed wire fence told us where South First Creek School had been; no sign marked the spot and no man-made artifacts remained visible from the road. The grass had grown up thick and green where our feet once trampled it to bare dirt, and recent rains had set the prairie blooming with the small, close flowers we both remembered. The wild parsley we called cat's paw, curlycup gumweed, and broom snakeweed glowed yellow and gold. Here, the lick of scarlet globemallow and pincushion cactus, there, a sprinkle of cool lavender and pale blue in the low mounds of moss phlox.

We poked around through the grass, keeping one eye and one ear tuned for rattlesnakes, and found the concrete step that once led into the school's entryway. With that to center my gaze, I could see a vague outline of the building in the vegetation and on the south side, a couple of shallow, parallel troughs in the grass where our swing set had been. We laughed at how tall the grass had grown at the western end, where the outhouses used to stand. The old South First Creek building had been sold to a Sun Prairie rancher to use for storage, the outhouses relocated to the new school where they continued to serve well into the seventies. Eventually Second Creek School would boast a tiny indoor bathroom fed from an underground tank, but federal law still required all schools to provide separate bathrooms for boys and girls—hence the two propped-up, carefully patched, and seldom-used outhouses we'd just watched sell for a few dollars apiece. They had braced the north fence of the schoolyard for decades, fulfilling the letter of the law. Little else remained.

It was a beautiful afternoon, and we were in no hurry. I smiled as I shook off the buzz of town life and breathed in the absolute silence, the rich smell of spring sage after a rain. I was back in the cradle of my childhood, surrounded by everything, and nothing. Blank horizons marked north, Malta some fifty miles away, and south, where the Missouri River Breaks lay invisible, tucked below the surface. To the east, a slim blue streak marked the Larb Hills; to the west, the Little Rocky Mountains stood in silhouette, and though the profile had changed gradually since the seventies, I found my eyes drawn back to the huge bite dredged from the center of the range by Pegasus gold mines, the missing peaks visible a hundred miles away.

It was on the prairie itself, a short distance from the schoolyard, that

I found a solid piece of my past. There, half-buried in sod, were the rock houses built by a generation of grammar school girls in the fifties and sixties. Not three-dimensional except in concept, a rock house was made like a floor plan, with a rectangle of large, same-size rocks outlining the exterior "walls" and smaller ones marking off the interior rooms; gaps in the walls denoted doorways. The rest of the house existed only in our imaginations. For years we had played rock house during recesses when the weather was mild, returning to the same small plot when the snow drew back in spring, as a bird might return to its old nest. Every autumn when school began, we reseated any rocks dislocated by grazing cows over the summer, then scoured the prairie for more to expand and improve the walls. The best rocks were quite difficult to find, like the highly prized pink granite and the darker green-flecked fieldstones, and more than once I sneaked rocks to school from home in the back of the pickup.

I recognized my house at once by the layout, though I recalled it being much larger. The living room and kitchen made up over half the house, and the three small bedrooms alongside were just large enough for an adult to sit in cross-legged. Some old lessons survived with the stones— one did not step over the wall of a rock house. On that June afternoon, thirty-odd years after I had last done so, I walked around the perimeter and entered through the front door. Inside these rooms, we had enacted the social rituals of our grandmothers and mothers, the formal invitations crayoned one recess, guests assembling the next. We younger girls took our cues regarding proper rock house decorum from our elders, the seventh and eighth graders. The older the girl, the bigger the rocks used in her house, and the more impressive her collection of broken crockery and glassware scavenged from the homesteader's dump over a rise to the west. Bits of prairie foliage, even an insect or two, served as imaginary luncheon on the salvaged china. I'd been a fifth grader when the school closed, one of the last to serve "air tea" and grasshopper drumsticks on broken Depression ware to a circle of ranch women-in-training.

In the years that followed my leaving the ranch, I would find the landscape of my life reflected in the lives of women from many different backgrounds. In the company of other women writers, in listening to them talk about their lives, I had come to understand how we may be isolated by circumstances as well as by distance, and how our experiences, though geographically different, often translate into the same feelings. I had come to believe that what matters most is our story, what we tell ourselves and pass along to our daughters. But standing in the living room of my rock house, I was again reminded of the enormous power of this silent prairie and the whisper I made inside it. I had forgotten how easily one person can be lost here.

I left my house as I found it, settling into the sod a year at a time. Even our stories move underground eventually. The prairie will reclaim its squared corners and straight walls as it has gradually, patiently, taken back the teepee rings left centuries before. Driving the narrow, familiar road back to my parents' ranch, I felt a sense of peace, imagining my house hundreds, thousands of years from now, suspended far below the surface of the short-grass plains, five stone rooms that hold a part of me, still.

I can't imagine what my uncle must have thought when I called him from the University of Montana in Missoula in the winter of 1974 and told him I was going to be living in the woods that coming spring. I'm from Minnesota, and during high school I lived with my aunt and uncle in a suburb of Minneapolis. Most of our clan who had left Minnesota had stayed in the Midwest or had gone off to the East Coast. I chose Montana for reasons that included a bit of romanticism, a little hearsay, and for the most part a heedless whimsy, which I was big on in those days. And there I was in the second quarter of my first year of college, announcing that I was going to be living outside, or nearly so. My friend from New York and I were going to live in a tent, or possibly under a lean-to. Our plan was to continue our higher education but to live in Hellgate Canyon, the narrow chute through which the Clark Fork River enters Missoula from the east. We planned to settle in about a mile from campus, close enough so we could walk back to civilization every morning, handsomely begrimed and smelling of wood smoke.

What, my uncle wanted to know, had inspired my rather unusual resolution? It wasn't something easy to explain.

I am susceptible to the influence of books. When I think of my childhood I am more apt to picture pages from *A Fly Went By* than actual scenes inhabited by my younger self. The first time I read *The Lord of the Rings* trilogy, I spent much of one summer in Middle Earth, with only occasional forays back to the drab kingdom of Suburbia. Once, reading Thomas Mann's *The Magic Mountain*, set in a Swiss sanatorium full of feverish tuberculosis patients, I contracted, or willed myself to develop, a raging, hallucinatory fever, the worst of my life. And during winter quarter of my first year of college, I took a literature class, which I believe was called "Cowboys and Indians: Literature of Red and White." Of the books we read, I remember only two, Dan Cushman's *Stay Away, Joe*, which was good, and A. B. Guthrie Jr.'s *The Big Sky*, which was more than good. It was transformative, in the sense of having persuaded a citified teenager who possessed no skills or knowledge that would have done him any good in the wilderness to imagine himself a backwoodsman. How could I explain to my uncle that I wanted not merely to live in Montana but to live out, in my own small way, the story of Montana as constructed by A. B. Guthrie?

The Big Sky is mainly the story of Boone Caudill, a headstrong young Kentuckian who lights out for the West in 1830 in search of freedom, of unfettered wildness. I was not unmoved by the plot, or by the great tragedy at the heart of the book, but what stirred me most at the time were Guthrie's descriptions of the land itself, this "great sprawling magnitude of the west" that I found myself in. I was intoxicated by the grandeur of Guthrie's vision, by scenes like this:

> High along the slopes of the peaks the snow lay patched. Between the
> mountains and the Missouri was high, bare country, where a man
> on a rise saw buttes swimming in the distance and the distance itself
> rolling off so far that he lost himself looking into it.

In truth, Missoula was in a tight, hemmed-in valley, and Hellgate Canyon was more compressed still, but this vastly beautiful place was my new home, and Guthrie showed me large parts of it that I could not have found grander had I discovered them on my own.

And of course I responded to the lives of the mountain men. I wasn't much older than Boone, so the allure of living on my own, out under the stars, answerable to no one, not even to teachers of Western literature, was powerfully attractive. My friend from New York, after reading the book at my urging, fell just as hard for it. We wanted to be Boone Caudill and his friends, Jim Deakins and Dick Summers. In the afternoon, after our classes were over, we'd leave our dorm rooms in Duniway Hall and tramp up Hellgate Canyon. We'd build a fire in a swale not far from the river and sit there drinking quart bottles of Lucky Lager, smoking hand-rolled cigarettes, and palavering in our best imitation of our new heroes, larding our speech with "I reckon," "this child," and "I'm thinkin'." It was during those afternoons that we cooked up our plans to live outside. We both realized it was all a bit silly, but we didn't care. What did the people we passed our days with, mere students, know about the melancholic fatality the wide-open West engendered in thoughtful mountain men like Deakins:

> The feel of the country settled into Jim, the great emptiness and age
> of it, the feel of westward mountains old as time and plains wide as
> forever and the blue sky flung across. The country didn't give a damn
> about a man or any animal. It let the buffalo and the antelope feed

on it and the gophers dig and the birds fly and men crawl around, but what did it care, being one with time itself? What did it care about a man or his hankerings or what happened to him? There would be other men after him and others after them, all wondering and all wishful and after a while all dead.

I didn't try explaining all this to my uncle. He had been bewildered but compliant and had even agreed to let me have the money that ordinarily would have paid for my room and board. I'm sure he was relieved when our plans fell apart. The closer spring quarter got, the sillier the prospect looked. What finally killed it was the impossibility of finding a sufficiently secluded spot within walking distance of campus, for Hellgate Canyon was regularly traversed by numerous other college students, a smattering of older folks, and too damned many young kids, who were our main worry. We realized that our camp would be plundered and vandalized if it were anywhere near close enough to walk back and forth to school. We took some ribbing from friends when we gave up on our little dream, but I had no regrets. At eighteen, life-altering resolutions are as easily abandoned as conceived, and we had an awful lot of fun just imagining ourselves as mountain men.

If I gave up my plans to live like Boone Caudill, I never let go of *The Big Sky*. I read it through two or three more times, and for years it was my bedside book, the one I turned to when I wanted to read for a few minutes in the morning, or when I was nodding off at night but not quite ready for sleep. In a sense, it speeded up the acclimation process. It filled in some of the missing history and sense of place that people born here would have learned by osmosis. It didn't make me a Montanan. I still haven't figured out how long you have to live here before you feel comfortable hanging that label on yourself, but it went a long way toward making me want to be one.

That didn't prevent my whimsy from luring me back to Minnesota in the mid-1980s. But after five years in the Twin Cities, my wife, a native of Missoula, and I were so eager to move back to Montana that I accepted a job in Billings. In the past, I had never gone to Billings except in the company of the Missoula Flying Mules, a barely organized, nominally adult men's hockey team that played all its games on the road because Missoula in those days didn't have its own rink. Always coming here as an outsider, a challenger, had something to do with the image of Billings I developed, but my dislike for the town went deeper than that. The stink of the place alone from the oil refineries, the sugar beet plant, and a now-defunct meatpacking plant was enough to make us glad we were just weekend drop-ins. And unlike Missoula, with its loose, late-hippie feel and its large population of college students, Billings seemed to be a collection of arrogant oil men and go-getter business types in spanking-new cowboy hats and freshly ironed blue jeans. But the *Billings Gazette* had offered me a job as a night editor and Billings was in Montana and that was the main thing.

I had been in Billings hardly more than a month, in the summer of 1989, full of doubts and wondering what I'd gotten myself into, when I fell under the sway of another Montana book. I had just read *The California and Oregon Trail* by Francis Parkman, the great historian's account of his ethnographical sortie into the land of the Plains Indians in 1846. It was a fascinating read, but marked by a pervasive condescension toward the Indians. That was forgivable, considering when it was written, but I wanted more direct knowledge about Indian life. A friend recommended *Plenty-coups, Chief of the Crows* by Frank Linderman.

Plenty-coups was born in 1848, not far from the present site of Billings. In the late 1920s, nearly blind and not completely trusting his memory, Plenty-coups, aided by interpreters and sign language, sat down and told the story of his life to Linderman. Even in Plenty-coups's youth the lifestyle of the Plains Indians was clearly doomed, but when he brought to life the world he knew as a boy, it was if that world would go on forever. The freedom that Boone Caudill struggled to extract from the West was given to Plenty-coups as a birthright. He had nothing to rebel against or to run from, only a promise to live up to.

"My heart was afire," Plenty-coups told Linderman. "I wished so to help my people, to distinguish myself, so that I might wear an eagle's feather in my hair. How I worked to make my arms strong as a grizzly's, and how much I practiced with my bow! A boy never wished to be a man more than I."

My own heart was afire. It was like reading ancient history, for like the ancient Greeks, Plenty-coups had dedicated himself to honor, harsh pleasures, and war. And like the heroes of the Trojan War, he always spoke in high praise of his vanquished enemies, making sure to point out how handsome and brave his victims had been. The Crow Indians raised their boys in an atmosphere of intense emulation, constantly inspiring them with examples of bravery and endurance. The young boys learned to run by chasing butterflies, which they would catch and rub on their bodies, hoping to obtain their powers. They swam in the rivers at all seasons of the year, dodging ice floes in the winter. When he was a young man, Plenty-coups said, he could run from sunup to sundown without stopping, and you believe him. If there are not so many rapturous descriptions of the land here as in *The Big Sky*, it is because they are not necessary. It is a given that there is no finer spot on earth. As another Crow chief, Ara-pooish, said in a famous speech, "The Crow country is exactly in the right place. Everything good is to be found there. There is no country like the Crow country."

Plenty-coups's book immediately altered the way I looked at Billings. It was no longer a cowtown that had changed into a crass, rough-and-ready commercial burg. Now it had a past and a context that stretched back beyond the edge of written history, and its landmarks seemed full of mystery and meaning. Just as *The Big Sky* had speeded up my internship as a newcomer to Montana, *Plenty-coups* made me love this part of Montana, in just a few days, in a way that I could not have loved it at all without the book. And when I finished it, a friend took me down to Pryor, on the Crow Reservation, to the two-story wooden house where Plenty-coups had lived in his old age. We sat under the same cottonwood trees that shaded Plenty-coups as he dictated the story of his life to Linderman. We peered into his locked and empty house and we even presumed to make tobacco offerings at the little spring-fed pool near his house.

Older if not wiser by then, and having a job and two daughters, I harbored no dreams of going off to live in the mountains. But I couldn't look over the Yellowstone Valley, or off toward the Pryor, Beartooth, or Crazy Mountains without thinking of Plenty-coups. I took my daughters down to Plenty-coups's house and into the Pryors, and we swam in the Yellowstone River more often than my wife considered altogether prudent. I never quite shook the feeling of strangeness that came over me when I thought of Plenty-coups, the idea that this man who seemed so ancient and inaccessible had lived where I lived, and his house still stood, and he had died only a generation before I was born. I wasn't so fortunate as to have the circle of elders who counseled Plenty-coups when he was a boy and who affirmed the strength of the vision he had high up in the Crazy Mountains, but it seemed to me that books like *The Big Sky* and *Plenty-coups* were our elders, if only we would listen to them.

There were other Montana books that served as elders and that schooled me and moved me over the years. Norman Maclean's *A River Runs Through It*, James Welch's *Fools Crow*, Richard O'Malley's *Mile High Mile Deep*, all books that had to be read more than once and that grew on me and *in* me nearly as much as *Plenty-coups* and *The Big Sky* had. I haven't lived in enough places or read enough books to hazard an opinion on our relative standing, or even to know whether I sound laughably provincial, but it seems as though Montana is blessed with a disproportionate bounty in terms of natural beauty and the stature of our books.

Which brings me to one more, *We Pointed Them North: Recollections of a Cowpuncher,* by E. C. "Teddy Blue" Abbott. Like *Plenty-coups,* this is an as-told-to memoir, in this case dictated to and compiled by Helena Huntington Smith. The old cowboy, like the old Crow chief, didn't need much editing. As Smith says in the introduction, her main job "was to keep out of the way and not mess it up by being literary." It might seem strange that I'm including two ghostwritten memoirs among my three favorite pieces of Montana "literature," but here we are in the company of the ancients again, when the best stories were told by people who had lived their adventures, not simply narrated them.

Teddy Blue was born in England in 1860, twelve years after Plenty-coups. He came to the United States in 1871 and settled with his family in Nebraska. Soon after their arrival, his father bought some cattle in Texas and Teddy Blue was allowed to join the drive to Nebraska, the family thinking it would be good for the health of the "poorliest, sickliest little kid you ever saw," as Teddy Blue described himself. Teddy Blue was soon a bona fide cowpuncher, going all the way from Texas to Montana for the first time in 1883. He tells his story more or less chronologically, but no one ever enjoyed a digression more. And these are not the digressions of a scatterbrained old man. Teddy Blue knew he was telling the story of a heroic group of men that he was proud to be part of, and he wanted to get every detail of their lives down: their gear and their clothing, their grub and their methods of working, their ways of fighting and thinking and taking pleasure. It was a life of incredible hardship and danger, where dismemberment and death awaited the smallest slip. When the cattle were on the move or had to get to water, the cowboys stayed in the saddle so long they would rub tobacco juice in their eyes to keep awake. And it was no use complaining: "If you said anything to the boss, he would only say, 'What the hell are you kicking about? You can sleep all winter when you get to Montana.'" Fat chance. Those cowpunchers were so fired up by the time they hit a wide-open town like Miles City, Montana, that they might have gotten more sleep on the trail.

"I never had time to gamble," Teddy Blue said. "I couldn't sit still long enough; I always had to be up, talking, singing, drinking at the bar. I was so happy and full of life, I used to feel, when I got a little whiskey inside me, that I could jump twenty feet in the air. I'd like to go back and feel that way once more. If I could go back I wouldn't change any of it." The whole book is like that—vivid, unrepentant, electrifyingly alive. I have sometimes thought there might be a connection between extremely difficult, hazardous occupations and the flowering of a language lively and direct enough to encompass them: witness Melville aboard a whaler or Twain piloting a steamboat. As Smith says of Teddy Blue's English, "Of all the varieties of speech in the United States, I don't know any that for color and violence can touch the authentic Western American." I was smitten by his language and by his evocation of a glorious, fleeting chapter in the history of this state. The plains and rivers of eastern Montana took on new meaning for me, and Miles City, which I barely knew before reading Teddy Blue, has fascinated me ever since.

In these three books we have the three great themes of early Montana: the twilight of the Plains Indian tradition, the mountain man's glory in that brief era when a European could at least pretend to share in Eden, and that even shorter period when the open-range cowboy was king, when a man lived in the saddle, and there wasn't a fence to be seen all the way from Texas to Montana. But these books that have shaped and re-shaped the way I feel about Montana have more in common than geography, and they describe more than mythological lives. In each, there is a feeling of great sadness at the end being near, the curtain coming down. When Plenty-coups was a boy, his powerful vision was of "buffalo without number" coming out of a hole in the ground. When they finally stopped coming, they were all suddenly gone, and then out of the hole came countless more bulls, cows, and calves. But these were all spotted buffalo, "strange animals from another world." They were the white man's cattle, which Plenty-coups had not seen before he dreamt of them. It seemed impossible, but come they did, and then the buffalo were gone. Plenty-coups speaks of the transition with a note of noble fatality, only noting, not complaining. In Guthrie's fiction, Boone Caudill makes an attempt to hang onto the vanishing past. He takes a Blackfoot wife and wants nothing more, he thinks, than to live as an Indian, only to realize at the end of *The Big Sky* that he himself had a hand in killing paradise. In real life, Teddy Blue married the half-Snake Indian daughter of Montana pioneer Granville Stuart, and he quotes with approval what his friend, the artist Charlie M. Russell, said of the Indians: "They've been living in heaven for a thousand years, and we took it away from 'em for forty dollars a month."

You want Plenty-coups and Boone Caudill and Teddy Blue Abbott to be twenty years old forever, but it can't happen, even in the pages of a book. And Montana can't just be this beautiful, uncomplicated place. As our stories tell us, it is haunted by all the things that cannot be undone.

The call came at 11 p.m., when sleep had finally defeated the relentless replay of the day, the corral dust in his nostrils, the din of bawling calves, the sight even with his eyes tightly shut of bovines in constant motion through sorting of cows from calves, then of heifer calves from steer calves.

Shipping day had been relatively uneventful, though accompanied by the familiar tightness in his stomach on this single payday of the year. There was the saddling in the dark, the ride out on snorting horses that knew, too, what day of the year it was, their blood hot with the frost of October. His steers had filled three stock trailers, his own and those of two neighbors, while the heifers, not qualifying as replacement prospects, were sent up the chute and into his old cattle truck. And when the calves were finally weighed and he slumped into his pickup, the check from the buyer lighter than he'd hoped but heavier than he'd feared, he drove slowly into his lane and walked at half speed toward the penned, bawling, calfless cows. He checked the latches on every corral gate, supplementing the strength of each with a twist of baling wire. Cows, the ultimate mothers, can do strange and wild things when you send off their calves.

And then, in the car now, since he didn't feel up to unhooking his trailer from the pickup, he made a quick trip to the bank to deposit the check. The reckoning with the banker could wait a day. Supper with his wife—she hid well her disappointment at the amount on the deposit slip—was followed by a shower, bed, and an hour of involuntary calculations on his mental balance sheet before, finally, the first soft touch of sleep. And then the phone rang.

She identified herself with a name vaguely familiar, a new resident in the subdivision that just last year had been the ranch of a neighbor. What she said made him sit bolt upright. "I think there's something wrong with your cows!" Visions of a broken corral, his herd loose on the highway, eased slightly when she clarified. "They just keep mooing."

"Well, we shipped calves today. When you wean you always have to lock the mother cows up for a day or two. They always moo."

Her tone turned testy. "They're keeping me from sleeping. Can't you do something about it? Quiet them down?"

"No." She hung up. He started to explain to his sleepy wife this baffling call about a yearly event as normal and predictable as Christmas, the weaning of calves and the bawling of their mothers, when the phone rang again. This time it was the dispatcher at the sheriff's office, reporting that a neighbor had called to complain about his cows. "Anything wrong out there?" she asked.

"No. We shipped calves today, that's all. She thinks I ought to be able to tell my cows to shut up."

The dispatcher laughed. "Go back to sleep, Bill. Sorry."

We would laugh, too, in the days that followed, join in the ribbing. "Hey, Bill, got those cows trained yet?" But it was a nervous sort of teasing. And Bill shot back that it would be our turn one of these days, that perhaps the dispatcher next time wouldn't be a ranch girl, and we knew, too, he was probably right. Things were changing.

With Bill on my mind, I curry Partner, the big black colt, though I have no real reason to ride to the hills. His coat has touches of new winter hair, but not enough to hide the smooth, hard muscles underneath. I swing on blanket and saddle, cinch up, and slip softly my father-in-law's favorite bit into the gelding's mouth. Then we're off in a swift single-foot. We sweep down the lane and over the bridge, Partner's shoes thumping the planks in four-four time, the solid reverberation a familiar and welcome sound.

I point Partner toward the hills of our eastern range, toward the valley wall of brown grass studded by green juniper and blood-red buckbrush, and let him lope into the breeze. He crossfires, starts off on a lead in front that does not match what he's doing behind, so I rein him in and start over, and then he's fine. We canter across the flat pasture and begin our ascent. I rein the gelding back into a perfect head-nodding running walk, satisfied that he has become a horse of the sort prized by my father-in-law Elmer and his father Magnus before him.

We skirt Indian Coulee, where Magnus found a Crow tree burial when he settled this ranch in the 1890s after the tribe's agency moved east a second time. A single horizontal stick remained when Magnus's granddaughter Emily pointed to it many years ago on one of our first horseback rides together. Elmer could remember when most of the platform was still there, and Magnus, I've been told, when tufts of blanket blew in the breeze, revealing the bones beneath. Probably the occupant of the platform died during the measles outbreak the Absaroka suffered shortly before leaving this land to white settlers. For a reason I can't explain, I've always thought the deceased was a woman, an older one. Nor can I fully explain why this spot has become so important to me that I can't seem to write a book without finding a reason to mention it.

The pull of the slope warms Partner, who drops his head from its normal proud position to better handle the hill, his hind legs pistons, his breathing deepening. But he does not try to rest. When I stop to let him blow where the cow path threads through stunted fir, he takes three deep breaths and then signals his wish to get it done. So we lunge up the remaining grade and top out on a knoll under 360 degrees of endless sky, and here the horse is willing to stop.

The Beartooth range of the Absaroka Mountains stretches from our southeast to due west, a blue wall marbled by caps of snow that finger down each watercourse. Northwest, jutting sharply from the plain, are the Crazies, named, they say, for a woman whose mind broke down under the strain of westering. A touch of rein on Partner's neck swivels him right. To the north on this very clear day I can see the tips of the Snowies, a hundred miles away, and swiveling farther, to the east, named for Lewis and Clark's sergeant, the Pryor Mountains. It is big, it is beautiful, it is open. Many of the recent changes cannot be seen from here.

I will ride Partner on a clockwise circle around the range, progressing north along the top of the valley wall. To my right is a rolling plateau, gradually descending toward Beaver Creek. To my left, down the sharp slope I have just climbed, lies the deeper valley of the East Rosebud. Across it I can see the western half of our ranch, the old log homesteader's barn on the hill, and below it, irrigated hay fields. Now, in October, enough green lingers in the alfalfa field below the ditch to contrast with the brown above. Yellow-leafed cottonwoods line the banks of the ditch, their roots watered now for a hundred years by the work of Magnus and a hired man he imported from his native Bornholm, the Danish island. From what we can tell by water rights documents, Magnus and his helper spent seven years getting water two miles down the valley by hand-digging the entire way. So full of boulders was the ground that even a horse-drawn slip would not work. It was all pick-and-shovel work, squeezed whenever possible between other ranch tasks.

Emily and I now face the probability of a nine-unit subdivision spanning this ditch on the land above us, nine separate sets of ornamental fences for us to cross each time we walk it or check it on horseback. Our legal right to access and maintain the ditch is secure, but enforcement in Montana is anemic. It will take just one ill-tempered buyer of a new "ranchette" and a padlocked gate to make us hire lawyers to retain what we already own, not a happy prospect. I put it out of my mind and congratulate Partner on failing to spook at a covey of Hungarian partridges that noisily flush at our feet from the sage.

At the head of the next coulee mule deer, a few does and fawns and a small buck, lope casually out of our way on pogo stick legs, their hooves dislodging small stones that clatter down the slope. We top another rise and look to the valley floor at a neighbor's house located very close to the site of the second Crow Agency. Magnus knew the agency—corrals, outbuildings, and an adobe fort—from horse-buying trips. After emigrating from Denmark in 1885 at age sixteen, he had settled in central Montana near White Sulphur Springs and, with a cousin, set up a dairy to supply miners with products they craved. As a sideline he traveled by rail to Crow country to buy horses from the tribe, spent a few days breaking one of them in what must have been a crash course, and then herded the rest two hundred miles home to train and sell over winter. On those trips he found his ranch, our ranch, and when the valley opened to settlement, he bought out homesteaders and squatters and assembled the spread he wanted.

Spanning a valley and bisected by the East Rosebud River and a major highway, the ranch consists of dryland hills, irrigated hay fields, and a cottonwood bottom along the river. There is a discernable ledge along the base of the eastern hills where the county road lay before being moved toward the river to service the homesteads that were springing up. The ranch was once larger before a split to satisfy two sons. What remains could, in the best of times, support a single family. For our generation, the third, two full-time teaching jobs have been required to keep it, as they say locally, "out of the hands of the Californians."

I spur Partner up the knoll onto high ground that will furnish my last view across the valley before I turn east. The hilltop mansion two miles to the west no longer stands alone, for a large subdivision of twenty-acre plots spills down the valley to its right. In *Sketches from the Ranch*, I told of my discovery of this first of many hilltop homes, called it "a wart on my landscape," and felt some embarrassment later when I discovered its occupant was a very nice man who I had reason to believe had read my book. And there lies the paradox.

Partner's body language shows his disappointment at our turn to the east. Perhaps, like me, he believes that the only two directions worth a damn are west and north. More likely he was hoping to turn toward home. But he doesn't resist the long, gradual descent toward Beaver Creek, though his gaits roughen with the downhill direction. Toward the bottom, where our range runs out, I can see debris remaining from the Dickinson homestead and recall tales of a woman who thought nothing of assembling a basket of her recent canning, then trotting the several miles over the hills to visit Emily's parents. They were social, those homesteaders, social and physical. It was nothing to walk a few miles for a cup of coffee, something sweet to eat, and a chat with friends.

I know the Dickinson place well from rides after errant cattle. The location of the homestead on a south-facing slope is another study in contrasts. The homesteaders did not need lessons in being "green." The buildings, below the crest of the hill, faced the low winter sun, and the barn was dug into the hillside, earth-sheltered. The chicken house faced the same direction, its south wall consisting of many small glass panes to capture precious heat. On the northwest side of the buildings, blocking some of the prevailing wind, was the shelter belt to which the family hauled water from the spring below, establishing the roots so well that some of the trees still live. Although the homesite affords a glimpse of the mountains through a cut in the hills to the south, view was secondary. The family could have seen the entire Beartooth range from their front porch by building their house upslope a few hundred yards onto the ridge. But they would have suffered for it.

For many of the modern immigrants, view has eclipsed all other considerations. Not many miles away there is a large house built on the very top of a steep little hill, a tiny, pointed, isolated butte. The building looks like a precariously balanced nodule, and its occupants must be extremely athletic because in no direction from the house could they step without great risk of a tumble all the way to the bottom. The owners must not be concerned about the wind or about accessibility during winter. A house in Florida or Hawaii probably serves them for the tougher half of the year.

But the paradox. For every one of these new arrivals who waves his wealth like a magic wand, who spells out to you very clearly very early that his financial accomplishments elsewhere translate into superior power in this new environment, there is another who is kind, even admiring of your occupation. For each who stands by her fence, hands on hips, and claims that in spite of your water rights more than a century old, you now have no right to enter her property to maintain the ditch that brings you water, there are many who respect the culture and the laws and want to learn of them. There are the usual benefits of an immigrant population of varied background and education, enrichment for our local institutions. New friendships, too, come readily.

The cattle trail has now touched my east border fence, and Partner, glad for the change in direction, lunges through a coulee bottom still green from spring water at a place we can safely cross now, but that would have been boggy during spring. We cruise south along the fence line, climbing back to higher ground, looking for breaks in barbed wire that in some places is as old as the ranch itself. We top out in a smooth saddle on a ridge, and now the Beartooths and the Pryors loom larger, as if our little ride has made significant progress toward them. Mountains do not look the same day to day or even hour to hour. They seem to have their ups and downs, like living things.

It is here I try to tell myself to quit whining. I have, after all, more space around me than 99 percent of the humans on the planet. Why, then, does it take so little as houses on the horizon miles away to make me anxious, even claustrophobic? Besides, it's not as if subdivision were something new. Everything my race has done since its first arrival under this big sky has been subdivision of one sort or another. The railroad split the prairie, broke what the Sioux called the "Great Circle." The Homestead Act divided this land optimistically (and against the advice of John Wesley Powell, a man who really knew it) into 160-acre plots. Indeed, a few remaining cedar posts still standing far off the fence line Partner and I now follow are reminders of a time when half a dozen families inhabited this range on little, starveling farms, prosperous during a few rainy years before nature made its correction.

An urban sister-in-law, shown this range in my four-wheel-drive pickup, said, "I can see condos up here." I turned to her innocent face, as horrified as if she had cursed my religion. A vision of security, safety, and normality to her was one of destruction to me. And I wonder at just how, in a single lifetime, I have become such an archetypal Westerner, a Daniel Boone (or perhaps an A. B. Guthrie Boone), so dependent on open space and the ability to evade the constructs of civilization.

But maybe it did not happen that fast. Except during stints in the Marine Corps and in graduate school, I have never lived in a large city. I grew up in tiny Dakota and Montana towns, the son of a minister who had among his oldest possessions, purchased during his college years, a double-bitted ax. He told me once, half chagrined, that he had bought it during a brief preoccupation with the idea of homesteading in Alaska. And before him, there were Norwegian fisherman who found their open territory on the treacherous waters of the North Sea, and before that, of course, Vikings who escaped tiny terraced farms by pointing the prows of their ships toward the ultimate space, the great unknown lying to the west. In more modern times, Norway lost fully half of its population in a few years spanning the opening of the twentieth century, most to homesteads on the American prairies.

The craving for space, of course, ultimately displaces space. It's a perpetual Western motif, groups coming for beaver pelts, gold, or land, and then, by sheer numbers or waste, destroying the very things that attracted them in the first place. And one group displaces another. Magnus and others, seizing opportunities provided by the US government, displaced the Crows, who, quite possibly, 150 years earlier, had displaced someone else. The ranching generation is now being displaced by those who have other visions for the land. I don't begrudge anyone for wanting a chunk of this valley, for wanting twenty acres with a view, for craving more space around them than the suburban yards they have sold. But as the space fills, the thing that attracted them, too, will diminish.

In a television interview, A. B. Guthrie Jr. paraphrased the Bible regarding the West. He said it should read, "In the beginning was the Word, and the Word was 'Change.'" Mountain men, cattlemen, miners, homesteaders, ranchers, and retirees have come in succession. And as Partner and I hit our south fence and turn west, and I let him lope in long, easy lunges, each with the rise and fall of a wave on water, I, too, think in biblical terms: "For everything there is a season, and a time for every purpose under heaven . . ." The Ecclesiastes poet does not say whether it is bad or good. It simply is.

On this last leg of our circle, I ride toward a horizon now lightly streaked with red, sunset coming quickly on this October day that is truncated in a way that surprises me, mild as it is. Now, though, there is a bit of bite in the gentle breeze, so I slow Partner to a brisk flat walk, reach behind me, and shake my down vest out of the saddle strings behind the cantle. We reach the ridge on the left side of Indian Coulee, pausing on this highest place on the ranch before our plunge down on the trail through stunted fir that we ascended earlier. I can see our ranch buildings as if from a low-flying airplane and to their south, the new houses.

Turning back to look east I catch the light at just the right time, my favorite time, those fleeting minutes when the entire landscape turns reddish brown, the color modulating through blended shades of yellow and pink before my very eyes, the sage flats and brown fall grasses showing a beauty they reserve for the waning moments of the day. The Beartooth Mountains are purple now, and the western sky toward which I ride, blood red. Partner feels good beneath me. I can smell his warmth, his scent mingling with that of sage and the fir trees through which we descend. As the breeze cools, I find myself hoping for the cold, wet smell of coming snow, and for the other smells that will follow that, the spring smells, the sweet placentas of birthing animals, the chinook winds thawing the ground beneath the snow.

A cow moos in the distance. On a trip to Spain, Emily and I descended on Andalusian horses a similar valley and heard a similar cow, and our guide said, "There's something comforting about a cow mooing down in the valley."

At the barbed wire gate I slide off Partner to open it and let us through, my legs needing a moment to shake out their kinks, a problem I did not used to have. The gate lever is a rusty piece of steel some two feet long and an inch wide that I scavenged from the pile of scrap by the blacksmith shop. In the fading light I look at it closely for the first time. It is not the product of a factory. It is a handmade part for some machine, perhaps a mowing machine or a plow, hand forged, I can tell, because I can see the folds made by several pieces of steel heated by pedal-powered bellows, then pounded into a single piece. Crafting this iron bar must have involved an afternoon's work, probably by Magnus, bent over the anvil in our little red blacksmith shop whose forge and bellows are still intact.

By the time we cross the irrigated fields it is dark, the light in our kitchen window bright. I tie Partner to the hitching rail by the tack shed and with practiced hands unsaddle and brush him by feel. He takes oats from my hand, then joins his buddies in the pasture and begins to graze.

Emily will have supper. She will ask me about my ride, as she always does. I will tell her that it was very good.

Russell Rowland | CHASING THE LAMB

When I was sixteen, I accepted my grandfather's invitation to spend the summer of 1974 working on the family ranch in southeastern Montana. Late one night, I caught the mail truck in Billings and rode to Ekalaka sitting between the driver and one other passenger. At sixteen, I wasn't about to fall asleep on the shoulder of one of these men I didn't know. So I stayed awake, head bobbing, for the 250-mile trip. In Ekalaka, I transferred to a smaller mail truck (actually just a pickup) that would travel the remaining sixty miles to the ranch. To my weary dismay, the driver was eager to visit. She talked for the entire sixty miles, which took several hours because she was obliged to stop at every rural mailbox.

By the time we arrived at the Arbuckle Ranch, the sun was making its appearance along the vast horizon of eastern Montana, and the only thing on my mind was a long nap. I had never stayed up all night. But as we pulled into the gravel drive, my mother's brother, Lee, came rushing out of the house.

"There's a fire at the Thomas place. Come on, let's get your stuff in the house."

No point in mentioning that I hadn't slept all night. For the next several hours, we dipped burlap bags into barrels of water and beat the fire to death.

Although I had spent my entire life in Montana and Wyoming, this was my introduction to the real American West, to a place where the task at hand is not determined by mood or whimsy. It was the most significant period in my development as a young man. Working twelve- to fourteen-hour days formed my body and my mind and gave me a new perspective on labor. The work felt purposeful and real in ways that no other job ever has. We were working to keep animals alive—animals that would one day feed other people. Everything we did contributed to that end, whether it was stacking the hay that would feed the cattle in the winter or docking lambs to prevent disease. It was selfless and satisfying in ways I've seldom experienced. I also learned that I could do things that seemed beyond me. I learned to operate heavy farm machinery, shifting hydraulic levers while I drove, before I even had a driver's license. Alone, I moved hundreds of head of cattle. I tossed seventy-five pound bales of hay and watched my arms grow from thin reeds to . . . well, slightly bigger arms.

When I decided to become a writer, it was only natural that many of the themes that emerged in my work were closely related to that time and place. First, it was the people. My characters were often stoical, and most of their dialog was coded, or terse. Sometimes these characters seemed out of place in the stories I tried to tell. But when I plopped them into the Montana prairie, they came to life. I now know the reason: this is the place I know best; these are the people I understand.

I have since lived in twelve other states, as well as the District of Columbia. I've spent a half century on this planet and had the opportunity to compare most of America to the place I grew up in, the place I call home.

I've also spent half of those fifty years evaluating from afar how the West has formed my image of myself. Most of my family was working class, with a long string of ranchers, mechanics, and welders, but I did not grow up with clichéd Western role models. Although my father always wanted to be a cowboy, he didn't hunt or fish. He didn't even own a gun. He didn't beat my mother or rant about the Indians. He was a guest teacher on the Northern Cheyenne Indian reservation for two years, and he loved his students. Although he rode saddle broncs and bulls on his college rodeo team, it wasn't until he tried his hand at being a rodeo clown that he found his comfort zone. He excelled at bullfighting, which allowed him to exercise both his talent in athletics and in entertainment. Rather than playing the tough guy, he had free rein to make light of that role. In many ways, he embodied both the old West and a West that has evolved since his boyhood, where there's less pressure to live up to the old myths. But those myths are still strong, and I have struggled to grasp my role as a man growing up between these two worlds.

One winter day when I was still a teenager, Uncle Lee and I were driving around the ranch when we saw a herd of deer in the distance. I had never shot a deer, and my uncle suggested this would be a good time. He had a rifle in the pickup, so we made our way around the perimeter and positioned ourselves in the direction they were traveling. I had very little shooting experience, so I missed my first few attempts. I started to get frustrated and embarrassed, which only made me more determined to succeed.

With one shell left in the rifle, we finally headed off the herd at just the right angle. They came bounding gracefully in front of us. I jumped from the pickup, propped the rifle against my narrow shoulder, and fixed my sights on the closest deer. I fired, and to my surprise, she dropped. My uncle circled the truck, laughing and cheering, and threw his arms around me. But I was fighting back a sick feeling in my stomach. I couldn't reconcile how beautiful that animal had looked racing across the pasture and how I'd crumpled that same beauty in an instant. I've never been opposed to hunting, but I've never done it again.

Of course I'm not the first kid to feel this way about hunting. Maybe most hunters experience that initial reaction and keep doing it anyway. But I think this experience symbolizes a common struggle among Westerners—the fight between what we're expected to be and what we really are; the question of whether we embrace Western attitudes because we believe in them or because we feel compelled to fit in; and the fact that some of the qualities that are attributed to us apply, but some don't.

In many ways, this is no different from the experience of teenage boys anywhere. The pressure to fit in inspires idiotic behavior and angst for teenagers all over the world. But in the capital "W" West, everything is magnified by legend, by myth. We have a reputation to uphold, and that's not always a good thing for confused teenage boys. Or for grown men and women. For example, when I started drinking, I took the job damn seriously, and my genetic makeup combined with the underlying pressure to be a real Western man sent me on a short but dramatic journey into a treatment program.

What I wonder finally is whether the last frontier of the West might be the internal journey, the search for how each of us fits in this mythical place. From as far back as I can remember, there was an underlying feeling that growing up here meant that we shouldn't expect to be as sophisticated as those exotic folks to the east or even the ones on our own coast. The idea of going to an Ivy League school never entered my mind in high school, but I later realized that I had the credentials to attend just about any college I wanted.

The West has long suffered from an inferiority complex. Westerners have been reminded in ways that are often subtle, but always clear, that we are interesting in some of the same ways that cavemen or headhunters are interesting. We are reminders of a past that was brutal and lawless. And we are often expected to perpetuate these myths, making occasional appearances in the press for our modern day outlaws, our mountain men, or our Unabomber, and producing art that reflects the same old stereotypes. We constantly struggle with the possibility that, if we step out of

these roles, we might not be taken seriously. And yet we're not taken seriously when we stick with the roles, either. Even those who have achieved
success in their artistry are considered regional and are often dismissed
by the elite.

In a sense, it's understandable that we hang onto the myths or perhaps
address the myths from a slightly different angle. Because the myths are
interesting and because the relationship between the past and the present
is always part of a region's history. We do have a violent history, and it's
important to acknowledge how this affects the people who live here today.
We are descended from people who were shaped by labor, people who
could fix just about anything if you gave them enough time. But there are
also those among us who have traveled the globe, lived in cities, and have
just as broad a perspective as any Easterner.

The more places I've lived, the more I realized the old adage that my
people are really no different from people anywhere. But what is different
is that Westerners have a history that is as hard to overlook as a ten-gallon
hat. We know that the wild wild West, where men were tough as nails and
women were just as tough but still looked good in gingham, is a myth. But
not entirely.

Life in the old West was sometimes a thrill-
ing adventure, but it was mostly just brutal. Suicide rates were (and still
are) high, and rates of alcoholism and mental illness would have been just
as high if anyone had acknowledged them. There was very little that was
romantic about life in those early days, whether you were a cowboy, a
farmer, an Indian, or a miner. Work was persistent and strenuous. Minorities and women were treated like pack animals. People lived in constant
fear—fear of the elements, of disease, and fear of the scores of ruffians who
found their way West. Deserters from the Civil War, problem children
from wealthy Eastern families, and garden-variety outlaws all found safe
haven in the West, where the law was often as lawless as they were. And
in many areas of the West, the lack of water was a scourge. Among other
things, it made personal hygiene difficult, which invited disease.

The real West was a children's graveyard. It was a series of misguided
schemes that drew people in hoards, from the gold rush to the Homestead Act to outrageous propaganda from the railroads. It was ranch hands
frozen in snowdrifts, trying to escape the relentless winds. It was senseless slaughter by both whites and natives fighting for what they thought
they deserved. And it was bad information.

Nobody told the pioneers that 160 acres of this land, the amount available through the original Homestead Act, couldn't possibly support a

family because there just wasn't enough water. Nobody told them how hard it would be to live in a shack in winters that reached forty below zero. Or that the worst part was not the cold, but the isolation of living miles from the nearest neighbor in a tiny, poorly constructed house.

For every Annie Oakley, there were thousands of widows left with a houseful of hungry children. For every William Clark, who found wealth in the copper mines of Montana, thousands of men died in mining disasters because of the lack of safety standards. For every publicity hound like George Armstrong Custer, thousands of cavalrymen died fighting for land that meant nothing to them. And for every John Clay, who made a fortune running cattle, thousands of anonymous cowpunchers quietly fought their loneliness by drinking themselves to death in isolated bunkhouses.

The people in the West learned not to talk about their problems because life was hard for everyone, and you didn't want to be the one to complain. A grieving mother didn't mention the baby she'd lost the week before because four other women in the room had lost a child in the past year. Not only that, but part of you believed that you deserved it, for having been hoodwinked into coming out West in the first place. There was a core of guilt and shame that lived in the hearts of those early Westerners. We stole this land, and for the vast majority, what we got in return wasn't exactly bountiful. It's easy to spot a guilty unease in the self-effacing attitude of most Westerners.

It sounds bleak. But here's the important part of the story. Despite all of it—the deceit and the loneliness, the guilt and the fear—many of us stayed. We're still here.

So what was it about this place that made people stay against all odds, despite the broken promises? What held people fast to the dry Montana dirt? What was it about the badlands of South Dakota that kept people pushing their team into one more blizzard to pitch one more wagonload of hay for their cattle? One answer, of course, is that many of them couldn't afford to leave. Most of the early pioneers gave up everything they had to come West and establish lives here. They had no money left.

But there had to be more than that for many of these early settlers. Was it that direct connection to the land? The majesty of the mountains? The quiet drama of the open prairie? Or was it the people? The country dances, the card parties every Friday night, the fact that neighbors showed up at five in the morning to help with the branding, to raise your barn, or to help dock your lambs? Was it the fact that everyone within five miles hauled barrels of water and gunny sacks to your ranch to fight a fire in the buttes?

It was all of these things . . . the shared experience, both of the brutality and of the joy. The satisfaction of watching your very own cattle get fat from the rich prairie grasses. It was the feeling I got when I was sixteen, riding alone in a pasture where I could neither see nor hear anyone for miles. Where I could smell the sweet and sour sagebrush and hear the twittering melody of the meadowlarks. I could admire the rows of hay I'd cut the day before. I recognized the ewe I'd pulled from the bog, the one with the twisted horn, and knew that if I hadn't found her, she'd still be there, long dead.

That was also part of the real West. But for many of us, it no longer is. I never worked on a ranch again, despite the power of that experience. The new West is filled with people who've never been on a horse, people who wouldn't know a baler from a cultivator. The new West has people who oppose hunting and don't eat the red meat that has provided a living for so many of our families and towns. People who prefer a latté to a shot of whiskey. It has become more and more like any other place, with Walmarts and Costcos in towns that were once considered insignificant by big business.

So what does living in the West mean today?

I've thought a lot about the fact that many of us are descendants of those who stayed, and that those who stayed were probably the most tenacious and the most resilient of the people who "settled" the West. These are qualities I see in most of my family, as well as in myself. And as it turns out, they are the qualities that helped me become a writer.

But the thing that may be most Western about me is a strong desire to make a connection to wherever I am. The Arbuckle Ranch was two miles from the nearest neighbor. They did not have telephones until the 1940s. The people in that small county in southeastern Montana had to work hard to create a sense of community. In today's world, where human contact is in our pockets, just a few finger punches away, I have tried to imagine what it must have been like to be so far from people beyond your own family. I've wondered how the people of that time dealt with losing family members, or losing a year's wheat crop to a hailstorm, or losing half their cattle in a blizzard, without the resources we have come to expect.

They had no support groups for post-traumatic stress or for the loss of a child, no twenty-four-hour helpline for suicide prevention. There were no cowboy therapists. Even if there had been, the ranchers I knew would never have talked about the fear or the grief or the depression because they wouldn't have put a moment's thought into whether they had those feelings. I've tried to imagine someone from my grandparents' generation responding to the question "How are you doing?" with something like "I feel a little depressed today," or "I'm dealing with some issues," and it just doesn't fit. It's like picturing my grandfather in a tie-dyed shirt.

They relied on each other in a very different way. They did it without talking about it. They relied on each other by working together and by providing companionship. And more than anything they relied on the knowledge that doing what needed to be done each day was not optional. They could not afford to call in sick or take two weeks of vacation each year. They couldn't afford to let their fears or discouragement get in the way of doing what needed to get done. They had no sense of being entitled to anything except what they themselves had earned. This fostered a sense of duty and independence that made them very productive. But it also created a stubborn reliance on self that didn't allow people to admit that they were having problems or to ask for help.

I still see this dichotomy in my people as much as I fight it in myself. The need to gather, to create a sense of community. And the stubborn determination to solve our own problems. I see it in the way our history has played out and in the way we approach our future.

The West is a series of stories about promise, disappointment, and perseverance. But it is the last of these that is probably more fundamental to our identity than anything. Whether it is the Native Americans and their persistent hope for justice, or the determination of the ranchers to hang onto their land despite little promise of making a living, or the continued efforts of the Western culture to be considered more than a novelty, we do not give up.

The West has continued to crank out its own unique brand of products, some of which capitalize on and some of which attempt to steer away from the stereotypes. But how much has the rest of America resisted anything that goes against what they expect from us? What is it about the Western myths that has become so important to people outside of the West? Especially now that our lives are so much more like theirs? And on the other hand, why is it that the Western experience is so often dismissed, as if people who work with their hands are somehow less insightful than city dwellers?

For me, living in the West today means having a choice to embrace or ignore the old myths. I live in Montana despite the lack of publishing opportunities here. I loved Boston, San Francisco, and Seattle. But the pace here suits me. The people here understand me when I talk, and that has nothing to do with accents. They share my language. I choose to write about the relationship between the people and the land although many people think the subject has become irrelevant. I do it because I believe that each time we tread a path, we learn something new about it. I'm still trying to understand the significance of our history, which is constantly changing. Although our relationship with the land is not as intimate as it once was, there is still a relationship, and it is the way this relationship continues to change that affects who we are and what is important to us. We are a region that was shaped by its resources—agriculture, mining, logging, etc. As those industries die out, we find ourselves in the position of having to form a new identity. Another new West.

One day on the ranch that summer of my sixteenth year, my uncle and I were moving a flock of sheep when one of the lambs had a moment of panic and took off running. I hadn't had many opportunities to show off my skills as a horseman yet, so I spurred my horse and drew a rein across his neck, and the chase began. I gained ground on the lamb until my horse's nose was even with his shoulder, then the little bastard stopped dead in his tracks, circled around behind me, and kept right on going. This act of insubordination only made me more determined, so I dug my heels in deeper and spurred my horse forward again. He pulled that stunt three more times, and each time I fell for it.

Finally, I gave up, called him a name, and started back toward the flock. Just a few strides into my retreat, I turned around to see how far away he was, and the little tyke was following me back, his ears flopping.

It took me thirty years to understand the lesson in that chase. Each time I moved to a different state, I tried once again to find the same kind of happiness I had known working on the Arbuckle Ranch. I moved all over the country, chasing that lamb. And I did manage to find a different brand of happiness in each place I lived, whether it was the culture-laden squares of Boston, the DC museums filled with our history, or the never-ending flow of creative energy in San Francisco. But none of this ever felt quite right. When I moved back to Montana in 2007, I brought the life experiences and the images of those other places with me, and they provided a dramatic contrast. They made my life richer, and they glorified what I have here. Which is not to say that Montana is better than those other places. It just means that it's better for me.

When I drive across the prairie of eastern Montana, where there is often nothing but open space for miles in every direction, the silence and the immensity fills me up like oxygen. I look at this land and understand how some people would see nothing interesting at all—it's seemingly flat, and without trees. But I have the advantage of that sixteen-year-old version of myself sitting next to me, reminding me what it feels like to live and work out here. Reminding me that this is where I learned that I can accomplish more than I know. Like the landscape of eastern Montana, the people in the West often need a slower, closer look to be appreciated. The intricacies of our people are often as subtle as a gentle slope or a hidden water hole.

More than anything, I am connected to this place by the spirit of my younger self who still wanders along these open fields. This is where mind and muscles came of age. When I returned, I didn't even have to look back to know that the best of who I am and of who I can be was trotting close behind.

Annick Smith | THE SUMMER OF NOW

The stones are warm under my bare feet. End-of-August grass is yellow and crinkly, and grasshoppers bombard my legs like a squadron of tiny airplanes. I have walked this path from kitchen to yard every summer for thirty-eight years, seen my small sons grow into men, and held the tiny trusting hands of granddaughters. But when I look down the V of Bear Creek's pine-clad canyon to the valley of the Big Blackfoot River or raise my eyes to the scarred ridges of the Rattlesnake wilderness—when an easterly breeze riffles my hair, long turned from black to white, and the rise of sun warms my cheek—I shiver with pleasure as I always have. The mountain morning glows like a ripe peach. I want to devour it.

But it is never forever now. Beyond the constants of dawn and sunset, change attacks stasis from inside and out. This morning I smell change in the texture of air, a tang more bitter than sweet, a coolness of sharper degree. And I see change in the quality of light—the clean white light of summer's end.

The trees see it. Shorter days signal the trees to turn inward. Sap has begun its retreat. In the tapestry of forest that surrounds our meadow, leaves of the vine maple are tinged red, wild currant is yellowing toward brown. Soon, we will witness first frost. Perhaps snow. But predictable Mars will burn in the southwest tonight, an elbow's length from the half moon. And I will sail the light I was born to—the only season.

What does it mean to grow old? Doesn't growth imply movement toward maturity, not over the hill and away from it?

"It means you're growing wiser," says my son Steve.

"That's not for me to say," I reply. "Do you think I'm wiser?"

He smiles. I might have smiled in a similar way if my father had asked me the same question, for the answer is both yes and no. Steve Deutch, my son's namesake, had been a successful photographer as well as a sculptor, but as he aged from his seventies into his eighties, it seemed to me he became sadder rather than wiser. He mourned the loss of commercial work, which he equated with manhood, and walked hesitantly into a retirement that offered not only financial stability but the artistic freedom he'd always desired. But freedom came late, compromised by arthritic pain that crippled his body while failing memory, delusions, and hallucinations gradually took over his mind. The result was escalating despair, bitterness, and anger.

True, my father had periods of gentleness, good humor, and love—especially when his children and grandchildren came to visit, or when he kept company with fellow artists and old friends. He was generous to a fault, strong in his opinions, and had moments of insight unmitigated by sentimentality and tinged with irony. He found refuge at our summer home on Lake Michigan's shores, observing cardinals in oak trees, frozen spindrift piled onto our sandy beach, and the black menace of a thunderstorm approaching across placid waters. Nature induced a meditative state immediate and sensual, quite different from his responses to our family and the historical world, which were as acute as his best photographs and honest to the point of cruelty. Maybe clarity of vision is the wisdom of elders.

My mother Helene Deutch acted out a different story, coming into her own at the age of ninety, after my father had died. Although once a photographer herself, she had turned her energies to caretaking—taking care of her three daughters and their children, also her aged mother, and finally enduring the long decline of her husband. Now it was time to take care of herself, and to allow herself to be taken care of. I believe she actually did grow wiser. Wisdom rounded the sharp edges of opinion and stubborn pride that had made my mother so difficult to live with. As years accumulated, she became more open and understanding, until as she approached one hundred her resistant mind was overwhelmed by ravages of age. Then she grew compulsive and child-like, resigned but not bitter, holding on to her delight in life and the sense of humor that defined it.

Grow. Old. How do those words fit together? My mind jumps to old growth. Old growth is a forest with big trees, like the forest I am trying to preserve beyond our meadow. There, in a few precious patches, ponderosas, tall and wide girthed, with thumb-thick layers of reddish bark that interlock like pieces in a picture puzzle, create an umbrella of shade called "over story" where sun cannot reach the ground to nourish young trees. That's why the big trees stand alone on brushy hillsides, stately and slowly dying—ponderosas in their clusters, harboring red-tail hawks and great-horned owls who look down with hunger at mice and songbirds, rabbits and squirrels, predatory as we are.

"Cut 'em down when they're mature," says the forester. "Before they rot."

"But rot is a condition of old growth," I say. "We need rot."

Hopefully it will be slow rot, not the disease of beetle infestation that is infecting our forests like an unchecked virus. Slow rot starts in cracks or lightning strikes or in some rabbit's burrow, while the rest of the tree inches skyward. An old tree will grow and rot for dozens of years past maturity. Half a century. Maybe more. Here is one old fellow I love, a grizzled guy two hundred years old at least, leaning toward the creek. Who knows when gravity will take him down, roots giving way, the great tree falling, the sound like dynamite exploding, shaking the earth, damming the creek, changing its course. Decay will accelerate with years of snow and rain, but the trunk may still be visible a hundred years from now, returning to earth while it nourishes seedlings that thrive in sunlit space opened in the over story when the old tree fell.

I ask myself why I treasure old growth while the forester wants to cut it down. Certainly, my love is connected to beauty. I stand in filtered green shade, look up to long-needled crowns two hundred feet above my head, and find my true dimension. Here, I am a pointillist dot in the canvas of nature and it feels correct to be a small, connected being. Here, even the moose is small. And the bear. They find shelter under the old trees as I do, but what do bears know of beauty as humans conceive it?

Beauty is a side effect. What matters is the shelter. This old growth provides homes for owls and elk and the elusive moose and her new calf who bed down where the grass is bent. There are berry thickets for bears and hollows for coyote dens and thick branches where mountain lions wait to pounce on a large mammal like me or that browsing deer. I stand on top of the cliff above my house and look out at the low mountains that flow in every direction. Most of the big trees in the pine, fir, and larch forests around me have been cut down. The rest are in danger. This is another way to perceive the growth of age. Friends get sick and die. Others rise to unforeseen heights. Finally, inevitably, the gnarled survivors stand alone before they fall.

"Your house is made of logs," says the forester. "You had to cut down some big trees to make *your* home."

"My house is recycled," I reply with righteous pride. "Those timbers are one hundred and ten years old."

"Someone cut the logs," he says. "I see you're building a deck. Where the hell do you think those two-by-sixes come from?"

He's right. Old trees have offered me shelter. But only when they've been cut down.

Seventy-three and counting. That's me. When I look into the mirror with my 250-degree magnification spectacles on, I see the sagging skin of my grandmother's face. Serena, not so serene. The nagger. The weeper. The wondrous maker of Hungarian delicacies. *Csirke paprikash* (chicken paprika), the color of burnt orange and thick with sour cream. And *uborka salata* (cucumber salad) swimming in vinaigrette. And *langos*, a fragrant fried yeast bread like Indian fry bread but not so heavy, slathered with butter and honey. Grandma Beck was softer than I am. Prettier. Her hands were more agile, and her face more fallen. Had I known as a child what I know now, I would have loved her better. I would have been forgiving.

My face is more wrinkled than my grandmother's because I have lived in Montana for almost forty-five years, choosing a life exposed to wind and sun and the cold dry air of many winters (not to mention fifty years, on and off, of smoking). But the rough brown pre-cancerous spots on my brow were not born of the West; they are souvenirs of a childhood spent sunning on Lake Michigan's beaches—days and years when suntans were marks of beauty, not danger. If I live past ninety, I hope I will not fade gently, as she did, but will be transformed into the big-nosed, white-tressed, broomstick crone in my granddaughter Tilly's fairy-tale book. Or maybe I'll look like the wife of Modoc Henry in Edward S. Curtis's portrait, a Klamath elder with rheumy eyes under her beaded cap, deep-knit frown lines, and a mouth slightly twisted above chin furrows that spread neckward like channels in a river's delta.

When I was young and romantic and new to the West, I wanted to age like the Indian women I saw at powwows and in historic photographs. "You can read their lives on their faces," I said. "And the stories are beautiful."

I imagined shawled women in moccasins gathering camas bulbs and huckleberries, tanning deer hides, riding horses, bathing in rivers, caring for children in the mountains or plains—lives spent in all weathers, heavy with sex, births, and husbands, and with hands busy beading, weaving, or baking, crafting hands like those of my Hungarian grandmothers. Aged Indian women seemed to be counterparts of the venerable yellow pines I loved, only with the tree rings exposed. But I did not know, and still can't know, the anger, violence, and despair of their lives, and losses both physical and cultural. I can only empathize with the toll a history of dispossession and defeat can take, and the strength and patience and humor of endurance.

Now that I've lived my own losses and faced my own storms, I'm achieving that weathered look I once desired, and I'm not sure I want it. The knotty face of old growth does not seem as beautiful on me as it did on those unknown others. It would be better, I think, to look like Jane Fonda. Or Catherine Deneuve. Not with an artificial mask such as Dolly Parton has constructed, or—God help us—the face of Joan Rivers. No, just a hint of Botox on cheeks and mouth, a tasteful eye job, and the most sensitive possible lift of neck and chin.

Of course, I was never a great beauty like Jane or Catherine, so there is not so much to preserve. But in the mirrors of my mind, I am still an earnest fourth grader with French braids to her waist. And a long-necked nineteen-year-old bride with black hair cropped short as a boy's. And the hippie mother on my book cover photo, standing surrounded by her four sons outside their log cabin, wearing irrigation boots, bell-bottom jeans, and a red bandana that holds back her tangle of prematurely graying hair.

Yesterday in yoga class, we were practicing balance. It was the tree pose, *vrksasana*, pronounced vrik-SHAHS-anna, recommended for relief of sciatica and flat feet, both of which I suffer from. To do the tree pose you must start from the mountain posture, *tadasana*. "Feel your feet resting firmly on the floor," says our teacher. "Raise your big toes and little toes at the same time, release them and feel the insides and outsides of your heels. Now let your upper body stretch toward the sky. . . . Open your collarbones. . . . Breathe. Relax your chin muscles and stomach muscles. Breathe."

Only after we learn to stand as mountains will it be possible to become a tree. We shift weight to our left legs. "Now root your left leg into the earth," says our teacher. "Imagine the roots going down, down, down."

We lift right legs to rest on standing thighs and swivel lifted knees sideways, resembling herons or storks but not any tree I've seen. The tree part comes when we spread arms horizontally at shoulder height, then fold them into a praying position and raise them above our heads. It's an elegant pose, if you can get there, the trunk foot rooted, the other leg triangled to the side, and hands raised like supplicating branches.

To keep balance, it is best to focus on a spot on the floor or slightly above floor level and hold that focus as long as you can. And it helps to press the lifted leg into the standing leg while resisting with that standing leg.

"I push too hard," I tell our teacher. "And then I fall over." Balance has never been my strong point.

"You always push too hard," pipes up my friend Judy, a writer and former ranchwoman who, like me, will say bluntly what she thinks.

"See," says our teacher Serena, "see how old Annick is, and she's still pushing too hard!" Everyone titters, and I can't help but join them.

Serena is also past sixty, with cropped gray hair and a rollicking sense of humor—rigorous but not pious in the gooey ways of some New Agers. She struggled through a West Texas ranch upbringing, eventually journeying to India to work with Iyengar himself while trying to live up to her name. Our class is packed with university students, and today we regulars are dwarfed by supple youth. By regulars, I mean a group I have christened the Yogettes, who have been coming to this five o'clock practice twice a week for six years. I share the honors of being oldest with a friend who is a retired English professor. The rest, ranging downward in age to their mid-forties, include the aforementioned Judy, as well as a professor of American Studies, a high school English teacher, a geriatric nurse, a dentist's office manager, a visual artist/poet, and Becky—the other grandmother of Tilly and Elodie—who has come from Tennessee to help her daughter and my son care for the girls. Over the years, we have learned to accept the limits of our bodies while transforming them into vessels stronger, more flexible, and yes, more balanced. We can be downward-facing dogs, cobras, triangles, and trees.

After the flat-on-your-back relaxation/meditation called *shivasana*, we fold our blankets, roll up our mats, and walk out the door, ready to share a bottle or two of wine and a potluck gourmet dinner at one of our houses. We have, I think, found a recipe for growing old. First, spiral toward some balanced center; next, repeat disciplined actions until they are part of your circuitry; try not to push too hard; and, finally, know that each moment might be transformative. It is important to remember that after yoga practice, this recipe calls for jokes and Cosmopolitans, or if you are me, a tall gin and tonic.

Growing old has nothing to do with living in the West, but perhaps it is easier for people like the Yogettes to accept the necessary rot because we are rooted or transplanted by choice into a world where people are dwarfed by a landscape that is imminent and wild and dangerous. This end-of-summer day, the air is smoky from Bitterroot forests on fire. In Glacier National Park, glaciers are melting before their time. I know, I know . . . eventually there will be new forests, and valleys in the glaciers' wake, and rivers that cut through earth until bedrock is exposed.

I will not live to see the outcomes of a planet grown warmer, but here in Montana, in a valley surrounded by mountains, watered by rivers, and sheltered with forests, my friends and I can still see the red shine of Mars in a blue-black sky. And this morning, as I took my Labs out to pee on yellow meadow grass in the peach-colored dawn, I noticed a pile of bear scat under the thorn apple tree by the Little House. If I am lucky tomorrow, as

I have been in past Augusts, I might take my granddaughters by the hand and point out a bear cub standing upright under that thorn apple tree. He will be reaching for the sweet, pitted, black fruit on the spiky branches and stripping them off with his teeth.

"This is a real bear," I will whisper, "with real teeth," and we will shush our mouths so he won't be scared off, and we will keep our distance, for the mother bear is surely on guard nearby. Like me, she is fattening for hibernation. The change of light tells us winter is coming, but summer's fruitful end is now.

THE NATIVE HOME OF GOVERNORS ON HORSEBACK

If you heard about the man who kicked off his campaign to become governor of Montana by swinging a medieval battle sword on horseback in the middle of downtown Billings, you probably thought, "Only in the American West."

Such a thing could only happen in a region so caught up with cowboys and horses, so eager to see them as more than vocation or transportation, so willing to hand over important policy decisions to a man who speaks in such symbols. Only in the West could a potential candidate have sat down to think about how to go after the most important job in his state and apparently concluded, "Well, first I need a horse. Then maybe a weapon." Only in the West could such a candidate expect to be taken seriously.

And Glenn Schaffer was taken a tiny bit seriously. In February 2004 he posed at the offices of the *Billings Gazette* on a white stallion named Big Dog Thunder Horse and said that his campaign motto would be "Honor, Above All Else." He cited Hannibal, the Carthaginian general, as his example. Announcing that he would campaign across Montana with his horse, he said, "I will not ask for money, but for water and shelter for me and my steed."

The *Gazette* put his story on the front page.

I couldn't fault the newspaper. I found it a tremendously readable story. Partly, I found it refreshing to have a candidate for statewide office admit his ignorance about the economy and promise only to try to set a good example. Furthermore, his platforms of reducing the cost of child care and building public respect for law enforcement officers made a lot more sense to me than anything the outgoing governor had done. And I was delighted to read a political story that wasn't analyzing the candidate's fund-raising strengths or intraparty reputation.

But then it wasn't really a political story. It was clearly pitched as human interest, a fascinating local individual involved in an unusual enterprise. Glenn Schaffer, the *Gazette* was saying, was a typical Montana character. You can understand a lot about a region by looking at the human interest stories that run on the front pages of a local newspaper.

In this case, the story made me happy to be a Westerner. I was glad to live in a region that had such a clear sense of itself. Schaffer didn't strike me as any less ridiculous a gubernatorial candidate than Jesse Ventura— but where the former Minnesota governor had made his reputation as a professional wrestler, we had a cowboy. While both professions involve a good deal of symbolic good and evil and both make for fun Halloween costumes, a genuine cowboy also possesses actual skills that can earn a real if paltry paycheck.

I didn't vote for Glenn Schaffer. He never filed the paperwork to be listed as an official candidate, never even followed through on his plans to announce a running mate chosen "not on the basis of a resume, but on spirit, heart and soul. It would help to have someone with experience in the Legislature." He had his fifteen minutes of fame on the front page of the *Gazette*, then disappeared.

But I've kept thinking about his story, based largely on a tiny little hard-to-reconcile fact buried deep in the original article: when he mounted that horse in downtown Billings, Schaffer had lived in Montana only four years.

I've come to see Glenn Schaffer as important not because of anything he did in politics but because he represents an underappreciated trend: it's the newcomers who feed off (and thus feed) our Western myths.

Do you see the West as the frontier, a place where you can reinvent yourself? Then you're probably from the East. Do you equate wilderness with unspoiled purity? Then chances are you're from a coastal city. Do you see the concept of honor on horseback as proving your electability? Then maybe you're a recent migrant from Pennsylvania.

Certainly, when I moved west at age twenty-six, I was gung ho for the mountain image. I immediately bought cross-country skis and a mountain bike. I acquired a dog and hiked with her constantly. I felt inferior for not being a rock climber, telemarker, or winter backpacker. I was re-inventing my life, emphasizing and even discovering the activities and character traits that represented the "real" me, which had been unfairly suppressed by my previous residence. Every time I found more of the real me in the West, my spirit surged with delight.

But then I met Montanans who hadn't made the two-hour drive to Yellowstone in decades.

As a newcomer in a small town, I quickly volunteered to serve on boards and committees to preserve and strengthen our community. And I soon learned that without the newcomers' enthusiasm, many such organizations would wither and die.

I developed a passion for Western literature. Then I met my wife, who grew up in eastern Montana, and learned that she prefers Dostoevsky.

Friends tell me of similar situations around the West: in Wyoming, newcomers embrace the horse-packing image; in New Mexico, they build in adobe; in southern Utah, they follow the Ed Abbey legends. It's the people from elsewhere who most love and sustain the old myths.

The more time I spend here, the more I alter my picture of typical Westerners, the ones whose character is no longer defined by where they *used* to live. (When exactly did you cross that line—after twenty years of residence? only if you're native-born?—is a question for another essay.) The more time they've been out West, the less they're defined by horses or cowboys or wilderness or quaint small town cafés. Many of the ones I've met prefer snowmobiles, four-wheelers, Harleys, or similarly motorized updates to those clunky romantic traditions. Many need economic development and see wilderness as an obstacle to it that puts their region at a disadvantage compared to the rest of the nation. Many want the sort of good-tasting food that's ubiquitous in California and believe they can find it at an Olive Garden.

In other words, many Westerners want . . . what everyone else in the country wants. The longer you've lived out here, the more you've done without the latest trends and conveniences, the more aggravated you may become at their absence. Ask a harried corporate executive what she most wants out of life, and she may say she wants to be a cowgirl. Ask a woman herding cattle, and she may say she wants cell phone coverage so she can be better connected to the world while on roundup.

I'm not saying this is good or bad, just inevitable. Progress—the anti-mythology—is as much desired in the West as anywhere else. To my mind, two factors distinguish the West from other regions. One is that our wide-open spaces cause that progress to arrive here more slowly than elsewhere. But although some people mistake change-behind-the-times for a lack of change, this difference doesn't affect our culture as much as the second difference: the West is full of newcomers who are attracted by the old-time mythologies.

You might move to Atlanta for a job. You might move to New York for the museums. You might move to rural Missouri because of a family connection. In any of those cases you'll still embrace progress. But the West has a far greater percentage than any other region of people who arrive because of a mythology of the past. They love horses and come to a place where the horse dominates. They love wilderness and come to a place where they can experience it regularly. They love John Wayne, or Hunter S. Thompson, or Georgia O'Keefe and want to live in a region that hasn't progressed past identifying with their idol.

Yes, I'm speaking in broad generalizations here, but I do so for a reason: it's really interesting when the stereotypes meet. These myth-obsessed newcomers don't have the power to stop progress in its tracks—nobody does—but their efforts to do so create an exciting tension. Just as wildlife finds the intersection of two ecosystems (say, forest and meadow) to be the richest habitat, I find this intersection of myth and anti-myth to be a vibrant culture, a place I want to live.

Let me explain it with an example. When he taught in the environmental studies program at the University of Montana, Don Snow told me he thought the school's great reputation came from the way it took kids who thought they were environmentalists and turned them into Montanans. I took him to mean that the environmentalists had come with a starry-eyed view of nature and its essential goodness and had suddenly been surrounded by practical, friendly Montanans with a bias toward getting things done. In other words, both archetypes have value, but the most substantial value comes when either is exposed to the opposite perspective.

That's what I'd like to think the West as a region tends to do as well. It takes people who thought they were cowboys—or skiers, or loggers, or hippies, or miners, or outdoor recreation junkies, or budding real estate moguls, or . . . whatever they came to the West for—and turns them into Westerners, which is something less romantic, but more functional. We are, all of us in the region, caught somewhere in that transformation. We live at the intersection of myth and reality, and everybody gets entertainingly confused as to which street is which.

When Glenn Schaffer gets on his horse to run for office, he's part of that mix. When the *Billings Gazette* (and, for that matter, I myself) report with such glee on people like him, so are we. We are yet another set of relative newcomers reinvigorating Western mythology. In Schaffer's case, many of us are saying, "Isn't the West full of unusual characters?"

It doesn't matter whether the West really has any more unusual characters per capita than anywhere else. The point is that people like me want it to. Our beliefs that the West is full of unusual characters, that it's full of cowboys, or wilderness, or individualism, fuel the very culture we seek. Merely by pursuing our mythic dreams, we perpetuate them.

I've tied my personal view that "characters" are the ultimate Western mythology to Glenn Schaffer, which may make you think I celebrate him only because I think he's a bit of a wacko. That's not entirely the case. What I admired about the *Gazette*'s article was the way it showed Schaffer grasping the heroic elements of the Western vision. I saw direct parallels to 102 years previously, when another Pennsylvanian also grafted the concept of honor onto a horseman and paraded that image around in the media. In that case, Owen Wister dubbed his creation *The Virginian*, and publication of his novel did much to enshrine what we now think of as the cowboy myth.

Wister did it because he fell in love with a region of epic landscapes, big and bold enough to support mythic constructions that he consciously modeled on stories of the Bible and King Arthur. Wister couldn't imagine *The Virginian* happening in the Pennsylvania of 1902, any more than I could have imagined the grand spiritual structure of the life I wanted to live happening in the Massachusetts of 1990.

We may occasionally bump into the limits of those visions. We may forget that the West is not entirely peopled by taciturn, honorable men riding the open range nor by idealistic granola crunchers leaving no trace. That forgetfulness may lead us to enact policies that reduce our quality of life. But even then, we do still have those epic landscapes. If in another 102 years they are not still inspiring newcomers to run for governor on horseback, I believe they will still be inspiring similar characters to similarly deep spiritual quests in pursuit of the reflections they see on those landscapes of qualities of the human soul—qualities of goodwill, honor, and hope.

I came over a rise and rode down into the gully, a few scraggly trees hiding the water hole. And there was the bull, big and dusty and not lonesome at all. My guess was that he was so satisfied by having grass this close to water he wasn't even missing his real job, which was to cover as many of the Spear-O cows as he could for next spring's calf crop.

We'd been looking for him for two weeks, and Torrey had mostly given up, thinking he must have escaped to chase down someone else's cows. Fences hadn't been around all that long anyway, not on the Spear-O. For that matter, they hadn't been around all that long in the Rosebud, the same range Custer crossed, ignoring the warning signs, to ride into the US Cavalry's darkest moment. I knew Custer's bravado charge had happened only seventy years earlier, but when you are thirteen, seventy years seems forever. It was 1944, and what little I knew about our history was already fading behind the war in Europe.

That war had everything to do with my being on the Spear-O. My father was a cavalry officer. At Fort Riley we'd even been quartered in the same house once assigned to Custer. But the horses we rode were more important than the houses we lived in. We were on them often and with them always, which was part of the reason my older sister left college for a wartime marriage to Vic Johnson, a young Navy pilot from Montana whose mother was a Spear. My sister had grown up schooling Army remounts; Vic had grown up gentling the Spear-O broncs. And they both loved the new music, loved to hear it but loved even more to dance to it. That seemed to me the other part of the reason they'd fallen in love. With swing music taking over the country, they were a natural. . . . And, as it turned out, it was almost as natural that I became their ward.

I was practically an orphan by the time they married. My father's narrow escape out of Burma and his new job with the battle-scarred 1st Division had driven my mother over the edge. My being wed to the football games we played on Washington's busy streets hardly helped. Her breakdown was serious; Vic's letter to me was as well. "The Spear-O is a family affair," he wrote. "It's hard to get help. My brother lives three miles above the main ranch. He could use someone who knows horses."

What boy scratching around for an identity could resist? Particularly a boy with nowhere else to turn.

When I was put on the train for Montana, my mother was already in the psychiatric ward of St. Elizabeth's. We didn't know, of course, that my father was wading ashore on Omaha Beach—and surviving to make it up the cliffs and establish the first command post. But if we had known, it wouldn't have changed anything. My mother was already undone. And in a way, I was too. As soon as the war broke out I became sure—through whatever reasoning drives a boy's thinking—that my father would die. That I must face it. Not complain. Accept the inevitable.

It was a journey, reaching Montana. After Chicago, a flood stalled us on the tracks for two additional days. And when I finally got to Sheridan, there were four more before I would be delivered to Torrey's, which was about as remote as you could be in the Rosebud. Not only was it three miles above the main ranch, which was three miles of potholes up Corral Creek from the "good road"; it was also sixty miles of washboardy "good road" from the paved one that ran north from Sheridan into Montana. And there were lots of ranchers to visit along that graveled road. As it turned out, I was not only considered part of the family, I was also a celebrity, of sorts. Everyone wanted to know about my father.

Meeting Torrey at last was a relief. He was mowing in Corral Creek's bottomland. He got off his tractor and shook my hand, saying he "sure could use a good hand." He seemed a foot taller than I as he showed me how he'd converted a cow camp into a home for his little family. He'd even built an eight-by-twelve-foot cabin part way up to their spring. There was a bed in it, there was a kerosene lantern, there were feather quilts. . . . It would be mine.

I was in a different world from those football games along the streets of Washington—and from my mother's fears. Everything here was real. Everything here was a responsibility. If I didn't digest what I was to do the first time, I could digest it later—by doing it again.

After dinner, Torrey showed me the barn. It was partly collapsed, but the corrals were holding and beyond them was a grazing pasture for saddle horses. Three of them, he told me, pointing out a paint and a sorrel and a stocky bay, would be my "string." They didn't look like they'd ever been curried, certainly not like the shiny remounts of Fort Riley, but I was relieved to see them. Horses, at least, I knew something about.

He gave me a stack of books, mostly Zane Grey novels, showed me how to work the lantern, and left me in the cabin. Light lingers in the Rosebud, and I was hardly ready for sleep. I went back to the barn, found a tack box with some rags and saddle soap and began to clean up the saddle I was to use. The leather was beginning to crack. I'd never ridden a Western saddle before, but if that was my only option, I wanted it serviceable. We'd saddle-soaped our tack after every ride at Riley, but then at Riley there wasn't nearly as much required of a boy as there was going to be on the Spear-O.

When it got dark, I went back to my cabin, got the lantern going, and started in on *Riders of the Purple Sage*. It turned out I would read Zane Grey's novels most of the summer. They were exciting, but they had nothing to do with the life I was living. I could actually taste the life I was living. You couldn't taste Grey's stories.

　　　　　　　　　　　　　I'd never had so much to do. On the domestic front, I brought in the half-wild milk cow each morning, gathered eggs, caught up the horses we might need, killed any rattlesnakes lurking around the barn. "Kill 'em if they're close, let 'em be if they aren't" was the rule, which I followed without much drama after warily dispatching the first few. There was also laundry to be done with a wooden-handled plunger and a crank ringer. And there were the Johnsons' two kids to care for when Torrey and Adrienne left to have some fun, the two-year-old still in diapers, the four-year-old showing me how the diapers worked.

The only thing wrong with that task was that I had to stick around to see that the children didn't get into trouble. I couldn't saddle up and go off to do what needed doing on the ranch front: fix a gate, patch a fence — do whatever took me away from all that needed completing by taking me into a country that was complete already. Being at one with that country meant everything to me, comfortable as I was with the family making it possible.

I loved my work, though my duty behind the baler, an ancient contraption that pounded hay into bales, was miserable. Two of us bounced along behind, each perched on a seat attached to the baling chute. I poked baling wires through to be hooked by the Crow Indian opposite me. Wheat chaff covered us, clogging the kerchiefs over our mouths, the Crow never complaining as I cursed and grimaced at the blood dripping on my legs from a crushed rattler or rabbit or whatever got scooped up with the hay in our clanking progress across the fields.

But the baling duties soon ended, replaced by the magic of the horse roundup. Moving horses was different from herding cattle. Fearful of spooking them in a wrong direction, we kept our distance, watched them pool together from afar as they sought out open gates and negotiable draws, like flowing water working its way down to fill the corrals. Once there, we separated them — colts for weaning or castration, mares for breeding, a few for gentling, most back out on the range for next year's decisions.

The idea was *not* to throw a rope, as Zane Grey's heroes did. You carried your lariat, calmed your selection until you could slip a noose over a head. I understood all that, even won a compliment from Paddy Ryan for catching up a wild-eyed three-year-old.

A compliment from Paddy Ryan was no small thing. He'd succeeded the great Yakima Canutt in winning the Roosevelt Trophy as the nation's best bronc rider. I didn't know who Yakima Canutt was, of course. But then I didn't know who I was. All I knew was that Paddy Ryan had singled me out. I was walking on air.

Not long after the horse roundup, we had the Davis Creek gathering. The Spear-O leased grazing land from the Cheyenne and the Crow. Davis Creek—the same drainage Custer had used to cross the Rosebud and ride into the Greasy Grass—was Crow.

We were spaced out on the ridges at dawn, each of us flushing cattle from the ravines before they could brush up for the day. Once on the flat, we held them for branding and castrating, Junior Spear himself healing this calf or that, dragging it to the branding fire where two Crow wrestled them down to do what needed doing. It was rough work. All I could think of was how much I wanted to do it myself.

In late summer, I wrote an aunt telling her I was going to stay and go to the Kirby School there in the Rosebud. Torrey, both amused and surprised by how serious I was, even said he'd back me. Kirby, now not even on the map, had a population of six. The one-room school was better populated, but was still known mostly for educating a cowboy who'd become so bored waiting out a winter that he'd enrolled. The cowboy was a grown man; his teacher was eighteen. No one, not even Paddy Ryan, knew if she'd actually taught him to read. All they knew was that he'd enjoyed it and caused no trouble.

For me, however, there would be no Kirby schooling. The aunt sent back tickets to Washington, where I would be headed in September.

That news was a sadness to me. A few nights after I'd found that bull, Torrey had sent me back to push him over the ridge to a water hole where lots of mother cows gathered. The bull wasn't hard to move, but it took time and I was thankful. Everything seemed right, my paint and I pushing along the dusty bull, each of us taking his own comfort in the country.

The bull seemed pleased to join the others, settling in as though coming home. I watched for a bit and then made my way back across the divide, taking my time as the cool came in and the shadows lengthened. I got in at dark, grained my paint, and went to my cabin to read Zane Grey, knowing nothing I would read could touch what I'd just done. Bringing that bull home seemed to have brought me home too. I was just too young to make sense of it.

My mother got leave from St. Elizabeth's so she could meet my train. I was wearing my Western hat, my boots, and carrying my lariat. She walked right past me. I almost missed her too, so worn had she become.

After that we worked things out. When the war ended we even began putting our family back together. I did a hitch in the Marines. We lost Vic, his plane exploding on a flight. I went on to college and thought about writing, as all English majors must, in their aimless ways. What I didn't realize was that I already had my topic. I just needed to find my way back to it.

It took a long time, but finally I did. I may have left Montana, but Montana never left me. After college I headed back, this time to pack horses and mules into the Bob Marshall country. I stopped at the Spear-O so Torrey could show me the diamond hitch, but I didn't need it. We would pack Deckers, not sawbucks, which didn't really matter. We would pack into some of the West's highest country, which did.

I've packed into a lot of high country since, tying all sorts of hitches in Montana and in the Sierra and in that life of the imagination that finally brought me home. And it was the West that became home, though not the made-up West of Zane Grey or the West of the shoot-'em-up writers with their formulas. Nor was it the new West of McMurtry's city novels or Stegner's novels of discovery. It wasn't even the West of the gifted memoirists like Maclean and Kittredge. But it was a West big enough to hold them all—and more: it was the West primeval, which to me is the true mythic West, the one that draws so many of us back to make of it what we can.

Now, almost as many years after I found that bull on the Spear-O as that day was after Custer's misbegotten charge, seventy years seems like the blink of an eye, and the history of the West not much longer. In a way, all of us on the Spear-O were a part of it back in 1944. In a way, all of us are a part of it now, if only to say good-bye, remembering how it shaped us, realizing it will shape fewer and fewer, knowing it will soon be gone.

Of course our chapter won't end with the drama that silencing Custer provided for the Sioux and Cheyenne. We can hardly take arms against ourselves. I just didn't understand, at thirteen, what a prescient statement those gathered tribes made when they swarmed over Custer and—just for a moment—stopped a nation. They surely knew they would lose, be tracked down and killed, or given the long death sentence of the reservation. But what a statement they made for living with the land rather than reshaping it to meet our every need—and in our own image.

Today I find myself with them in ways that surprise me. I can't seem to leave the land, even as it seems to be leaving us. It's stuck in me like a first love, holding on even as I watch it pillaged, its waters diverted, its mountains torn open, its solitude violated—all of us using it up because we can't teach ourselves what the Sioux and Cheyenne knew in their hearts: we belong to the West more than the West belongs to us.

Watching it leave us brings in a sadness impossible for me to express—but it also brings me home. I have to believe that if we can understand what we had—and lost—we may be able to preserve something of what is left.

It is, after all, where the waters begin.

Melissa Kwasny

THE IMAGINARY BOOK
OF CAVE PAINTINGS

Late winter in Montana, well below freezing, but we have come to the dry-lands anyway, where the views are magnificent and unobstructed to the southern ranges. The brown prairies, rolling like bolts of suede, are dotted with patches of snow that gather on the north-facing sides of the coulees, patches that look, from afar, like small herds of white-furred animals. The mythic snow-deer, we decide to call them. We walk to a ruined homestead where my friend likes to pick around—*poor family, such a hard life*—finding nuggets of glass that age has turned translucent aqua and lavender.

Despite the harshness, the cold and unrelenting wind, there are always unlikely marvels. Today, for instance, we suddenly find ourselves in the midst of a bluebird migration, forty, fifty, maybe a hundred rising into the air, landing on the barbed wire fence, then dropping to the sage and cactus-covered ground to catch worms. Farther down the path, more, that trick wild things play of disappearing into a surface—dun prairie or bare tree—until you see one figure, which enables you to see the many others. Something brown and large runs across the road, ducks into a ditch. We stare into the dry grass, the forked broken tines of dogwood that look like ears and then, they *are* ears, black tufts of a lynx, up on its haunches to stare back at us. We watch it through binoculars: the green golden eyes, the dramatic black and golden stripes above them, its face the mask of an actor in a mystery play.

It is said that even after the reindeer disappeared in parts of Siberia, they still occupied a place in the mythology of the people, who dressed their horses in masks made of leather, fur, and felt and adorned them with life-size antlers. For most people today, an encounter with a wild animal *in the wild* is rare, provoking feelings ranging from fear to awe to a kind of honor that they have been chosen for such disclosure. Even in dreams, animal sightings are felt to be special, symbolic, as if they were ambassadors from some more ancient realm, a realm far deeper than the human. In A *Field Guide to Getting Lost*, Rebecca Solnit writes that "animals are the old language of the imagination; one of the ten thousand tragedies of their disappearance would be a silencing of this speech." Having lived in

Montana for over thirty-five years and never having seen a lynx, an animal nearly eradicated in the eastern United States, I, too, feel the presence of something calling to me beyond my understanding.

On our way home, we encounter a blizzard, a lovely one, each flake so large and distinct that we can see the landscape between them. I am driving and suddenly, something else catches my eye. There are drawings on the rock face of an outcropping of large boulders we are passing. Pictographs? Yes, there is an arrow, a few tally marks, perhaps a figure. What figure? An animal? It is astonishing to me that I haven't seen them before, or that no one else I know has mentioned them. Even though this is a backcountry dirt road, people drive by here every day, must have passed them for at least a thousand years. Maybe two. A certain slant of light? That unmistakable rose-orange of hematite against the snow? We get out of the car to look closer. Like the lynx that, running across the road, had caught my eye, this, too, seemed to come out of nowhere, as if a door had opened where there was no door.

According to archaeologist Mavis Ann Loscheider Greer, as of 1995, 626 rock art sites have been recorded in Montana. These sites consist of pictographs (paintings on rock surfaces) and petroglyphs (images that are etched or pecked into the rock). The oldest known pictograph on the western plains is an image of a black-painted turtle on the back wall of Pictograph Cave outside Billings, which produced AMS (Accelerator Mass Spectrometry) dates that averaged 2,145 years before present (BP). The oldest petroglyph site nearby is in eastern Wyoming, where a hunting scene has been dated as early as 11,300 BP. The images range from simple handprints and finger marks to elaborate anthropomorphs and zoomorphs—figures that resemble humans and animals, respectively, but that also display decidedly un-human characteristics such as having no arms, or many arms, or no head, or the head of a bird or beast. Nested arcs, hand smears, spatter marks, knotted chains, concentric circles, gargets, handheld wands, pubic fringes: the rock surfaces house a world of imagery with an archaeological vocabulary all their own.

Montana, of course, is not unique. People have been pecking and painting images into rock all over the world, with Australia having the longest continuous tradition, perhaps over 40,000 years old, and an engraved piece of ochre found in a cave in South Africa has been dated to 77,000 BP. The Paleolithic pictographs that were dramatically discovered by schoolboys in the Lascaux cave in 1940, and in the Chauvet cave in 1994, have been studied extensively. Yet, in the Mojave desert, petroglyphs have been found that have been determined with radiocarbon dating to be from

11,200 to 16,500 years old, easily rivaling the antiquity of Lascaux. In California, pictographs have been dated to 14,070 years BP. Early explorers in America found rock art nationwide. Almost every state has recorded them. Most pictographs and petroglyphs, however, have been found in the West, where our mountains provide dramatic caves, cliffs, rock shelters, and bluffs on which to make the images.

Who made them? The Missouri River corridor was a busy prehistoric travel route. The hunting culture along the Smith River, which flows through central Montana, was at the southern edge of the ice fields and was an active hunting area twelve thousand years ago. Consequently, the Smith River has the highest density of recorded sites in the state. Greer says that it is possible that some of the art was made by early Kiowa people, before they were pushed to the south, or by the Salish or Kutenai people of the western part of the state, who used this corridor for buffalo hunting. In different areas, art has been attributed to the Pend'd 'Oreille, Blackfeet, Crow, or Gros Ventres, though most of these modern tribes, like the Blackfeet, have only been on the plains four hundred years. Many tribes say that the rock art was made before their people came to this area. A Blackfeet elder told anthropologists James D. Keyser and Michael A. Klassen that "a well-known Foothills Abstract Tradition site on the upper Sun River was not their doing, but instead had always been known by them to predate their arrival in the area."

What we do know is that people have inhabited the Plains for thousands of years, and yet, there is little physical evidence of their presence until recently. We know that early peoples traveled from Asia and Siberia over the land bridge of the Bering Strait twenty thousand years ago, following what is called the Old North Trail through Canada and down into Montana. That trail is still visible in places, as dry and fragile and isolated as the prairie is, lodge stones and travois marks sunk deep in the long ago mud. "To have gathered from the air a live tradition," Ezra Pound wrote in his *Cantos*, yet he was writing in Europe where the traditions were still alive in the languages spoken around him, in the ruins and cathedrals, cities and roads, rather than something caught on the twigs of aspen, buried under the stones of the creek. Uncannily, though, most people who have lived long in the West can testify to an ancient human presence felt in even the most suburbanized areas, especially so in those places that are, to use a word telling in its connotations, *undeveloped*. It is an apperception of something long absent and yet continuing, a presence murmuring under the surface that we hear in the rustle of cottonwood leaves or in the emptiness of the prairie.

Many years ago, I heard an interview with the writer N. Scott Momaday who, when asked his definition of sacred land, said it was land made sacred by the acts performed there. It was land consecrated by human ceremony. Pictographs and petroglyphs are often found not only in the most spectacular settings—steep limestone cliffs rising straight up from a creek crossing, enormous caves whose mouths look out over wide valleys below them, rock shelters at the confluence of rivers—they are also often located in isolated, even almost inaccessible places. That what is called "rock art" was used to *ceremonialize* these sites is clear. Entire cliffs can be found, washed with red ochre first before any images were drawn on them. There is evidence that people did not live in these places, but rather traveled to them, sometimes carrying pigments mined hundreds of miles away. The amazing fact that these sites are everywhere, that they surround us, and yet few people pay them any mind, that most of the time they exist unprotected, even painted over or scratched with graffiti, makes me think that most modern people see them as we see rocks, trees, animals, and plants—that is, we don't really see them. They recede into the background, the *setting* against which we live our lives.

Yet, like an earthquake rumbling below the surface, like weather or the moon, the fact is that they do exist, that we in the West live here, surrounded, in our canyons and mountains and watersheds, by a visionary record, as well as a record of the visionary, that spans thousands of years, perhaps thousands of people. We talk about the uncovering of the Paleolithic caves, the surfacing of the Dead Sea Scrolls during World War II in a cave in Egypt, the discovery of pictographs in a similar manner. It is instructive to look at the words we use—uncovering, discovering, surfacing, by which we mean found, or revealed. The mysteries that are revealed are essentially the mysteries of those who lived before us, and hence the dead, and are often found in places we might think of as under the earth. In fact, instead of the word *undeveloped* we might instead use the word *under-developed* in speaking of these sites, as in an underworld of images—songs, figures, presences—that has developed just below the reality of what we call our time.

The poet Clayton Eshleman speculates in *Juniper Fuse*, his book about the European cave paintings, that we might think of these discoveries as "a retrieval of depth, of a bottomlessness that is not simply absence but one complexed with hidden presence and invisible connections." Given that many of these images took generations to be discovered, that they "dis-appeared" from any human account and then were "found" again, makes me think of wisdom surfacing counter to the currents of the upper world. Here in the West, Clovis points—the points on the tips of spears, an amazingly difficult mode of hunting that predated the use of bow and arrow—surface in fields and dirt roads after each torrential rain. Teepee rings, sweat lodge stones, even medicine wheels emerge after centuries of being buried under soil and dust. A friend is hiking mid-August and feels cool air emanating from an outcropping of limestone. Investigating, he finds a shaft that he drops into, then an opening just large enough to squeeze through. It opens up into a cave whose walls are covered with paintings. When was the last time a human being set foot in this place? Who were they and what were they doing?

an intimate and age-old kinship between
the earth and human inwardness

ROBERT POGUE HARRISON

We enter Hellgate Canyon, in central Montana, by a dirt road well traveled by hikers, hunters, and campers, but most especially by rock climbers who can be found almost every day scaling its steep limestone cliffs. Just before the small creek crosses the road, we stop and park the car, deciding to experience the site the way peoples hundreds of years before us would have seen it. The canyon makes a sharp turn, creating the illusion that its walls have closed, but as we walk farther, it opens, and we face a thirty- or forty-foot-high and ninety-foot-long rock wall that has been painted orange-red to arm's reach. On top of the red ground, which is pockmarked from fallen spalls, is a powerful and mysterious constellation of images ranging across the entire wall: handprints, dots, finger smears, a chaotic array of intricate lines and enigmatic groupings that on further inspection are human-like with upraised arms or possible wings or horns. Some figures we think we recognize: a cat's head, a knotted rope, an arrow pointing to a basin. The light changes and, as we stand there, the images fade in and out, an entire world, a ghost population facing us, then turning to rain streaks the soft color of strawberries or the flowers we, incidentally, call Indian paintbrush.

We cross the creek by foot. The Forest Service has worked to preserve the site, removing most of the graffiti and preventing erosion from the trail, though we notice a pile of human shit and toilet paper near the water, and a crazed motorcyclist revs his motor and drives up and down the canyon furiously as if trying to get us to bring our attention back to the twenty-first century. Close up, the figures again play their tricks with light; some are more distinguishable from the lighter red behind them; some disappear altogether. The creators of these images used "hematite or iron oxide in powder form, combining it with plant juice, blood, urine and animal fat," says local archaeologist Sara Scott. They painted with their fingers, brushes, and sticks. Sometimes they carried the pigment far from their favored deposits or, as in the Missouri River drainage, found it nearby. In Victoria Finlay's book, *Color: A Natural History of the Palette*, she speaks of the universal regard for ochre, a word she says originally meant pale yellow but has shifted to the red we think of now: "In Swaziland's Bomvu Ridge (Bomvu means 'red' in Zulu) archaeologists have discovered mines that were used at least forty thousand years ago to excavate red and yellow pigments for body painting." Ice Age hominids in Europe used ochre to paint their dead and line their graves, as well as to decorate shelters and figurines. In the West, the varying colors of the red pigment have been used to date pictographs and to categorize them into traditions, an orange and medium red like this color being favored by peoples in the Middle and Late Archaic periods, ca. 5,000 to 1,000 BP.

There is a small cave to the right of the cliff, just big enough to lie or sit in, which muffles the roar of the creek as it echoes off the canyon walls, the roar of the wind patrolling its corridors, ever-restless wind-snake and the restless water. Here, one can rest one's restlessness. Over there, the small stick figures emerge, chthonic, from the cracks in the cliff and go walking across the horizontal surface, chained at first in lines that seem knotted as they stretch out and then transformed into humans with wings, with upraised arms. What a spirit might look like if we could see it. Or what spirit might become inside the earth. Scott writes, "Many prehistoric groups viewed the surface of rock cliffs as veils between our world and that of the supernatural. As people penetrated the rock surface with paint affixed to their hands, they entered and interacted with the supernatural world."

The fact is that the paint really does enter into the rock's chemical composition so that it becomes, literally, the rock. "When freshly applied, the pigment stains the rock surface and seeps into microscopic pores by capillary action," say Keyser and Klassen. A mineral skin of silica or calcium oxalate also forms on the rock walls, due to rain washing over their surfaces, so that the painted image, in time, is no longer on or behind the surface, but *is* the surface and really looks as if it were emerging out of the rock itself. That is why the pictographs last. They have found their way in. They have also, one might say, found their way out. Over and over in my reading I have encountered the idea that the creators of the pictographs believed that the spirits emerged from deep cracks or crevasses in the rock face and, indeed, the evidence seems to point in this direction: a bear whose hind leg appears to be ready to step out from a dark cleft, lines of anthropomorphs streaming out of a natural indentation, starbursts and arrows pointing to a fold.

Much has been said about the way the stags, bison, and aurochs depicted in the European caves take advantage of natural formations in the cave walls, as if the image were actually suggested first by the rock and then coaxed into a clearer depiction by the painters, the possibility that the painters were "touching what was already there." One thinks of the horses at Lascaux, swimming through the waves of darker-colored rock below them. Something more seems at play, though, both in the cave walls of Lascaux and the North American rock art that I have seen, more than the interaction between features of the rock and the imagination of the painter, more than the outlines of shadow and light suggesting images. If it is true what Scott says, that people believed that these were spirits emerging from these cracks, not *representations of spirit*, then the figures painted on the cliff walls are not only similes (what the rock face looks like) but also metaphors (what rock has been transformed into). Not only a place to house the dead but also a place for them to appear. Perhaps it is as John Berger imagined it in writing about the Chauvet cave in France: "When an apparition came to an artist, it came almost invisibly, trailing a distant, unrecognizably vast sound, and he or she found it and traced where it nudged the surface, the facing surface, on which it would now stay visible even when it had withdrawn and gone back into the one." Perhaps the pictograph images are necessarily both, a crossing where the outward force of spirit moving through rock into visibility and the inward movement of the human imagination toward invisibility meet. In the process, it seems, the images would naturally become distorted. Again, as Berger imagines: "Things happened that later millennia found it hard to understand. A head came without a body. Two heads arrived, one behind the other. A single hind leg chose its body, which already had four legs. Six antlers settled in a single skull."

The pictographs at Hellgate Gulch have been calibrated to range from 1,020 to 1,360 BP and, because of their age, their location, but most especially because of the images painted here—hand streaks, anthropomorphic figures—they have been classified as typical of what is called the Foothills Abstract Tradition, the making of whose images are attributed to shamans, initiates, or those on vision quests. According to oral traditions, the torsos of many of the human-like figures are elongated to indicate that these are spirits or shamans who have squeezed between the cracks in the rocks or have been manhandled or torn apart by the spirits of previous shamans they encountered inside them. In many of these sites, red-painted hands or "spatter clouds" are superimposed on the images or they are scratched into and over with something sharp. The scratching may have been to partake of the power that had been released at this sacred site, or it may have been to collect some of the paint to reuse now that it had sacred meaning. The hand smears may have been a way to participate or place oneself in an ongoing dialogue with those who had been here before, adding one's own paint to the rock and thus, symbolically joining one's ancestors. A public site such as Hellgate was probably visited by different artists and initiates over centuries, including four or five episodes of site use and "at least a dozen (and probably many more) visits by different artists who added images over many years."

I try to imagine what it might have been like to enter these foothills from the broad and sun-filled Valley of the Missouri, to enter the cool and vaulted limestone canyon not knowing what lies ahead, to turn a corner and be confronted by this strange cliff, bloodied and honored with paint that must have been brilliant in its time, a line of spirits proceeding from the rock toward you as if out of the past, each figure surrounded by unreadable but potent magic signs. Was this the site of a puberty rite, a place young people were taken en masse to introduce them to the mystery and ancientness of the worlds they were born both into and out of? Were they fasting? Were they singing? How else might they have been prepared? There is a possible prefatory spot, a staging area we read about but missed before we entered the canyon. We find it on our way out, a large red arrow pointing toward the site, placed low on a bluff so that one might see it from afar. In the dust below it, we find a thick braid of sweetgrass, dried out but intact, that someone must have left relatively recently. Impossible to imagine what people who were first brought to this cliff felt or saw or heard, what power that simple arrow must have had for those already anticipating something sublime and perhaps terror-filled—that unambiguous sign, the universal hieroglyphic for the word *Enter*.

"To be human means to come after those who came before," writes Robert Pogue Harrison in his book *Dominion of the Dead*. The word *human* comes from *humus*, he reminds us, as in the soil, which is an ongoing amalgamation of what once was alive and is no longer, is rotting and transforming and is on its way to becoming alive—and useful—again. "Just as we are always preceded by our forebears," Harrison writes, "so too the ground in which we lay them to rest has always already received the bones of others—'others' in the most radical sense of the term, including that of other species, many of whom have died on our behalf." Rock, literally, is our oldest form of earth. Grandfather rock, my Cree friends taught me to call it. To be human, one could say, means to *under-*

stand that one comes after those who came before. We stand under that knowledge, transfixed as those long-ago initiates must have been, unsure of what to make of our experience but carrying now these images inside us, images that offer us a deeper gaze into this place we, who live here, call our home.

Walter Kirn | LIVINGSTON BLOWS

Mostly, it comes at us from the southwest, from the general direction of Yellowstone Park, and once the battering begins, it doesn't let up for days, sometimes weeks. When it starts it feels like normal wind, like ordinary rushing air, and people in town respond accordingly, removing laundry from clotheslines, shutting windows, and taking care to hold their car doors firmly when they open them in the grocery store parking lot so that the gusts don't catch them and bend them backward past the mechanical limits of their hinges. It's potent when it hits Livingston, this wind—forty miles per hour isn't unusual, and sometimes it's closer to sixty, or even seventy—but to say that it "gusts" is inaccurate, actually, because it's incessant, vast, and deafening; the equivalent of a roaring wall of water unleashed by a catastrophic dam break. But that's wrong, too, because walls of water pass—they wreck what's in front of them and then subside. The wind in Livingston isn't like that, though. Its source seems inexhaustible, immense, as though it extends all the way to the Pacific and perhaps even across it, to Japan. After the wind has been raging for a few days, one imagines the world must be out of air completely—or maybe the wind has managed to circle the globe and is hitting us a second time.

But that's just Act One of the atmospheric drama, when the wind in Livingston is merely wind. Over time, it turns to something else. You find yourself walking south on Callender Street, headed to Sax & Fryer's dry goods store to buy a calendar or a box of pencils, your body angled forward against the gale, your ears picking up the rattling of cables against the shaft of flagpole by the post office, when suddenly what has seemed until that moment like a meteorological event feels like a mythic, spiritual event—a terrible contest pitting you, with your petty, inconsequential will, against an immeasurable elemental nemesis. A sense of profound subjugation soon descends. How defenseless you are. How defenseless your neighbors are. With whatever they're carrying tucked against their bellies as their hair whips chaotically around and their clothing flaps and flutters crazily, they push ahead, pursuing their goals, their errands, but their efforts seem farcical, trivial, contemptible—no more important in the scheme of things than that blue plastic trash bin skating on its side down an alley and out onto the sidewalk, where it finally comes to rest against a wall and out of it spills a profusion of diapers, beer cans, magazines, paper plates, and plastic milk jugs, some of the refuse skidding over the curb and into the middle of the street. In the path of an oncoming car you watch a whiskey bottle spin in place for a moment before it's crushed, allowing the next car to drive over its splinters. They skitter, tinkling, across the pavement, and as you set down your right shoe to cross the street one of the splinters lodges in your sole.

Vanity. All is vanity, the Bible says. You make it into the store and buy your calendar, but does knowing what day it is really matter now? Do plans matter? Schedules? Appointments? Not at all. Suddenly, all that matters is taking shelter.

But there is no shelter to be had. When the wind in Livingston turns monstrous, even life indoors becomes unstable. I'm in my apartment downtown, at my computer, e-mailing a colleague across the country, when the glass in the windows in front of me bows inward and seems to be on the verge of shattering. Then, just for an instant, the power goes. My half-written message is lost; I failed to save it. I decide that instead of working I'll read a book deeper inside the building, in my living room, but concentration proves impossible. Between every sentence, the turmoil shakes my brain. My entire two-story building, made of stone, is rocking like a table with a short leg. Is this how the apocalypse will feel? Someday, the geologists predict, the great volcanic plateau of Yellowstone Park will heave upward and erupt, sending dense clouds of ash so far and wide that much of the West will be buried, overcome. Could that awful entombment be any worse than this, though? This all-consuming nonstop turbulence that doesn't kill you but, after a few days, starts to make you wish it would.

I plug a pair of headphones into my stereo and turn the music up loud, but it's no use. I can't hear the angry god now, but I can feel him. Everything trembles, shivers, rumbles. The disturbance is palpable inside my cells, deep in their mitochondria. Wind comes from the outside, but this seems to come from within. This is another creature, chaos itself.

Which may be why Livingston, in its windy months, is not a town or a place but a condition. A mental condition, progressive and severe. Sitting at the counter at Pinky's diner, we spoon up pea soup and stare silently ahead. The waitress is nestling a paper filter in the basket of the coffee-maker, but none of us notice this, none of us can see her. We're looking past her into a gray depth that may as well be our own minds or souls, and what we're beholding, what we're witnessing, is their gradual decomposition. This morning, for no reason we can think of, we fought with our spouses, we hung up on our parents, we snatched our kids' toys and threw them in the trash. After breakfast, we had jobs to do—walls to sheet-rock, packages to mail, paychecks to deposit at the bank—but we skipped them, we blew them off, went back to bed. We took aspirin before we lay down, though we weren't sick. We poured ourselves glasses of water but didn't drink them. We've begun to behave nonsensically, destructively, yet somehow, although we know better, we just can't stop ourselves.

It's madness. Today, when I finally rose from bed at noon, I went out-side to move my car so the cops wouldn't issue me a ticket for leaving it in the same spot for over three hours. But my car wasn't where I remembered parking it. At last I spotted it a block away. There were only two explana-tions for the sight: the weather had managed to move a ton of metal sev-eral hundred feet during the night or my brain was disintegrating, which seemed more likely—especially when I climbed inside the car and tried to insert my key into the ignition, couldn't do it, and realized that the prob-lem was that I was using a pencil.

It occurs to you after two weeks of howling anarchy that your mind, like the big McDonald's sign that used to stand on a pole beside the free-way but now lies in dozens of pieces in a parking lot, has been ripped from its moorings and reduced to shreds, which are hanging on faraway tree branches and stop signs. Though a lot of those stop signs are gone now, too, of course. After seventeen days of flexing, twisting pressure, the monster has snapped them from their metal posts and sent them sail-ing off like Frisbees. Sometime next spring, when you're fishing in the Yellowstone, you'll snag one with your hook and drag it up. That, or you'll scrape the hull of your new drift boat against the TV satellite dish that was whisked from your roof in the middle of the *Tonight Show* and carried, *Wizard of Oz*-style, into the heavens, leaving you staring at a dead, dark screen while sipping your fifth double bourbon of the evening.

Once you've accepted your madness and hit the sedatives, life gets easier—temporarily. In the eye of the psychological hurricane that has been raging for two weeks, there comes a soothing interlude, though brief, of philosophical serenity. All existence is flux, you understand, and mo-tion, change, and unpredictability are the essential facts of life on earth, accounting for its miraculous dynamism. Over in Bozeman, where the air is calm and maintaining fixed routines still possible, the people have yet to learn this lesson, you sense, but someday they'll be forced to, and you pity them, because the revelation will leave them stunned. Your period of composure ends abruptly, though, when a Styrofoam carryout box of Chinese noodles rises from the top of a full dumpster and is flung at high speed directly into your chest, dripping peanut oil on your new coat. That's when the panic resumes. This might not end. It might last forever. But you won't last forever. Nor will your marriage, you suspect. And now that the satellite TV is gone, there's no escape from the nights of nonstop bickering.

The radio is still working, but you can't listen to it. Its inaccurate weather reports have made it hateful. Three days ago, it was reported that the siege would end by yesterday morning, but out near I-90 the truck stop parking lot is still, this afternoon, packed with at least a dozen idling semis that dare not drive on any farther toward Butte or Billings lest their trailers be swept into the ditch and their pallets of hand tools or crates of frozen chickens spilled willy-nilly over the embankment. Also, because the overpass is closed, located as it is near a narrow canyon that concentrates the gale, the truckers who are inclined to take their chances have been forced to detour through downtown, blocking the intersections and slowing traffic, which is why you turned back when you set out for the drugstore a couple of hours ago. You can refill your Valium prescription tomorrow.

This is the point where most everyone in Livingston considers relocating to kinder climes. Remember that trip to Key West two winters back? Those temperate, soft breezes off the Gulf? You sunburned your pale northern torso there, it's true, and were forced to spend three days in bed at the motel, but maybe it's time to empty your savings account, rent a big U-Haul, and put this hell behind you. Then you remember: you spent two-thirds of your savings last winter, repairing your ripped-up roof. The remaining third went for those sessions with the therapist who told you, because his office was in Bozeman, that inner distress has no geographic cure and that blaming the weather for your unhappiness is a symptom of paranoia and immaturity. Fulfillment and peace, the therapist assured you, result from coming to terms with imperfection, not fantasizing about escaping from it. That's when you wrote the fellow his last check and told him where to stick it before driving back to Livingston and holing up at the Murray Bar all evening.

And then, without warning—the way it started—it stops. You're at the self-service car wash when it happens, attempting to direct the nozzle's spray at the two-inch thick layer of mud on your front fenders. The spray has been arcing backward into your face, but all of a sudden the water starts shooting straight. Your wild, tangled hair lays down flat atop your skull. It's hard to believe it's over, and so you don't at first. You brace yourself for more turmoil. You wait. But nothing happens. All is still. You finish rinsing off your filthy car and resolve to drive back to the house immediately—but only after buying flowers to pacify your wife, who's close to leaving you. Now that that the three-week fury has abated, there are many messes to clean up. Some involve your family and friends, while others involve your house and yard. For example, you'll have to return your children's swing set to its upright position, which will take considerable faith, since it's likely to be blown down again next weekend. Rigging up a new satellite dish will take faith too. But what choice do you have, really? None. Besides going back to church next Sunday, none.

That's the hardest thing about the wind in Livingston: picking yourself back up once it dies down and knowing that it won't play dead for long. But because this is also the hardest thing about life in general, anywhere—resuming the fight that can't be won, persevering in the struggle that never ends—perhaps it's not so bad that you reside here. Or so you tell yourself as you use both hands to grip the crossbar of the fallen swing set and heave it up off the lawn with all your might just as your cap goes flying off your head and lands in the compost pile twenty feet away. But perhaps, just perhaps, it won't last this time, you tell yourself. Perhaps it will swell and subside this time—just wind, after all.

Once the swing set is up, you hurry to fetch your cap. Your fool's cap. Which you run after, but never catch.

William Kittredge | WHERE SHOULD WE BE?

Can artists be anything but regional? Does physical location matter? Sure, if you've got attention, success, and money in mind. You stand to sell more books or other artistic products if they are of interest between Boston and Baltimore. Publishing houses tend to be there, and national museums and theaters and galleries and newspapers. The most influential critics work there. Is that "eastern power corridor" a region? Sure it is. Do tastemakers in the East wield more power than they merit? Probably. The bicoastal extension of that domain is in Los Angeles, with its museums and art house theaters and influential movie business. Are the eastern power corridor and Southern California the best locations for artists courting attention and career-sustaining wealth? Seems that way. But what does physical location have to do with creating the actual art?

Robert Helm was an artist who lived in a farmhouse outside Pullman, Washington, a western college town. He died recently but his work is in the Whitney and the Museum of Modern Art. In the 1980s, when Bob was just getting into those museums and high-end New York galleries, critics labeled him a minor provincial regionalist. Bob went back at them with the truth that regional doesn't necessarily equate with minor and/or provincial. Artists have no choice but to work with and imagine about what they have learned, knowledge that they may come across on the streets of Manhattan or on the plow grounds of Poland or Montana or out in the far, sad deserts of Darfur.

It's always seemed that art more often that not originated in particular times and places. The *Iliad* and *Don Quixote* and *Moby Dick* and Shakespeare and Sophocles and Lascaux and the carvings of Haida and Tlingit artists along the northwest coast of North America and Bach and Mozart and Giotto and Goya and Michelangelo and Mark Rothko all worked in places that can be located on Google maps. Seeking locating narratives, those artists found psychic versions of homelands not only in places where they happened to live, but in myths and legends and histories and the evolution of the various arts from artist to artist. Revealingly complex stories evolve in such mental landscapes and lead to what Aristotle called "recognitions," moments of insight, positive or negative, about the working out of histories and lives. Both the artists and their audiences are led in conservative and protective, or radical and innovative, directions, often both at the same time. This is true for figurative artists and for abstractionists, like Jackson Pollock. Art can't help but be physically and psychically local. *Housekeeping* and *The Meadow* and *Rock Springs*, among my favorite Western American books from recent years (my bias is obviously toward traditional prose), are equally located in versions of actual places.

After leaving in 1967, and visiting only occasionally since, my interior life still resonates around Warner Valley, far out in the thinly populated Great Basin—off to the west, juniper mountains. Jagged lava-break rims loom against the skies. I still see those rims in my mind's eye quite precisely. Deep Creek and Twenty Mile flood Warner in the spring. Greasewood badlands stretch toward Idaho. The valley is landlocked, fertile with deep peat soils and abundantly watered, a fine and isolated end of the line in which to be a child. At the age of six, I went out on an old gelding with my mother's assurance that nothing could go wrong so long as I took care to not fall off. I did fall off and walked home. But I didn't come crying to dinner. That would mean I couldn't be trusted to ride out into the Thompson Field and watch muskrats slither in the mud and baby ducks paddling after their mothers. So I bit my lip. What work I've done since resonates with emotional connections I was fortunate enough to find there.

Richard Hugo wrote of seeking "triggering" towns that might incite his poems. I grew up in my own triggering location. But that doesn't make me anything but fortunate and has little to do with the significance or lack of significance of work I might get done. The work gets done where it gets done—originating in anything and anywhere that spark emotional significances the artist values and a sense of consequences that follows on those significances.

In his dealings with the eastern artistic establishment, Robert Helm cherished a line from Whitman, who said that New York was a fine place to sell vegetables but not much of a place to raise them. "But I didn't quote him," Bob said. "I just remembered what he said and held my temper when some fellow said I didn't deserve success because I hadn't paid my dues—I hadn't lived in Manhattan or Brooklyn."

Clearly, our dues aren't paid by living in one place or another. No doubt vegetables *are* raised in New York, and certainly wonderful art is created there. But fine work is brought off all over the place. Ingmar Bergman wandered the stony beaches of his barren island off the coast of Sweden and recognized that he needed markets for his work. They are obviously easier to find in locations that are populated and wealthy. Bergman took his films to Stockholm and the world. Physical location counts big if we're thinking about access to audiences and the wealth to sustain the work. But it doesn't determine whether our work is minor or provincial or for the ages or whatever. Everybody knows that.

Alyson Hagy | SELF-PORTRAIT AS THE
STRONG AND SILENT TYPE

Have you ever wondered why there isn't any sexy literature written about the American mountain West?

I have.

I think it's because of the mules.

I know, my answer is nearly as ridiculous as my question. But consider these facts. Folks come—and stay—in the rugged parts of the West because those places *are* rugged. We have wide-open spaces and (fairly) pristine landscapes. Beyond the few metropolitan areas that cling to the high plains or deserts, there are no crowds, no traffic, no malls, no damn taxes. Folks come here because their mouths will be scoured dry by fresh wind each and every day. Folks *stay* here because the stars in the night sky are more numerous than the decent jobs. And we don't care. We like it that way. Westerners take pleasure in the romp of deprivation. We think it's fun to be thrown off a horse.

We are not a bodice-ripping people.

After a dozen years in Wyoming, my own habits have been eroded down to a few manageable essentials: work, being outdoors, and conversations with friends about what life is like in those parts of America where you can safely order seafood. There is not much need to discuss politics in Wyoming. Politics barely exist in the Equality State because everyone purportedly shares the same credo: Leave Me the Hell Alone.

This is not the way it was when I was growing up in the South. In the South people didn't want to be left alone. They wanted to talk, and they especially wanted to talk about other people. They wanted to gossip about the school principal, the preacher, the dairy farmer with the cross-eyed sons, the circuit court judge and his girlfriends, the hairdresser with the albino pig. They wanted to chatter. And they could not complete even the simplest task, such as mailing a letter at the post office, without launching into a raucous and very public soliloquy.

I have a hard time getting Westerners to talk. They are not profligate with their stories. They do not relish scandal, perhaps because their grandfathers and grandmothers left the more arable parts of this nation on the heels of some sort of bad behavior. Westerners do not easily talk about one another, and they can be zipper-lipped about themselves. This, I think, partly explains the dearth of sexy literature. Sexiness depends upon seduction. And seduction usually depends upon language. A love-seeking man or woman cannot truly maintain their right to remain silent during courtship unless they happen to own that fail-safe aid to the pheromones—a really good-looking dog.

Southerners are wed to their stories. They cannot pass one another on the road to the tobacco warehouse without swapping whoppers. Over a couple of lively centuries, natives of the American South have cultivated the ability to talk themselves into and out of trouble. This trait is doubly necessary because the Southerners I know *love* their trouble. The newspaper from my Virginia hometown is a biweekly testament to poor judgment. A woman falls in love with her father-in-law and torments both of the men in her life until shots are fired. A state Alcohol Beverage Control agent serves illegal corn liquor (which has been seized during the bust-up of a three hundred-gallon still) at the retirement party for his boss. An erstwhile dealer in prescription drugs reports his "partner" to the sheriff because the partner tried to pass off aspirin tablets as Oxycontin.

Which brings me to the mules.

For I think I have discovered what truly turns a Westerner's crank. It's not a glimpse of firmly toned legs encased in fishnet stockings. It's not a set of brawny biceps. And it's definitely *not* trouble. What Westerners desire more than a new set of winter tires is competence. You can make a Western man's face flush to pink if you describe to him the afternoon you spent sighting in your rifle. You can inspire an impassioned hip shimmy from a Western woman if you can weld a straight seam. Just ask the crowd at the Third Street Bar & Grill in Laramie. Third Street is a shameless hangout for law students from the University of Wyoming, but many a future prosecutor has had his fires quenched when he was unceremoniously dumped in favor of a Carhartt-wrapped heavy equipment operator who drives a snowplow for the state.

Do you really think those stumpy guys who call themselves bull riders get the girls because they've been air-flogged by a Brahma? I will admit there is some manufactured glamour to rodeoing, but it's a flat-out guarantee that those boys can also tweak the clutch on a snowmobile, hang sheetrock, deliver twin calves at midnight, and play a mean game of cribbage besides. Westerners know how to *do* things, especially with their hands. And they are damn impatient with those who cannot.

Thus, the mules. Everyone I know who has deigned to develop a relationship with a mule complains about the creature. A mule is too fat, too bony, too fast, too slow, too single-minded, too unfocused. Mules are hard to please at feeding time, and they are even pickier about their companions than they are about their grain. Mules are stubborn. Mules are stupid. Mules come in for more verbal abuse than mothers-in-law. Yet, no one wants to leave the hammer-headed hellions behind. Pack trips, hunting trips, day rides into Yellowstone. My friends are forever loading up their mules. Sure, they own hard-footed mustangs and svelte Arabians that can glide under saddle all day. But they never leave their mules, not if they have the choice. A mule is a Leatherman tool with ears. You can use one for almost anything.

My own involvement with mules has been mostly positive. I made fun of a fat, short-legged jack once only to watch him dance his way into a steep river canyon with the quick-footed grace of the running back Barry Sanders. The jack was carrying the whiskey and red wine in his panniers. I should have known better than to tease him. I needed him to get his load to the campsite. I did have the good sense not to cuss him out when he decided to bray like a teen hooligan at two o'clock in the morning. I ate my humble pie later in the week when I had to scramble out of the canyon on foot. There is nothing that silences a yackety Southerner quite like a two thousand-foot ascent at high altitude. This may be the only hope I have of achieving any status as a stoic denizen of the West. Keep me exhausted. The fat mule, light-footing his way upward far ahead of me, wasn't even breathing hard.

It's important to me that Westerners hold competence in high regard. It means our communities are filled with jacks-of-all-trades, and that's never a bad thing, especially if you're a daydreaming writer who has the skill set of an LA housewife. It means meetings are shorter and your boss is likely to be the kind of person who believes in a meritocracy. So what if the packed movie theater is dead quiet before the show starts? So what if the bars are more likely to break out into bouts of fighting or dancing than supple verbal debate? It's cold most of the year in the West. We are almost always layered up to our nostrils in clothes. Maybe the natives have earned their relative silence and reserve. As to whether most of them have, on occasion, used their competent hands to heat up the blood of another man or woman, I leave that for others to determine.

It is worth noting, however, that almost everyone I know in Wyoming truly, madly, deeply loves to visit Las Vegas. What am I to make of that? There are white tigers in Las Vegas. And pirates. But I have yet to see a good, hard-working mule anywhere on the Strip. This makes me wonder. What happens in Vegas stays in Vegas, or so they say. Maybe keeping that kind of sexy promise is a Western competence all its own.

BLOOD WEST

> *But I reckon I got to light out for the*
> *Territory ahead of the rest . . .*

HUCKLEBERRY FINN

The West begins in runaway blood; it ends when the lifeblood stops running. The rain shadow of the 100th meridian bisects flatland Nebraska between lowland farmers and high plains ranchers, climatically eastern rainfall and arid West. Native tribes, both hunters and harvesters, have straddled the line for thousands of years. Growing up in the lee winds of Wounded Knee, near Chimney Rock on the North Platte River, taught me something about sundown trails, tribes overrun by settlers, and where our westward treks might end.

My corner of the West came with the Chisholm Trail emptying longhorns onto the newly tracked coast-to-coast railroad after the Civil War. It was the western dumping edge of the Homestead Acts, a town called Alliance for the merging of two rail lines. Native tribes living there called themselves Lakota or "allies." The North Platte River banked sunset trails from Omaha and Kansas City—Indians and Mormons trekking on the north side, pioneers and adventurers on the south in "The Great Migration" west. Where streams flowed people could survive on the high plains, both Native and migrant, though collisions were bloody. Native points of reference keyed on trees and water, sun and wind, stone and stars.

Rooted things stand magical on the gusty prairie, and water gives life. "I see men as trees walking," Saint Mark's blind man tells Christ of a global icon. Flatland cottonwoods run to water, their leaves rounding into hearts, their twigs snapping open with stars: "wind-loving trees," the Nebraska writer Willa Cather noted in *The Song of the Lark*, "whose roots are always seeking water and whose leaves are always talking about it, making the sound of rain." Cottonwoods anchor the West in river loam and raise migrant spirits to the skies. Plains tribes ceremonially replant them at the Sacred Hoop *axis mundi* of the Sun Dance.

Make no mistake, it's rough, spit-dirt country with unrelenting winds. Immigrants lean west into the gale and fear being sucked back east where they came from. Wind-chafed skins tend to be leathery, appetites large, eyes cataracted, responses curt. For centuries, Native peoples moved seasonally north and south among the bison herds, until the bison were mostly slaughtered and the surviving Indians herded onto reservations. When my turn-of-the-century pioneer ancestors—Lincolns, Whitmans, Warricks, Johnstons, Giles, Sumners—got to western Nebraska, they weren't sure where their there was. Many settlers, dissidents, rejects, and westering prospectors peeled off from fatigue, dispirit, fear, or disgust before they reached destined Colorado, Montana, Oregon, or California. The remnants tended to be sodbusters and cattle ranchers like Robert Thompson Lincoln from Wisconsin and Patrick King from Texas, Indian killers and grizzled homesteaders like the gunslinger Doc Holliday from all over the West and the Swiss immigrant Old Jules. Jules Sandoz is buried today just south of Carhenge, a Stonehenge replica made of junked cars in a fallow wheat field outside my hometown.

At the turn into the last century, my ancestors homesteaded along the North Platte shallows and Good Streak buffalo runs north of Bayard, Nebraska. Chimney Rock stood sentinel over the river. To the west stretched the Great American Desert of Wyoming, Utah, and Nevada. W. D. Johnston, my mother's ex-Scottish grandfather, fought in the Civil War and came west to police Indians out of Fort Laramie. Farther up the "Nile Valley of the West" in the Wildcat Range on Scott's Bluff, a teen Oglala Lakota nicknamed Curly had his quested vision of a horse so wildly alive it never touched the ground, hence the legendary, gray-eyed *Sunka Witko*. Crazy Horse took his stand with Sitting Bull, Red Cloud, Touch-the-Clouds, and Gall at the Little Big Horn—Plains Indian martyr and spiritual warrior of a buffalo-hunting nomadic culture plowed under by Manifest Destiny. At the century's turn, my great-grandparents on both sides settled down as farmers, plumbers, railroaders, teachers, carpenters, and clerks in Bayard and Bridgeport, dimpling the northwest Panhandle. Everyone went to work every day; no one went to college.

You learn something about human nature growing up in a small town in western heartland America. Locals learn where the sun rises and sets on the horizon in all seasons. You figure out that most railroads go east and west, and that every good farm has a light on at night. When you get lost, you are told to circle back home across an endless prairie. Plants and animals, angles of light and shadow tell you things about a human place in it all. Observers note sunflowers by dirt roads, hollyhocks in backyards, barbed wire fences and windbreaks, wheat fields in harvest and cornstalks in fall pheasant season, frozen furrows in winter and spring plowing. By necessity, folks know to grieve the losses and to celebrate the newcomings of life—births and deaths, anniversaries and discoveries, departures and homecomings.

Residents build houses to live in for a lifetime, not for equity or resale. Living there, kids find out about basements—storing preserves, coal, tools, home brew, dogs and cats, work and laundry rooms, lumber and hunting gear. Neighbors learn to make peace with neighbors, no matter how cranky or feisty; they aren't going away. Friends learn to welcome visitors when they drop by unannounced, and in turn villagers know to drop everything when someone needs you. In a city it's easy to close the door, hang up, just say no; in small towns, commitments turn on yes, certainly, just ask. By listening, you learn that men and women discuss, negotiate, cuss, and carry out accepted roles without grousing big time, most of the time. Both cross over to help the other in a pinch—who cooks or washes dishes, who digs the garden or greases the car, who feeds or disciplines the kids, who cleans up after the pet or runs the vacuum. It's not big-cheese living, but good lives work out here.

By God, you learn about going to church, Boy and Girl Scouts, volunteer fire departments, local police, PTA, dog catchers, drunks, teetotalers, drifters, and permanent fixtures—a pond or river, a valley or butte, a summer storm or winter blizzard, a back alley, county road, or state highway. You figure out whom to trust, when to step around, what will tell, who's watching over you, and since villages turn on gossip, kindness, spite, and grace. As a boy, you take to fishing and hunting and fighting and competing and sharing. Football is king. Emily Osborne, Big Red coach Tom Osborne's aunt, taught me to play piano at five when I was dreaming touchdowns. Emily's brother Howard Osborne was the Presbyterian village preacher who buried my father. Most residents honor the ancestors, pay respect to the old ones, observe family history. *A people without a past*, the Plains Indians say, *are like a wind in the buffalo grass.*

So you know about your relatives, your kinships, your cousins and aunts and uncles, grandparents and descendants, teachers, and rivals. "We are all related," the Sioux say, *Mitakuye oyasin*, even when competition and recalcitrance leave not a few men bunkhouse lonely, too many women cabin-fevered. No one really fears being alone short-term, but ostracism or isolation threaten long-term peace of mind in a land where distance italicizes human frailty. And soon enough, we take our place among the elders, the old neighbors, the community advisors as the grown kids coming back from faraway places with scars and stories and gray-streaked thinning hair.

My relatives have taught me to get up early and work hard, then to put down the work at midday and eat and rest with others. Pacing is everything, gumption an expendable resource. You learn early to take the time to speak with a child, to thank someone for a meal or a clean shirt, to value a man's honesty, or simply to admire a woman's grace, quietly. Working agrarian people regard animals as essential to human life and respect real living things. Everyone goes back to work, and works hard all over again, and at the end of the day turns back home and smiles for the release and the reward of laughter with your own people. Day work well done, evening sleep. And next day they come back for more of the same good hard life. It's worked like this for a long time in small towns around the world and remains essential to grounded survival in the West.

There were realities in northwest Nebraska that I didn't inherit by blood or learn on my own. These lessons came more through the human grace and good fortune of adoptive kinship in a town called Alliance— Lakota tribal ways from Pine Ridge and Rosebud Indian reservations to the north. Nick Black Elk was a local healer along with his second cousin Jenny Lone Wolf, our south-of-the-tracks family Sioux matriarch, and both were cousins to Crazy Horse. Their tribal celestial axes crossed with the ever-present sun or spirit *Wi* rising daily in the east and setting in the west. The sun's cyclical mortality was kept moving by *Takuskanskan* or the "Spirit-that-moves-(what)-moves." That's all the medicine men could say when asked about God. And the ever-changing moon or *Hanhepi-wi* waxed and waned across the north-to-south, star-filled axis of the Milky or "Spirit Way." Here, the ancestors have all "gone south" with the migrating herds of four-leggeds and flocks of wingeds, returning seasonally. This is a mythic prairie, natural as buffalo grass, pothole lake, and clay sod rooted in the extended family *tióte*, or "home place," my adoptive Lakota brother Mark Monroe taught me. *Mitak' oyasin*, "we are all related," even the took-ins. The four-winds horizon embraces a curved plate tipped at the edges, circling back home.

So I grew up hardpan where the West begins, ducked the redneck sweat holes of knuckle-busting work, and lit out for college on the West Coast. I've taught modern literature, writing, and American Indian Studies for forty years at UCLA. It's good work if you can get it, and the vacations aren't bad. These days I fly weekly, going on twenty years, between my daughter's family near the university in Los Angeles and my golden homestead in Santa Fe, New Mexico. This kind of touch-and-go mobility seems truly Western in the twenty-first century. But I annually go back to "flatwater" *Nebrathka* (Oto), and there I have a second home with the Mark Monroe *tiospaye*, my extended family in south Alliance, where Indians lived in tents when I was a kid.

Over forty years ago, Mark took me in and taught me the Lakota commitments of familial kinship—how to "give back" when given a break or a chance, how to sit still and listen to the other's long story, how to learn from adversity and laugh in the face of terrible odds. Humility, courage, wisdom, and endurance staked the four corners of natural virtues among now-day Indians. Poverty is no picnic, injustice no church social, racism no block party. My White-boy upbringing had turned a blind eye to Native suffering and survival (3 percent of the original four to six million eradicated inhabitants of five hundred different tribes in the contiguous United States), so I had some things to learn.

My life changed at the end of the sixties when Mark adopted me into his tribal family as a *hunka*, or younger brother. We shared the warrior name *Mato Yamni*, meaning Three Bears, and Old Man Bear became my guardian spirit. We built social and educational programs together, created an Indian Center in south Alliance, fed the hungry at noon over four decades, and bussed the ill to the Pine Ridge reservation hospital twice a week. Our center helped dropouts complete GED high school requirements, counseled alcoholics and pregnant mothers, cleaned up vacant lots, ran Boy Scout troops, organized quilting parties, and put together AA programs. We wrote state grants and canvassed church charities, worked with medicine people, nurses, doctors, and town councils. It was uphill hard work with weekly breakthroughs and perennial setbacks. Over the decades things got better for Indians in south Alliance. They tended to stay sober, hold jobs, speak clearer, improve their homes, go to school, get healthier, and live longer. As yet there's no parity with *Wasichun*, or "fat-taking" Anglos, but we're closing in.

It's time to redefine the frontiersman. With four decades of tribal work back home and educational activism out West, I've come to see that being a man, indeed human, Native and émigré, asks an allegiance to care for kin as well as strangers—not just defending and fighting for cultural rights and human decency, but raising children back home and parenting the needy down the block. There's no one way to do things out West. Big skies, open prairies, pioneer pluck, and the great mysteries (*Wakan Tanka*) of the West granted me growing room over a lifetime. This largesse may have something to do with an unchecked boyhood, exploratory adolescence, demanding manhood, and human survival along sundown trails into the unknown. "Don't fence me in," as the old song goes about home on the range.

Here's where I've come to rest growing up in the West: crossing the tracks in south Alliance and nurturing my daughter as a single parent kindled a consideration of others beyond frontier self-preservation and academic advancement. This othering (of not-me) grounded kinship spiritually and strengthened life-purpose, so that getting up early still awakens needs beyond coffee and toast. For forty thousand years or more, Indians have bedrocked western hemispheric cultures, and let me tell you that fathering a daughter straightens the spine. Not limited to tribal societies or solo parenting, "helping out," as Indians say on the rez, remains critical to folks with essentially each other against an invasive technocracy of self-interested getting and spending, rushing and forgetting. "Family and friends," my Irish cousin kept saying before he died of cancer last summer. George was a Vietnam Green Beret, a real Westerner, a true man.

Macho models out West may be evolving from cowboy to caregiver. Raising my daughter singly made a man of me, nothing fancy or new. Together and singly through hard times and plenty, my pioneer ancestors tended families migrating west, and each step toward the sun meant new territory, new challenge. Just so, it strikes me that a man can father a child but must *follow up* parenting for a lifetime—from daily chores, to guidance during adolescence, to discipline, empathy, and consistency in helping as she matures, to grandfatherly back-up during the golden years. This means talking with her, holding her, even being held by her and her family through a lifetime. Gentleness is not divided by gender, miles, or age.

Men have come a long way in loving partners and taking in strays, hearing out enemies and tolerating differences, feeling compassion for those less fortunate. Turning a frontier trope, a *real man* learns to walk the extra mile, shake the neighbor's hand, and work overtime around the kitchen; among Indians, he tells good stories, sings old songs, and sits down to laugh through the losses. So being a man down West, it seems at this grandparental age, takes a full heart, *cante ista*, the Lakota say, "seeing from the heart's eye."

Where are we today? There are surely many ways to be masculine out West, not all of them white-knuckled, gritty, or gut-checked. Since Chautauqua is a stump rite back home, grant me a few guiding precepts: Being a man on the frontier, by way of a child's needs or the misfortunes of others, is not a novel concept, though Americans have let some traditional fathering values slip in the ruckus over gender equity, tax breaks, sexual preference, and homeland security. As tribal and pioneer models intersect, no gender or culture has a lock on caring. To speak in moral terms, a man's strength can be tempered with kindness, and discipline does not work without compassion; indeed, courage has no value without clemency. Barack Obama calls this "disciplined hope."

Warriors coming home have worked toward these delicate balances of power and grace through the ages. "The swift and natural observation of a man," W. B. Yeats characterized a westering Odysseus, "as he is shaped by life." A man's integrity, intellect, and courage remain critical to our collective survival and going on, given the arrogances of power, mechanistic tools of destruction, and ill wills of declining empires. *Bring 'Em On* or *Wanted Dead or Alive* rattle like tin cups. Being a western man today is no less demanding than it ever was, but hopefully less taciturn or trigger-happy.

Over five centuries the western frontier has etched an exacting horizon, and changes are in full swing. Our sisters are counterbalancing tradition in role reversals—single mothers raising kids or solo women entering the managerial sweatshop. Women total nearly 65 percent of college enrollments today while many young men are being educated in the home, minding children, running the kitchen, and joining the community.

Let me put all this in terms of a traditional Lakota tale that I heard decades ago from Lionel Bordeaux, the president of Sinte Gleska College on the Rosebud reservation in South Dakota. Once there was a smartass duck who thought he would prove his solo toughness by not flying south with the others during winter migration. The plains winds blew, the temperatures plummeted below zero, and the snow piled over the forage. Pretty soon the hapless duck was starving and knew he had to fly south after his kin. The duck got right over a barnyard and passed out and fell to the ground. A cow was walking by and stopped and crapped on him. Under the warm manure the dumb duck came to and thought it was spring, so he started quacking. A hungry cat heard the noise and dug into the manure and ate the duck.

Now there are three tribal morals to this cautionary tale. Everyone who dumps on you is not your enemy. Anyone who pulls you out is not necessarily your friend. And if you find yourself safe and warm in a pile of *chesli*, that is, cow shit, keep your mouth shut.

Amen to that, brothers and sisters, down West.

Lee Ann Roripaugh

MOTHERLANDS AND MOTHER TONGUES: FIVE REFLECTIONS ON LANGUAGE AND LANDSCAPE

I. I WANT TO BE A COWBOY, BABY

Of course I want to be a cowboy. I have a cowboy hat, a brown plaid Western shirt with snap buttons, Lee blue jeans with a leather belt hand-tooled for me by my American grandfather, and sometimes I am allowed to wear one of my father's bolo ties. Dressed as a cowboy, I am gender ambiguous. It is one of my favorite outfits.

Of course I want to be a cowboy. I want to ride broncos in the rodeo like my father when he was young, bottle-feed orphaned sheep at the ranch my American grandparents used to own outside Lander, Wyoming, shoot rattlesnakes in their apple orchard. I wield my father's toy pistols from when he was a boy—in love with their realistic detailing and sinister heft—although I am forbidden to play with them outside. In the backyard of my parents' house, in Laramie, Wyoming, the Caragana trees snap and explode their seedpods in late August like cap guns, and I'm an outlaw crouching behind the Nanking cherry trees, fending off a hail of bullets. Inside, my father's manual Olivetti studio typewriter sounds like distant artillery fire.

Of course I want to be a cowboy, but with my thick dark hair, inherited from my Japanese mother, and my ambiguously mixed-race features, I am always, instead, the default Indian in playground games with other children. In elementary school, at Thanksgiving, I am never, ever a pilgrim. Each year, it somehow becomes obligatory that I wear my hair in braids and don a construction paper headband with an Elmer's-glued-on feather. It's not so much that I don't *want* to be an Indian, but rather the unspoken *impossibility* of my ever being a pilgrim—or a cowboy, which of course I *want* to be—that troubles me. It is through these gestures of obligatory categorization and exclusion that my tenuous state of never quite *belonging to* or *belonging in* the American West is constantly made apparent to me.

2. SNAPSHOTS

Cowboy is not the only mask I adopt, however. My childhood pictures show me wearing multiple costumes, in a bizarre array of highly stylized poses: prancing jazz-handed baton twirler in a pink-checked dress and a white headband, sailor-suited sailor, professor wearing my father's mortarboard and contemplating a copy of *Winnie the Pooh*, ballerina in a yellow tutu assuming the dying swan pose. Most of the pictures are taken on top of the dining room table, cleared off to function as a makeshift stage. The photo shoots are lengthy, tedious, and there's much poking, prodding, and primping. My father goes through rolls of film. My mother choreographs these photo sessions with the grim determination of a drill sergeant. The psychotically perky poses she insists I assume are obviously culled from vintage mid-century children's sweater pattern booklets such as *Clark*, *Spinnerin*, and *Bernat*—featuring well-groomed, well-mannered, dimpled and doe-eyed, wholesome *white* children. My mother consults these booklets heavily, along with a book in Japanese called *The American Way of Housekeeping*, as guidebooks for assimilation.

My mother is big on coaching. Before taking me to tea parties, she drills me beforehand, asking me potential questions, to which I deliver the answers she's provided for me ahead of time—answers occasionally accompanied by coquettish physical gestures she's also devised. (When wearing the cowboy outfit, for example, if someone asks my name, I'm supposed to turn around, one hand on outthrust hip in reference to the leather tag on my jeans, and exclaim, *Lee!* If someone asks what my father does, I'm supposed to reply, *My father's an Arthur!* It's supposed to be *author*, but sometimes things get confused between my mother's accent and the limitations of my own budding vocabulary.)

And so rather than being spontaneous or candid, picture-taking in my family becomes a highly performative, formal—and very Japanese?— affair. My mother is tense and critical, while I sulk in cranky boredom. But of course, there's much more at stake for my mother than the mere capturing of snapshots. In retrospect, I think she's clearly fashioning and manufacturing images—images intended to represent her own Americanness, or perhaps more importantly, *my* Americanness. When I think about these snapshots, I think of the underlying sense of strain, the feeling that making these images is terribly difficult work, that they are a product of trying too hard, that the *deliberation* that goes behind all the costuming, choreographing, and posing—rather than capturing the 1950s wholesome

Americana my mother seems to be insistently striving for—reveals instead the tricky and unspoken cultural fault lines underlying my parents' miscegenated marriage. (It is Laramie, Wyoming, early 1970s. It is post–World War II, post–Korean War. The Vietnam War flickers in menacing black-and-white footage on the television.)

As if this weren't enough, these images have to pass muster on two continents, for these are the pictures my mother also sends to her father, my Japanese grandfather, as representation and validation for the life she has chosen—with a "Yankee," no less—in America.

But still . . . where *am* I—indeed, *who* am I—in these snapshots, underneath these costumes, behind these masks?

3. GOOD LEE HUNTING

My father teaches me how to shoot: shotgun, rifle, handgun. In the fall, he takes me hunting: dove, sage grouse, antelope. I use the rifle and shotgun that belonged to my American grandmother, with a shortened stock for smaller arms, and my father makes cross-sticks to steady my rifle when hunting antelope at long distance through a telescope. I am an overly sensitive child, but I like to shoot and am fascinated by the biology of the gutting, the skinning, the dressing.

My American grandfather taught my father to shoot and took him hunting, and now my father has taught me to shoot and takes me hunting. I don't want to be a girl or a sissy about this. I want to please my father, make him proud. I am very troubled by the killing, but there is still a small part of me that is secretly pleased. Even in Wyoming, most of the girls in my junior high or high school classes typically don't go hunting with their fathers or brothers. Every fall, my father takes pictures of me in my orange hat and vest with my shotgun and my sage grouse, or my rifle and my antelope. It is a rite of passage. There are trophies. It is vaguely Hemingway-esque. One year drunk hunters swing by in their truck to admire my downed buck, and when they get close enough to see my braids sticking out from under my hat, they yell, *Goddamn, it's a girl*!

My father is a writer. I frequently fall asleep to the explosive clattering of his typewriter in the dining room as he writes late into the night. A novelist, short story writer, and poet, he will eventually become the poet laureate of Wyoming, and he refers to himself as a *cowboy poet*. Of course I want to be a cowboy poet, too. Whenever my father publishes a poem, he puts it on the refrigerator with a magnet, and I ask to have my crayoned drawings magnetized to the fridge as well. Soon I am obsessively writing—journals, poems, stories—and eventually my father lets me use one of his cast-off manual typewriters.

My father writes and teaches Western literature. His novels, stories, and poems deal with Wyoming ranch life, as well as the culture and landscape of the American West. In the same way I intuitively understand the element of gender and racial transgression inherent in shooting and hunting with my father—how many Asian-American girls, after all, are raised to go hunting in Wyoming with their fathers?—I also intuitively understand the element of gender and racial transgression inherent in my writing. Or maybe what I mean by this is that I intuitively understand that to write as my father writes, about the things my father writes about, is to write within a certain Western literary tradition, and from a subject position that is frequently male and typically white. It's not that I'm not given female authors and poets to read—because I am—or that I'm not given writers of color to read—because, once again, I am—but rather that there's no available literary mirror to reflect or speak to my jumbled nexus of subject positions: biracial Asian, growing up in the American West, slightly confused about gender, possibly queer. And so instead of following in my father's footsteps, I train to be a concert pianist. Asian-American girls *do* play the piano, after all! Years later, when I write my first poem containing something that resembles Asian-American content, I'm so confused by what I've done that I have to ask my mentor if it actually even *is* a poem.

It is during one of our hunting trips that my father tells me, for the first time, the story of my parents' marriage. How they met when my father was drafted into the army during the postwar occupation in Japan. He was assigned to work in the personnel office at Camp Ojima, where my mother had taken a job—apparently as somewhat of a lark and with the lackadaisical intent of *typing like the sound of rain dropping*. They began a secret courtship, then entered into a secret yearlong correspondence when my father returned to the United States. Following that year of separation, my father came back to spend a summer in Japan, during which time they resumed their secret courtship, and my father convinced my mother to run away with him—culminating in their eventual elopement at the end of that summer on August 6, 1955, ten years after the dropping of the atomic bombs. Later on, when I ask my mother why they decided to get married on August 6, she tells me it's because it was the day she *dropped the bomb on her father*. I'm never really sure if she's joking about this or not.

4. JAPANGLISH

My mother speaks Japanese to me when I am an infant and a toddler, because when I first start to talk, I speak a cryptic form of Japanglish apparently indecipherable to everyone but myself. My mother panics and immediately ceases speaking to me in Japanese. One of her fears has always been that I won't speak proper English. Given my father's profession, she feels my English-speaking skills will be under close scrutiny. She doesn't want to be blamed if I am English *handicapped*. Does it seem to her as if *her* English-speaking skills are under scrutiny? Does she feel, I wonder, English *handicapped*?

It's a strange thing, not being able to speak your mother's tongue. I do know a handful of words and phrases, mostly having to do with food, and when my mother's Japanese friends come to visit, they often forget to switch to English and ask me questions in Japanese, which I am somehow able to answer in English. My mother's surprised by this, asking me later how I know what they are saying. It's not that I can translate verbatim, by any means . . . at best, I only recognize a sprinkling of words here and there. It's difficult to explain, but somehow I instinctively *know* what the conversations are about.

The small amount of Japanese I do know falls much more easily, almost naturally, from my tongue than the German or French I end up studying in high school and college—perhaps this is from consistently having the intonations and rhythms of the Japanese language in my ear. Is it possible people come into the world "hard-wired" for a particular language? And if so, what does it mean to have given up a mother tongue one might otherwise have been destined to speak? And if language is in any way a filter through which we perceive and interact with the world, is it possible we turn into completely different people altogether when we speak a different language?

I've carried with me for a number of years now a marvelous discussion from an online Asian-American writers' group about how many of us, as children, experienced some type of early "thorniness" with a missing or lost second language. We went on to speculate that perhaps this was one of the things that informed, at least in part, our need to write. I love this notion of a second "lost" self—a Japanese-speaking self, a "ghostly double" self—whom I might be trying to recover through my writing. A second self ironically recovered only through an obsessive mastery of the English language. A second self who isn't divided into binaries: American or Japanese. A second self who can speak to her own mother in her mother's native tongue. But still, as much as I might try to write *toward* this second self, I also understand that such an act of recovery will never actually be possible.

The gaps in translation, the things that don't get said, are funny and awful at the same time. When my first book of poetry comes out in 1999, my mother takes the volume to her ESL class at the University of Wyoming to show her ESL buddies. One of her Chinese friends reads the first poem in the book, "Pearls." As a child, I used to love the sound of my mother speaking Japanese on the telephone. I thought it sounded so beautiful, like the sound of birds, maybe sparrows, and I used to think she knew how to speak the language of birds. Inside my head, I had a special name for it. I called it "bird talk." The poem "Pearls" was written in the voice of this child, and early on in the poem the speaker says her mother "does bird talk" when the Mormons come to the door. When my mother's Chinese ESL friend reads this line, she asks my mother, "Bird talk? Is she mean like pigeon?" My mother hears, and understands, this question to mean, "Is she mean like pidgin?" As in Pidgin English. And no amount of explanation on my part ever since has convinced my mother that this is *not* a poem in which I'm accusing her of speaking Pidgin English.

I would like to learn to speak Japanese. I would like to go to Japan someday. But at my age, the acquisition of a second language, hard-wired or not, is difficult and slow going. I have a Rosetta Stone program for Japanese that is quite good, which I work with, on and off. But although I have made some small progress, I can still only say the most trivial and absurd things. *O-hayo gozai-masu.* Good morning. *Sakana wa oyoide masu.* The fish is swimming. My mother is getting older, and time is running out. How will I ever be able to ask her the important questions? How will I be able to understand her answers? Will she always be asking me things in Japanese, and will I always have to answer back in English—leaving to faith that the part that gets lost in translation will somehow be instinctively *known*?

There's a children's book in which a girl's favorite doll is magically given the ability to speak for one hour, and during that hour the girl and her doll have to say all the things that went unsaid before and that will otherwise have to go unsaid afterward. I loved that book. Lately, I think maybe I loved that book so much because I was a girl whose Japanese mother stopped sharing things with her in Japanese because she wanted her daughter to speak only perfect American English. I sometimes wonder if I could speak Japanese fluently for one hour, what my mother and I would say to each other. Sometimes I call her on the phone and practice my Pidgin Japanese on her. *O-hayo gozai-masu,* I say. *Sakana wa oyoide masu.* She laughs at my poor Japanese, answers me in chipped English.

5. HAUNTED BY LANDSCAPE

I am haunted by landscape, by the terrifying beauty of mountains, in particular, which I miss with the sort of internal, gaping, physical ache typically reserved for a lost beloved. I think best, and feel the most clarity, in the emotional and intellectual expansiveness of open sky. Is it possible for people to be "imprinted" early on by a particular landscape? And if so, what does it mean to leave, or give up, such a motherland? And if landscape is in any way a filter through which we perceive and interact with the world, is it possible we turn into completely different people when we move to an alternate landscape?

And yet there is an anxiety, too, in this landscape that haunts me. It is a gorgeous and occasionally inhospitable terrain upon which it is difficult to find a foothold, absent the usual tropes of outlaw gunslinger, pioneer, colonizer, entrepreneur. Indeed, it is a terrain upon which it seems inappropriate to assert the right to *claim* a nonindigenous foothold or place.

Growing up, I am haunted by the shadows of Heart Mountain, where 10,617 Japanese-Americans were interned inside barbed wire fences and monitored by armed guards during World War II. I am haunted by the racial slurs thrown my way on the elementary school playground. I am haunted by the memory of the doctor's son who lived across the street and who molested me when I was nine and who continued to live across the street from me until I finally fled Laramie for college. Years later, I am haunted by the image of Matthew Shepard's broken, pistol-whipped body tied to a fence and left for dead in my hometown. Laramie, the Gem City of the Plains.

I sometimes dream of this landscape, and it's half-nightmare, half-rapture. In a blog post detailing one of these dreams from last year, I wrote:

> Coasting down foothills into Laramie. My father's old gray Jeep: vinyled and squared, filigreed in lace cuffs of rust.
> Rockies' chilled crust thrusts up hard, distorting the horizon.
> Perspective all askew: Mountains much too large and much too blue, looming up much too close too fast. I am not a child, but I slide back and forth in the middle of the front bench seat, knees jogging the gearshift. The parents in the car are not my parents. *Alco's* cracked neon on the left closed down years ago. Lost effervescence of wind-bobbled balloons frantically bubbling in the no-longer-there car lot. Clouds spill down off the mountains, twisting into dangerous, spiraling wraiths.
> *Are those tornadoes?* I ask.

They flame in the too-loud wind like black dry ice, slivered with bright threads of lightning.
Is it war? I ask.
They dervish off the sagebrushed plains toward the road.
You have to stop. You have to pull over, I say. *I'm not wearing a safety belt.*
The sound of unfurling metal, burning, shattered glass, hot wind. Everything goes blank.
An eyelid blinks open to sunlight, emptiness, the heart-shaped white behinds of curious antelope retreating. Empty car, empty highway, everyone else gone. Mountains' bright prong ringing an empty town. Radio's static crackle, then chipped advertisements, like faded billboards in the wind:
it's Joe Albertson's supermarket . . .
on a sesame seed bun . . .
you're in good hands with All State . . .

I can't let it go. The landscape is too much a part of me and therefore an indelible part, too, of who I am as a writer. My relationship to the landscape, though, is not one of inscription, engraving, or carving out and conquering through language. While these histories, mythologies, narratives, and texts clearly inhabit, mark, and inform this landscape, my relationship to them, for many reasons, is vexed. Yet even though this landscape has been exploited as a fantasy space upon which to enact and write familiar frontier tropes, I think it simultaneously *resists* them, too—serving as a fantasy space in which standard paradigms can just as easily be interrogated, deconstructed, complicated, and unraveled, thereby allowing room for alternate, erased, marginalized, or new kinds of histories, mythologies, narratives, and texts to emerge and interact.

I'm a hybrid in every possible sense of the word—biracial, bisexual, combined of East Asian and American Western sensibilities—and as such, I can't help but be the sort of writer whose interaction with the American West is complicated by these aspects of my identity. And although I am never entirely an Asian-American writer, or a Western writer, or even a queer writer, I am consistently an interrogator, a deconstructor, a complicater, and an unraveler—one who remains haunted by this liminal fantasy space, this frontier, this landscape with its hyperbolic vastnesses and dangerously stunning beauty. I cannot let it go.

I was with a hot girl on a hot August night in Casper, Wyoming, 1975, in the backseat of a car at Mile-High Drive-in, when I heard the lines of dialog that distracted me greatly from the matter at hand. I lost my concentration as well as my place, so to speak.

The lines came from the clunky steel speaker, which stretched from a post by a cord to the car window. The speaker was turned down, so as not to distract those of us in the backseat as well as my buddy and his girl in the front. All I knew about the movie playing was that it was the second one. Months of drive-in movie dates had taught me that if things weren't cooking in the backseat by the second movie, they never would. And things were cooking.

I was to be a sophomore in high school. My worldview existed almost entirely of girls, wrestling, fishing, and pointless vandalism involving alcohol, tobacco, and firearms. (In fact, my group of pals liked to joke that the ATF was named in honor of *us*.)

In the back of my mind (really far back at that moment), I was considering signing up for the high school newspaper. And I was in the midst of reading *Catch-22* on lunch breaks from my job on a sheep ranch outside of town, which was blowing my mind open. The book, I mean.

But that night, despite the fact that I didn't really want to listen, I kept hearing these *lines* from the speaker:

From Slim Pickens, playing modern-day stock detective Henry Beige: "Ah man, take a look at this slug. This is from a .50 Sharps buffalo rifle. Damn, this is getting downright romantic . . ."

From Elizabeth Ashley, the sultry and whiskey-voiced wife of the rancher whose cattle are being shot and butchered with a chain saw: "Come on, goddamit. I want some Gothic ranch action around here! I want some desire under the elms! I want to see some smoldering blazes down at the old corral!"

From the American Indian father of Sam Waterston, one of the rustlers: "There is a sickness among our people. It's a sickness here worse than alcohol or dope. It's the pickup truck death. And there's no cure for it . . ."

And I remember disengaging from the hot girl, sitting up and pasting my hair back into place (I had hair then) and trying to squint through the steamed-up front windshield at the screen.

Something in this movie was connecting with me in a primal and completely unanticipated way.

I wondered out loud, "What *is* this?"

"Shut up," said my buddy in the front seat. His girl said something worse. So did mine.

"What is the name of this movie?"

More abuse.

I turned up the volume on the speaker for a Jimmy Buffett song called "Livingston Saturday Night."

You got your Tony Lamas on, your jeans pressed tight,
You take a few tokes make you feel all right . . .
Pickup's washed and you just got paid.
With any luck at all you might even get laid.
'Cause they're pickin' and a-kickin' on a Livingston Saturday night . . .

"Did you hear that?" I asked, after a line about "snuff queens." Hell, I *knew* some snuff queens: girls who dipped Copenhagen. I'm not so sure my hot date wasn't one of them. She *was* a ranch girl, after all.

They kicked me out of the car, which was fine with me. The hot girl smoldered alone in the back seat. My buddy and his girl resumed what they were doing.

I remember sitting in the gravel in front of the car, leaning back against the bumper. I sipped a warm beer and cradled the speaker like a baby and watched this movie that spoke to me in ways I couldn't believe. It was as if this second feature at the drive-in, this nameless movie I had never heard of, had been made for me personally.

Which still holds true to this day, I'm afraid to say.

Here's the *Wikipedia* entry:

Rancho Deluxe is a comedy western film that was directed by Frank Perry and released in 1975. Jeff Bridges and Sam Waterston star as two cattle rustlers in modern-day Montana who plague a wealthy ranch owner, played by Clifton James.

The film also stars Harry Dean Stanton, Richard Bright, Elizabeth Ashley, and, as the aging detective Harry Beige hired to find the rustlers, Slim Pickens.

Jimmy Buffett contributed the music, and performed within the film in a scene set at a country/western bar . . .

The script was by novelist Thomas McGuane . . .

It's that last part that's especially formative.

I doubt even my favorite novelist and literary stylist Tom McGuane (who lives and ranches in southern Montana) himself would say *Rancho Deluxe* was a great movie. It bombed, and reviews were wildly mixed. Roger Ebert wrote, "I don't know how this movie went so disastrously wrong, but it did, and the story must be a sad one." *Ouch.*

McGuane must have liked it some, though, because he told essentially the same story—*tight-assed ranchers hire a stock detective to root out happy-go-lucky cattle rustlers*—in *Missouri Breaks*, with Jack Nicholson and Marlon Brando. But I digress.

The thing about *Rancho Deluxe* for me, on that hot August night, was it provided clarity and answers to questions that were burbling up in me. I had real curiosity about this place I grew up in—Wyoming during an energy boom. Think cowboy hats and hard hats, our bucking bronco license plate on energy trucks coursing down the highways, three-generation ranches being sold to stockbrokers and movie stars, cows standing idly by, chewing grass while drilling rigs rammed more pipe into the ground.

Which made me wonder, was this still the West, or not? And if not, what the hell was it? And if one tends to kind of like that Old West rhythm and drivel—as I did and do—how does one square it with the postmodern world?

Rancho Deluxe helped to show me the way.

The laid-back, almost meandering story line of the movie featured items, issues, and attitudes that—for the first time for me in movies, music, or literature—lived in the world I actually occupied. It was filmed on location in Livingston, Montana. We're talking pickups, cowboy hats, gun racks, snuff queens, out-of-state landowners, prize seed bulls, vast lonely landscapes, chain saws that won't start when the pressure's on, ranch hands who were formerly hot-comb models or telemarketers, fly-fishing from drift boats, and bawdy barrel-racing cowgirls. For the first time, the Old West and New West were fused together into something hip, funny, sarcastic, and startlingly original.

And the writing!

The characters in the movie are from the West or of the West, but I noticed something right off that has stuck with me always: the only characters who spoke in "Westernisms" (dropping the "g's" off of words, using colorful and corny cowboy phrases like, "Let's git down the road a piece to Ole Wyomin'") were the ranch owner (John Brown), who'd sold his Eastern beauty parlor empire to retire on his new Montana spread, and Slim Pickens, who really *was* authentic and used his corny talk as a ruse. The other characters spoke clearly, without accent, in complete and brilliant sentences.

Unlike characters in so much fiction about the contemporary West (and certainly most movies), the characters in *Rancho Deluxe* were of the modern world and accepted it, but still chose to live and celebrate the place. They weren't trying to strike it rich and get out. They were comfortable in their own skins, and they accepted and embraced the unique culture without a second thought.

And unlike cinematic or literary portrayals of the contemporary West (still, sadly, to this day), the characters didn't grunt and spit and kick at the dirt *jes' tryin' to find the right words to say* or speak in a slightly drawling Southern accent, as if Georgia was in the next county. They talked like real people I knew: clear, literate, with a nod toward modernity and at least a dollop of wisdom.

The American Indian antihero (Waterston) in *Rancho Deluxe* didn't speak woodenly without conjunctions or in that sappy romantic child-of-nature hogwash so often used by novelists or screenwriters. He talked like a real person: funny, down-to-earth, self-deprecating.

Say what you will about folks from Wyoming and Montana, but we don't talk like rubes.

Thomas McGuane opened up a new and exciting front for me. After that night at the drive-in, I started reading everything he'd written. And I found out it wasn't just me. He was nominated for a National Book Award, and Saul Bellow called him "a language star." I found out he studied under the brilliant Wallace Stegner, so I read him as well. His fellow students and colleagues were of similar cloth: Jim Harrison, Richard Brautigan, Edward Abbey, Ken Kesey, Wendell Berry, Larry McMurtry. Westerners. I read them all.

The protagonist in my novel *Three Weeks to Say Goodbye* is a Montanan named Jack McGuane. In tribute.

McGuane, like his gang of literary mischief-makers, accepted the modern West as it was and wrote about it. He was (and is) openly contemptuous of the phony and romantic vision of the West still propagated by the poseurs among us. And he did so in novels, stories, and screenplays that were (and are) equal parts comic, sardonic, bleak, bitter, knowing, and self-realized. He writes about real people in the real West as it was and is. People who have jobs, problems, and dreams and who are not obsessed with the mythic West of the 1880s.

Or, as the movie poster said:

Oh give me a home, with a low interest loan,
A cowgirl and two pickup trucks.
A color TV, all the beer should be free,
And that, man, is Rancho Deluxe.

Back when I was very small and my father was a giant and always in a hurry, I remember trotting along at his side, trying to keep up with his long-legged stride. I have come across such scenes in fiction, and I have also heard friends describe similar experiences from their own lives. Often, the father is not only a giant but also a bad guy, oblivious to his little girl's needs, or consciously insensitive, or downright cruel. But in my own memory, the sun shines on a slant and the grass is still wet with dew. The day vibrates with purpose and I feel a strength in my legs, a capacity in my lungs, a competence that, looking back now, I realize was completely at odds with my age. My father is going to work, and he has asked me to come along.

Perhaps we are heading for the shop, where my little hands will be able to fit the grease gun to a nipple deep in the baler, a task that had left my father in a sputtering rage the night before. Or maybe we are heading to the pickup to take salt and mineral to the cattle. I'll "ride shotgun" to get the gates and I'll use my own pocketknife to open the sacks of supplement. Or perhaps I am older, ten or twelve, and we saddle up and head out for the high country to find a bull missing from the roundup. The critter isn't in the first pasture we check, or the second, or the third. By the time we find him, sick with foot rot and on the fight, my father's colt has played out and is no longer useful. He stands to the side as I do the hard and dangerous work of getting the bull headed home. The bull tries to take me time and again, sometimes feinting and other times charging. Twice he hits my stirrup but my horse is already pivoting out of the way and we escape unharmed. If he becomes too dangerous, my father will suggest we leave him for another day, but my horse is working well and I am one with him in this intricate and dangerous dance. Finally, the bull turns down the trail and limps off like it was his own idea all along. We arrive at a neighbor's corral at dusk, after having ridden thirty miles or more. We put the bull in a pen and call my mother to pick us up. A cloudburst explodes just as she arrives, and we slip-slide the gumbo road home through thunder and lightning and blinding rain as my father tells her how he couldn't have gotten the bull out of the hills without me. It's true. If I hadn't been along, he would have come home empty-handed. We both know this, and it makes us feel good.

Time passes. Twenty-five years slide by. Sun plays in this memory, too, but this time it is high overhead and relentless. I am newly married, sitting on the stoop of my home in Salt Lake City with Kristi, a dear friend who has come to visit. She and I are catching up, talking about this and that, and the conversation meanders to our childhoods. "I don't remember a single time in all my growing up," she says, "that my father, or any man for that matter, took me seriously—or even really saw me." And then she starts to weep.

We have been close for many years, Kristi and I, and we know much about the hurts and joys of each other's lives. Still, I have never known her to express such naked pain before. I reach out to her in that hot noon sun, and it strikes me for the first time that many, even most, women our age must have had similar experiences. I have my own hidden wounds, many of them caused by men and some by my father, but being consistently dismissed when I was a girl does not number among them.

Simply by closing my eyes, I can place myself in the dining room, halfway between the kitchen and the living room of the big ranch house in Wyoming where I was raised. I can hear the deep rumble of the men talking in the living room and the quiet murmur of the women in the kitchen. And I can feel, even now, the pull, the inevitable attraction, toward the real talk, the hard clean stories of the men.

Every gathering ended up like this, with the men in one room and the women in another. No men ventured into the kitchen but some women found a place in the living room. These were the women who worked outside, who could handle a rope, who knew about the treatment for diphtheria or poison weed. Most of them will admit what I tell you now: the softer talk of women bored us. It was all recipes and babies, a drone of necessary but unremarkable information. Just family stuff. The men's stories were about horses and cows, weather and danger. They were about competence and consequence, about what happens when you make a wrong step, and how you recover or you don't. The air was full of raucous laughter and palpable respect. Now you tell me: given a choice, which room would you choose?

I must have been a wild one as a child. For the first two or three years that I attended our rural neighborhood's one-room school, I was the only girl. Even before that, I hung out with my older brother, Blade, and his friends. I learned to ride, to fight, to shoot, to swear. I remember wanting to be a boy, and I remember thinking it unfair that the boys tried to keep me out of things simply because I was a girl. But I also remember feeling a certain conceit because I was a girl and I got in anyway. I was certainly aware of the differences between us and I remember noting with pride, though probably only to myself, that I had seen every boy in the neighborhood pee, but they hadn't seen me. I'm not talking about peeping, sneaking around in the bushes, trying to cop a view. Because I was "one of the boys," they answered the call of nature unself-consciously. I was not enough one of the boys to do the same. The fact that I kept score indicates that I wasn't really one of the boys at all.

And then there were the times I had girls to play with. With boys, I rode horses. With girls, we actually *became* horses, and I can still remember those magical moments of transcendence when we first urged our horses into comfortable lopes. I was a chubby child, but my awkwardness fell away when I was on horseback. My mount and I became a single creature, sleek and strong and graceful. We inhabited a world of perfection and in-finite horizons. This is what the boys didn't know, would never know, be-cause however much we wanted to step into their world, they didn't give a hoot about ours. There was dismissal in this, but also freedom.

While we were still in grade school, my best friend from town, Carol, and I rode fifty miles from the ranch to Cheyenne Frontier Days, the annual rodeo. We took two days and spent the interven-ing night at a ranch halfway. Our exploit landed us on the front page of the paper, and afterward people asked us if we hadn't been afraid, out there all alone. Of course not, we answered. We weren't alone. We had each other and we had our horses (and, after all, we'd followed the road). If the truth were known, I suspect we were a little disappointed that the trip had been so uneventful. But we basked in our mobility, and in others' perception that we were daring girls.

A few years later, when I was twelve or thirteen, I wanted to break a colt. I was offered one out of our mare and stud bunch. These colts were notori-ously hard to handle; only a handful had ever been broken and many ended up as bucking stock in rodeos. But I picked out a big bay yearling whose mother, the men said, had more sense than the others. They roped him and tied him to a snubbing post in the round corral. It took me the rest of the day to sweet talk my way up to him. I'd take a step toward him, he'd quiver with fear and the whites would show all around his eyes; then he would explode, fighting the rope, twisting and kicking and striking. I'd take half a step back and keep talking to him until he calmed down. In time, I'd take another step forward. Finally he let me touch him for a second before he went wild; a bit later he let me rest my hand on his shoulder. By the end of the day, I could stroke his neck, talk to him as long as I wanted, tell him how handsome he was and that he had no reason to be afraid. In another two or three days, I could walk up to him loose in the corral.

That summer, I taught him to lead, to lunge, to be comfortable under a saddle. The next summer, I started to ride him and he soon turned into a sweet and willing horse. Some time later, I learned that our foreman had bet another of the hired men a hundred dollars that I'd never get on. I didn't like the foreman. He was of the old "kick 'em hard, buck 'em out, and wear 'em down" school, and I was convinced this was the reason so few of the colts had turned out. But as pleased as I was to think he had lost his money, I was even happier to realize that another of the men had backed me.

If those years had their moments of pride, they also had their awkward epiphanies. I remember a day when we were moving cattle and I rode along behind the herd, swearing effusively. I used words I had learned from the boys, who had learned them from the men, and I used words I'd learned from the men directly, since I worked with them almost as much as the boys did. I was having a great time, chirping and ki-yipping and cussing as cowboys are wont to do when they ride behind cows, when suddenly I broke off mid-syllable. What stopped me? As I look back now, I simply don't know. It's as if I suddenly heard myself and was shocked, which means that I must have caught some clue wafting on the wind from the men around me, or even from the universe at large, that my behavior was inappropriate. It's not that I quit swearing from that moment on (I still swear more than, say, my husband), but I changed from being truly foul-mouthed to indulging in only an occasional "shit" or "damn."

A second memory: one day in school, Blade and I got into a terrible fight. This must have been during the years when I was still the only girl. At any rate, we were both young enough that we were evenly matched in strength, something that would soon change forever. I had him pinned to the floor and I brandished a ruler with which I intended to strike him. The sun glinted off its metal edge, and in my memory, it loomed as lethal as a saber. I suddenly became aware of my own violence, and let the ruler clatter to the floor. I don't know how the fight ended, but neither of us sustained mortal wounds. And I don't remember for sure if that was the last time I ever fought a boy, but I rather suspect that it was.

And a third recollection: my family went to a party at the Hirsig Ranch.

It might have been Christmas or perhaps the gathering after a brand-ing. The whole neighborhood was there, as well as several families from town. I jumped at the chance to play with the Hirsigs' two daughters, both younger than I, and the half-dozen town girls of various ages. We ran in a pack. Buddy, the Hirsig girls' father, was younger than my own and more playful. He was Marlboro man handsome and had infinite patience. We were all crazy about him. At one point, we swarmed around, begging him to pick us up. When my turn came, I crawled up into his lap, as I had seen other girls do, and I snuggled up against him. I remember distinctly stroking his cheek. And then suddenly I grew hot with shame and slunk down, only to be replaced by another girl. Again, what happened? Buddy did nothing wrong, nothing lascivious. But where did I learn my own seductive behavior? What made me suddenly conscious of it? Why did I feel such shame? It was as if I suddenly became aware of the difference be-tween being a tomboy, an identity of which I was passionately proud, and being a daddy's girl, *any* daddy's girl. At some level I must have recognized that I could cuss (mildly) or I could coo, but I couldn't do both.

These memories are united by an underlying current of eroticism and by my growing awareness of the threat of exile. If my friend Kristi suffered from being dismissed, I realize now that I was learning not to garner too much attention. More than anything else, I wanted access to the world of men, which is to say, in my particular circumstance, to the world of na-ture and animals and physical work. If I were too wild or too sexy, access could be denied or could become dangerous, facts that served to smooth my rough edges.

Looking back, I realize that I was often confused by the mixed mes-sages that every girl receives. (Boys receive mixed messages, too, though the messages are different.) My parents encouraged me to become as com-petent outdoors as my brother, and yet I also understood that I must be quieter about that competence, just as in the classroom I shouldn't raise my hand too quickly or let it be known if I had aced a test. I watched my great-aunt Marie manage her ranch with a similar subterfuge. "What do you think we ought to do today?" she'd ask the men when she lined out the day's work. If they didn't suggest what she thought needed doing, she would tenderly, mysteriously, nudge the conversation around until they came up with the idea she had in mind all along. In the world where I was raised, a woman could do anything she wanted as long as nobody noticed.

Where was my mother in all this? The short answer is, in the house. She was not a tomboy, horses frightened her, she did not particularly enjoy hard physical labor. But neither was she a typical housewife (whatever that is). She was a good-enough housekeeper and an excellent cook. She also kept the books and made out the payroll, did much of the hiring, drove to town for parts. She belonged to service clubs and lobbied for the Stock Grower's Association. When I was in fifth grade, she started teaching our one-room school.

In retrospect, she was a remarkably self-contained woman. She never minded staying alone in our house fifty miles from town when my father left on business; whatever worry she felt when one of us came in late from riding, she managed to conceal. If she were to describe the partnership she shared with my father in business terms, she would probably have given herself the title of executive secretary; he was the CEO, but she knew she was essential. She also kept a certain part of her life for herself, through friendships and reading. She loved both conversation and ideas; she subscribed to a variety of magazines and a book club, and I remember once she took a correspondence course from the Metropolitan Museum of Art.

Though my mother was not herself an outdoorsy woman, she supported my tomboy ambitions. Since both Blade and I worked outside, she divided the domestic chores evenly between us, and she never tried to make me into a little lady (though I do remember her once sinking down in exhaustion in a Montgomery Ward dressing room when we were shopping for school clothes and I threw a particularly obnoxious fit about having to try on a dress). She greeted my advances in cowboy craft and daring with the same enthusiasm as she did those of my brother.

As much as I loved participating in the world of men, I also loved my mother's world, which was softer and gentler and much more intimate. We could talk about anything—work, men, sex, poetry, higher mathematics, baking—and we spent hours together in the kitchen cooking or in the car driving the long road to town. But my mother's world was distinct in my mind from the more generalized world of women, something I imagined as much more boring, filled as it was reputed to be with babble about babies and recipes and other uninteresting stuff. My mother disparaged this world, as did most ranch women I knew. I thought this conceit particular to ranch culture until I left it and found that many women— including those who would never have deemed themselves tomboys— professed a similar superiority to mundane feminine concerns. It was as if we could believe in our own value, and that of a few handpicked friends, only in contrast to "women" who, as a group, didn't interest us much.

In her short stories and memoirs, Mary Clearman Blew, herself ranch-raised in Montana, often describes a certain sort of rancher's daughter who shadows her father and is his "boy." These girls are usually quiet, competent, slim-hipped, sexless. I recognize them; if I was never as quiet as some instinct told me I should be, androgyny still bought me safe passage. I started out working with my father but I soon began working with the other men, something that was possible—and comfortable—because I simply denied the possibility of sparks.

For the most part, it worked. In my entire working life, I have had only two uncomfortable encounters. One was with a young man my father had fired earlier in the day. I didn't know about his dismissal and was working with my colt in the meadow when he approached me. We made small talk for a while and then he followed me when I took the horse back to the barn. I grained the colt and turned him out. When I hung up the halter, the young man cornered me. I was scared but also excited; we had never worked together, but I had noticed him from a distance and I found him incredibly handsome. He took off my glasses and said, "You aren't so bad looking without these things," a line that didn't quite meet my young adolescent image of romance. Then he took off his hat and placed it on my head, saying, "Where I hang my hat is my home." I gave his hat back to him—I'd like to think without hesitation—and said, "This house doesn't take boarders," or some such line, not bad for a rank beginner. Then I hightailed it out of the barn.

The memory still gives me the creeps. Even before I learned that my father had fired him, I must have recognized that his advance had less to do with attraction than with simmering hostility. The moment radiated with a potential for ugliness. I escaped unscathed, but the experience left me aroused and confused; at a deeper level, it also warned me of the dangers that lurked around the slightest departure from androgyny.

The second experience came during my junior year of college when I returned to school after my mother's sudden death. Her loss had shattered me, and I suppose a certain vulnerability leaked through my careful armor. A professor made a pass at me. I still remember how shocked I was, and how upset. As before, with the hired man, I felt I was somehow at fault. I fled his office and from that point on, I avoided him. He had been a mentor and important advisor. Now I dropped out of his class and changed my major. This last step I had planned to do anyway, but the experience reminded me of what was at stake when sex got mixed up with things.

It was not, in my particular worldview, that sensuality was not allowed. *Flirting* was the problem, not romance itself. From ninth grade on, I almost always had a boyfriend; those times I did not and was "available" were excruciating. How I connected with boyfriends in the first place is somewhat of a mystery. I was not one of those girls who drew male attention from afar. Instead, I almost always connected with my boyfriends within the context of shared interests or work—through the high school speech program, or in college seminars, or later, at professional conferences. There, I followed unwritten rules. Our involvement could not threaten my work. In other words, we had to be peers; I could never have gotten involved with someone I worked *for* rather than *with*. The move from collegiality to kissing was always painful for me, and I was terrifically relieved when that period of limbo came to an end. Safe within the sanction of an acknowledged relationship, I was at ease with my own sensuality. And outside that relationship, I was "taken" and therefore sexless—which meant it was once again safe to work with men. A primary relationship, in other words, let me move freely in the rest of my life; based on such utilitarian concerns, it's not surprising that my love life was a shambles. I was in my mid-thirties before I felt secure enough to be unpartnered, which, ironically, seemed to be the necessary precursor to meeting a man who could be a true partner and peer.

I was not the only tomboy I knew throughout my girlhood. In time, the two Hirsig girls started school, and Jennie Mai Bonham moved with her family to a ranch nearby. The four of us formed our own small gaggle of gutsy girls, roping and riding and working for wages. As my world expanded, I met others. We had our conceits. We could move comfortably in the world of men, and we knew what secrets we needed to keep in order to get along. We claimed our places among women, too, often with a certain sense of superiority that we learned from our mothers.

In time, I found my way from that one-room school in Wyoming to Yale. The summer after I graduated in 1977, I returned to the ranch for the restorative grace of hard physical work. One Saturday I went to a bull sale with my great-aunt Marie and we watched a family I will call the Browns bid on a bull. "Sold!" the auctioneer said, "To Jim Brown."

"And Jane Brown," Jim's wife piped up. A self-conscious twitter ran through the crowd; after the sale, as people gathered outside for ribs and baked beans, they joked with Jane, but the humor masked a palpable level of discomfort. Jane worked side by side with her husband and everyone knew it. She was often acknowledged for it. But she had *asked* for recognition, and some unwritten rule had been broken.

Like Jane, many of the women at that sale worked outside in virtually every capacity. They broke horses, they worked cows, they bought bulls, they decided what equipment the ranch needed and they knew how to run it. They took pride in their strength and confidence. But many also felt the tenuousness of their position, for they seldom had a bedrock right to the land. If they were a daughter, they had less chance of inheriting the ranch; if they were hired hands, they had fewer opportunities for paid employment; if they were spouses, estates taxes were biased against them; if they were owners, they needed the cooperation of male colleagues.

Men were expected to work outside; to greater or lesser degree, women were "allowed." And if permission could be granted, it could also be withheld or retracted. A rebellious daughter could be sent home to do the dishes; an "uppity woman" could lose the cooperation she needed from her employer, husband, ranch hand, or banker. Women had good reason not to draw attention to themselves.

But there was another side to this reticence, and it is harder to nail down. Many of us liked that male world with its clear rules and apparent lack of sentiment. We didn't want to draw the distinctions that would separate us from it. And we also liked that second world we inhabited, the one the men knew so little about. We had our secrets and our power. If work outside was a privilege, it was also a choice, something our brothers seldom enjoyed. Bound by fewer traditions, we could exercise more range in how we chose to tackle any given task. And if we could escape the drudgery of domesticity for the pleasure of work outdoors, at times we also escaped the drudgery of work outdoors for the pleasures of the kitchen. We had a place to go with our doubts and also with our secret joys, an alternative and softer terrain. We knew the limitations but also the freedom of being effective but unsung.

Some ranch women wanted recognition; others wanted to stay in the shadows. The truth is, many of us wanted both and in any case, the world was changing radically around us. The year of the bull sale, 1977, was also the year that *The Women's Room*, the best-selling feminist novel by Marilyn French, came out and marked the spread of a contemporary women's movement into suburbia and small-town America. And though rural women often disparaged the language of the women's movement, they forwarded its agenda on their own terms. When I was a child, I knew of no ranch women in positions of recognized authority. By the end of the seventies, they were being elected to public office, teaching on university faculties, and serving on the boards of banks and stock growers groups. In 1985, Jo Ann Smith, a Florida rancher, was elected president of the National Cattlemen's Association; four years earlier, Sandra Day O'Connor, raised on a ranch in Arizona, had been named to the United States Supreme Court.

Some years ago, I joined ranch friends for dinner in Jackson Hole, in the shadow of Wyoming's Teton Range. Mary Mead and Margy Wilson were a generation older than I and they had experienced the evolution of ranch women's roles firsthand. Mary ran the family ranch and had served in executive positions with the Wyoming Stock Growers. In 1990, she waged a spirited, if unsuccessful, bid for governor. She was a force in the state. Margy, raised near where I grew up in the southeastern part of the state, saw the family ranch go to her brother, but she was a partner in a drugstore in Wyoming and owned a macadamia nut farm in Hawaii.

But that day we didn't talk about professional successes. Mary and Margy had just come in from working cows, and on the way home they had ridden through a meadow of yearling heifers. On a whim, they dismounted, wrapped their horses' reins around a fence post, walked out to the center of the meadow, and lay down. The ground was cool even in the warm October sun, and the low autumn light made everything golden. Mary and Margy lay there, looking at the sky, not talking. In a few moments, a heifer came over to sniff them. Then another came, and then another. Soon, a dozen young cows sniffed the two women who lay still, trying not to laugh, looking up at all those pairs of long white eyelashes, listening to the heifers' soft huffing, taking a pure and sensual joy at being objects of curiosity. This is the secret life of girls—and just one of our many conceits.

When pine beetles arrive in a lodgepole forest, they burrow into the pines and nest their eggs inside. If the trees are healthy, their sap can slow and even prevent this drilling. If the trees are weakened by drought, they cannot ward it off. If the winter is cold enough and the timing is right, the larvae hatched from the eggs will die, trapped inside the pines. If the winter is too warm, the larvae will survive into the spring and more beetles will emerge and attack other trees, and soon, if the drought and the warmth continue, the forest will die. The pines turn brown. The best hope then is that the pines burn before they fall. If they burn, the forest will clear itself and regenerate. If they fall before they burn, the forest becomes a ruin. Downed trees, if they burn, may render the topsoil sterile for a few years or maybe more; one ranger I encounter says that downed trees are less likely to catch flame, and so instead, the collapse of the forest may create an impassable maze, and the big life sustained by the forest—the moose, the elk, the bear—will depart, and the forest will lie dead.

In 2000 I began driving south out of Wyoming a few times a summer, to Grand Lake and Winter Park, and I could watch the spread of the beetle kill in the West, massive and inexorable, thinking words like *massacre* and *catastrophe*, words the newspapers also used to describe the millions of dying acres, the beetles heading north, until one drive in 2008 I saw it at Chimney Park, on the Wyoming side of the border, and read, later that summer, that by 2012, 90 percent of the lodgepoles in the Medicine Bow forest I live alongside would be dead, the old alabaster thrust of the Snowy Range encircled by a sea of brown. Because of course the state line means nothing, and my ability to think it did was magical in the bad sense; because the drought and the warming air were here too, and ever more difficult to look away from.

On that dying route south lies Granby, Colorado, and in Granby in 2004, a man constructed a tank out of a bulldozer. The inside of the tank was perfectly enclosed, without windows, and equipped with a video feed and gun ports. The man felt he had suffered obscure but grievous wrongs at the hands of the local government. One day he permanently sealed himself inside the tank and drove into town, where he bulldozed the town hall, the local library, and the newspaper office, among other buildings. One of the Denver papers ran pictures of cops standing on top of the tank firing uselessly at the hull. When the driver was done, he shot himself inside the thing he had made. No one else was hurt.

My friend Gary and I talked a lot about this man that year. One night a few weeks after the event, I was with Gary and his wife Kelly in their RV, driving south to Winter Park, and when we got to Granby, Gary pulled off the highway and drove the RV through the dark to each of the sites the tank had hit, the wreckage shining in the RV's high beams. The next day I caught a ride home with someone else and Gary returned to Granby. What happened there spoke to him. Me too.

Someone Gary talked to said that a few locals were aware the man was building the tank, saw him at work during that long year of construction and intent. Why didn't they intervene, we asked later, and I tended to think they were familiar enough with that kind of grief to know it can't be interrupted. I'm not sure what drew Gary to the story, but for myself, I know that I am interested in the way some people can find forms of expression for their sense of loss that I can only recognize as such in the aftermath and can never imagine for myself. I know what it feels like to have plenty of violence inside, but my expressions of it have always been unoriginal—gunning the old Ford Bronco through ditches at the stable, flipping the three-wheeler as a teenager, experimenting, in my adulthood, with various forms of aloneness as extreme as I could make them. But all that feels pretty mundane compared to the extravagance and creativity of the acts in Granby. I feel a little awe. I think of the tank as a kind of shrine, a shrine to the man's anger and to his losses, losses that must have felt tangible although they were not measurable, an estrangement from a rightful state of being he had not intended to inherit and never occupied but still felt the terrible death of. A place to put and hold that death as well as his own, a place that acknowledged, even venerated, their charisma and draw. I think. I may be mistaken to call it a shrine, but I think of the year of careful building, like a bird constructing its nest or a beaver constructing its intricate dam, the inside of which is unthinkable; or like the shrines I saw from the buses in Mexico, tiny enclosures wreathed with plastic flowers and gas station bunting at the sight of which the bus drivers would cross themselves; or like the shrine my friend Joe bought for me there, a pink plastic clock radio housing figurines of the Virgin Mary and Christ on the cross and one Christmas bulb that lights when plugged in. Like the wild animal you didn't expect to see, like the horizon you don't know how to look behind, like the dead forest collapsed inward on itself and resistant to burning.

It's possible to wonder if the word *Western* denotes anything at all, whether applied to a place or a self. The West as an idea seems mostly employed as an advertising notion, and other times as a form of cover when one wants to take shelter from thinking too much about the wider world; the self's about the same. So the question might begin with when the West exists and when it doesn't, who calls it into being and why. It's nothing profound to notice that when the West is called up, it's mostly called up to say how pretty it is, or to mourn it, or to mourn oneself, or to accomplish all of those things at the same time. We bring it into being mostly to say it has passed, passed over, sifting out of the air out beyond the horizon. Many of the people who call that West up call it up to hear the defiance in it, the righteous dismay at what's forcing its way in, what's killing us off. But underneath that you can hear the faint thread of relief, the relieved inward turning. It's easier to be dying, to be a thing fading into the past. One can be angry at the present rather than live in it. One can make a shrine of one's assumed dispossession. White people live in the West and say it's dying. People who construe heterosexuality as a moral code and an admirable personal quality gather the West to themselves like a robe and bemoan its ruination. That happens everywhere else too, of course. But to love to die, to make it a way of life—to me that's got a Western air.

I tend to like it. I grew up in eastern Pennsylvania, and nothing much felt eastern-Pennsylvanian to me, except maybe the Astroturf my Italian-American relatives installed in their yards and the accent that seemed more like a speech impediment. It's interesting to move to a place that makes a defensive fetish of itself, that freezes up, that sees to its own fucking-over so that no one else can commit it. I'm not complaining. The West has probably unfit me for life anywhere else. But I don't think I believe in the West when it believes in itself. I believe in the West when it's running scared and is maybe smart enough to see that but unable to change it, having already killed itself so as to preserve its sense of self-destiny before the bigger forces steal it away.

If the West feels like anything to me these days, it feels like a long dying. So I've got nothing new to say. I know the dying's happening everywhere. What makes it different here is that it may just be easier to see. At least for me, it is easier to see whole histories of dispossession laid bare and how we fear them and enshrine them both. The world is difficult, and we shrink back from it bit by bit. Isn't that what we celebrate when we celebrate the advertising version of the West, its slowed-down pace and sweet quiet? That's not necessarily bad; some other animals kill themselves when there are too many of their kind around. But that shrinking is a smaller kind of dying. And the dying is here in other ways, too. We find ways to love our dispossession and inflict it on others; we live because we dig the remains of the long dead out of the ground, send them elsewhere to be burned, and speed the world's dying a little bit more as we do so.

A good scientist would remind me that the world's not dying, just changing, and that's true. What I mean is the death of what we know, the familiar world, the lodgepole pines going brown by the millions, unable to hang on in a world we've made convenient and too warm. I believe in the West most when I drive to the Snowy Range each May and see the advance of the beetle kill, catch myself flinching away from the dead stands, see myself trying not to see, trying to pretend it's not so bad, that the kill hasn't advanced, that maybe the 90 percent death rate the scientists predict has been slowed and turned back—none of which is true. It's when I catch myself trying not to look that I believe in the West. It's what the West does to me: lets me look away and see myself as I do it. I would wish that means I'll see more clearly, see what I fear to see or don't know how to see, see my own dispossession rolling in. See the unfamiliar world arriving, and not turn away.

Gretel Ehrlich | WHERE THE BURN
MEETS THE DEAD

Cora, Wyoming. Where the burn meets the dead the trees look almost
alike. They are human-like and disturbing, black arms on one slope,
brown needles on the other. I'm trudging down a steep slope carrying
a pack. Last summer and the summer before much of the West was on
fire. Now charcoal limbs mark my jacket and face as if to remind me of
what's still to come, more conflagrations, more dead trees. The ground is
black. Crushed ash cakes my boots instead of snow. I've been camping at
eleven thousand feet where it's still spring, wildflowers ebullient along
every foot-wide stream. Water falls from snowmelt. Up higher, terminal
moraines hold hanging lakes where tiny pieces of drift ice float, reminding me only that all the ice in the world has begun to melt.

Now sore-footed and raw-minded, I tramp down into the world of the
living from the realm of high granite where arrowhead-shaped peaks rise
straight out of lapis lazuli lakes. In a week I've seen almost no birds, only
a few beleaguered pikas that are dying from global heat. Driving home
from the ninety-five hundred-foot-high trailhead, I return to the everyday
world of the living. A herd of antelope looks up, their tiny brown manes
fluttering in the breeze. Raptors swoop and a lone coyote slinks along the
side of the road.

For the first time in my life I'm relieved to be out of the mountains.
The austerities of granite no longer hold me as rapturously as they once
did since now, in this last quadrant of my life, and perhaps the lives of all
humans on this planet, I want to feast my eyes on what my friend Edward
Hoagland calls "the world's infinite harmonious unruliness." Unruly it is,
as climate change brings weather chaos and the resultant human and animal migrations. With great sadness I change Hoagland's word "infinite" to
"finite," knowing that every aperçu equals a minute. I want to see everything as I run out of time. And now.

Home to my off-the-grid one-room cabin with its walls of windows. A
weasel flashes by, its black-tipped tail flicking time—an hour here, a season there. Sandhill cranes tip and tilt past the French doors. Twelve female
antelope and their twins press into a small herd, a "harem" led by a male

as a prelude to their slow progression to winter range in Wyoming's Red Desert. Theirs is the largest migration corridor in the lower forty-eight, albeit one torn asunder by highways and houses. Last winter a herd of antelope lingered too long near Kelly, Wyoming, and after it snowed four feet on Christmas Eve, they tried to make their way over the Gros Ventre Mountains and drowned in head-high snow. When friends made a track for them with snowmobiles, they refused to use it since it did not follow their migration path. That's how precise the wayfinding instincts of antelope are, which is why we have to make sure it's not obstructed by traffic, houses, and natural gas wells.

Jane Hollister, a friend in her hundreds who grew up on one of California's historic Spanish land-grant ranches said, "The ranch determined me." Not that she stayed there and saw nothing else of the world. Quite the opposite. She married a journalist, moved to China, walked on the Long March with Mao, and studied with Jung in Switzerland, but at the end of her life returned to the ranch, by then divided into hundred-acre parcels though still functioning as an undivided whole. She lived in a handmade house in the fourteen thousand-acre ranch's most remote corner and looked down on the lavender folds of the coastal range and beyond to Point Conception. Now she's dead and I've moved back to Wyoming from Jane's family ranch, after a short hiatus, to a piece of ground that faces a hundred-mile-long wall of granite mountains.

I watch as planes of light loosen at the corners, then shift with shifting clouds. A revetment and its chasm light up. A blue heron flies between two lakes, a blue line connecting them. Meteors stain the sky with gold. A moose lowers himself down into a pond, ears flicking bugs as water closes over the top of his back.

Late thunderclouds pile up into a chiaroscuro mass, a veritable altar from which hailstones are thrown, bouncing ludicrously through sagebrush and grass. Mountain-walking, mountain-watching, I invoke Ralph Waldo Emerson's idea that we must allow ourselves to be "moved by strange sympathies," by the siren lure of otherness, the indigenous as well as what Buddhists call "original mind," and to lie in the thigh-tight grasp of forested moraines between which thousand-acre meadows and string lakes lie.

Where to begin? About how Wyoming has determined me, I mean. With the eye, I suppose. Oh, the eye. Grab it, it's wandering. Put it into my forehead, there, in the cup of bone, the iris closing against Wyoming light. A breeze scratches the cornea, the eyelid heavy now, weighed down by heat, then snow. But opening again, always opening onto ice-carved moraines, a landscape in negative, revealing only what's left after the central ice has scraped by.

And the ear, the pathetic human ear clamped back against the head. I cup my hands to make animal ears and listen to the one black wolf at the edge of the timber sing its song. Mornings, the tin roof bangs with each change in temperature, booming another day into being. At the local bar I hear disgruntled talk about us socialists and think that at least we've risen from being pinko commies. But it pleases me that in the mix here, my Wyoming friends up the road—a logger, a postmistress, a carpenter, a ranch hand, and several cowboys who live in remote cowcamps all summer and feed elk with horse teams and wagons all winter—are thoroughly radical. But the climate emergency is bigger than any of us. We can effect small changes but we can't fool the planet, though the beauty the Earth gives out day after day like alms continues to beguile me, making it hard to believe the bad news. In view of the fact that there may be a large culling of the human population, I'm on the lookout for a cartographer who will draw a map with no human references at all: no roads, county or state lines, no railroads or airports, only game trails, ponds, rivers, and mountains, and the seasonal flyways the birds take to get the hell out of here when it begins to snow.

My maternal grandfather came west by oxcart from New Brunswick the same year John Muir walked a thousand miles to Florida. My grandfather waited until early winter to make his two-month-long trip when the ice had come in and he could get his heavy animals across the frozen lakes and rivers to Stillwater, Minnesota, where his French-Canadian nephews rolled lumber down the St. Croix River to his newly built sawmill, which later, he lost in the Depression.

I came alone to this part of Wyoming by pickup truck, the first time in 1975, and again, after a few years away, in 1993. Having lost "everything" twice in my life, a loved one and then a ranch, I bought this small piece of land after only a glance, writing out the check on a huge glacial erratic, then left and didn't return for a year. I lived in a tent while a neighbor built my cabin from scratch. Like my grandfather, he cut timber and milled it, then, as he likes to say, made it stand upright again as a cabin.

I no longer raise cattle, pull calves, feed hay by horse and wagon, fix fence, or irrigate hayfields. Instead, I look and wander. I put lime in the outhouse and dirt on the compost pile. The kitchen garden at eight thousand feet is small.

I sit with my legs crossed. The seasons change and waves of birth, death, and destruction continue. The word in Chinese for Buddhist practice, *mo lien*, means literally, "grinding-firing," as in the grinding of a brick into a mirror. Not an instrument of narcissism but a mirror in which one can see the inner workings of mind, the delusions and fraudulence, and the way doing nothing can sweep it clean. Spasms of loneliness come less often. What is it that I'm separated from? What's there to lose, except everything, and we're losing it anyway.

Too thin. The way time curls out from a single morning. Is time smoke? Global temperatures rise even though we have snowier winters. Perhaps we should carve totem poles like the house and mortuary poles I saw in British Columbia so that our narratives might be compressed, shoved down the neck of a bear, through the paws, and out the base of the throat, into the top of the head of a raven below until we finally understand that the skins of the Earth and the hides of every animal are permeable, how when we lift up, standing, eyes open, thinking, seeking, seeing, we are many interliving systems and beings, woven and one.

Wind flicks and shoves. House logs shudder. Sun is out on one side of the cabin, and it rains on the other. The wind that drove storm clouds down the face of the mountains turns and brings them back again. In dreams I hear beetles nibbling through pine bark, into the thin softness of cambium and the trees' circulatory systems, right into the phloem and xylem, its blood and bodily sugars. The grinding-firing body laughs at itself and lies down on one side to face whatever comes. Yet I'm breathing, and my dog, who I keep thinking is dying, lives on.

Evening. Internet service has been suspended by a tornado that cruised through. A large black column spun toward my cabin. I battened the doors and windows and slung my ancient dog in a towel to carry her down a few steep stairs to the crawlspace where we keep our wine. At the last minute I called my husband and asked him to wish me luck. Sardonic to the end, all he said was, "Take a corkscrew."

The black storm veered behind a low hill at the last minute and continued on to become a real tornado. Later, after midnight, a great horned owl perched on top of my nonworking satellite dish and screeched a song across the meadow to his loved one. We need so very little.

Now as I write, rain is beginning to fall on parts of the mountain. A whole season goes by like a single leaf spinning. On the moraine, beetle-killed trees stand trunk to trunk with the ones that burned. I go into the middle of them, up the elk trail, the moose trail, and look around. Here a Doug fir lives, there, a lodgepole is charred; over there, an aspen is turning gold, and beside it, white bark pine branches droop, the clumped needles brown and dead. I look at what is parched: ground, leaf, trunk, pinecone, but nowhere can I find any mending.

Tick, tick. Hands reel by a numbered, unlit face. Frost slides. The roof glistens. A thin cerulean band snakes across the blackened shoulders of the mountains. Body of earth. Dying, broken, burning. How does this place determine me? Womb and crypt, and once a refuge that gave solace, its embrace becoming mine. Now the blue snake of light that shows at dawn above the cordillera fattens as if it had eaten something, and smooth-backed wind-clouds pile up like thought. There's a flush of faint gray, a scrim against positive feedback loops that amplify global heat, and then it's day.

A Chukchi proverb pinned to my wall says: "The owner of the world is Earth." Too many of us have had it wrong all these years. We thought it was ours. Now we behold loss. Money, polar bears, pine trees, ivory gulls, frogs, starving children, goat herds, all like loose change slipping through our fingers. What's gone is gone and we can't replant whole ecosystems.

Mares' tails sweep eastward and a line of rain, like hair, falls from a black cloud. Thunder booms, reverberating in a long tinny whistle. Night comes. All those years living in the Arctic, I didn't miss darkness at all. Now it clamps down like a curtain lowered too fast. Yet, helping my old dog out in the middle of the night, the Milky Way draws me into its north-south slide and I free-fall in starlight. The poet Joseph Brodsky said that the sole purpose of evolution was beauty. I concur.

Quarter moon, orange at the mountaintop, swinging beneath dark clouds. Stonehouse, a fourteenth-century Chinese hermit wrote: "I sweep the steps when the west wind is done. I make a path for moonlight."

Stephen Graham Jones

TWO ILLUSTRATIONS OF THE WEST, *THE FIRST BEING SECOND-HAND, THE SECOND FIRST*

So my friend's telling me all about this drive he made the summer before. One of those rambling cross-country treks, the back of his little truck stacked three-deep with liquor store boxes, about half of them books, meaning he's got enough weight back there that he has to keep stopping, spraying down the radiator.

And my friend here, who I'm thinking would rather go nameless, when he tells a story he uses his hands a lot, like he's drawing you a picture with them, and he narrows his eyes to cue you to focus, to watch, and he leans forward out of his chair just enough that you lean forward as well, so that what you're doing here's stepping into this world he's creating. Seeing it all as he did, as he still does.

Where he finally gets to with this story, where he's been going all along, is the last leg of the week, way up some winding mountain road that didn't look so steep on the map. Because of his radiator, he's been ducking the interstates when he can. More service stations there, sure, but the traffic's a lot faster as well, doesn't make allowances for a truck chugging steam up from the grill.

Framing the drive like this, too, back roads instead of big roads, him as some kind of outcast hero just skating along on luck and the inevitable kindness of strangers, it's another way he reels you in. Even if you haven't made stabs across the country this stupid, then, the way he tells it any-way, you kind of wish you had, you think you probably would, and that's when he's got you: when you *want* to be him, easing into this next town of seven or eight hundred, the air in the cab tacky with antifreeze, so that you're having to drive with your head out the window, your arm down along the outside of the door, patting the truck forward another few feet, to the green hose looped on its wagon wheel hanger.

As for the name of this town, I'm going to pretend not to know it. Call it Idaho, or Oregon, Utah or Wyoming, Colorado or Montana, maybe even the north parts of California.

So I'll skip the part where my friend gives his name to the attendant who comes out to help, and I'll skip the elevation, not get into whether sheep or cattle were run here, or if they still are.

The radiator instead, hissing, my friend's right-hand glove still wet from the last stop.

When he finally gets the cap backed off it skitters there, steam whistling out the sides, and the attendant eeks his mouth out in something like sympathy—my friend and him about the same age here—takes his hat off and rubs the heat from his forehead.

"How far you going, now?" he asks, his voice up at the end like he doesn't really want to know the answer here.

In reply my friend laughs his slow-motion, tolerant laugh, and soon enough the two of them have the hose wedged through the grill, the water washing over the front of the radiator, and they're sitting on the tailgate just watching the day pass, the attendant shrugging that his family's been here for nearly a hundred years now, in this one place. It's in answer to my friend's seemingly indirect questions; he's maybe going to write a story about all this, if he makes it to where he's going. One thing he writes down in his mental notebook, repeats to me, is the attendant's phrasing, how he's "seen it all come and go, and then come back around again."

My friend never writes this story, of course. Without his hands, his eyes, your presence right there with him to urge him, to get him through this again, maybe even make it better in the telling, something's lost, can't get translated to the page. Almost immediately, writing becomes an exercise for him, is no longer a real experience.

Certain phrasings, though, odd wordings, he's a machine with those, can call them up like his own birthday.

I don't know what he's doing now, this friend.

We lose track of each other not long after he tells me this one last story. Not so much on purpose, intentional-like, but more by mutual consent. Which is to say we just stop looking for each other one week, and then that week becomes a month, and now it's been years.

Because this story's always there between us?

I don't think so, no.

But I can't seem to forget it, either.

At some point in the afternoon of my friend's story—and he's like this, has this effect on people—the attendant looks up the steep slope directly behind the gas station, asks when exactly does my friend need to be getting back on the road?

They can each still feel the engine, ticking down.

No other cars are passing.

My friend's response, just catching the attendant's face for an instant: "What you got?"

Cut to the attendant rubbing his mouth with the side of his hand, his eyes still fixed up the mountain.

"Most people don't know about this, I don't guess," he says, wiping his hand with his grease rag now. Balling it back up into his pocket, casting around for witnesses.

That's all it takes to get my friend's little truck easing over into an empty slot—pushed, not driven—beside the town wrecker, the windows up in case of rain, the *Open* sign above the cash register flipped over to *Back in a Minute*.

That sign isn't meant to be ironic here, either. This story doesn't end with my friend getting jumped in the woods, barely getting away with his skin—or not—and it doesn't end with them coming back to his suspiciously absent truck.

No, where this story ends is in my friend's apartment the following semester, him biting his lip a bit, saying that all that's what he *thought* was going to happen, sure. He even had a screwdriver in his pocket just in case.

But maybe he wouldn't need it, right?

He laughs about this part, some. Those are the last words for every one of his adventures: *Maybe it'll all work out, yeah?*

This time, for him, I guess it does.

Getting up the slope, not to the top of the mountain but not that far from it, he guesses, it takes the better part of forty-five minutes. He's breathing hard, not used to the elevation and embarrassed by that, trying to hide it as best he can, and this is the part where I lean forward a bit, can see the two of them stepping into a flat little meadow, mostly out of the wind.

It's a sheep shack, a herder's hut, I don't know what they call it.

Or, if this is cow country, it's just some outbuilding or another, set up here for firewatch, maybe.

Either way, it's old but was built strong, has stood against the wind and the snow for, according to the attendant, at least eighty years now. Probably longer.

My friend nods, looks all around, thinks he could live in a place like this, maybe. Someday. That this is all you need, really, might be where all his adventures have been taking him.

Or not.

He steps inside, I mean.

On the walls, like they were painted just by slinging buckets, and spattered on the rafters some, and probably on the floorboards if there weren't beer cans and magazines ankle deep, there's blood.

At least that's what the attendant says it is.

Supposedly, eighty years ago some of the Indians around here, of no particular tribe, they were causing the usual problems—stealing livestock, scaring women, living—so finally the men of the town, as it was then, they'd had enough, and cornered those Indians up here one winter, drove them into the shack, the hut, the cabin, whatever it is.

At which point my friend doesn't have to finish the story, just shrugs it away, laughs it off.

Me, though, I can't seem to.

Every broke-down place I see now, I mean.

This is Montana, this is Idaho, this is Washington and California and Colorado.

And this, the second illustration, it's Utah.

Maybe three years before my friend's story, when he still had a name and I didn't even know it, I was driving from Somewhere, Texas, up across to Someplace, Washington, I think, though it could have been Oregon as well.

I know it was Utah I was crawling across, though, in some bad joke of a car.

In my head, the memory's half-crossed with another from-Texas trip, one that started at two in the morning, punched through a blizzard and ended at the hospital in Colorado where my brother was in a coma because he'd stood up to somebody in the cafeteria of Columbine High School, but for that trip I had a friend, and baseball bats, but the police were waiting for us, and we had to drive all the way back without even seeing my brother.

Which is to say, stupid trips, yeah.

My friend knew what buttons to push. What questions to ask to have got me to tell him this story in the first place, back when I still wasn't talking about it.

It's the same as his, though, I think.

The West, it's painted with blood.

And I know it was Utah this time because at some point all the sameness finally got to me, and I had to pull over, feed quarters into a phone, ask the operator to tell me where I was, please.

As it turned out, it's illegal, or was then, for her to give me anything more specific than the state I was in. She tried, though, told me to look at the phonebook—gone—to listen to the radio, and she talked for a bit, too, probably too long, asking what I was doing, how could I be this lost?

"It's a big place," I might have said. Or just hung up softly, more like. Turned around to study all this space.

Surely I'd hit a rest stop soon, with somebody who could tell me something, or maybe a service station, a truck stop. Maybe even a town, though at this point in the trip I didn't so much believe towns were real anymore.

An hour or so later—time didn't matter, just my gas gauge—I coasted into the slotted parking lot of a rest stop. It looked like the last outpost at the edge of the world, but I was more dramatic then, I'd guess.

I slipped the car into park, locked the doors against all the people surely hiding out in the scrub, and stumbled over the curb to the men's room, my feet half-dead from the last few hours, the sun harsh. It's stupid, but I felt like the cowboy in the movie, his horse dead ten miles back, some sort of town wavering in the distance.

First, though, a pit stop.

And I was wearing sandals anyway, not boots.

Usually I won't remember details like footwear, but here, it matters.

I looked back one last time to the car that I secretly hoped would end up stolen—it wasn't even mine, I think maybe I was delivering it for someone—and ducked in through the doorless doorway, careful not to push myself along on the wall, the shoulder-level grime on it pretty permanent.

Because the restroom was cinderblock, it was cool inside, like standing in a wet shadow, and, like most rest stop buildings, the state hadn't committed any electricity to this one. All the light there was leaked down from some opaque sheets of fiberglass, I think, so the sunlight was weak enough that, white urinals, yeah, that's the ticket. Easy to find in the dark.

Going by the empty parking slots, I was alone here, too. The only person in all of Utah, maybe.

Still, because all the stall doors were shut, not swinging, I didn't whistle or talk to myself, anything like that.

Just step, step, forward.

Except.

This is where the sandals matter. Where I wish I'd been wearing boots, like usual.

The floor was flooded, it felt like, sounded like. Smelled like. Meaning at any moment, the water collected on the tile could rise up above the level of my sandals, slide under the sole of my foot.

I stopped walking immediately, waited for my eyes to catch up with the haze, so I could take my next step with all necessary care.

In that interim, though, the contours of the restroom taking better shape for me, the sandal on my back foot, the one I'd been stepping up with, it kind of sucked back down to the floor.

Like I'd really stepped in something. More than water.

I cringed, prepared myself for this, and finally got the nerve, and the dilated pupils, to look down, see what I'd walked into here in Utah.

Blood.

The whole floor of the bathroom, under the stalls, the urinals, the sinks, it was all blood. And the reason it had pulled my sandal back down to it was that it was still tacky, hadn't yet congealed.

I studied the stalls again. Much, much closer. Swallowed, looked behind me as well.

This is Utah.

This is Utah and this is Montana, this is Colorado and this is Idaho, this is Washington, this is Oregon.

This is the West as I know it.

And, because I had no suspicion where I was, I couldn't even tell the attendant at the next station about this. What I could have told him, if I'd wanted, was that now there were footsteps in all that blood, walking the rest of the way to a urinal, and that there were sandals in a trash can somewhere along the road, but I don't have that gift of talking to people my friend has, and the attendant, he wasn't asking anyway, so I paid for my gas, drove off deeper into all of it, no map, just the vague idea that I needed distance, was probably going to have to drive all night to get it.

COWBOY UP, CUPCAKE?
NO THANKS

I do not like to gut fish. I grant you that a trout's fluorescent-colored guts are interesting to poke at with a stick and examine, but only once in a great while. Mostly they're just slimy and smelly, and they get your hands all germy, which, if you are camping, say, in the Colorado mountains, is already an annoying problem, because stomach ailments at eight thousand feet are never fun.

I'll say it again: *I do not like to gut fish.*

Okay, so I'm not eligible for the Cool Western Women's Club.

I write about the West and the people out here, and read books about us, and have to say I'm fascinated by the women I find. You know, the tough broads who populate the pages of books about the West. Women who hunt, camp, ride horses, and fish—and relish it all. The women who live on ranches or fall in love with ranchers. Or the women who have kayaks on their Subarus and suntan marks on their feet from their Chacos, or the women who fall in love with said suntanned kayakers.

Don't get me wrong: I am, in part, this sort of woman. I'm a ranch kid who now owns a Subaru, criss-cross suntan patterns are visible on my feet when I'm not wearing cowboy boots, and I am apt to fall in love with thoroughly Western men, most particularly my husband. So while I'm similar to my fictional counterparts, I must assert that I'm also not them. Women of the West are a lot more than what I sometimes find on the page, frankly. And as a writer, and a reader, and an observer, and a self-appointed philosopher and cultural critic, I have to say: I'm starting to get a little worried.

Co-creation. That's what I'm thinking about lately. How books create our identity, and our identity gets captured as characters in books, and back and forth it goes like some frenzied feeding machine. I read, I reflect, I transfer. So do you. Writers write about real people—we get our inspiration from somewhere, after all. Meanwhile, in contradiction to what I just said, writers also single out interesting characters in order to write singularly interesting stories—and then real people, who read these books, are often inspired to live up to these unique characters we've just invented. In other words, we co-create each other.

Admit it, half the women in this country thought they were Elizabeth Gilbert of *Eat, Pray, Love*. Or wanted to be. Likewise, out here in the Wild West, we like to see ourselves in Pam Houston's *Cowboys Are My Weakness* or Melissa Bank's *The Girls' Guide to Hunting and Fishing*. We like to see ourselves in the characters of Louise Erdrich or Alexandra Fuller, whose book *The Legend of Colton H. Bryant* (which is about a man, but plenty of women are involved) mentions the famous bumper sticker, which has become doctrine for Western females, "Cowboy Up, Cupcake."

I like these authors (some are friends of mine), and I think their books are fabulous, and I think these books have taken us in new directions. But lately I've been thinking that we're just not quite there yet, and personally, I'm getting mighty tired of getting back into the saddle when I damn well don't feel like it. Especially when it's a fictional character egging me on.

Recently, I had a male friend admit to me—with a sweet, sheepish smile on his face—that on his last solo camping trip, he got a little scared. There are bears and weird people out there, he pointed out. He still *goes* camping, he *likes* to camp, and in fact he fishes (and guts fish) every week, but he's prepared to admit to chinks in his armor.

Amen, brother.

I think Western women would like to admit to the same chinks.

In most of our past literary history (and thank god it's over), the West has been portrayed one way: men were the focus; they were quiet and stoical, they had a bunch of broken dreams, and they sure as hell could not have been scared of camping alone at night. There was an absence of minorities or women, except as characters who reflected something about the man. And most of all, we had this romantic, mythic West thing going on.

But then big changes happened. We evolved. We quit talking about gunplay and instead started talking about other compelling stories. We quit being so romantic and nostalgic. New voices became part of our literary dialogue; voices of minorities and women, for instance, who had characters more complicated and interesting than the single silent unafraid cowboy.

But I wonder if we just backed ourselves up into another corral. Maybe the myth has not gone away, it has simply changed: Western women are now cowboys in pink chaps. Or fisherwomen in waders.

I'm afraid our books have romanticized us yet again. Are we all to be fishing, camping, kayaking, outdoorsy, tough, strong, wild women?

There are plenty of women in the West who aren't outdoorsy, don't fish, don't camp, hike, or fix fence. What about those of you who live in subdivisions, neighborhoods, apartment buildings, and mansions? What about a single and lonely Chicana mother on the streets of Denver, or the single and lonely transplant from LA who is gay and living in a new subdivision?

Are *those* stories being told?

This is a gross oversimplification, but we writers try to write about compelling stuff, in part, so that you readers will buy our books. So we *do* write about the air and space and mountains and ranches in the West because that is, in part, what makes the West interesting. And frankly, we *are* influenced by space, terrain, weather, and nature. It's true that if we have an inner cowgirl (or camper), it's sure to come out in the West—that might be why we're here, and yes, we've got the space and the place and the activities and the culture to egg us on. It's true that when I look out my window to the mountains, my heart does a little shimmy. So we write about the people who know these places and spaces—because they, too, are what make this place interesting.

We also write about them because that's probably what New York publishers want—they like certain patterns to hold. Well, to be really honest, it's not only New York publishers. I think *we* want the patterns to hold. They give us a sense of who we are. Or who we want to be.

Case in point: I wrote a short story about four naked people in a hot tub in the Denver suburbs contemplating swingerdom. This was at the request of the *Rocky Mountain News*, a paper I used to enjoy (before it went out of business), and I was proud they were publishing a series of fiction to celebrate Denver. My piece, as it turns out, was rejected for being too overtly sexual (a lot of my work gets rejected for that reason). To me, that piece was an accurate story about accurate occurrences, but it has sex, so I sent the story to a California publisher, who took it, and I mailed the *News* a more conventional Western tale—a loner ranch hand woman who falls in love with a vet in a small ranching community. That, they liked.

Don't get me wrong. I'm glad they took the piece, I'm glad it's published. But as someone who is called a "Western Writer," I'm getting cranky. Western women sit in fancy hot tubs and contemplate extramarital sex, too.

Perhaps feminism in contemporary Western lit got sidetracked: we were finally heard, all right, but often only in a predictable pattern of masculine/cool/romantic West ways. And maybe we like it. We don't want to be ordinary, with ordinary sadness playing out across ordinary landscapes. So we acquiesce and don the pink chaps and go fishing, sometimes not because we love it, but because we feel as if we should. And in the meantime, we forget to admit that chaps (even pink ones) are uncomfortable and the waders really start to stink.

Besides the ranching women who live all around me in my little rural hometown, there are also painters and musicians, army personnel and homemakers. There are women suffering from anxiety, schizophrenia, and bipolar disorders. There are women who are meth addicts, illegal immigrants, homeless women, and hyper-rich women who live up on the hill. Our literary canon will be complete when these stories are included, too.

Books have a lot of power, after all. They show us how to live, or how we could live. They make us less lonely, they connect us, and they embody ways of being human. In certain surprising ways, art is what makes us more real.

So we writers better damn well get it right. And there are times when we've fallen down on the job, constricted by cultural mores, paradigms, and trends in publishing and readership. I think our characters are valid, but they're not complete.

So, here's my wish: I want the full spectrum. Especially when it comes to how being out here in the West defines us. I hope women get fair treatment in books and magazines in the years to come. I hope we read about how motherhood just sorta stinks sometimes. And how non-motherhood stinks sometimes. And about politics, poverty, wealth, sex, sexual orientation, class issues, overpopulation, and climate change. So I leave the river guides and fly-tying to other heroines, and I will focus on my own guts rather than those of fish. Because a good book's job is to expose real lives, the blood and heart inside us all.

Patricia Nelson Limerick   THE FATAL WEST

> *I was sorry to have my name mentioned*
> *as one of the great authors, because they*
> *have a sad habit of dying off. Chaucer is*
> *dead, Spenser is dead, so is Milton, so is*
> *Shakespeare, and I am not feeling very*
> *well myself.*

MARK TWAIN

In the early twenty-first century, a surprising number of writers and intellectuals, activists and politicians are poaching on the professional turf of morticians and funeral directors. You can choose among a wide variety of accents and emphases in the nonstop series of memorial services for the West. Mourning the devastation of ecosystems, the loss of free-flowing rivers, the homogenization of once distinctive communities, and the constriction of a legendary freedom, Westerners have established themselves as the master practitioners of eulogy and elegy. We once knew a better West, the memorialists declare, but now we have lost that West, leaving us to get by on our memories.

The funereal genre of Western thought and sentiment draws from sincere and deep feeling, and it deserves no mockery. But having acquired an unchosen expertise in the experience of coping with the deaths of individual human beings, I am not of much use when it comes to grieving for a region. For all the injuries, losses, wounds, and lesions inflicted on the West in the last two centuries, the funerals seem strikingly premature. There is nothing in the troubles of the West that approaches the finality and irreversibility of a human being's death.

With a remarkable capacity to trigger rapid-onset nostalgia, the West has for decades echoed with laments over its decline and impending disappearance. People who were in California in 1848 bemoaned the narrowed opportunities of 1849, and the forty-niners did not waste a minute in lamenting the degeneration so evident to them by 1850. Whatever the enterprise or adventure at issue, the good old days yielded, and still yield, instantly to ratty disappointment. Before-and-after contrasts are regularly accompanied by a deep sigh of regret.

On August 18, 1805, on his thirty-first birthday, Meriwether Lewis went as far west—in attitude, not latitude—as he was going to get.

> This day I completed my thirty-first year, and conceived that I had in all human probability now existed about half the period which I am to remain on this Sublunary world. I reflected that I had as yet done but little, very little indeed, to further the happiness of the human race, or to advance the information of the succeeding generation.

As he descended into the canyons of despair and self-reproach, Meriwether Lewis celebrated his birthday in a very Western manner, pulled into melancholy by the contemplation of the brevity (which he drastically underestimated—there must be a lesson in that!) of his stay in "this Sublunary world." Hundreds of readers have scratched their heads over the peculiarity of Lewis's line of reflection. How did a man of such achievement, in the midst of one of the world's great explorations, cook up the idea that he had "done but little, very little indeed, . . . to advance the information of the succeeding generation"? Distinctive torments visited the mind of Meriwether Lewis, as many commentators have noted when trying to understand his troubled death. But on his birthday in 1805, Lewis was making a point far bigger than his personal sorrows: a river of melancholy runs through Western experience, and a surging awareness of death sometimes turns that river into a flood.

Human efforts to dam and divert the currents of sorrow have been correspondingly intense and widespread. Much of Western conduct has demonstrated the way in which efforts to deny death have led to the overproduction of bravado. The West, thousands of boosters declared in the nineteenth century, was such a healthy place that people who had come there to die could not do so, despite their best efforts. This casting of the West as a place set apart from time and mortality has never lost its appeal. Mortals, after all, have reasons to find this a pretty nice idea.

Conjuring up an image of the West as a place where the life force drives back death was a logical, opposite, and equal reaction to the abundant encounters with death that the region has delivered. There is no better way to feel gratitude for one's own claim on life than to stand in the presence of death.

On the overland trail in the mid-nineteenth century, the emigrants could not avert their eyes from frailty and death. Cholera ravaged the travelers at the start of their journey, and scurvy waited for them at the end. Drownings and accidents with firearms took far more lives than did Indian attacks. Many diarists kept a running count of trailside graves. Stark cliffs and piles of rocks evoked thoughts of the ruins of departed civilizations. In its scale and extent, the West made human beings feel tiny and dwarfed, reminded of their transitory and insubstantial claim on life. Deserts pushed all organisms to their edge, and thirst carried a direct threat of death.

And yet every thought of death reasserted the strange, precarious, and miraculous status of those who still lived.

For many who moved to the West in the last half of the nineteenth century and the first years of the twentieth, every breath was a contest between life and death. For respiratory afflictions, particularly tuberculosis, high elevations and dry air could hold back the progress of the disease. But the rush of health-seekers to the West also added to the visibility of human frailty; in a pattern that did not interest Hollywood, Western invalids considerably outnumbered hardy cowboys, prospectors, outlaws, and sheriffs.

"In the midst of life, we are in death," the *Book of Common Prayer* says, which more or less sums up the personal and professional game plan for historians. We spend the lion's share of our lives immersed in the stories of people who were once very alive and who are now very dead. And if our professional preoccupation with death should flag (though I can't imagine how it could), the aging process will keep us on point.

The universality of death might seem to make region irrelevant. And yet, facing off with death, region does not necessarily yield ground. My father died in 2002. My mother died in 2003. They grew up in Brigham City and Salt Lake City, and they always got their bearings in and found their homes in landscapes where mountains soar up, in the most intensely vertical way, from valleys and flatlands. After living in Southern California in places where mountains seem almost at right angles to the desert floor, my mother and father died in Las Cruces, New Mexico, where the land had the configuration they had always preferred. A good share of the time now, when I look at foothills and mountains rising sharply from flatlands, my parents' deaths are the next link in my chain of thought.

Inserting itself into death's dominion, region is entirely flexible in its choice of medium. In January 2005, I made my maiden visit to the legendary Elko Cowboy Poetry Gathering. I had a fine time, giving a speech, seeing old friends, making new friends, immersing myself in Westernness up the wazoo. On Friday night, January 29, 2005, I was in a state of great cheer, dining with unexpected company (the noted Western artist Willie Matthews and Steve Miller of the Steve Miller Band!), walking at midnight in the midst of an unpredicted blizzard, wearing shoes that were not made for deep snow, and feeling very happy because I had only myself to hold responsible. If I did not like having wet and cold feet, I could vigorously condemn myself, and then, with equal vigor, defend and exonerate myself.

On Saturday, my husband called to say that he had decided against picking me up at the airport because he was having episodes in which his sight and hearing seemed unsteady. He had had his first stroke in 1996 at the age of 48, so there was no peace in this news. But a friend who is a doctor told me that he did not think this was an emergency. When I got home from Elko, Jeff spent much of the weekend listening to the CDs I had brought back with me. Cowboy music filled the house. On Monday night, after a neurologist had recommended a night of observation in the hospital, Jeff had a massive stroke, and on Tuesday night, his life ended. Living by myself for the first time in more than thirty years, I kept playing the albums from Elko. I cohabited with cowboy music.

Our feelings about the West's history share an under-recognized kinship with our feelings about our own journey through time. With a disturbing finality, our youth, and many of the people we knew when we and they were young, have left us. The West we knew when we were young has departed with an equal measure of finality. If we are not constantly on the alert, the story of our own journey—from life to death, from strength to weakness, from a sense of our invulnerability to the recognition that we are playthings of forces larger than ourselves—will set the terms of the story we tell of the West. Given the opportunity, we will take nostalgia for the vitality of our youth and nostalgia for the West's golden age, and we will tie them into one very persistent knot.

In the late 1980s and the early 1990s, a bunch of us wrestled with the passage of time and attempted to engage in a generational transition in the field of Western American history. Some of the older generation performed this maneuver with grace and even elegance, welcoming and encouraging the upstarts, whippersnappers, and young Turks. Others did not do anywhere near so well. A memorable group conducted themselves like grumpy and shortsighted runners in a relay race. At the moment when a more conventional person would hand the baton on to the runner waiting to take his place, some of the established Western historians kept a firm grasp on the baton and used it to wallop the young.

So I knew I would have a choice when I got older. I could interpret the approach of my successors as an unwelcome indicator of my own impending decline and death. Or I could welcome, encourage, and sometimes, trying hard to stay on matters of substance, joust and spar with those successors. There is no fudging the fact that revising, rethinking, and critiquing the ideas of their elders must be part of the next generation's to-do list. "Welcome, young folks!" we codgers and geezers must practice saying. "It is great to have you join us. Dissect our ideas, reveal our shortcomings, prolong our opportunities to keep our wits sharp. Let us enjoy each other's company while we can."

The happiness and sorrow of human life converge in these reckonings with our impermanence. We live in a narrow niche of time between those who die before us and those who will survive us. Passing through this world, we are negotiators and diplomats shuttling between our predecessors and our survivors.

When I was widowed, I walked. As if I were a character in a novel, following the designs of an author overly impressed with her gift for symbolism, I walked every day in the open space at the edge of town, where the Rockies' foothills rise dramatically from the floor of the valley. I walked uphill, and I carried with me the weight of many departures: my mother, my father, my first husband, my brother-in-law, my aunts, my uncles, my mentors, and my models—Wallace Stegner, Norman Maclean, Page Smith, Vine Deloria Jr., Barbara Sudler Hornby, Alvin Josephy, Dean May, Mel Coleman, Sam Arnold, Gene Hollon, Martin Ridge, Hal Rothman, Chips Barry, Jim Roser, Jackson Turner Main, Randy Jones. Walking in Boulder's open space, I pursued, hunted, stalked, and gradually approached that most self-evident and most impenetrable truth: life goes on.

The Boulder open space where I regained my spirits is one among thousands of areas in the West that retain a breathtaking grandeur and beauty. Contrary to many laments over the decades, Westerners have not been irreversibly evicted and expelled from Eden. Quite the contrary, we have been granted a visa that allows us to travel back and forth, visiting, departing, returning, and leaving again. The words from the Wilderness Act describe the earth as well as they define wilderness, maybe better: the world is, like federally defined wilderness, a place "where man himself is a visitor who does not remain."

An awareness of our transitory state proves to be as productive of exhilaration as of gloom. Midway through this essay, I left it to take care of itself and find its own conclusion while I went to hear my stepchildren play the violin. My timing in taking up with their father was fortunate on various counts, and one of them was this: at the time our courtship accelerated, the children had just made the transition from the earliest stages of violin instruction. My exposure to repetitions of "Twinkle, Twinkle, Little Star" was brief. They were soon playing music that brought pleasure to the listener.

At this concert, Dylan, then eleven, played "Long, Long Ago," a song I had learned when I visited elderly people in the retirement homes of Santa Cruz forty years ago.

> Tell me the tales
> That to me were so dear
> Long, long ago,
> Long, long ago.
> Sing me the songs
> I delighted to hear
> Long, long ago,
> Long ago.
> Now you are come,
> All my grief is removed . . .

No one, it is important to point out, should be tempted to believe that word "all." Grief never agrees to a full and complete removal. But when an eleven-year-old violinist plays "Long, Long Ago," grief knows that it's time to back off.

Devotees of nostalgia, Westerners are not going to stop telling dear old tales and singing old songs. The memorial services, funerals, eulogies, and elegies for the real and true West are very likely to continue. But every now and then, we might ask each other, "Does anyone know any *new* tales and songs that might be worth hearing?"

The more directly we look at death, the better our chances of answering "Yes."

A SHAPE-SHIFTING LAND

Writing personal stories about the landscapes we love is a radical act. A protective act. A celebratory act. Even an act of desperation. It is also an intimate and sensual act. Sometimes I crave the Western earth like food, or breath, or sex, or water. I cannot imagine hungering for another landscape in quite the same way, nor can I imagine writing about another landscape in quite the same way.

I have watched the territory of my Western homeland expand, from the mountains west of Denver, Colorado, to the suburban farmlands rimming the South Platte River, to the rounded peaks and short-grass prairies of eastern Wyoming, to the purple skies and brittle landscapes of New Mexico, even to the red walls and muddy rivers that the canyon wrens of Utah call home.

When I first moved from the ranch in Wyoming where my son and daughter were reared back to Colorado, and then to the suburban desert near Santa Fe, I felt mute, disconnected. I looked outside the window to the desert beyond and saw nothing familiar. I found no comfort in the distant purple horizons—the Jemez Mountains, the Sangre de Cristo range, the Sandia Mountains. Nor in the vast desert. I missed the oak-covered draws and the sunlit meadows. The faces of the junipers and the piñons were not familiar. I found no elk tracks or porcupine tracks on my morning walks. Where was the boneyard that cradled my old mare's scattered ribs and the vertebrae of her hollow spine? Where were the cows and calves? Where was the hill with the grandparent trees?

I began to journal about this muteness. Soon, I heard coyotes at night. When spring came and the desert plants bloomed, I recognized penstemons and wild legumes, sand lilies and blue grama. Suddenly, the suburban wildness was speaking a familiar language. As I wrote, I listened to this unspoken dialogue and began to recognize myself *within* the landscape. One morning, while hiking a snow-covered hill to the east of the subdivision, I discovered three sets of coyote tracks and one set of frantic rabbit tracks. Soon, the tracks converged, racing around a piñon tree.

Bits of fur and blood told the rest of the story. I named the hill "The Place Where the Rabbit Died."

Keith H. Basso, in his book *Wisdom Sits in Places: Landscape and Language Among the Western Apache*, tells us that Western Apache place-names were created by their ancestors—names like "Gray Willows Curve Around a Bend," "She Became Old Sitting," "They are Grateful for Water," and "She Carries Her Brother on Her Back." Each of these names tells a story.

Once, when hiking in the Big Horn Mountains of Wyoming, where I spent a summer month alone in a remote cabin, I sat on a granite overlook prying apart cougar scat to see what the animal had been eating. The storm clouds gathering over the mountains spiraled above in dark gray swirls. The sun streamed through the clouds in one narrow break. A golden eagle rode the thermals. Goldens, abundant in the Big Horns, are found in mountainous areas on all continents. They will defend a territory as large as a hundred square miles. The bald eagle, found only in North America, defends a single cone-shaped section of air directly above his nest.

Do familial ties make a difference, I wondered, when defending territory? Often, back on the ranch in Wyoming, the female cattle of three generations would stand side by side, waiting to be fed—grandmother, mother, granddaughter. The grandmother, whether Old Red or the Reisland cow or the longhorn, would defend her pile of hay against the other cows and heifers, but never against her kin. In what way do our stories defend who we believe ourselves to be?

It makes sense that a golden eagle needs to claim and protect a much larger hunting area than a bald eagle, for the mountains do not yield up nearly as plentiful a meal of mouse or snake or fawn, as the rivers and lakes yield up a bounty of fish. If writers of the West are predators hunting stories, perhaps we are goldens claiming the vast expanses of a shapeshifting land with ever-changing borders.

What happens when two writers claim different truths about the West? When our experiences lead us to different conclusions? I confess, I am both predator and protector, tearing at the flesh of stories that claim to know *all* the West, yet loyally clinging to the truth as I see it in my one corner. The West is a landscape of deserts and mountains, lushness and aridity, great rippling plains and blinding white sand dunes. No two ecosystems are alike. What is true for Utah's San Juan County is not true for the Black Hills of eastern Wyoming. All Native Americans are not Indians of the Great Plains, and they do *not* all live in teepees. Chicanos and Hispanics have different stories to tell, as do urbanites and suburbanites. All

are unique. Yet the tension created by our differing and sometimes con-
frontational stories is vital to our survival. It hones our senses, keeps us
alert, and energizes our lifeblood.

Perhaps, like the Aboriginal people of Australia, our stories keep this
land alive and in a state of perpetual, mythical creation. James Welch said
that the landscape in *Perma Red*, an exquisite novel by Debra Magpie
Earling set on a Montana Indian reservation, "borders on mythic." Earling
writes:

> She thought of rainbow trout, their dense eyes watching, the scales
> ringing along their backs as they bit up toward the small white
> wings beyond water. There was a pause in the reed grass as a deep
> breeze pulled dust toward a higher place. The red-winged blackbirds
> were quiet. She looked closer at the bloated cottonwood roots that
> stretched to the pond edge. A slow current writhed silver and then
> green in the sleeping shade. She threw a rock toward the pond, saw a
> sudden lap in the water, then more waves, the smooth familiar wiggle
> parting grass, small hiss. She had come to know the language of the
> fields, the thin weave at the roots of grass. Snakes.

Sometimes, we must learn the language of the land through silence.
In the chapter "Layers of Time in a Silent World" (*In Search of Kinship*), I
write about my maternal grandmother who, at the age of eleven, discovered her mother had slit her own throat and who, at the age of eighteen
living as an orphan with her aunt in Northern California, became deaf
because of a tragic error. In 1910, she was married off to a man whom my
mother would later refer to as "the black sheep" of his family. A short time
later, my newlywed grandparents headed south to homestead in California's relentless desert country.

> I see her, deaf, in the quiet stillness of the Mojave, searching her arid
> garden for a half-hidden rattler. A snake shakes a warning, but only
> the desert scorpion hears . . . was this why you loved the desert so,
> grandma? In the desert it was easier to forget your sudden growing up.
> Easier to forget that fateful day when the doctor poured acid in your
> ears. Easier to just be. Shed your memories, begin anew. Be reptilian
> for a while, let the new skin thicken.

My paternal grandmother's sudden growing up was of a different kind,
her silence a culturally imposed one. *There are some things it's better not
to talk about.* Her birth certificate read simply: Helen Denishia Terry.

Born November 11, 1894. Potapo Creek. Choctaw Nation. Indian Territory. I longed to find this place and to stand on its shores, to hear some whisper of her long-ago presence.

Finally, in the summer of 2007, I traveled east with my partner John, a member of the Cherokee Nation, on this long-awaited pilgrimage. At the Confederate Museum near Stringtown, Oklahoma (an old logging town), we browsed through history books and discovered my great-grandfather's name within the pages. Apparently, he hung out with the notorious Starr clan, a group of renegade Cherokees who bootlegged whiskey, stole cattle, and thieved horses. In 1889, he was with the outlaw Belle Starr when she was murdered by a shotgun blast from a dirt farmer. He later testified at her murder trial. This was the same year he married my great-grandmother, whose mother's name is listed only as "Mahala" on court records.

We left the Confederate Museum and headed for the backcountry road that would lead us to a wildlife management area and hopefully to Potapo Creek, one of dozens of tributaries flowing into a ten thousand-acre wildlife management area eleven miles east of Stringtown on Greasy Bend Road. When the railroads expanded westward, dozens of small sawmills sprang up along these branches. To discover the creek where my grandmother was born meant to also discover a family legacy, for years later my father would be born in a logging camp in Trail, British Columbia. These are stories of motion, each begetting the next, each a part of the mythic creation of the West.

Thick brush and tall grass flanked the backwoods Oklahoma road down which we drove. Giant trees—pines and deciduous trees, hardwoods and evergreens—embellished the hillside. One flamboyant tree (a mimosa, I later learned) spread out huge, flower-laden branches like the spines of a pink umbrella. Scissortails. Mockingbirds. Cottonmouths. Copperheads. Red-tailed hawks. Opossums (Southern roadkill). According to a wildlife brochure, bobwhite quail, eastern wild turkey, white-tailed deer, cottontail, coyote, bobcat, raccoon, doves, wood ducks and mallards, fox and gray squirrels, and screech owls all made their homes there. In the winter, bald eagles roosted in the trees near the banks of the reservoir and largemouth trophy bass, catfish, and crappie populated the waters year-round.

When we found Potapo Creek, there was no drum roll of ancestral celebration, only a narrow bridge, a meandering creek, which quickly disappeared into the dense brush, the sticky feel of humidity on my skin, and the flutter of birds flitting from tree to tree. I stood on the bridge overlooking the creek and tried to imagine a logging camp set up along its banks, tents pitched, women cooking over open fires, horses and mules harnessed up to hauling chains, the sound of trees being felled in the woods.

I imagined my great-grandmother washing clothes at the creek with an infant wrapped in a shawl beside her.

The creek yielded up only these few hints of earlier times. Yet there I was, one hundred and fifteen years after my grandmother's birth, hundreds of miles east of my Western birthplace, surrounded by trees rooted to a landscape that served as a bridge between generations. I inhaled the muggy air and could almost feel my family stories and the boundaries of my perceived homeland expand as the heavy air filled my lungs. My breath felt languid and slow, like a silty river moving over a bed of alluvial rock. If I were to name that place as the Western Apache name their places, I might call it *The Place Where Memories Lie Heavy*.

Where I live in Colorado, at eight thousand feet with thin air, regal mountains, and open vistas, inhaling is an act of survival. Writing stories about the West *feels* like an act of survival. During times of war, humans couple with abandonment, as if the intimate act of making love counterbalances the threat of extinction. In fact, it does. In the West, where nature is besieged by development and drilling and the homogenization of culture, we make love to the land through our stories. We flirt with the land. We court it. We tease it into the bedchambers of our hearts. We explore its inner realms. We massage the flesh that layers its mythic bones, all the time feeling as if we are accomplices in an ongoing betrayal.

Some imply that when we feed the stories of the past, we create a serpent that circles around and devours its own tail, that the future of the West should no longer be anchored to a mythic past. Yet the future of the West is not a stagnant or linear thing. It rises up out of the same soil in which the past is grounded, then returns, a breathing circle of motion. And each story that we write about the land, whether we love it or hate it, whether we agree or disagree, is part of that perpetual creative manifestation.

I moved west to escape the East. I stayed west to inform the East.

This took place in the late 1960s, when the antiwar movement and its cultural twin were both flowering. There's that window of opportunity many of us have in our early twenties when there's nothing—love, family, job, mortgage, school—to batten us down. "Arizona," someone suggested with a nod and a wink. "Arizona." I knew nothing about the youngest of the lower forty-eight, except that Barry Goldwater and marijuana both came from there, and I thought, any place where those two elements are both at play is worth investigating. I jumped through that window of opportunity and landed in Tucson.

A squat two-bedroom adobe in a working-class neighborhood full of similar houses rented for $150 monthly. A friend and I took the place. My bedroom window looked out on a couple of lonely saguaro, and every morning I awoke to a B-Western movie set. An active antiwar movement was in place and I found the freelancer's oasis—a fertile town with no one else writing for the underground press or sea level magazines such as *Crawdaddy*, *Fusion*, or two-year-old *Rolling Stone*. I could take part in affairs that mattered and write about Southwestern mythology at the same time. For *Crawdaddy*, I wrote about the real Rosa's Cantina in El Paso and the copper smelter workers who sipped away their afternoons at its bar. For *Fusion*, about the acid cowboys of northern New Mexico. And the biweekly *Rolling Stone*? They put me on retainer, sending me fifty dollars an issue simply to be on call and to give them first dibs on story ideas. I arranged for a hipster country band to play for imprisoned draft resisters at a minimum-security federal prison, then wrote it up for the *Stone*. Like that.

The people, the issues, the land, the air, the music, and yes, the language. All these ingredients constructed my new West. I grabbed a picket sign to march for farmworkers in front of Safeway. I joined another demonstration against a university's Mormon beliefs of racial inequality. (That was at a college basketball game. Boy were we popular.) Late one night, I ran with a secretive group called the Eco-Raiders and wrote up their efforts to combat urban sprawl. The war against Vietnam was a constant reminder of global issues, while the desert Southwest taught me the fragility and permanence of the land.

I had not just moved to the American West. I had moved to a region with an odd-angled line running through it, the international boundary. The north of Sonora and Chihuahua had much in common with New Mexico and "dry-faced Arizona," as Jack Kerouac called it. Mexico too became part of my faculty, and I, one of its pupils. I spent time in Bisbee, Silver City, Cananea, Walsenburg (Colorado, but who's counting?), El Paso-Juárez, Morenci, Cd. Chihuahua, Douglas-Agua Prieta—many of these towns with huge mining and smelting operations. They were more than just colorful destinations on the map.

I cannot explain why I am attracted to mining camps and their stories. Traveling through the towns where copper, zinc, and coal rise to the surface and get processed, I've found a genuine kinship with miners and their families. Certainly it cannot be envy: I have no desire to descend hundreds of feet underground and extract ore or calibrate explosives in a shaft, nor do I want to drive mammoth yellow equipment pitched on tires three times the size of a pickup truck. It cannot be common background, either—the mining communities and I have no shared past. Still, time and again I have been invited into miners' homes and felt privileged to listen to family histories and collective memories, to hear cherished songs explained, and to read unpublished letters. It's been an honor—one-sided, as far as I can determine—and I've benefited by it enormously.

Back in the late 1970s the two thousand-mile US-Mexico border was a warm and inviting place (still is to a certain extent, though no one believes me anymore). I traveled that Third Country sandwiched between two large powers, listening to *fronterizos* and writing down my impressions. Only one other writer was traveling the frontier at the time, a fellow from the *New York Times* who invited me to contribute pieces to his newspaper. And so I wrote about the American West for people back East—very part-time, nothing more than a stringer, but in a region full of life and rough edges.

They asked me to report conventional stories such as court cases, regional angles on national trends, and curious university research, but what assignment editors valued most was stories pitched from the field— all the more so, I discovered, if they evoked the Old West with dirt roads, dusty boots, and barbed wire. Their notion of the Southwest was matched by my compulsive attempts to fulfill it, and soon, in deference to my editors, I put a sign over my typewriter:

Remember: Cowboys amble, businessmen stride, mariachis stroll.

One day I learned about a Yaqui judge who had helped a Jewish retirees' club unearth the old Hebrew graveyard at Tombstone's Boothill Cemetery. The rededication ceremony was to take place later that week. This Old West story linked Jews, cowboys, and Indians—a threefer! I breathlessly called the National Desk. Instead of the usual follow-up questions, I was immediately green-lighted with an open-ended word count and a photographer.

Interpreting the Southwest for the East, I tried to give an accurate picture, though my credibility only went so far. To file a story, we'd type or handwrite our copy, then read it over long distance to the recording room in the bowels of the old Times building on West 43rd Street. A battery of transcribers would monitor our calls as we dictated our stories into their machines. We e-nun-ci-a-ted each word, especially names, which we'd spell out, and always spoke dis-tinc-t-ly, even giving punctuation commands. The transcribers would call back if they had any questions, period, paragraph.

In one story from the frontier's smallest bordertown, Antelope Wells, New Mexico, population two, I wrote about the annual cattle crossing that attracted cowboys, livestock brokers, Department of Agriculture inspectors, ranchers, and customs officials from both countries. On my way to file from the nearest pay phone five miles away, I colored the story, describing the strong chuckwagon coffee served to gathering vaqueros at daybreak by "a few Mexican cooks." The next day I was chagrined to read in the Times that the event attracted "a few Mexican crooks."

I liked interpreting the West for the East, and in chitchat with an editor one warm day he asked about the racket in the background. "Oh, that's the swamp cooler," I replied, as matter-of-factly as if I had said it was my dog barking. "The what?" I explained that a swamp cooler worked on the principle of a cool damp towel tossed over the metal grill of an electric fan. This led to a major conference among editors on the Desk, all of whom were intrigued with this exotic contraption—should they assign a piece on the poor man's air conditioner? (They did, but not until much later, and then to another contributor.)

One story I wrote included the word "campesinos." A copy editor called back, insisting that I blend a translation into the article. I blanketed my exasperation and asked if he would agree that campesino is one of those foreign words that has been absorbed into contemporary English. The line went silent for a moment. "I'll tell you what," he finally said. "I'll learn Spanish if they'll learn Yiddish."

Touché.

One morning the phone rang at seven o'clock, usually a warning that someone on the East Coast didn't understand time zones. It was an editor at *Esquire* who, after describing a story he wanted pursued in Texas, asked if I would, and I believe these were his exact words, "mosey on over to Houston." I informed him that if we both started moseying at the same time, he'd likely mosey into Houston before me.

                    The rhythm of the Southwest, its natural continuity and occasional brute force—I suppose that's what keeps me here. I tried to move away. Twice. Once to the San Francisco Bay area, and another time to Austin, Texas. Neither venture lasted more than six months. Both times I maintained my post office box in Tucson. I knew.

Thornton Wilder lived in southern Arizona at various stages of his life, once in Tucson in the mid-1930s just weeks after *Our Town* had opened on Broadway. One early summer day he was asked how he liked his temporary home. "I like it very much," he answered, then tempered his reply. "There are three disadvantages, two of which would be curable. I miss a great library to browse in. I miss great music. And I came at the wrong time of year."

The library problem and lack of great music have both been cured, but not Wilder's third disadvantage. In more than four decades of living here, from my first arrival one August, I've never grown accustomed to the unrelenting heat of the summer, never liked it, and annually grumble that this summer will be the last one I spend here. The sun bores a hole through your skull until it singes the synapses in your brain and renders you powerless and stupid. Like Thornton Wilder, I came at the wrong time of the year.

The rest of the year I need the desert. Not all the time, please, but inhaling a good whiff of it now and then keeps the lungs satisfied and reminds me that I'm not too far from the dread unknown. I need the border for its anarchic sense of reality. I need Bisbee, Arizona, population sixty-eight hundred, for the stumbling satisfaction it conveys. I'd like a good river and more green, but then it wouldn't be the desert Southwest.

TASTING A SENSE OF
PLACE IN THE ARID WEST

Like many people around the world whose families include political and economic refugees, I have spent a good part of my life trying to find *home*. I was born and raised around sand dunes in a more humid place, but left it for good when I was seventeen. And yet, while I did not grow up in a desert, for much of my life I have been coming and going from the Sonoran Desert lands within a two hours' drive of Tucson in what we call "Baja Arizona."

I would occasionally leave for a spell, to work up by the Grand Canyon, or over around the Big Bend, or up in the hills and valleys of northern Italy, or along the Pacific coast of Mexico, but I always found that I was hungry for something those places lacked: the taste and fragrance and cadence of an exceedingly dry land, one I truly loved.

Every once in a while, I instinctively knew that I must come home to be with friends and family around Tucson, and it seems that my trusty pickup, Old Paint, could surmise that as well. On my first night of living back in Baja Arizona after an eight-year hiatus, I found that truck's steering wheel turning in my hands, so that Old Paint suddenly veered through the intersection at Grant and Campbell into the parking lot of one of the best used bookstores in the entire world.

It dawned on me that my pickup—just as any devoted horse knows in its enormous heart—sensed deep down in its carburetor that I was hungry to reconnect. It drove me to the bookstore, perhaps again sensing that I needed to read some of my old favorites from authors of the desert borderlands. Perhaps a *Bean Trees* by Barbara Kingsolver, a *Garlic Testament* by Stanley Crawford, or a *Taco Testimony* by Denise Chavez. . . . The pickup truck's sound machine knew that I needed to hear some songs by Linda Ronstadt, or even better, from Lalo Guerrero, accompanied by Los Lobos or Ry Cooder . . .

In any case, when the pickup came to a halt, I climbed out and walked right into the bright lights of the almost-never closed *Hissing Mouth of the Gila Monster Used Books.*

It is not just a market for old books and records. Before I had even a moment to glance around for a paperback novel, an LP, or an eight-track tape, I smelled something that stopped me in my tracks. A middle-aged Mexican-American woman with a silver-and-gold smile sat inside the entrance to the bookstore, a towel strewn across the basket in her lap, and a few aluminum foil packets shining up out of the uncovered corners.

"Tamales!" she cried.

I sniffed. "Tamales de elote?"

"Seguro que sí. Es la temporada . . ."

I swooned. "Una docena, pues, dos docenas, por favor . . ."

It was the summer smell of chlorophyll, the sweetness of a cool desert evening, the mouth-watering texture of a steam-roasted mass of creamy corn kernels and cheese shaped by crumpled corn husks and caring hands. If God had ever imagined creating a food that could embody the glory of the summer rainy season, She must have made it manifest in green corn tamales. They are as close to Sonoran Desert manna as mortal beings will ever taste. They remind us that the desert can feed us, nourish us, in myriad and sundry ways.

The next morning, I ventured out before dawn, chaotically wandering around like a senile naturalist lost in the midst of a city. But Tucson doesn't exactly seem like a metropolis to me; it feels more like a patchwork of neighborhoods, barrios, y colonias packed tightly into the same desert valley like so many sardines jammed into a greasy tin.

The more I walked the summer streets of Armory Park neighborhood, Barrio Viejo, and Barrio Anita—their quelites and mesquites and verdolagas growing out of every sidewalk crack and every pothole—the more I felt as if I was crawling around the aging, disheveled body of a former lover, a woman I had not seen since her youth, but whose exaggerated curves, dimples, and curls I vaguely remembered.

And yet it was not her shape so much as her fragrance and flavor that I remembered more deeply than words can call forth. Even before I turned a corner onto a pathway I had not trod for decades, I inhaled her aroma. There was a faint but lingering perfume emanating from a night-blooming cactus down the pathway, which I could smell even before I could see the thorny succulent itself, its limbs akimbo from years of homeowners building fences of different heights to serve as its props. After spotting the source of the nearly spent fragrance, I stood on tiptoe to gaze at its still-withering blossom. It was luminously pale and at that hour, sort of ragged, like an old nightgown that had endured far too many midnight frolics. And yet it remained so sensuous—I daresay, *erotic*—that the whole lot of negligee designers working for Victoria's Secret could never have surpassed its skimpy elegance. The mere sight of a night-blooming cereus flower was enough to send me off into those pollination dreams that punctuated four summers of my life nearly a decade earlier.

With a whiff of that blossom, I realized I was back living in a Sonoran Desert city for the first time in eight years and that I was once again hopelessly in love with the place. I am older and crankier now, so I am also aware that I am much more frequently irritated by Tucson's tackiness than I was when I first arrived here more than thirty-five years ago. And yet, even my irritability does not last long anymore. I can forgive my lover for trying on an outfit or two that really doesn't suit her.

The difference between then and now is that back then, I was in love with Tucson as both an abstraction *and* as a physical entity; that is to say, I was enamored with the *idea* of being in love with a desert place. As of late, I don't care much for abstractions anymore. As poet-doctor William Carlos Williams famously scribbled in chalk in the bottom of his rusty, rain-soaked wheelbarrow, *No ideas but in things.* Here in the desert, my wheelbarrow remains so dry that it hardly rusts, but I have belatedly come to realize that all this talk about gaining a *sense of place*—as if such a thing were merely a concept—simply misses the mark. What I am feeling today is a deeply visceral yearning for—as well as a hedonistic pleasure in—the *senses of place* embodied by Tucson, which come to me through my sensory organs long before reaching the synapses of my brain.

What I am saying is that you could blindfold me, spin me around for a half-day in a centrifuge, drive me to any one of a dozen cities on the continent, and I could still tell you which one was Tucson solely by its aromas and its sounds, its textures and its flavors. At the very least, I would know I was back in Baja Arizona. I would not have to read a sign or take in a single visual cue. The senses of place that this desert city emanates are not at all intellectually crafted indicators of this city's distinctiveness; they are subconscious cues most of us automatically respond to within months of calling this place home. They trigger what goes on in our sympathetic nervous system, in our pleasure center, hence, the deep etymological connection between *placer* and place.

Now, I don't think I can rationally convince anyone that such subliminal relationships exist. Instead, I might simply lead a visitor down the arroyo, through the barrios, and into the centro, until her senses became as engaged as mine have become these last few weeks.

One morning after a long night of gentle rains, I meandered over to El Tiradito, the historic shrine on Simpson just off Cushing Street on the edge of Barrio Viejo. I was not there to read the interpretive signs or to light a candle; I was there for the laying on of hands. I opened my palms and stroked the wax-covered walls and benches left smooth and greasy by the burning of prayer candles. Sweethearts and mothers had stuffed photos of their loved ones in every available open niche between the old adobe bricks. Red-hot candle wax had spilled its story out on every horizontal surface, and some of it had dripped down the ledges to form stalactites that produced a dull sheen. That shrine became my touchstone, my tactile means of feeling all the souls who had prayed and hoped and wept in this place over the centuries. I even ran my hands over its giant hedge of prickly pears, its curvaceous green pads jutting out in every direction, its lipstick-red fruits dripping with sweetness.

Fragrances and flavors. Textures and tempos. These things linger, lodged in our memories, as dormant as Sonoran mud turtles lying deep beneath the dry, cracked clays of drought-wracked *charco*. And then suddenly, they pop up again through the mud and slime and turbidity of everyday life, to remind us that we are *home*, not permanently exiled in an alien nation.

The most obscure but rooted sense of place, by my reckoning, must be *tempo*. How, during the heat of the summer, the desert slows down, down, down, near to the point where social life seems nonexistent. Old-time Sonorans had the perfect minimalist response for the newly arrived who would greet them and ask them what was going on there during that particular desert summer.

Puros guicos en la calle: No one but whiptail lizards are dumb enough to be out on the street in this heat . . .

And yet, when the desert picks up the tempo, there is much to be had. One glorious fall years ago, after the heat had dissipated but everything in the desert remained in bloom, I decided to visit the San Augustín Cathedral for a Sunday morning mariachi mass. Although the music was good, the homily was hackneyed, and my eyes began to drift around the cathedral so that I could see just who it was that I was among. Some of the oldest, wealthiest Spanish-speaking families of the Old Pueblo filled the front pews. Behind them were the harder-working immigrants who had arrived in Tucson just one or two decades ago, but had already become owners of tortillerias, carnecerias, and cafes. And behind them was a hodgepodge of Jack Catholics, tourists from out of town, Refried Christians, and the like. But the Truly Faithful, I noticed, lingered by the backdoor—dark-skinned men with slicked-back hair, wearing threadbare, sharkskin suit coats and faded guayaberas from the Salvation Army. These men crossed themselves at the beginning and end of every prayer, went down on their knees with every confession or admonition, and shouted "amen!" or "hallelujah!" with each priestly proclamation. And yet, I could see that they were treading water at the back door, as if they were saving up their energy so that they could begin swimming furiously as soon as the wave of a spiritual flash flood washed down upon us. I was not sure what form this spiritual catharsis might take, so I watched and waited.

And then the priest announced that it was time for the Kiss of Peace: "I give you Peace, Peace I give you; go out and share the Kiss of Peace among your neighbors."

I saw that an elderly man, one who had hovered close to the back door throughout the entire mass, was suddenly on the move. He slicked his hair back one last time, secured a button to close his sweat-stained suit jacket over his protruding belly, and then he began moving up through the rows. As he approached a family, he would first shake the father's hand, wave to all of the children, and then kiss the man's wife right on the lips; after which, he would move on to the next family and do the same. He toured the pews, kissing dozens and dozens of women as he went. Some looked stunned while others grinned, offering him a brief hug or a wink of recognition. Even among the wealthiest families in the cathedral, he was embraced and kissed by every woman, from pregnant beauties barely twenty to octogenarian grandmothers bedecked in sequined hats that shimmered and sparkled like crowns. And then, when he reached the end of the very first row and stood before the priest, he genuflected, crossed himself, and exited, stage right, out the cathedral door and into the desert garden.

That anonymous elder taught me something about pacing one's self in the desert, whether in the city or the country: move slow as a desert tortoise during those hot dry spells, but always ready yourself for something more, for some wet luscious kiss may suddenly come your way. We all need such a kiss to awaken us to where we truly are, where we want to be. Perhaps those two *wheres* will fall—or at least genuflect—into perfect alignment . . .

Denise Chávez

ENTRE MUNDOS/ BETWEEN WORLDS

I was born and grew up on the Mexican border near El Paso, Texas, in Las Cruces, New Mexico, a place defined on the northeast side of town by three large crosses, commemorating the many travelers who passed through here in the early days of settlement, and on the south by the road leading to México. Many of these early settlers on either side of the Río Grande became statistics in a harsh landscape where the essential struggles for life, land, and happiness were ever-present crosses.

I know intimately, through both sides of my family, what it is to live on La Frontera/The Border, the southern corridor of Texas/New Mexico and México. My mother was born in El Polvo, "The Dust," Texas, near the Mexican border town of Ojinaga. Her grandfather, Nabor Rede, had been given a land grant to settle what was then arid land near the Presidio, Texas/Ojinaga, México border. "Vamos al polvo," the men used to say when they went to work. And that was about it. They were headed into the dust. The dust is what they knew, what I still know.

An unforgiving but profoundly beautiful desert landscape, the world of El Polvo was both a blessing and a curse as a young girl. My parents divorced when I was ten years old, and my mother returned each holiday and each summer to her roots. I found the small remote village of fewer than fifty people far removed from my known world of southern New Mexico, the safe boundaries of our Chávez family neighborhood, my aunt Elsie living down the street, my uncle Sammie down the block, several cousins within earshot. El Polvo was a stark and brutally hot place in the summer, a frigid blank in the winter. My Tía Chita, who rarely spoke English, had no indoor heating other than a few small and dangerous-looking moveable heaters that followed you to your sleeping quarters at night. In the summer we stayed indoors until late afternoon, spending our languid summer days napping, reading, or visiting family in nearby towns.

Tía Chita was an inveterate reader and started a lending library in her husband's, my Tío Enrique Madrid, grocery store, which went on to become featured in national magazines and television programs. But in those halcyon summer days, it was all hot and boring or cold and boring.

When I was in Texas a part of me longed for New Mexico, my errant and missing father, and our life before we were changed.

My father was from the barrio in Las Cruces called "Chiva Town," for the many goats that lived there. The dust and poverty of his hometown led him to seek his life elsewhere. He graduated from Georgetown University and returned as a seasoned lawyer to the world he knew and had tried so hard to forget, a place he both hated and loved. He was restless as the wind, and life as a married man and the father of two girls never suited him.

I have spent all my life moving between families, countries, and languages. I still wander back and forth between my two worlds and the third: a land that is sacred, undefined, without name, and resides at the core of my being. My heartland, my homeland. The oft-used term "Nepantla," the land in-between, comes somewhat close, but is still distant from the world I inhabited as a child, a world I still hold close. This other land/other space/no state needs no naming. To experience it is the only testimony of its true nature. And this is what the West is to me. It is my unchartered South, the unknown North, the beguiling East.

It is here, in this landscape where the living spirit of place, history, culture, and language reside that I have lived my life. A land of little rain, achingly blue skies and family, family, family. I never strayed from my knowledge of who I am and who my people are.

In those days, I also knew we lived in a land that was different from all other places and that my people were people who knew where they lived and belonged. They were proud of their Mexicanidad and also celebrated their life as US citizens. And yet their real country was family. They knew allegiance to the clouds as did my great-great-grandfather Francisco Rede, who was kidnapped by the Apaches, lived as an Apache, and greeted the sun with prayers and salutations on the little cerrito behind his adobe home. He knew no borders other than day and night, sun and moon, heat and dust. His legacy to me is the longing for spirit that would lead me to become a writer.

Prior to the Gadsden Purchase, all the land around them was México. No border existed other than the Río Grande. If you needed to go see your abuelita en el otro lado, your grandmother on the other side, you crossed in the chalupa, the little canoe carrying all kinds of foodstuffs, gifts. If you needed to ferry wood across for your uncle's new house, you carried the planks in the boats, where you transported live chickens or goats. You had to get across somehow, and no one was there to tell you that the land you always knew as home wasn't yours anymore and that you couldn't cross it.

I remember crossing the Río Grande near Redford, Texas, in a chalupa to visit friends Gaston and Roberto. When I crossed, all my culture and language crossed with me—there was no separation.

My work explores the multiple cultural dichotomies of life on La Frontera, saddled with its sad misconceptions, grand illusions, harsh realities, as well as its fierce beauty and surprising mercies.

As a border writer, I continue to explore the wonderful living hybrids of our frontera world. And in that world we go back and forth and back and forth, now carrying a chicken, now a plank of wood, now a story.

I grew up with border families with the names of Tashiro, Luján, Nakayama, Fielder, Chávez, Boyer, Salopek, Triviz, Barncastle, Stern, Po, Frietze, and Paco Wong, may he rest in peace, this Chinese Mexicano, patriarch of Chinese food in Juárez. My list could go on and on.

But our people, all of our people, did not always have a voice. Especially women. My New Mexico grandmother, Guadalupe Triviz Chávez, spoke softly. She, too, grew up in a dry dusty world. But that world was New Mexico, Las Cruces, place of ever-present crosses. "Mira, ay estan las cruces," the early settlers used to say, "there're the crosses, the descansos/ the death markers where people have died by the side of the road."

A child of Mexican-American parents, their parents being Mexican then American, there was never any misunderstanding about who they were. And language was, well, language. If you lived in El Polvo you were in El Polvo, and if you lived in Chiva Town you knew who you were, and whether you were Anglo or Mexican, you spoke Spanish because that was the language. Later, you spoke English as well because that was the language, too. And in that place of many languages, including Apache, you battled the same heat and lack of water, the same mosquitoes, and the same issues: poverty, a constant search for livelihood, life and hovering, ever-present death.

My mother, a teacher for forty-two years, loved language, and told me stories of how the ten members of her family would sit around on Sunday afternoons reading the various newspapers, journals, and magazines my grandfather, Eusebio, "Papá Chevo" had subscriptions for. A hard-rock miner in Shafter, Texas, he loved to read. He and my grandmother, María Antonia Luján Rede—"Mamá Toña" to her family, Mary Ann to some— believed in the power of education. All of their eight children graduated from Sul Ross University in Alpine, Texas, the first Hispano/Latino graduates in that part of far West Texas.

That West of my deepest understanding connotes a sense of reverence and hope. Imagine a place so heartbreakingly beautiful, so full of mystery and magic, and yet so harsh and unforgiving, a place so without borders or boundaries that the thought of borders or boundaries seems an aberration of the human spirit. It is this land—my land, my mother's land, and her father's land—that I speak about. That land is now controlled by the Marfa Sector of the Immigration and Naturalization Service (INS), the Border Patrol, and the Office of Homeland Security.

No one ever knew way back then that someday someone would be Los INS and the others Los OUTS.

This became the battleground where the young goat herder, Ezequiel Hernández, was shot to death by the Marines who were patrolling the border for a short-staffed Border Patrol. I've been to that place, I've stood on that land, and I know Ezequiel's people. My aunt was his teacher, she ran the library where he checked out books, and my grandmother was his grandparents' postmistress.

I have stood on that hallowed ground, near the makeshift rock memorial that marks the spot where he was gunned down by those who thought he was running drugs. And in the nearby shack where he stopped to rest those many cold nights, I have seen his art and name on the crumbling adobe walls.

I have looked out to the twilight blue Río Grande, been overcome by the incredible beauty that settles over you like a silken shroud, seen that brilliant and hauntingly beautiful purple red sunset, El Polvo's cemetery to my left, Ezequiel's family's home behind me, and wondered, who and what killed him? Why? And in what language? Whoever has the power has the language. That's the way it's always been, or has it?

As a writer, I am always looking to find the true voice among the many that I hear. Sometimes it is my voice. Sometimes it is the voice of others who are voiceless. Sometimes unknown and known voices whisper to me. Early or late, I try to listen.

Can I speak for them?

What do they say?

And *how* do I say what needs to be said?

As a writer, I am interested in what is sacred and what endures. And how we, as human beings, cling to the truth of our lives in an ever-altering universe.

El Polvo has changed over the years. It has grown somewhat with new families coming in although it is still remote, still stark, and still dusty. My Uncle Enrique and Tía Chita's grocery store is no longer open. It was closed years ago and little remains to testify to its vibrancy. The land is still dry, still dusty, the weather still extreme, either too hot or cold, but to me, it is still miraculous and full of incredible beauty. I wander back, as my mother did before, with hope and love, finding in my ancestral heartland a part of my deeper self. And it is because I know los diferentes mundos/the many different worlds that I can speak to the world within that resides within us all.

My work as a person of place is to be a transmitter of language and to do my best to celebrate the unique beauty and inherent power of that language no matter how distinct and different.

The pronunciation is Juárez, not Wwwarez.

Relleno, not ray-ano.

Ha-cienda isn't hacienda. Here's a tip. In Spanish, the *h* is silent.

It's Manuel Camuñez, not Manual Commune-ez.

But here's the rub: what if Manual doesn't want to be Manuel or even Mannie. We can only hope someday he'll realize who he is and where he comes from. That's the day we'll all celebrate. When peace is peace. When war is a word we don't understand, don't want to know. When the borders aren't so harsh and so brutal and when we have outlawed signs that celebrate 1,657 alien removals; when we realize our intrinsic nature as global citizens of this mother earth and can enjoy the salsa of our language and our cultures, because we want eggs with red and green chile, what we call Christmas style, and thank God we have a blue sky we can all share.

And the water, well, it belongs to all of us. I hope to see the day my Mexican brothers and sisters in Juárez don't run out of water as they are supposed to in 2010, and that Las Cruces and El Paso aren't two of the poorest places in the US, and that someday those overlooked and overburdened cows out there on the highway in the various dairies will have some decent shade. And that I don't have to worry that our daughters and sisters, young women from Juárez, will be beaten and raped and end up dead in vacant lots without the dignity of a life because someone saw them as disposable labor, sex objects, inconsequential nobodies who work in maquiladoras/factories for someone without a face. And that our mothers, fathers, brothers, and sisters don't end up tortured and slain in the revolution that is now happening on the borderland that is my home. That's when I'll celebrate.

But for now, I'm translating as fast as I can, for as long as I can. Because that's my job as a writer. To speak for those who can't, who won't, and are afraid to speak.

It's my job to explain my world to you. I'm the translator. The word crafter, the doctor of language and of a people's soul. And there are many fellow writers who translate the untranslated for you so that you understand as clearly as you can what it is to feel the heat, to appreciate the rain, and to hear a language, living and exultant. I am proud of their work. It is the heartbeat that gives pulse and meaning to our world. I thank them for their bravery and talent. They have taken great risks and they are appreciated. To change the words for anyone is dangerous. Still is. Will always be. People live and die by words. And to us, the translators, words are sacred.

The life, the ánimo of a people, resides in communication and translation. It is important to reflect on diversity of place and to celebrate the unique voices that have opened the many worlds to us, worlds unbounded by the restraint of the many perceived borders that limit us, hold us in check. I live in the formerly untranslated land whose borders to you may at first seem unclear. This essay continues that process of acculturation that has long been overdue.

My wish is that you will feel and then hear the grateful breeze that cools those interminable hot summer days, 115 degrees in the shade, then revel in a sunset with other-worldly lenticular clouds whose hues come from another world, a better world, a divine world.

The important thing to remember is that daily we move between worlds. It is a miraculous gift. The blue sky and the clouds are our brothers and sisters and sometimes our angry fathers. The land is our nourishing mother and feeds us without exception. And the animals are our friends. We are different, but not so different. We, if we choose, can navigate the many borders while retaining our cultural and linguistic legacies, celebrating the richness of our neighbor's lives, retaining what we deem sacred, should be sacred for us all.

Let us continue to live in and between the many worlds. Entre Mundos. The Many and the One.

David Lee | **MATINS IN THE CATHEDRAL OF WIND**

If I stay here long enough
I will learn the art of silence.
After I have given up words
I will become what I have to say.

RICHARD SHELTON, "DESERT"

If I stay here long enough
in this havoc of landscape,
colloquy where enormous rocks
collapse into each other,
this place of desert and sky
wrenched apart by stone walls
buttressed with crimson arches,
shafts of light or brilliant clefts
suddenly opened with a hush
like the quickly drawn breath
of ancient winds trapped
in cool silence of primordial dunes
pressed into stone, where
a rough-legged hawk rides wind drift
in a lazy helix, waits
for rising thermals above the
tortured wreckage of sand
and stone, creosote and desert phlox,
sky and jagged horizon, each
glimpse, touch, scent its own
mélange of belief,
trinity of grace, beauty, dignity

will I learn the art of silence
and through silence hear breath

from another world cross and spill
over the juncture, sough as the moon
folds its wings and rests
on the shadow of a limned bluff,
arroyos echo the deafening roar
as starlight tunnels its way
into labyrinth and from that echo
understand there are no geographies
in the language of man
whereby one may find wisdom,
only to live here long enough
in this most sacred of sanctuaries
and learn not silence
but the art of silence
and the knowledge there is
no art without faith in existence,
that frail detritus of belief,
or believing in belief,
the intersection between
stone and wind, light and shadow,
no more than a tatter of cloud
caught on a ragged bluff's selvage
in this valley of kings where
the sojourner lingers until

after words have been given up
like flung jewels stitched into clouds
where strands of sunlight glitter
in the La Sal's snow wedges,
now lifted by a wind tendril
into a flood of rushing light
westward like thunder to smash
against the Moab red wall
as it blisters the darkness
into trembling fingers of shadow
clinging to any rock crevice,
then scrapes downward
until all is ablush, as if God
slapped the desert's face
into brilliance, horizon
suddenly broken as arroyo

winds into absence of canyon
where earth fell
into a hollow beneath itself,
the world alive with the gift
of light: cloud shadows
race westward, up the mesa walls,
angle north, then leap
the horizon beyond sight;
cool silence of a salt dome,
the braided persimmon moon fragrance
lingering in beardtongue, peppergrass
and yucca, the bend of sunlight
into open lip of slot canyon,
manifestation of *beresith*,
the great command *let there be*
hurled into the void of darkness
until word became flesh
and drew first breath
of crimson wind and world
became living sanctuary,
body of divinity manifest,
the words given up,
transformed into most holy
of holies whispering through the wind

I become what I have to say
sunlight bent and cooled
by the flow into seep rock
inside the lip of slot canyon,
walls scoured clean by wind,
where glistens the amazing
white flower of sacred datura,
the burning bush,
a lingering votive candle
held in the open palm
of God's mind.

To the Utah Chapter of the Nature Conservancy

ON LANGUAGE:
A SHORT MEDITATION

It's gone from my speech forever I fear. I don't remember the last time I said it, the last time it didn't feel odd in my mouth as though I were pretending to be someone I no longer am.

I'd known it no other way throughout my childhood. As a young man, my father had left Oklahoma for the logging camps of Idaho to make a new life for himself and my mother. He was eighteen, the son of a sharecropper killed in a drunken car accident; she was the daughter of a hard-drinking gambler who had abandoned her. My father's graduation from high school was a mistake, he once told me — he should never have passed his classes and wouldn't have if not for the basketball coach who refused to acknowledge his star player's failing grades. My mother quit school when, at seventeen, she became pregnant with me.

My earliest memories are of our small line shack — a one-room wooden trailer built on wheels that could be hauled from one isolated logging camp to the next, no electricity, no plumbing, nothing but a woodstove for heat and a gas lamp for light. Always, our gyppo tribe — a few uncles, aunts, and cousins, one sawyer or another who was always named Swede — circled our wagons near the feeding streams of the North Fork of the Clearwater River, and nothing is more resonant and precious in my memory than the sound of moving water. We drank it, bathed in it, waded its shallows in the summer, fished its currents no matter the season. Deer, Elk, Orogrande, Reeds, Weitas, Mussellshell, Cayuse — all names of creeks I knew and can still recite like a nursery rhyme. Except I did not say *creek*. Like everyone else I knew — family, friends, teachers, preachers, the druggist we called Dr. Kimball because he was an educated man — I said *crick*. Lick Crick. Quartz Crick. Split Crick. And it sounded right.

Only lately have I become aware of its absence from my speech, and I feel a kind of grief setting in. I'm a tenured college professor with three degrees in English, the author of several books, but it feels as though in attaining my education and career I've lost some essential part of who I am, some last connection to the forces that shaped me.

My people's language was crick and ain't and every *g* dropped from ing. We went huntin and fishin and shootin. We drug rather than dragged our deer out of the woods and said of new stomping grounds that we'd never went there before. My grandmother said her house was so small you couldn't cuss a cat without getting fur in your mouth. My father's speech was peppered with Old World sounds and conjugations: he retched for the plowers to tighten a nut, he clumb the tree to pick them plums. Certain words in my family seemed to necessitate added or deleted syllables and sounds—Mandarian oranges, Napoleon ice cream—and some took on onomatopoetic validity: wing in my mother's mouth is *whing*, a fitting combination of object and action. We did not differentiate between pen and pin, between sit and set, and we did not lose a whit of meaning. The men told stories of fighting the forest fires that ran and ridged and crowned and blew up; of nearly being smashed (like the potatoes we ate) by the wind-broken top of a widow-maker snag; of how my great-uncle didn't hear the sawyer's call and *was* smashed by the felled white pine that drove his shinbones through the bottoms of his boots and still he lived a few hours; of the impatient mistake my grandfather made when he reached beneath to cable the load, how the stack gave way, crushing his head that swelled up like a melon and he was never right after that; of how the log my father had hooked to the boom swung crazy and hit the stump on which my young mother sat. "Bam!" my uncle would say and smack his hands together so hard that I jumped, then he'd pinch his fingers near-closed, "I'll be goll-darned if that ol' pole didn't miss her this much." Our stories of survival were alive with color and sound, each word—quickway, flume, blazer, buck, swamper, grappler, gyppo—holding its own miniature drama.

No television, no radio, but we studied the King James Bible because we were Pentecostal fundamentalists, and the dark and chanting rhythms of the Old Testament remain with me. My father read every line of Louis L'Amour's métier, stacks of paperbacks in the outhouse, and when years later he told me I wrote almost as good as Zane Grey, I took it as the highest of compliments. I read all the novels the traveling Bookmobile allowed me to cart away, each volume of Classics for Children and the set of encyclopedias they accompanied, every juvenile book-of-the-month selection that came to our mailbox in town. I knew polysyllabic words by sight, heard them phonetically in my head, and developed an unlikely Victorian vocabulary sprinkled with the names of exotic plants and animals found in the diaries of castaways. I used the word *cask* to describe a barrel and got strange looks from my grade school classmates. It would be years before I heard many of the words I'd read spoken aloud, and the wrongness of my pronunciation would become a lifelong affliction, like an accent I couldn't, and I'm not sure I want to, unlearn: drought will forever be *drot*; solder will never be *sodder* but a word that so obviously contains an *l*.

In 1970, we moved from the woods ninety miles southwest to the small city of Lewiston, where my father took a job as a truck driver and where I would become the first in my family to graduate from college. Even among the other Idaho students, many of them displaced homemakers and disabled millworkers, my words were strange. "You speak English like it's your second language," my literature professor once told me, and I didn't know enough to be ashamed. I'd visit my parents, and my father would scowl whenever our conversation bogged down with the niceties of grammar and diction: "Talk Okie to me," he'd demand, and I'd feel a different kind of shame. He meant don't you forget your place. He meant never think you're better than the people who brung you up. I became reluctant to speak during class discussion, hesitant to join in my family's vivid storytelling sessions. My life became bifurcated by language. Nothing I said sounded right.

Through the decades, my linguistic transgressions became fewer but have not disappeared. Like a person discomfited by a stutter, I've learned to rephrase a word whose pronunciation I am unsure of. Even now, there are words I've known only in print, heard only in my mind's ear, and have no idea how to pronounce without help from the dictionary. While giving readings, delivering a lecture to my class, presenting at an academic conference, I will suddenly stop and feel the old panic begin to rise: what if I pronounce bosom as my grandmother taught me—*boosum*? What if I regress, say *nekked* instead of naked? What if, like many Westerners, I say *warsh* instead of wash? How can I break the habit of beginning each sentence of intent with, "I've been meanin to . . . ?" I've turned uncommonly fanatical about correct use of the subjunctive and the exquisite difference between to lay and to lie, as though by having a firm grip on such syntactical subtleties I am somehow proving my lexiconical authority. "Language is my life," I often say, but whose language do I mean?

Once, while on a book tour in a big American city my parents would never visit, I was interviewed by a radio talk show host who asked, "How did you get from *that place* to where you are today?" I sat stunned into silence, once again humiliated by the question I'm so often asked, as though I were a feral child raised by wolves, miraculously come out of the woods blessed with the gift of speech. I have a rehearsed answer—that I read voraciously and that even people raised in backwoods Idaho can live a life of the mind—but I've never gotten over the sense of freakishness and suspected fraudulence that comes with the query. It touches the core of my discomfort—that somehow I've forgotten my place, that I'm a pretender in both camps, unable to return to my roots along the banks of those cricks, undeserving of my success in arts and letters that I've worked so hard to attain.

And even as I dutifully deliver my answer, I realize something else: I'm bored—bored right out of my ever-lovin mind. The stilted language we're speaking bores me. Talking *about* story rather than *creating* story bores me. The sound studio bores me as does the loud city and the staid, five-star hotel into which my publisher has me billeted. I'm bored by my nice black pants and Italian leather boots and the sameness of every interview I've ever been drug through.

"This just ain't real to me," I want to say. "I've been meanin to tell you about that time my uncle decided to bring down this schoolmarm bull pine. There he was in his Whites and stagged Filsons, notchin in a Dutchman, when that ol' ponderosa starts to pop, looks like it's goin to barberchair, and you know that will sure-nuff kill ya. He starts to jump . . . but listen, let's you and me go down by the crick, eat us some slam sandwiches and MoonPies, maybe drop in a crawler or two, and I'll tell you the rest of the story."

Now we're talkin'.

Ron Carlson | UTAH CABIN UNDER
HEAVEN, JULY 3

Today is Insect Day in this world, and the sun has invented all of these creatures who now work ceaselessly in the grasses and trees surrounding the cabin: the bees, ten kinds of bees, some who whistle or is it sizzle as they bump against the eaves in some kind of labor; and the flies, twenty kinds, some very small who still retain the ability to bite; and the gorgeous and feared horsefly on my shoelaces, standing there in twenty blinking facets, rubbing her forearms together as if rolling up her sleeves for the duties to come; and the little beetles, narrow as exclamation points, but less excited; and the one hornet all alone, dragging his golden quotation mark legs through the air, looking for a mate so they could quote something; and the butterflies through whose wings the sun shines completely, orange and brown, and flying in hiccups or so it seems to the inept human observer. The sun doesn't shine through many parts of his human body, maybe the shellbacks of the ears, but it doesn't shine through his rib cage, which he so desires. The trillion ants are imperturbable; they don't act like it is crowded, and the glistening black ants walk around like dogs, some of them wearing leashes and shiny colors. When the human spilled grape jam on the kitchen counter, suddenly there was a black ant. He'd found the mother lode, and he nosed the jam and then circled the sink to tell his three buddies back by the wall. The human interrupted their plan, and when he swiped them carefully up in a paper towel, they came popping out of it with a skill that goes back a millennium, survivors, but they were escorted thus quickly to the front lawn. Certainly they regathered there, all four, and the three asked the one with a purple mouth: what did it taste like? Is it really good? The human knows that he will see them again. And there is the little quick gray spider in the bathtub who always comes out when the human appears; the gray spider wants to see who's messing, and who the hell cleaned up all the flies? Does the human think he killed them for nothing? He's late for lunch.

It is a day of insects, but a human being needs to stand still to see them. To look at the ground is to see a cosmos in motion; there's an ant climbing a long blade of grass, three inches, and then, disappointed at the top, he climbs down. He thought this elevator went to the tenth floor. He hoped actually it went up to the hummingbird feeder from which the drop of sugar he'd chased had fallen. On hands and knees, the human can raise his gigantic head and see the far hills, Grizzly Ridge, imbedded with red rocks like jewels in a crazy present for the king, and between where his hands rest in the dirt and those rocks there are un-limited creatures blessing the earth, uncountable motions in brief lives, and the human wishes with his human heart, which is an imprecise in-strument, that he could find god here, that god would appear. But he may have. The human heart may not be the right tool for the job. It's like try-ing to paint a picture with a drum. Or something. The human knows he loves this world and that his sadness is a blessing of some kind, which will either be revealed to him or not, but he will use the days to breathe and to call himself to mindfulness, some of the time.

Debra Gwartney   PLUCKED FROM THE GRAVE

I remember a particular autumn when I was a girl in the late 1970s, traveling from Boise, Idaho, toward the town of Moscow. There were four of us
in the car on our way back to school after vacation, returning to a state
institution that our parents were fairly certain would reinforce, would
maintain, the Western ideal in which we'd been raised. We drove the
switchbacks of White Bird Hill and, some miles later, the twisty-turns
of Lewiston Grade. I crossed my arms over my stomach, closed my eyes,
and held back an inevitable queasiness by anticipating the flatter landscape ahead—over the last pass, I knew, lay the variations of yellow, the
textures, the subtle relief of the stretch of land known as the Palouse. The
north Idaho edge of the Palouse, that is, with its far edge in eastern Oregon, a region of subtle humps and hollows formed during the last ice age
and made fertile from a glacial silt known as loess, soil that is ideal for
the dryland farming of what seemed to me then as endless acres of wheat.

I was not yet twenty, not at all worldly, far behind my contemporaries,
I'm certain, in other parts of the world. I was a young woman who'd been
born and raised in Idaho, who was permitted to apply to only this university (which my parents and grandparents had attended as well); who
couldn't grasp, I realize now, the dream of a life other than the one defined
and prescribed by the time in which I was living, my place, my people. I'd
rarely left the state, unless I counted the travel made possible by books,
and in that case I departed regularly. I'd read, for instance, Hemingway's
short story "Hills Like White Elephants." I had some notion of the discussion between the man and woman but was more enthralled by the
geologic mounds that appeared in the distance of their conversation. The
great restless beasts. Driving into the Palouse that autumn day, I sat in the
back of my friend's car, having begged for a ride because my father forbade
me from bringing my own vw bug to college (he'd decided a car would
lead me into trouble). I stuck my head out the window, Steely Dan's "Hey
Nineteen" on the tinny stereo, and gazed at the rolling treeless hills of the
Palouse. Not like white elephants, these, but like brown women. Open,
vulnerable, sexual, though those were not words I could have applied then

to the rise and fall of hips, the goddess thighs, the swooping breasts, the tanned and angled shoulders of wheat crops. I knew only that the waving grasses trundling to the horizon, stunningly golden, both excited and re-leased something within me, as if a switch had been turned that admitted possibility and glimpses of wonder and peace, tantalizing and strangely forbidden at the same time.

The first woman of European descent to settle in the Palouse—the first white woman, like the women of my family, like me—was Narcissa Whitman. On July 4, 1836, she and another missionary wife named Eliza Spalding, together with their husbands and a contingent of guides, reached the apex of the Continental Divide, at South Pass in Wyoming, with wagonloads of household goods (at least some of their dishes, furniture, trunks of clothing had made it that far) and walked to the other side. That moment, according to journals the women left behind, wasn't one marked or celebrated *in* the moment, but regarded as simply another difficult mile on this more-difficult-than-they-could-have-imagined trek that had begun in upstate New York nearly five months earlier. Word soon reached the East Coast that women had not only crossed the jagged and untamed Rocky Mountains, but had done so with *wagons*, and the phenomenon known as the Oregon Trail was set in motion. Within a few years, tens of thousands of women and their own covered wagons—and men and children and dried goods and animals and furnishings—headed off to begin again in a startlingly new and distant land.

My own pioneer ancestors were among those who sought new life in the frontier West, and in this way I consider myself linked to Narcissa Whitman. She, especially in the wake of her violent death eleven years after her arrival in Oregon Territory, was regarded a hero by people like mine. An "angel of mercy." With her journey and her settlement in the far reaches of the West, she opened a door of sorts that my great-great-great-great grandparents strode through. These relatives also shared plenty of her attitudes about the frontier: an assumption that the land out here was their God-given right to claim as their own; a determination to stay put, to raise crops and animals, to bear children and teach them to be fiercely loyal to this place. They believed in the divide between men and women's work. Ideals that remain, even now, at the core of my family's sense of itself.

It's curious to me that Narcissa's primary aim wasn't to pave a path for the onslaught of new inhabitants. Instead, she felt she'd been called to save the godless heathens living on the far side of the continent before they were exposed to the vagaries of the inevitable settlers. I try to imagine the drive stirred in this young woman: a spiritual awakening at the age of eleven potent enough that she was compelled to give up every comfort, her home, a family that cherished her. A certainty in her heart allowed her to believe that pagan strangers in the wilderness would bend in gratitude at the message she'd come to deliver. Narcissa could have easily stayed in upstate New York, become a teacher as her parents had hoped, and married a kind New Englander. She was famous for her singing voice, like an angel's, and her beauty, her pious nature, her long strawberry blonde hair. Instead, she arranged to wed a man she'd met twice at most, a man equally consumed with the missionary spirit. They provided each other the means to travel to a strange country, for the church board insisted that only couples be sent to distant lands. She departed with her husband only a few hours after the ceremony, still wearing her black wedding dress, for a destination so mysterious that no other missionaries would accept the challenge. The others opted for Hawaii, Guam, anywhere but the dangerous and dark West.

In September 1836, Narcissa, pregnant, along with her husband and Eliza and Henry Spalding, reached Oregon Territory, a tremendous expanse of geography that then included Washington, Oregon, Idaho, and parts of Montana and Wyoming, and they began to plan the locations of their respective Protestant missions. The Spaldings went on to what is now Idaho, near current-day Lapwai, to live among the Nez Perce. The Whitmans set down on the grasslands of the Palouse, outside the town later called Walla Walla, about a half-day's travel from one of the West's first forts and smack in the middle of Cayuse Indian land. This was the tribe that the couple would try to convert to Christianity, though in the end not one Cayuse signed on to the Whitmans' rigid religious views; most particularly, the tribal members could not accept the missionaries' notion of a fiery Hell.

The tribe the Whitmans settled among didn't refer to themselves as "Cayuse." That word derives from the French *cailloux* ("people of the rocks") and was used by French trappers. (The origin of the word "palouse" is French, as well: *pelouse*, meaning, "land with thick grass.") The Cayuse called themselves "the superior people." They lived on land they identified not as rocky, but grassy, Waiilatpu—"place of the rye grass people"—and they relied on bulrush, known also as tule, for their baskets, some of their clothing, and longhouse dwellings that could withstand the region's bitter winds, snow, and rain. The Whitmans, for the eleven years they lived in this place, also called their mission Waiilatpu—

their one concession to the native language—though Marcus cleared and burned the grasses around the compound to introduce the Indians to the plow, to dig irrigation ditches, and to make way for expansive gardens that would feed his family and a growing number of pioneer visitors. He yanked up the rushes, planted wheat, and built a mill. In her writings, Narcissa, believing she was right to excoriate the Cayuse for a belief system she'd traveled all that way to eradicate, refers to the Indians as "heathens" or "savages." She once wrote that they "have been serving the devil faithfully," thereby feeding her own need to portray these people as desperate for redemption.

Despite her single-mindedness, her tunnel vision, I have become fascinated with Narcissa Whitman over the past few years. Part of my intention—or obsession—involves seeking hints of my younger self in her younger self, drawing a line of sorts from the first Caucasian woman to settle in the West to those of us still here, deeply rooted 162 years after her death in the attitudes she brought with her. I'm not so much taken with her fervent evangelism as drawn in by her willingness, her eagerness, to give up everything she knew and loved to set off on an unprecedented trip. I understand now that she unwittingly provided a course and a rationale for thousands of pioneer women, including my ancestors. I've read her journals and letters, chock-full of praise for her Lord and the fanatic determination to turn souls in His direction. But at times, under the thick layer of hallelujahs and amens, I've detected a tender vulnerability, a yearning for her mother's "pork and potatoes," a plea for any of those she'd left behind to come to Oregon and ease her loneliness. In other words, she was complex and conflicted. Human. It occurs to me, as I read Narcissa's language, the beat of her own syntax, that she was in over her head before she'd even left St. Louis. I wonder if she'd made a choice that she began to doubt—traveling with a relative stranger into a dark mystery, an unknown and unknowable land. Rather than turn back, each day of the trip, each day of the eleven years at the mission, she took to shouting ever more loudly about God's purpose for her. Putting together the numerous accounts that have been written about this woman, it seems she grew more hardened by disappointment the longer she stayed and, after the accidental drowning of her only child, two-year-old Alice, Narcissa became as impenetrable as stone.

Last summer, I asked to examine a rare book about Marcus Whitman, one volume within the vast holdings of the library of the American Antiquarian Society in Worcester, Massachusetts. I'd applied for a research fellowship at the library because I wanted to dig into my questions, some of them vexing, about the real Narcissa Whitman—not the myth, not the icon, but the actual woman who might teach me something about those who followed her West, and who might reveal to me my own calcified inclinations. I had started my research some months earlier at Whitman College in Walla Walla, where a lock of her hair set in a simple frame rests chillingly atop a filing cabinet in the basement archives. I sat at a table while the young archivist there gingerly slid a set of her letters from a sturdy box—letters written on the journey to Oregon Territory and from her new home as well, her fine, straight handwriting barely decipherable on the original paper, now crisped and yellow. Once I delved into the research materials in Massachusetts, I read books about the people who swept in to take advantage of the bloodshed that took place on November 29, 1847, at the mission. Eleven years after the Whitmans' arrival, the Cayuse killed them and eleven others, just as the movement to launch a government in Oregon was at fever pitch—reformed mountain men and early settlers were actively pushing for laws and regulations to protect their lands and commerce. White people were slaughtered at Waiilatpu, violence was translated into fear, and fear into governance, all within the great billowing cloud of Manifest Destiny. Out of Narcissa's death came laws that increased the rights of white settlers and that provided justifications for chasing off or killing native peoples. Narcissa was instantly cast as innocent, as martyr, and the complicated woman she was—a lonely woman, a woman who wanted to serve God on her own terms, a woman who had surely contributed to the conflict that led to the murders—was simply swallowed up.

The book I'd requested at the American Antiquarian library was delivered to a small carrel, as was protocol, and I set it on a dustless plastic cradle (more protocol), and squeaked open the cover on stiff and unblemished paper that had remained unread for decades. Peeling apart the pages, I happened upon a blue piece of paper tucked into the middle of the spine—onionskin thin, extraordinarily delicate, and maybe four-by-six inches. The note was folded in half; I unfolded it. I held the paper in my palm. On one side was pressed a feathery green leaf roughly the shape of a Christmas tree. On the other side, written in the leaf's rusty shadow, was the following notation in tiny, formal handwriting: "Plucked from the grave of Eliza Whitman, October 12, 1848."

Finding the note exhilarated me, but what was written there rubbed me wrong, for no two women were more unalike than Narcissa Whitman and Eliza Spalding. Documents regarding Eliza's sojourn with the Nez Perce describe her calm demeanor, her placid presence. She, too, had been deeply religious, but she'd learned the Nez Perce language, accepted some of their ways as her own, made friends in the tribe. The leaf pressed into the paper had been picked from the resting place of the fierce and determined Narcissa, who had died at the hands of those she'd come to save, not Eliza Spalding's. Seeing her name confused with another's not even a year after her death filled me with an odd frustration, a sadness that she had been so quickly forgotten.

That day in the library I abandoned reading the book and concentrated instead on that blue piece of ephemera. I tracked down its donors, Edwin and Harriet Chase Marble, born in 1828 and 1830, respectively, which would have made them teenagers when the note was written. Was it one of them, or perhaps one of their parents, who'd gone out to Oregon Territory in the late 1840s? If so, why would an Easterner stand on a heap of soil over the mass grave of people who'd been killed eleven months earlier? There was no specific place of interment for Narcissa then. Her remains, dug up early on by animals, had been combined with the body parts of others, all of whom were reburied in a shallow hole and covered with a wagon bed topped with dirt. Waiilatpu in October 1848 was nothing like the tourist attraction it is today, with tidy displays, a well-marked gravesite, a memorial atop a hill, and, on the valley floor, white lines painted on the golf course-like grass showing the shapes and sizes of the mission buildings, weirdly reminiscent of the perimeter paint around a body at a murder scene. In October 1848, the war the new government of Oregon had declared on the Cayuse was raging; the Cayuse, despite clever tactics, were losing, with their people hidden, half-starved, in the mountains. A few local mountain men—Joseph Meek, Robert Newell, Wesley Howell— had stormed onto the mission grounds not long after the killings to help with the reburying of the dead and to pick up pieces of Narcissa's strawberry blonde hair strewn across the quiet compound. Who else besides the military and these rugged individualists would have reason to visit the scene of death? Why would someone tear a leaf from a plant growing in the rubble, carry it all the way to Massachusetts, and press it flat? And why did that person, who went to the trouble to place the folded note in a book about Marcus Whitman, conflate the two women's names?

Perhaps whoever did it was thinking of young Eliza, daughter of the Spaldings, who'd been in residence at Waiilatpu during the attack. Nine years old, she emerged from the violence and was returned to her mother eerily unscathed. But the horrific images of the killing spree that took place in the Whitman compound, along with the terrible anger built up in the Cayuse community toward the Whitmans, and Narcissa in particular, were sharply on the minds of those determined to establish white settlements in Oregon Territory. Panic in the aftermath of the violence led to a decimation of the Indians drastic enough that not a single full-blooded Cayuse is alive today.

I was unaware of this history when I drove over the mountains to Walla Walla, Washington, one weekend during my senior year of college — traveling west now rather than those north-south trips back and forth from school. I had forgotten about Narcissa Whitman, a historic figure I'd last studied in the fourth grade during Pacific Northwest lessons, and failed to notice that we were a few miles from where she'd lived and died. The purpose of my trip, with my mother and sister in 1979, was to buy a wedding dress. A long drive — 125 miles from Moscow, two and a half hours, more switchbacks until we reached the Washington version of the rolling brown-women hills, miles of wheat under a brilliant spring sun. To this day, I'm surprised that my mother went along with the plan, as there were plenty of dress shops in Boise. But I'd seen a particular dress in a magazine, a gown I was sure I had to wear to my May wedding, with layers of Victorian lace, a creamy scalloped hem, and a train fit for royalty.

Maybe I had an opportunity to reconsider what I'd committed to during our quiet drive out of Idaho and into Washington, out of one corner of the Palouse and into another. I was twenty-one, scared out of my mind about leaving the cocoon that college had become for me, my nearly perfect grades and lofty conversations (so they seemed at the time) with English major friends about lines of poetry and passages of prose. I was unsteady about leaving the provincial reality that was Idaho, yet incapable of other considerations, of finding a job, attending graduate school, traveling to distant places. I'd opted for what seemed the easiest and most logical step into adulthood. I would marry a boy who both awed and troubled me deeply.

Perhaps I let some of the panic I had hidden about our relationship bubble up in me as we drove to Walla Walla, but I don't remember a single such thought. It seemed the thing to do, getting married. And so my mother transported me to the shop, to the gown that was in the end too expensive. My sister, who wed soon after me, and I chose another, with less lace and a more conservative train, to wear at our respective weddings. The trip was accomplished, the gown purchased, another stone set, another detail that made it impossible for me to change my mind. I've sometimes felt angry at my mother — why didn't she say something, why didn't she point out the obvious disasters facing me with this boy-man who I'd soon meet at the altar? But of course I would not have listened to her. Her arguments would not have mattered. That was what young women in Idaho did: find a husband, raise a family. She had married my father at a ridiculously young age, already pregnant with me. I, too, was pregnant on this shopping day, though my mother didn't know it. I'd hardly let myself know it. Another unconscious stone firmly set, this baby on its way, the most convincing strategy yet to keep me headed toward the only future I would let myself consider.

Last spring, many years divorced from that first husband and our children raised to adulthood, I returned to Waiilatpu, which I have visited several times now. The day was hot, and I sweated all the way up the steep rise of Memorial Hill. At the top, I stood next to the marble column erected in tribute to the white people who had died at the mission on November 29, 1847. There is still no memorial there for the Cayuse, nearly half of the tribe dying from measles brought with the wagon trains, and hundreds of others killed in retaliation for the deaths of the missionaries and others at Waiilatpu.

When I first began reading histories of Narcissa Whitman, I wanted to despise her for the damage she had done, for the changes she'd set in motion, some of them severe. Because this young woman had a religious fire in her breast, many people lost their lives and their lands. But is it easy to draw that straight line after all? Narcissa's own intentions, if her journals are to be believed, were to have an effect on a small group of people, not to broadly influence white settlement in the West. I'm convinced that significant changes were an unintended consequence of her mission. Narcissa's death didn't stir a desire in the new government of the Oregon Territory to do away with the Cayuse, but the Whitman Massacre, as it's called to this day, provided exactly the right excuse at the right time for wiping out the once mighty tribe and opening the way for Anglo immigrants—many of whom would become farmers and who would supplant the native grasses with vast acres of wheat.

On the afternoon of the attack on Waiilatpu, Narcissa pulled the tomahawk from Marcus's head and packed his wound with ashes from the fireplace, an act that probably extended his life by some hours. Survivors said that he spoke to her before he died and that she spoke to him. And then he was gone and she was left alone to manage the dozen or so women and children in the house with her and to face the mayhem outside—men being hacked and shot, buildings trashed, fires started. Her husband was dead in the living room, her only biological child was buried at the bottom of the hill, her mother and sisters gone from her life for more than a decade. She was profoundly alone, facing impending demise.

On this last visit of mine, I walked back down the hill and over to the shady section of the grounds to the communal grave (in 1897, the bodies were disinterred, reburied with dignity, marked with a marble slab) of the thirteen people killed at Waiilatpu. Narcissa Prentiss Whitman is listed second among the dead, after her husband, on the weather-beaten stone. I stood there for a moment and thought of my own failures whose implications and consequences strike me as considerably smaller, private failures that few others know about, but that, nonetheless, have hurt people I love. A young marriage I should not have entered into, and the children we brought into the world who are still reeling from the sparrings of their parents. My four daughters understand I was a product of my time, my culture; they realize that if I was to have the future I vehemently claimed to need, it was necessary for me to break out of my conventional marriage. But did that explanation warrant the unraveling they had to endure?

There at the gravesite at Waiilatpu, I pulled from my bag a scan of the blue note with the plant impression I'd found in the book, and squatted to the ground, searching for a piece of matching vegetation. Before long, I found a feathery green weed growing in shade. Tansy. The same species of plant rooted in the same place in 1848, perhaps planted by Marcus or Narcissa as part of a medicinal herb garden. I reached over to pluck a second leaf from near the grave. Then I tucked it in my pocket for the return trip to my room downtown at the Marcus Whitman Hotel. Now the bit of foliage rests between two sheets of parchment paper, dried and flat, in a book about Narcissa Prentiss Whitman—a woman who altered the West whether she meant to or not—that lies here on my table.

Robert Wrigley | TWO POEMS

PROGRESS

You begin to fear all the nowheres are somewheres now.
Everywhere's been discovered. Is there anywhere you can go
and find a hair-netted octogenarian wrangling a walker
and four massive, camp-sized cast-iron skillets full

of Sunday dinner fried chicken at 9:00 a.m.
and ask if she's serving breakfast, then have her say
"Sure thing, hon, but you'll have to wait on yourselves"?
Remember how pretty you were? Well, your sweetheart was

beautiful and all you wanted was some
sunny-side up eggs and bacon with hashbrowns
a white boat of peppery pan gravy,
and a mason jar of homemade apple butter

you'd have to pry the disk of wax out of
and dollop on your toast with a long-shanked teaspoon.
These days Main Street features two antiques emporia,
a coffee shop, and a wine store offering Friday night

tastings of the latest regional Cab Franc cuvee.
The café's become an office dealing in view lots,
weekend lakeside rentals, and time-share condominiums.
That was twenty-five years ago, you tell yourself.

The old chicken-frying woman probably never saw
what's become of the place, though what with the baskets
of brightly colored artificial geraniums hanging
from the vintage lamp posts and the new pocket park

with a memorial to the loggers of yesteryear,
she'd probably approve. There's a new high school too,
and according to its electronic marquee sign,
not only is there a girls' basketball team but they've won

the state three-B championship for the second time this year.
And probably the granola and yogurt breakfast parfait
with seasonal fruit from California's central valley
you had this morning was better for your arteries anyway.

Your sweetheart's still beautiful and you're willing
to settle for distinguished or fairly well preserved,
but the jam this morning comes in those tiny single-serving jars
sealed with a stirrup of foily paper, and you remember

how that morning's apple butter was explosive with cinnamon
and cloves, how the tang came from the cooked
to submission red and golden mottled peelings,
and how the old lady wheeled and toddled

over to the kitchen doorway and called you back to
"Try this for a finish up," and it was a plank of sweet cream
strudel still warm from the oven, a perfect square of butter
liquefying itself on top, and you and your sweetheart split it

and because of it all fell more deeply in love than before,
and after paying the ridiculously tiny bill and thanking
the kindly cook, drove up the lake road and found
a perfect spot in what is now an eighteen-hole, pro-designed

golf course, and made love on a grandmotherly quilt,
within a body's length of the cold clear water,
and lay there for an hour in the sun, as naked and at ease
as no one in that place will ever be again.

COUNTY

County of innumerable nowheres, half its dogs
underfed and of indeterminate breed. County
of the deep fryer, staples in glass against mice,
county of horned gods and billed hats. Sweat county,

shiver county. The hallowed outhouse
upholstered in wooly carpet, the sack of lime,
time out of time, county of country music.

Insufficient snowplows county, county
of the blasted doe all winter in a drift, dust sift
and feather duster county, county of the quo
all status is attached to. Of batches and bitchdogs
howling, of rowels and boots, of soot wash,
of the chimney sweep's red beard,
of the songless radio preaching to no one in the shed.

County of the deadly road, of the shoat pig roasted
in a pit. County of molasses, hobo coffee,
and sugarless soft drink, county of the methamphetamine
picture window, of the padlock and massive hasp.
County of tools and dewormers. Curry comb
and salt block, black pepper gravy, red-eye venison,
blood sausage, county of Bud Light girl posters.

Treblehook county, chum county, bear bait
and dead wolf county. County of the coyote pelt
nailed to the barn door. Bruised woman county,
of men missing one or more fingers, single-finger
wave county. Pistol alongside the cash register.
Pitch-dense firewood county, county of the fearful
and fearless, of the distant mysterious school.

Target-poor county, distant Walmart holyland,
malodorous pulp mill and paper plate county.
County of the hundred-yard drive to the post office,
oddly familiar faces among the wanted posters,
four-hour drive from the county seat county,
unadopted highway, county of no return.
County of August always somewhere burning.

Beercan-bejeweled barrow pit county, hardly
one bullet-unpunctuated county road sign county.
County of the ATV and ancient Indian trail
into the high mountains. Get your bull or buck
county. On-the-way-to-somewhere-else,

doe-see-doe, hundred frozen casseroles
after the funeral, go to heaven county,

blister and blister rust county, Jahweh trailerhouse
county, unassisted living, county
of the Gospels and the *Penthouse* under the bed.
County of tenderness and terror, of almost
universal skepticism, Jesus country county.
County of the cell tower stipend, everywhere
and anywhere, boneyard county, county

a day's drive from the end of the open road.
Softshell Baptist county. Pentecostal pancake county.
County of illusions and of hard facts. Rock
and broken shock, rock and roll aught-six
save your shell casing. County of not quite breath-taking
vistas, of the for sale sign, of timothy and brome,
spring and autumn slaughter county, meat county, home.

Our lives move forward in fits and starts, just as erosion reduces to rubble the redrock cliffs of the Colorado Plateau. Frost pries away slabs of stone in winter. Rocks crash into canyons and roll to a stop where they sit, waiting, until a flash flood moves them downstream, rounding their edges. Each boulder rides the chaotic churn of floodwaters, comes to rest for a time, then again pulses down canyon, headed for the sea.

And so we live—tumbling, careening, and ricocheting off events and people, finally slowing to a stop, becalmed. Our journey shifts, and we lift once more into action. We rush into a new chapter of life and suddenly encounter unforeseen barriers that demand a change in direction. Eventually, we all come to rest in the great ocean.

Maybe this metaphor appeals to me because I love the slickrock canyons of the Four Corners more than any place on earth. I'm equally sustained by the peaceful times—leaning against a sun-warmed alcove, basking like a lizard—and the lively times, when something extraordinary happens, when stormlight creates a moment unlike any other, when a new person comes walking around the bend and life changes, subtly or forever.

In that long-ago spring of 1976, the side canyons of Utah's Escalante River were remoter than they are now, and they are still pretty remote. My two buddies and I had driven without incident in our hand-me-down family sedans across the Circle Cliffs to the Moody Creek trailhead. We found no other vehicles parked at the end of the road. Once we set off on foot, we weren't expecting to see anyone else for the next week.

We did expect thrilling canyon country wilderness. In *Slickrock*, published by the Sierra Club five years earlier, Ed Abbey and Philip Hyde had revealed what we might find—and asked for our help, insisting that if we visited this place, we then took on the responsibility of adding our voices to those seeking to protect "a piece of wild Utah that ought to remain that way." We signed up, lifetime members of the chorus, for we were the generation that came of age as the environmental movement first galvanized

America. When we went off to college and paid our first dues to the Sierra Club, Stewart Udall was still secretary of the interior. In 1970, those first Earth Day demonstrations took place on the grass in front of our college dorms.

We made camp at the junction of East Moody Canyon and the Escalante. In the lengthening iridescent light of late afternoon, we wandered up East Moody Canyon. Each rounding curve brought new walls. Desert varnish streaked the crossbedded sandstone, black swaths across lavender and vermillion. Here, the color fields of Rothko; there, the bold strokes of Franz Kline.

One wall in particular drew me. I moved my tripod this way and that, aiming my camera past piñons and junipers to a canyon wall reflecting purples and mauves, textured with fractures and cracks. The light had bounced down between canyon walls from the sky and the stars, distilled to an unbelievable saturation. I had never seen such surreal and intense colors. Later, I realized Philip Hyde had photographed the very same wall for *Slickrock* and for his Glen Canyon portfolio. Over the years as I published my pictures of that place, I captioned them "Hyde's Wall."

We tore ourselves away from each mosaic of rock, tree, grass, and lichen in the endlessly changing gallery and strolled on, tantalized always by the next bend. We came to an amphitheater, the canyon's curves arranged to form an echo chamber with three reflective surfaces.

A trickle of water in the streambed was enough for the frogs and toads. On that springtime evening they were calling enthusiastically, the cricket-like trill of red-spotted toads and the plaintive bleat of Woodhouse toads advertising their readiness for sex. Spadefoot toads added a third melodic line, a sawing snore, while the final accent came from the ratchety bark of the canyon treefrog—my favorite. They took turns, calling across the alcove, each song echoing individually and distinctly. Stage right, stage left. Then a pause, and a call from back in the cheap seats. We kept our distance to avoid silencing them. They created a fully three-dimensional audio space, and to lie back against a boulder and listen to them felt both intimate and voyeuristic.

We left the frogs and toads to their night music, returned to camp, and sat on cottonwood logs on the little rise along the river where we had rolled out our sleeping bags. To our surprise, a young man our age, lanky and bearded, appeared from around the upstream bend, alone, walking down the Escalante through a last shaft of sunlight in the absolute middle of nowhere. He came over to greet us, and we offered him a cup of tea.

He was scouting for Outward Bound, assigned to lead a course through these canyons in a few weeks. The conversation drifted to politics, for our car radios had been buzzing with news about the 1976 presidential primary season on the drive over from Colorado. We joked about covering our "Udall for President" bumper stickers to make our vehicles appear innocuous to the local anti-environmentalists, and we lamented the fact that it looked like Mo Udall, Westerner and conservation champion, was going to lose the Democratic nomination to Jimmy Carter.

Somewhere in this back and forth, the lone hiker said with a grin, "That's my dad," and then introduced himself as Mark Udall.

How do such encounters with land and people play out in a lifetime? Mark invited us to join a Udall family river trip the next month, and I got to know him better. His cousin Tom rowed our raft on that trip through Cataract Canyon. I followed Mark's career and stayed in touch occasionally as he worked for Outward Bound for twenty years, served in the US House and then as a US senator elected from Colorado in 2008—the same year his cousin Tom, Stewart's son, became a US senator from New Mexico. The two new Udall senators carry the burden of stepping into their fathers' legacy. Mo and Stewart had created new national parks and wilderness from Alaska to Cape Cod.

I know that no member of Congress understands the spirit of the red-rock wilderness better than Mark. No other representative or senator has spent weeks living in the backcountry of the Colorado Plateau. Senator Mark Udall now has the power to speak for the wilderness he loves. I hope he will seize that chance. But he's turning sixty now, a long way from the twenty-five-year-old backpackers we all were in East Moody Canyon thirty-five years ago. He's a politician, a Democrat in a purple state. He has to get reelected. He has to be careful.

Mark's father, Mo, had to resign from Congress twenty years ago when his Parkinson's disease had become too severe; he died in 1998. Mark's uncle Stewart—Tom's father—died in 2010 at ninety. The generations bump along. I finally had the chance to interview Philip Hyde by phone in 2005 a few months before he died and was able to tell him my story about Hyde's Wall. Our tutors, our elders—Stewart Udall, Mo Udall, Wallace Stegner, David Brower, Georgia O'Keefe, Vine Deloria Jr., Ed Abbey, Ansel Adams, Philip Hyde, Eliot Porter, and the legendary founder of Canyonlands National Park, Bates Wilson—all are gone.

The survivors grow older and older—Glen Canyon's singing poet Katie Lee and southern Utah explorer Kent Frost, both over ninety; river runner Ken Sleight (Abbey's model for Seldom Seen Smith) and the artist and naturalist writer Ann Zwinger, both over eighty.

As we all tumble toward the sea, the land itself changes. Flash floods create new rapids, rockfalls enlarge arches. When we hiked the Escalante in 1976, the reservoir in Glen Canyon was still filling, not reaching high pool until 1980. Twenty-five years later, with drought and climate change, Lake Powell dropped so low that some of those side canyons along the Escalante began to reemerge, resurrected from what I had assumed would be permanent loss by drowning. The climate crisis and global environmental changes have decimated amphibian populations, even in remote and pristine places. I haven't seen or heard a canyon treefrog in the redrock backcountry in many years.

Like Mark Udall, I'm turning sixty this year, and, inevitably, I've been reflecting on all of this change. I don't feel old, but I realize that my childhood in the 1950s was nearly as close to the nineteenth century as it was to the twenty-first.

Slouched in the backseat on family vacations to the Colorado Plateau and the Southwest, to the Cascades and the Rockies, I tallied the national parks and monuments I visited. I made lists of parks I yearned to see. My photo album from my teens consists of row after row of snapshots from the viewpoints at national parks, all carefully labeled.

When I read in *National Geographic* about a new national park in Utah—Canyonlands, established in September 1964—I was fascinated. The writer told of discovering never-before-photographed arches hidden away in the sandstone maze of The Needles. I reveled in the fact that, just a few hours from our home in Denver, someone could still be an explorer like Lewis and Clark or Jedediah Smith.

My geologist father made sure we visited that new park the very next year. We dared the crossing to the Island in the Sky across the one-lane width of The Neck and bounced out to Grand View Point to unfold ourselves from the car, stunned by the view.

I still stop to photograph at those viewpoints—and I still define myself as a Westerner, right down to my yearly visit to the dermatologist to burn off the skin damage from a lifetime of walking through the dazzle of the Western sun.

In complementary essays, the Western writer and big-picture thinker Charles Wilkinson and I have tried to organize our understanding of this changing West. We have been watching those chunks of sandstone alternately resting in the sun and wrenched downcanyon as we try to make sense of these cycles of change.

Wilkinson posits four Wests. His First West was Native, distinctly rooted in land-based communities and extending into historic times only to the Spanish missions. His Second West began with the 1848 discovery of gold at Sutter's Mill. The Big Build-Up of dams and power plants that began at the end of World War II jump-started the Third West. In both of the latter Wests, he laments, "the land is considered a commodity and an amenity."

Wilkinson thinks we are ready to create a Fourth West, believing that a sufficient number of Western citizens now realize that we live in a "sacred landscape," that "we finally do know what we have and what we have to lose." He notes that Wallace Stegner was imagining this Fourth West when he yearned for a West with a "society to match its scenery."

My own scheme parallels Wilkinson's. I call my "First West" the Bedrock West—the land itself, an extravagance of mountains and deserts and two hundred Native cultures still intertwined with the holy Earth.

Landscape dominates this West. Redrock canyons insist that you acknowledge geologic time. Plains and deserts, and the sky above them, create spaces so expansive that they can fill you with exhilaration and dread. Mountains rise precipitously to bar you from neighboring valleys that a raven could reach in a ten-mile flight on a good updraft.

We Westerners must measure ourselves against this land. Drought, cliffs, distances. Alkali, uranium, cheatgrass. While South Carolina squabbles over how best to address the bitter heritage of slavery, and Illinois insists on extending corn and soybean subsidies forever, Utah and Nevada and Wyoming argue about the highest and best use of millions of acres of public lands—drylands that remain public because they were too challenging and difficult for anyone to actually live in and try to farm or ranch, with or without the help of slaves.

When non-Indians came here, we thought we had arrived on a blank slate, the Great American Desert. But to create that blank slate, first we had to nearly annihilate the Native peoples. We spent decades being brutal—to Indian people, to the wildlife, to the land itself. And as we moved on, we mythologized this era of callous conquest as the Old West (West Number Two). After a few more decades of complacency, we chucked that worn-out myth in favor of a New West that would somehow combine the realities of the place with dot.com fantasies.

My Third West, the New West, is urban. Today more than 80 percent of Westerners live in cities. More than half of American Indians live in cities, mostly in the West.

Identity doesn't come automatically in the modern West. We might be cowboys, but we have to decide if we are mythic cowboys or Sundance catalog cowboys, trumpeting our trendiness with our freshly purchased apparel—or if we just happen to be folks who work on a ranch and know a lot about range management. We might define ourselves, in part, as Western skiers or river runners or hikers, but we may well have grown up in Newton, Massachusetts, or Toledo, Ohio, before we came west.

Back in those green and fertile places, our relationship with home ground is simpler, more predictable. The Interior West, the Desert West, is a shape-shifter, as Native storytellers understand. Living in a landscape where the bones show, where the Earth itself reminds us daily of its history, we will do well to take the long view.

Now that the New West hasn't panned out quite as we hoped, we try reclaiming our imaginary identities as rural Old Westerners, to no avail. We are still looking for guidance, for a clear path into the future.

Like Charles Wilkinson, I imagine a Next West, a People's West, a Fourth West, where, with a new awareness of the true nature of our home, we finally acknowledge that we will always live enmeshed in Place—and that to find our way we must collaborate in creating a community rooted in healthy relationship, with each other, with the land.

But even as we writers and historians try to categorize and analyze the West, it keeps changing; it keeps challenging us. Just when summertime flash floods sweep a canyon clean, a hard winter wedges free a new succession of rockfalls to block our way.

The latest challenge looms large. The Colorado River Basin lies squarely within the crosshairs of global climate change. Rising average temperatures are certain to bring warmer summers, more rain than snow, decreased spring runoff, and more frequent wildfires. Fewer and fewer canyon treefrogs will call from potholes and desert streams. Climate change will push every living community uphill until alpine tundra and alpine animals, like pikas, can retreat no higher and will be pinched right off the mountaintops of the southern Rockies. What will we do for water in this increasingly dry century?

In the canyons of this dynamic home place, in the tricky cultural currents we must navigate, my aging generation is running out of time to make a difference. Sixty isn't old, but clearly we can't dawdle.

Our edges are rounder, our destination closer. Gravity and time turn out to be equally inexorable. This same arc through time deepens our relationships with the places we love. We never leave that tribe that Abbey and Hyde insisted we had joined the moment we set off down the canyons of the Escalante. The redrock wilderness has granted us refuge, repeatedly. The universe has provided us with a lifetime of chances to speak up for these remaining fragments of wild ecosystems.

Let's take full advantage of these last few winding and glorious bends, missing no opportunity for joyful adventure and rising to each occasion calling for advocacy as we tumble toward the sea.

Terry Tempest Williams | FRIENDSHIP

"Was it daylight or at night, you saw this rock?" Elizabeth asked. "Daylight,"
I replied as the sliver moon, blood-orange, rises over her shoulder. We keep
walking, this clan of ours on uneven ground through knee-high grasses and
candlestick forms of gentian, three feet tall. Some of us are walking arm in
arm so as not to stumble—Lowry's young bright eyes see a glimmer of light.
"Look, there, a boulder," she says. We keep walking. Rick speaks of rattlesnakes, but not to worry, the cold makes them docile. Brooke speaks of faith,
but remains skeptical about finding one particular boulder, call it an erratic,
in all of Centennial Valley. What is driving me is my desire to share and the
thought of one more touch of flesh to stone to the moans of bison who came
to this place and rubbed their shoulders with time again and again in a circle
around this rock until what was once hard became smooth and polished and known.

Amy Irvine) RED

> *The bereaved [Demeter] lighted her torch*
> *and from Aetna's rocks cast the shifting*
> *glare of the mighty flame . . . as she followed*
> *the traces of the dark ravisher [Hades] and*
> *the great wheel-furrows in the dust . . . [the*
> *giant buried beneath Mount Aetna] himself*
> *re-echoes her wild wailings, and illumines*
> *her path with bursting fire . . .*

THE RAPE OF PERSEPHONE, *STATIUS,*
THEBAID 12. 270 FF: LATIN EPIC C1ST A.D.

April 3, 2008. The storm came rolling across the sky like a chariot ablaze. It hit the mesa as I trudged up our dirt road to the garbage cans. Like a thousand small locusts, red dust pelted the trash bag slung over my shoulder while the two new pups—border collie-heeler mixes from the same litter—tried to take cover between my legs. Then suddenly they were rolling away like tumbleweed. I tried to shout to them, but my mouth filled with grit. Voice and eyes were sandblasted, breath snuffed. It felt like the end of the world.

For hours, the storm raged. Buds were scoured from trees while tender green shoots were battered back into the ground. When it was all said and done, every fertile beginning had been laid to an early end.

Even after the winds died, dust lingered in the air like sepia. And when the people of the Four Corners could finally make out the prominent incisions in our skyline—the fourteen thousand-foot peaks of southwestern Colorado's San Juan Mountains—even the old-timers were amazed to see their snow-laden peaks coated the color of rusted metal. Not just flecked or lightly tinted, but thoroughly painted. Looking at the horizon was like looking through a telescope at Mars.

Jayne Belnap, a veteran scientist for the United States Geological Survey, had predicted this. By 2050, she anticipates that the region's soil instability "will be equal to that of the Dust Bowl days."[1] Much of what gets caught up in prevailing winds is loosened by aggressive activities on public land. Analysis of the federal government's data of areas managed by its Bureau of Land Management found that, in just the last few years, off-road vehicle use has increased 19 percent, the number of oil and gas wells— accompanied by a host of new roads, rig pads, and settling ponds—has expanded 24 percent, while acreage dedicated to livestock grazing has risen 7 percent.[2]

A senior air resource specialist at the agency that oversees these activities was quoted in the *Washington Post*, saying of the dust storm: "In the big scheme of things . . . it's not that big a deal."[3]

But the proof was in the rivers. Satellite imagery would show that the dust had been lifted from denuded portions of the Colorado Plateau, the redrock landmass that occupies much of southern Utah and northern Arizona, and a physiographic province that contains millions of acres of public land. After crossing our mesa in southwestern Colorado, the storm dumped most of its debris on the high country of the San Juans where major tributaries to the Colorado River, one of the West's most vital waterways, are formed. The layer absorbed the sun's heat, exponentially accelerating the spring thaw of the snowpack beneath it. In mad, incomprehensible torrents, the water rushed by. Downstream, reservoirs were drained just to accommodate the inundation. And then the water was gone just as quickly as it had come.

The San Miguel River. The Gunnison and Dolores. And the San Juan. We stood on the banks and watched, wringing red-stained hands. We turned to one another and wondered: just how, come summer, would we quench our many thirsts?

To inhabit the Southwest as home is to dwell at one end of the visible spectrum. Passions or furies, we see it all in red. A nearsightedness manifests and we fail to remember, even in the face of climate uncertainty, the region's aridity, the memories of our own nascent mythology. Instead, we saturate the land with promises, we project onto place the slaking of limitless desires.

I was born to this landscape, and still the only claim I can make honestly is this: to be a daughter of the desert is to have been born to Demeter, the goddess of fruitful sustenance. She rages at our forgetting.

Red granules fall like dry tears. Somewhere above the fallout, I can hear my mother's wails.

NOTES

1. Juliet Eilperin, "Dust Storms Escalate in West, Raising Environmental Fears," *Washington Post*, April 23, 2009, www.washingtonpost.com/wp-dyn/content/article/2009/04/22/AR2009042203685.html.

2. Ibid.

3. Ibid.

To be truthful, in our family there was eventually no clear line between religion and fly fishing, either. We also lived at the junction of great trout waters, but not in Norman Maclean's Montana. We grew up in southern Idaho and eastern Washington. Our father was a coach and a teacher who loved history and mathematics. He read to us from Shakespeare, the Bible, and Mark Twain, but after our mother left him he went quietly insane until he received legal custody of all three of his children, and so my brothers and I were left to assume that our mother was never coming back to our father again, and she never did.

My father had taught Indian kids in school before he and I moved to Inchelium without my brothers to spend our first year without her. In fact, from the time my father took his first job in a public school at Blackfoot on the border of the Fort Hall Indian Reservation, my father continued to teach Indian students until he retired thirty or more years later. From our family's Blackfoot years, I remember two Indian students in particular: Lloyd Babbi and Neil Tres Hand. Lloyd Babbi may have been the finest point guard I ever saw play basketball—and I've seen a few, including not only those I played against during my brief tenure under Eddie Sutton at the College of Southern Idaho in Twin Falls but also those I played against in pickup games at noon in Bear Down Gym when I was a graduate student at Arizona during the glory days of Lute Olson. Every starting point guard for the Wildcats eventually made his way over to Bear Down at noon and so did the shooting guards like Steve Kerr and big men like Judd Buschler.

But Lloyd Babbi had all those extra things besides fine training: he could leap tall players with a single bound, sprint faster than an antelope, and see behind his head. He made everything difficult appear easy and graceful. Long before John Stockton ever set foot on a court or Mark Few ever picked up a whistle, Lloyd Babbi led the Gonzaga Bulldogs to their first appearance at the NCAA's Big Dance.

Neil Tres Hand played basketball, too—what young American Indian doesn't?—but Neil excelled at football. Under the protection of a helmet and faceguard, a game uniform and pads, Neil Tres Hand transformed himself from a gangly, introverted, too-tall, good-looking college kid into a warrior who specialized in intercepting passes and decapitating opposing quarterbacks. Unlike Lloyd Babbi, however, Neil drank whiskey, chased older women, and struggled with grades. He played, when he was eligible, for the Boise State Junior College Broncos. One morning not long before my mother left, I woke up early and saw Neil sprawled on our living room couch in Boise. My father had just been fired as the sophomore coach at Boise High School, but several of his former high school players were always attending college in town, so it was never anything out of the ordinary to find one of them sleeping on our couch. Besides, it was a weekend in spring and everyone was asleep, including Neil, who was snoring with his mouth open. Neil had left a flask of whiskey on the floor, but he woke up before I could examine it closely. "You better give that to me," he said. He pulled himself upright, put one hand on his forehead as if to take his own temperature — or measure the power of his hangover — then he took a long pull from the flask, threw off the rest of his blanket, put his feet into his shoes, and walked out our front door in his underwear. After that we never saw or heard from Neil Tres Hand again.

I imagine that was the same door my mother walked through, too, on her way out, only my mother was sober, and she took my two brothers with her. I think the primary reason she left me behind was because my father threatened to kill her if she took us with her, and he might have, too, if she had taken all three of us. Still, there were other reasons she left me behind. She knew I could outrun her and sometimes outsmart her. Once, when she came to pick me up at Julia Davis Park in Boise, she tried to lure me into the same car with her "friend" George, the alcoholic truck driver she later married. I feigned indifference until I got right up to the passenger-side door and she had her hands on the front seat to make room for me in the back. As soon as she turned her head away, I did a one-eighty and sprinted all-out across the open grass for the Boise River. To my mother's credit, she caught me by the shirttails just before I could reach the water. Then she slapped my face all the way back to the car. She slapped me so hard that she seriously injured her hand. My ears rang, but only partly because she yelled at me the whole time: "Don't you ever . . . !"

Needless to say, perhaps, as soon as we covered the hundred or more yards back to the car, I pulled what she later called "the same stunt" again, only that time I made the river. And I never did get in that car with George.

Boise had two parks in those days, but we ought to remember that the city of Boise today bears little resemblance to the town I knew. One day at the "new" park, Ann Morrison, my father stopped the car after more or less telling me that my mother was leaving him. The car was a used 1955 Ford two-door sedan. I was outside it leaning my back against the door and facing my father when he said, "If she does leave, would you prefer to go with her or to stay with me?" He knew the answer before he asked the question, but I suppose he felt he had to ask it, anyway, just to be sure.

After she left, he asked me another question I'll never forget. This time I was sitting on top of the garbage cans near the back porch of our house when he pulled into the driveway and killed the engine. By this time, he'd wrecked the Ford and was driving the blue Austin, his "fishing" car. After he got out of the car and closed the door, he walked straight over to me. He looked me in the eyes for a few seconds, and then said, "What do you think, Jim? Should I just beat the hell out of him or should I kill the son-of-a-bitch?"

I confess I thought about the question for a second. After all, I'd thought about killing the son-of-a-bitch myself. Instead, I answered his question with a question of my own: "Well, I suppose you should kill him, but what am I going to do for a father while you're in prison?"

The tiny village of Inchelium on the Colville Indian Reservation just below the Canadian border on the upper Columbia River was only a pit stop for my father—he couldn't wait to "go home," and it nearly killed him, literally, to be separated from my two younger brothers—but to me, as a pre-adolescent, Inchelium was an eternity in paradise.

It was at Inchelium that I first began to write and to read voraciously, to hunt deer and grouse and pheasants and doves, to pick huckleberries and wild raspberries and chokecherries and elderberries, to dig camas with a "tookus," and to fish for salmon and trout with a dip net, a gaff hook, a bow and arrow, or a fly rod. It was at Inchelium, too, that I suffered the slings and arrows of outrageous injustice and the unbearable lightness and sweetness of my fatal attraction to dark women with skin the color of honey and hair as black as a raven's eyes, not to mention minds as quick and fleet as the creeks and rivers themselves. At Inchelium, too, I learned to play stick games, to dance, to sing, to drum, and to risk everything, not for love or money or fame, but for pride and dignity and humility and honor and self-respect and the respect of others. I learned the value of silence and privacy and vowed to never betray anyone I loved.

I had learned to ride on my grandparents' ranch near Declo by the time I was four, so Indian horses made a real impression on me. I had never shot a rifle off a horse before. At first, I couldn't believe anyone would be foolish enough to try, but most of my friends could do it, and I learned to do it, too, eventually, although it almost cost me a broken tailbone.

I came from a long line of Irish, French, and British storytellers. From hearing my father, my grandparents, my cousins, my uncles, and my aunts tell stories, I already knew that even my best friends would never pay attention to any story unless a lot happened in it very quickly, but at Inchelium I heard stories that went on for whole days and whole nights, some of them in English. I realize now that a few of those stories were true epics.

Because he was a coach, as soon as basketball season started, my father was gone a good part of the time, especially on weekends when his junior high, junior varsity, and varsity teams played games off the reservation at places like Republic and Omak and Newport. At first, I traveled with the team, singing forty-niners on the bus along with juniors and seniors who adopted me, and telling jokes and listening to stories, but soon enough I demanded to be left home in the charge of any Indian woman foolish enough to take me. Usually, that meant the mother of my best friend, Carl Seymour. Because I tanned easily to a deep brown in the summers, if I wore a hat, as I usually did, at first the tribal game wardens and the state police treated me with distant curiosity whenever they checked the Seymour car for drugs or alcohol or poached game. Every morning Carl's stepfather woke us up at sunrise. If we wore pajamas to bed, he made us strip to our boxer shorts and run the lane to the mailbox and back twice in our bare feet without stopping. I thought this ritual would surely end with the first snow or the first hard freeze, but I was wrong.

At another friend's house, I learned to sweat. In fact, I came to love the sweat house, although I still grow timid when it comes time to jump in the creek, especially in freezing weather when someone has to clear ice from the hole. From living on my grandparents' farm, I knew all about outhouses, too, which only increased my respect for the immaculate inside bathrooms of most of my Indian friends. In fact, maybe even a majority of my Indian friends tended toward the bourgeois. One night while Carl Seymour and I were lying on our bellies watching an episode of the Lone Ranger and Tonto on TV while anticipating an elk hunting trip the next morning with his stepfather and mother, Carl turned to me and said, "Let's go watch some Indian television." His parents were out for the night. We were in charge of ourselves. His little brothers and sisters were all staying with relatives.

Carl fixed us both a ketchup sandwich on white bread, threw me a piece of venison jerky, and then led me outside in my shirtsleeves. We could hear crickets and frogs, so it must have still been early in the fall, and the moonless sky above us stretched from horizon to horizon as black as the Lone Ranger's mask, but it was also a sky filled with a billion planets and stars. We walked maybe a quarter of mile along a trail into the woods without a flashlight. I tried to use the one I had brought along, but Carl said it would make us "blind." Sure enough, it did. When we hit the camp where his family hung their meat in a locked shed, Carl started a fire in the ring near the smokehouse and the drying racks. Then the dogs joined us, appearing out of the woods like phantom wolves, startling me at first. Soon, we were all sitting around a good blaze that made our shadows jump on the walls of the shed whenever we moved. The dogs seemed to be restless and moving all the time. After maybe ten or fifteen minutes, I broke the silence and said, "What are we going to do out here?"

"What do you mean?" Carl asked.

"I mean, why are we here sitting around the fire? What are we going to do? Roast marshmallows?"

"We're doing it," Carl said. "We're watching Indian television."

Thinking back now, I suppose it must have been October because the next day after road hunting for elk and deer all morning, we spent the afternoon high up on some ponds and creeks, snagging eastern brook trout with treble hooks attached to spinning rods. Eastern brook trout, of course, are not really trout at all. They are char, and Pacific char (bull trout and Dolly Varden) had been part of the Colville diet for approximately eight or ten thousand years. Snagging eastern brook trout with treble hooks attached to spinning rods looks easy, especially since the eastern brook trout are highly visible in their spawning jackets. Every October they turn bright shades of orange and scarlet and deep crimson along their bellies, and the males go kype-jawed. Compared to kokanee and sockeye, whose entire bodies turn Christmas tree green and red at spawning time, I guess brook trout might be hard for some people to see, but we had no trouble seeing these fish congregated together in stages. Most were about eight to ten inches long, but Carl and his parents each caught several two and three pounders, which left me ambitious, lean, and hungry.

Of course, we fried some on the spot for a midday snack. Carl's mom cleaned maybe three or four dozen fingerlings quicker than I could say "Hi-ho, Silver! Away!" and then threw some dough into the grease to make fry bread. She cooked the fingerlings whole, with their heads on, and we ate them bones and all. The hot fry bread we spread with butter and huckleberry jam or chokecherry jelly. Then we went back to fishing. Carl's stepfather expected us each to fill at least one gunnysack. We naturally spent the late afternoon gutting eastern brook trout, and then we drove home in the dark. On the way, Carl's stepfather let him shoot a white-tail while I held the spotlight. We gutted it and then struggled to lift the carcass into the back of the pickup, which is where we rode, of course, huddled together against the cab for warmth, staring at Carl's little spike and the piles of wet gunny sacks full of gutted eastern brook trout.

As a teacher of American history and as a veteran of World War II, my father knew the US government was more deceitful than any coyote and more crooked than any stick when it came to dealing with Indians, past or present. "When it comes to Indians," he told me once just as we were crossing the bridge to Kettle Falls on a grocery run, "a politician shits out his mouth every time he opens it."

In fact, my father believed the West's greatest sin—its first and original sin—was the breaking of the treaties. "Your word, your promise, is sacred," he used to tell us. "It's really the only thing you have." Sometimes he'd fall back on the old homily, "A man is only as good as his word," but then he'd always add, "and his word is only as good as he is." My father loved his country, but he knew that his country was full of Indians his country had betrayed. As a realist as well as an idealist, my father knew further that his country was also full of Indians who had betrayed themselves and each other as his government had contrived for them to do.

For my father, the family was the center of the universe, and the universe centered itself around the family. Like the people we lived with at Inchelium, many of whom adopted us and cared for us and protected us as their own, my father also strongly believed that the family or the tribe or the clan or whatever we want to call it also included the places where we lived: the mountains, the trees, the rivers and creeks, the animals and plants. White people pay lip service to this idea all the time.

Traditional Indian people live it.

That's one reason reservation kids, no matter how talented, generally struggle and so often lose that struggle once they leave the reservation. Unlike most white people, young Indians from traditional families grow up knowing they are part of a sacred family that includes their mothers and their fathers, their uncles, their cousins, and their aunties, not to mention their brothers-in-law and their sisters-in-law, their second cousins, their third cousins, their nieces and their nephews, and perhaps most of all their paternal and maternal grandmothers and grandfathers, but they grow up knowing they are also literally related to sacred places— to sacred trees, sacred animals, sacred creeks, sacred rocks, sacred rivers, sacred mountains—that are no less alive and no less intimately connected to themselves and to their individual physical and mental health and general well-being than their human relatives.

Although I knew some very good Catholics at Inchelium where I later returned to coach and teach in the very same rooms where I had gone to school and where my father had taught before me, I never knew any Colville Indian who ever worried much about missing church. Likewise, the great cathedrals of Europe, Mexico, and the United States were merely outhouses, according to my father, compared to the cathedrals we discovered on our own each Sunday on or just off the reservation: a grove of cedars a thousand years old, for example, with a river running through it in sunlight and shadows.

That year we spent in Inchelium without my brothers, my father asked me to promise him two things: first, that if he ever got to a place where he would become what he called a "vegetable," I would help him die, and second, that when he did die I would bury him in a "pine box." He absolutely abhorred the idea of spending "good" money he had honestly earned and saved on a "fancy" coffin.

Unlike me, my two younger brothers grew up to become certified "Personal Wealth Managers," although they are also both very fine fishermen. They must be very good at their jobs because one of them spends more time fishing than he does managing his own or anybody else's wealth. Regardless, before our stepmother died a long, lonely, lingering death, my brothers helped my father sell his house, his tools, and, in fact, almost all his belongings and move into a "retirement home" where he could better care for her with the help of full-time nurses. Of course, we all know that "retirement home" is simply code for The End.

After our stepmother died, my brothers nevertheless continued to care for our father for several years by having him over to dinner on weekends and taking him fishing whenever they could. We also spent holidays together as a family, but once my father finally quit driving and could no longer leave the city of Boise on his own to visit his few remaining friends, he deteriorated quickly. Then, during a more or less routine surgery at a hospital, the surgeon nicked a bowel and despite "the best care possible" his bowels became infected and the infection spread. Toward the end, my brothers were spending $6,000 a shot two or three times a week in an attempt to control the further spread of the infection. Although my father couldn't speak with a tube in his throat, he was nevertheless highly alert and very much mentally alive during much of the time we visited him, and he kept looking at me in particular. I knew what he wanted, but convincing my brothers to end his "treatments" took every rhetorical skill I'd ever learned from him.

Worse, when it came time for my brothers and I to choose a coffin, tempers flared into flames. "They both look like miniature whorehouses," I said when they showed me their "final selections." "Besides, I don't believe your father would approve of spending $15,000 on a goddamned coffin. He made me promise him I'd bury him in a pine box!"

"He never told me that," one of them said.

In our family's way of doing things, not merely the majority but everyone has to agree.

After the "funeral director" finally (but reluctantly) showed us the very sort of coffin my father probably had in mind, my two brothers just looked at each other, and then they looked at me. The coffin was made of pine veneer and particleboard.

"Thanks," I said to Steve. Steve was the name of the funeral director. "Could you show us something in pine?"

Steve was gone a long time, but when he came back, he wheeled a shining coffin made of genuine pine into the room. "It's the last one of its kind," he said. "They aren't going to make any more of these babies. I had to run clear over town to our other shop to get it. What do you think?"

I looked at my brothers who appeared to be somewhat appeased. They both shrugged their shoulders.

"It's beautiful," I said. "We'll take it."

"Now nearly all those I have loved and did not understand when I was young are dead," my old friend Norman Maclean wrote, "but I still reach out to them." Whatever I am, whatever I have been, whatever I will be, I owe to all those I have loved and did not understand, my own father primary among them. Any good I have done in this world, I have done with them in mind, inspired by their examples. Happily, they are not responsible for my sins and omissions.

I have been lucky. I was born and grew up in the West. I left it briefly, once, to attend school (in the parlance of my family) "back east in Iowa," where for three long years I suffered from an acute fear that I would die without seeing another Western mountain. I've spent extended sojourns in Mexico and Canada, in the southern United States and New England, and I sincerely believe that travel enlarges the human spirit. Some of my truest friends live spread out across the planet, and while I'd like to visit them just to see their faces and to experience more fully the places they write about, almost all I know and love is right here where I have chosen to live and work. And unless I am otherwise persuaded by my beautiful, dark-eyed, captive wife, who has lived the last twenty-five years of her life in exile from her beloved Santa Fe, this is the place I intend to lay my burden down. However things turn out, when that time comes, I want my remains cremated, my ashes mingled with Tanya's (when her time comes), and the whole mix scattered on the wind from so high up that it settles on every mountaintop from Santa Fe to Lewiston. We want our remains to literally become a part of the West we love.

Meanwhile, despite the presence of the dams on the lower Snake, here at the Snake's junction with the Clearwater, the steelhead and the chinook have arrived in record numbers. I've been chasing them pretty hard with moderate success, using flies I tied last winter: Freight Trains, mostly, and Purple Perils. But I caught two wild fish on a Brazen Lady and one on a Whatka Blonde and another in September on a Blood and Brandy. For now, at least, we're home. And here's an idea whose time has truly arrived: I'm going fishing. In the words of a good friend, "Don't come with me. You stay home too."

I only seem to be a Westerner when I stand east of wherever someone at the moment says the West starts. This morning I fed the birds, checked the rain gauge from the monsoon last night, and then watched a young bobcat eat grass in the backyard while ravens in the cottonwoods raised a ruckus. I fielded a call from the East and talked to people in the documentary business who consider me a savage. It has been a long time since I thought the West even existed except as a historical moment in the conquest of land and cultures.

Last week, the bird sanctuary a mile upstream had to be closed to visitors because a mountain lion seemed to be stalking well-fed birders who were stalking gray hawks and violet-crowned hummingbirds. From my perch here, it is eighteen miles for a bird to the Mexican border and in that section three hundred and fifty Border Patrol agents prowl and drones almost silently skim the treetops, hunting Mexicans. There are checkpoints on the roads to make sure no unauthorized migration occurs. Meanwhile, the first rufous hummingbirds arrived last week on the return lap of their journey to Central America and southern Mexico. Even for a rasty group of creatures like hummingbirds, the arrival of the rufous is akin to having the area taken over by an outlaw motorcycle gang.

So based on the evidence, the case could be made that I live in the West and therefore I am a Westerner. But this claim is bullshit.

I have trouble with the idea that there is a kind of person called a Westerner. There have been days when I wanted to fire my .357 Magnum through the latest spate of photo books, all called something like *The Last Cowboy*. I have also toyed with burning down any art gallery that displays paintings of mounted Indians framed by rainbows, outlawing small statues of Kokopelli, and mutilating any pink coyote displayed in front of a home.

The region called the West has been a vast chamber where Americans denounce the federal government and feed off various forms of federal dole (grazing permits, irrigation districts, military bases, and the huge apparatus of a police state, now called in the best Waffen-us style, Homeland Security). But in the main, now that the slaughter of tribes is over and the hills have been gouged for minerals and the grasslands trampled by steers, the West is a place of cities, malls, golf courses, and tract housing.

If there is a West, it is not in our minds but under our feet. There are no real Westerners, but there is a series of deserts, mountains, streams, and *despoblados* that linger outside our home entertainment centers. This terrain is seldom glimpsed except through car windows or off the wing of a commercial flight. It is not a direction but a vast domain of limited rain and low population density. A place some of my fellow citizens consider godforsaken. A place I find one of my last refuges from the religious maniacs that infest my nation.

If a Westerner means a person created by the land and adapted to the land, well, we ran out of them some time ago. There are small pockets of resentment, saloons in the outback of the region where laborers gather over a beer and talk guns and weather. But the only current candidates I see for the role of Westerner are these brown people walking across my desert with very little water and food so that they can find new land and new lives. Of course, they face a standing army of twenty thousand Border Patrol agents who have been instructed to keep them out of the Real West.

As for the land itself, based on the current evidence, it will grow warmer and drier, the trees will migrate up the mountains, the grasslands will recede, and the human beings who have clustered in the cities will either make do with less water and less golf or they will leave. Should peace ever break out, an unlikely possibility given the penchants of my nation, the entire region will crater as the money of the military-industrial complex vanishes. The patches of the region that feed off fossil fuel resources will persist until they succeed in destroying this resource.

Eventually, the place will return to the natural flow of resources, rain, wind, sun, the four seasons, and the like. If anyone is still around then, well, they can become Westerners. Of course, by then, only a few fools will claim their identity is based off a direction.

The Real West will finally begin when both the name and the habits we now cherish in our films and other fictions are erased.

Maybe it will be called something unthinkable now. Say, something like Home.

Sally Denton   BEYOND THIS PLACE
THERE BE DRAGONS

"Nevada is ten thousand tales of ugliness and beauty, viciousness and virtue," Richard G. Lillard wrote in 1942. It was a place like no other, treated less as a land to settle than some alien fastness to be plundered, a colony valued only for what could be taken from it. Embedded beneath its lunar landscape was a fortune not even the greediest person could imagine. It was always a place to be used, one way or another. For three more votes in Congress during the Civil War and its electoral count in a potentially close 1864 election, Abraham Lincoln and his fellow Republicans made a state of the lawless expanse of one hundred thousand square miles. It was christened "Nevada"—Spanish for "snow covered"—with the motto "Battle Born."

Ten to fifteen thousand years ago, the region was a paradise. Fed by the effusion of retreating glaciers, emerald grass and bright blue lakes covered much of the region. For a time there was abundant animal life. Mammoths and camels grazed peacefully until devoured by saber-toothed tigers and giant lions. Some of the first humans of North America lived there as well, halfway between the Isthmus and the Arctic, their stone dart points embedded in the earth. Then, without warning, long after the Ice Age, "nature played violent games," as a 1937 California museum brochure described the mysterious events, and the land turned quickly into a sweltering hell. Water, animals, and people vanished, leaving to the mountains and desert only their chalky relics and scattered bones. Fearful of what might lay ahead, yet terrified to retreat, a pioneer passing through Death Valley in the 1800s warned fellow immigrants that "beyond this place there be dragons."

I am a fourth-generation Nevadan, shaped and inspired by this forlorn social and environmental history. Raised by a passionate Nevadaphile, I was taught to be proud of the state's exciting—if mostly down-and-out, boom-and-bust—history. I inherited my father's obsession with the land, the people, the culture. I even embraced our family mythology that *anyone* could make it in California with its golden climate and legendary fecundity. But it took grit and ingenuity, courage and tenacity to make it in Nevada, where as recently as the 1950s the population ratio was nearly one individual per square desert mile.

Imbued with this superiority complex about my roots, my strong sense of place naturally influenced my writing. So it came as a great shock to me to find that not only was the American West the poor relation of the Eastern literary elite, but also that Nevada was the bastard child of that benighted West. With its wild scenery, relaxed morality, Gold Rush ghost towns, gambling parlors, and whorehouses, Nevada inspired both awe and derision among New York publishers. I quickly learned that to be characterized as a "regional" writer—unless, of course, the region is the northeastern or southern US—was the kiss of death. To be labeled a "popular historian" is to be mocked and denigrated by academics, as the brilliant and gifted Barbara W. Tuchman often complained. To be a popular historian whose subject is the American West is to be doubly marginalized, as the talented independent historian Fawn Brodie found. With the publication of *No Man Knows My History*—her masterful biography of Joseph Smith—a "kind of Brodie-bashing cottage industry" was fueled by academics whose "criticism was rooted in a bald attempt to discredit her as a delusional woman who lacked the historian's ability to discern truth from falsehood," as Virginia Scharff, president of the Western History Association, put it.

Sadly, Western fiction writers have not been spared the bias. "It was the *New York Times* that broke his heart," author Timothy Egan quoted a retired Stanford English professor, referring to the king of contemporary Western writers, Wallace Stegner. "Stegner won the National Book Award for *The Spectator Bird*, which the Times never reviewed," wrote Egan. "He also won a Pulitzer for his best-loved novel, *Angle of Repose*, which the paper only noticed after the award, and then with a sniff."

When I won two Western Heritage Awards for my work on Utah's Mountain Meadows Massacre of 1857, and then was inducted into the Nevada Writers Hall of Fame, I couldn't help feeling slighted when my New York book publisher sent neither a representative nor even a congratulatory note to the ceremonies. I was a hick and the Western accolades were bush league, was the unmistakable message. But despite the at-once provincial and patronizing attitude of the Eastern media establishment, the stories of the West continue to ignite and inspire readers nationwide. The West, after all, embodies expansion and emancipation—the fulcrum of American ideology—and can no longer be dismissed as either aberrant or insignificant. Its politics, natural resources, economics, and culture are integrally tied to America's future. Whether the East knows it yet or not, the literature and history of the West is the literature and history of America.

Douglas Unger

CITY OF NOMADS,
CITY OF SECOND CHANCES

That sage, elder literary voice for the American West, William Kittredge, cites a statistic that 85 percent of the inhabitants of the region now live in cities. That seems about right, especially in light of frequent media features headlining the top twenty cities in the West for new job opportunities in high technology and so-called green industries. The last half of the twentieth century and the first decade of the twenty-first have been boom years for the West's urban centers: Tucson, Phoenix, Albuquerque, Santa Fe, Boise, Las Cruces, Portland, Eugene, and that metropolitan sprawl along the eastern slope of the Rockies that stretches from Colorado Springs up through Denver and Fort Collins clear to Cheyenne, Wyoming, as well as for that strangest new city—my city—Las Vegas. The pioneering delirium of its recent, unbounded growth is astonishing. In speed and scale, Las Vegas has been the fastest growing city of them all.

For a long time, it struck me as both ironic and just plain weird that my family and I ended up in Las Vegas and that my father, a part-time rancher and passionate even if transplanted Westerner, died here. Las Vegas is a place of historic contrasts between its classic cowboy emblem of "Las Vegas Vic" on Fremont Street, in his neon Stetson and cattleman's neckerchief, and the forty-story mega-resort casino complexes growing up along the Las Vegas Strip, their high towers of stacked, shimmering windows reflecting light like huge, glowing plasma TVs. The skyline has been transforming into something that resembles a kind of Miami, surrounded not by blue bays and ocean but by the vast brushy sea and mountainscape of the Mojave Desert. Thirty-eight million tourists throng through its attractions every year, making Las Vegas the largest adult-themed carnival on the planet. Recently, I've come to understand my family landing in such a strange, transient, urban jungle as this was in some way inevitable. After a lifetime spent wandering all over the West, in the end, there was nowhere better or more fitting for us to go.

I'm the son of what our more rooted, agrarian neighbors called, with no little contempt, a "suitcase rancher"—someone who buys a ranch mainly for recreational and speculative value, moving on and off the land with his suitcases for part-time residencies. After my parents' divorce—brought on in part by the nervous breakdown my mother suffered caused by the isolation and hardships my father tried to force on her by moving us into our first ranchhouse with only an unheated outhouse for plumbing and a hand-pump we had to prime each morning for water—my brothers and I grew up passed back and forth between Mom's East and Dad's West, and we spent summers and winter "vacations" on his ranches. His first place was a small grazing and hay operation in the rugged scrub oak foothills and ridge country midway between Steamboat Springs and Oak Creek, Colorado. Then Dad moved us to a more serious spread, a year-round cattle concern with about three dozen purebred Charolais, two hundred acres of farmed wheat and hay, and a BLM grazing lease—hard red wheat and cattle country—eighteen miles into the brushy arroyos and high plains north of Craig, Colorado, way off the highway heading up into Wyoming. The last ranch Dad owned was in the desolate short-grass prairie north of the Black Hills, the nearest town called Newell, population 312 (and fewer now, last time I checked) up in South Dakota—a corn, hay, and sheep operation out there all on its own, miles away from anybody.

My father was always buying ranches, forcing us to develop and work them, then, just when we got them running about right, he sold out and made us all move on. He fled real estate development and all the people it brought, selling out two steps ahead of the coming ski resort and oil shale speculation booms in Colorado, then well before the peak of optimum farmland prices in South Dakota, which made no financial sense whatsoever. He was too often overextended on his places, short of money to keep them running well. Still, "too many people," he would complain, then he would up and sell out for this and other reasons, some related to legal complications of his multiple divorces, but mainly due, I believe, to a perpetual impatience in his nature, an ever-discontented wanderlust that kept him obsessively driving around in his pickup trucks hundreds of thousands of miles all over the West.

When things went bad on the ranch—when two of his prize Charolais died of pneumonia one sub-zero winter, or when the hay baler broke down beyond repair under a catastrophic sun, drying out the hay until it was worth little more than straw—on impulse, he would leap into his truck and drive off in a rage, headed for Las Vegas, flat-out leaving us kids on our own to deal with and fix as best we could whatever misery he left behind. A few times, he came back a winner: pulling a good used hay baler or with two white, purebred replacement calves standing in the bed of his truck. Mostly, he lost. He answered our accusatory gazes with, "I didn't lose that much," and, "Hell, at least I tried." Las Vegas was a mystery—that place the old man took off for to try and turn around his luck whenever his luck went bad. We grew up feeling the place owed us something.

My father, Maurice A. Unger, was a transplanted Westerner raised in Patchogue, Long Island, about as far to the East in this country as it's possible to get. After World War II, he transformed himself completely into Western traditions and cowboy costume, right down to his Stetson hats, snap-button shirts, stovepipe Tony Lama boots, and the fancy Gross suits he wore for business or special occasions. He was an attorney who hated practicing law, so he turned to teaching at universities and wrote textbooks on real estate, real estate finance, and business law—his professing ever in direct conflict with how much he despised the real estate speculators that were, in his opinion, ruining the country. To give proper credit to the depth and sincerity of his passion for the West and all things cowboy, he was, while an assistant professor in the college of business, also the rodeo coach at the University of Idaho. Later, he taught for twenty years at the University of Colorado.

Despite, or probably more because of, my father's transplanted background, he significantly steeped my brothers and me in the solid agrarian traditions of hard ranch work. He planted us on his ranches, and he taught us the frugality and toughness of that life. We were fully exposed to the sun and chafing weather of the open spaces, and we grew up knowing how to work cattle, sheep, and horses (never trust an animal that big with a brain the size of a walnut, what I always say about horses). We learned what it is to till and harvest fields. And we spent a great many early breakfasts and noons at the cafes in town, listening to our father talking weather and livestock, grain futures prices, and the basic concepts of parity and price supports as he was making deals to lease out land on shares to other ranchers. Because of them—Irwin St. Louis and Pearly Green, Les Crozier and Pete Bosserd, their kids and wives, and a half-dozen cowboys and laborers who worked for us and generously taught us everything they knew—at least we grew up with some direct understanding of what it was: that very much less-than-mythic, physically punishing, hardscrabble ranching life out West. As for me, I was relieved and grateful to get away from that life as fast as I could at summer's end. Enough trouble and bad things happened that, to this day, being out in wide-open spaces or getting too close to nature causes in me an irrepressible compulsion to start chain-smoking. Still, I believe this is the story of the twentieth-century West: how most of the youth of my generation turned our backs on the land.

Some might say we failed, but that wouldn't be entirely true. Economies of scale took us over, and smaller, family-run spreads either melded into corporate agribusinesses, or, conversely, the land was cut up into little five- to twenty-acre hobbyist "ranchettes" by speculators who made themselves rich. My family wasn't interested in land speculation. I like to think of us now as people who kept spying something else up ahead, and so we decided to keep moving on.

In Las Vegas, people rarely stay in one place very long. And a high percentage of people living here are not the same people who were here ten years ago—a recent local survey claims almost half the population intend one day to move somewhere else. There are few storied landmarks or historical buildings—ones that might have been considered so, like The Sands, The Dunes, the old Desert Inn, the Moulin Rouge, all of "Rat Pack" showbiz fame, were routinely imploded in spectacular nighttime shows to make way for whatever came next. To a degree more extreme than in other Western cities, people keep moving in and moving out in a continual restless transience.

Las Vegas is a city of second chances. Losers are welcome here. And America sorely needs such a place. The untold truth of this country is that, for every success story, it's possible to find fivefold testimonies of people who have failed. For the past fifty years—not only during the recent, catastrophic Great Recession—workers were being laid off from jobs by the tens of thousands almost everywhere. Four out of five small businesses went belly up, nine out of ten farmers lost their farms, three out of every twenty professionals failed at their practices or, worse, their licenses in other states were revoked. More than half of all married couples split up in ruinous divorces. People were going bankrupt or getting stripped of everything they owned with increasing frequency. If Las Vegas and other boom cities in the West didn't exist, the country would have had to invent them all over again just to relieve the pressure. Perhaps more than any of these cities, Las Vegas offered a clean start. In Las Vegas, no one gives a damn where you come from; where you're going is all that counts. It's simple casino logic and the very essence of gaming that, with each new bet placed, the past ceases to exist; it's the future that counts, and Las Vegas is a city that keeps reinventing itself by its own improbable vision of this future.

In the boom years, almost anyone with an able body and a willingness to work could land a job here. Anyone who had failed elsewhere and could just get here, fully meaning to climb up out of defeat, powered by the earnestness of knowing he had less than a quarter tank of gas left in his car, could find a job in construction, the hotel and service industries, or in the professions. The promise was that if you were careful, steady, and turned up for work, you might be able to recover some success in life, even if modestly defined as a stucco tract home in the desert and a kid in college. So the city grew: the construction crews laying out concrete slab after slab after slab of the foundations and spitting out their millions of nails in a moving assembly line of strenuous labor and knuckle-breaking toil, putting up what amounted to the same half-dozen basic designs of ranch or two-story homes that spread out in a monotonous simulacrum from downtown out into Green Valley, then The Lakes and Summerlin and the Southwest, then on into the more luxurious developments that gradually crawled and grew into the black rock hills southeast on the other side of which is the craggy slope down into Boulder City and the sapphire blue of Lake Mead. In about thirty years, the big bowl of the Las Vegas Valley has been almost entirely filled, the desert wasteland transformed into real estate and dreams.

In all of this spectacular growth, Las Vegas never promised anything more than what it represents, though this is also the Las Vegas paradox. So many faux-themed resorts are rising up on the Strip and becoming emblematic of the place—a scale-model Eiffel Tower over a plasterboard Paris, a stage set façade of the New York skyline, robot pirate ships, gas-powered volcanoes, indoor canals at the Venetian complete with singing gondoliers, an artificial lake at Bellagio with spouts of water that dance to rousing music, and on and on it grows, all presenting itself with such patent medicine fakeness and overlayering of designs so baroque and busy that they clash beyond any human capacity to take them in all at once, now the absurdly packed-in, piled-up glass-and-steel futurism of City Center just opened its doors, the largest and most expensive resort hotel complex on earth—for all this showy fakeness, Las Vegas never pretends to be anything other than what it is. Even its gambling is thoroughly honest—the odds are published and easily available for any slot machine and table game; all anybody has to do is ask for them on a casino floor. With its hoopla of advertising, its games of chance, its chaos of fantasies, Las Vegas promises just exactly what it delivers—nothing less, little more. In sum: Las Vegas is a city of representations, and underneath them, it's the most honest city on earth.

My friend Dave Hickey—MacArthur Fellow in art criticism, also an unofficial poet laureate of Las Vegas—often says, "There are basically two kinds of people in the world, pirates and farmers," then he'll go on to assert an exciting, adventurous aesthetics of piracy as it applies to contemporary art and culture. After resisting this duality for a while, I now believe Hickey is essentially right, save that I'd add a third category to make a paradigm of dialectic: some people are nomads. They buy and sell, and, in journeying from market to market, they aren't nearly as treasure-driven as pirates. On established caravan routes, for which they require no more than hospitable space on which to pitch their tents and fresh water for their thirsty camels, nomads don't care too much for rapaciousness or pirate raids to carry off slaves and gold. They follow circling roads made by their own tracks. They end up owning little, only what can easily be transported, and they leave little of the plastic arts behind. Still, in most cultures, they are honored as carriers of the tale, song singers and story-tellers, bearers of tidings and news. For this, they are welcomed. Then they pack up and move on. This three-term paradigm—nomads, pirates, farmers—with migrations that span generations, can define a history of the American West.

Whether or not Las Vegas will keep growing through the new century or finally go bust for a lack of the water it uses up so wastefully—some experts predict Lake Mead might go all but dry in the next twenty years—or if it might erode away because of the continuing slide in general prosperity killing off the tourist industry, that mother lode on which the city was built, no one can yet say. If it does become some weird, haunted place of empty, sky-scraping ziggurats with blown-out windows left abandoned in the desert or dismantled and hauled off for salvage, piece by piece, it would be following a long tradition of past Nevada boomtowns from the era of the Comstock Lode and after—Virginia City, or Carson City, hardly cities now, yet once counted among the most populous urban centers in the American West—or becoming like the dozens of windswept old Nevada ghost towns still out there somewhere like phantom, floating islands off in the desert. More likely, Las Vegas will continue to be what it is—that teeming, postmodern carnival town people keep moving in and out of, leaving few if any lasting traces.

This restless transience and impermanence about Las Vegas seems to me quintessentially Western, in a sense similar to how the French theorist, Paul Virilio, in his book, *The Information Bomb*, speculates about what it means to be American: "The true hero of the American utopia is neither the cowboy nor the soldier, but the pioneer, the pathfinder, the person who 'takes his body where his eyes have been.'" A more grandly historical statement by Virilio describes this transience even better: "The United States was, then, still hungry—not so much for territories as trajectories; hungry to deploy its compulsive desire for movement, hungry to carry on moving so as to carry on being American."

It's more than fitting that my family's story should end in Las Vegas. My father was a man persistently uprooting himself and his children, taking his body where his eyes had been, heading toward that glimmer of something he had seen while driving through the empty spaces. He kept moving into them, onto a new piece of land, knowing all along it was a place where he could live but for a brief time. In the end, when his heart was failing, my brothers and I rescued him from his last, nine-acre mini-ranch in Idaho that was backed up against the Lemhi wilderness, where he lived all alone with a dog and a few sheep. We brought him to Las Vegas—where I had settled in to help build the new university—and where he knew he would soon die. Old stirrups from a saddle, my first deer rifle, my fly rod and fishing reels, historic old West photographs from Craig, Steamboat, and the Dakotas, a few worn farm tools and Indian artifacts are arranged around my writing office in Las Vegas now like rustic, nostalgic works of art—things that represent for me sources for two of my novels and a handful of short fictions already written, and at least one new book I hope someday to write: these are what remain.

We are a family of nomads. And I've come to a similar conclusion as my father at the end of his days: so little of it makes any difference, as economist Lord John Maynard Keynes once stated and my father liked to quote, "in the long-term, we'll all be dead." As in the old Irish saying, the West has gone the way of everything else. Everything has happened as economist John Kenneth Galbraith prophesied in *The New Industrial State*: the line between big business piracy and elected government has disappeared. Only the labor itself, with its quest and its movement on any given day, really counts. This is true also of language in the process of composition. Our stories are what we have, and what we leave behind—the only evidence that we were ever here.

Ursula K. Le Guin | PLACES NAMES

I

TO THE LITTLE BIGHORN

In the gorge of the Columbia
great grey shapes of mountain coming down
coming down
to the road
rain coming down
green forest and the rain coming down
and the river coming down.

Union Pacific going west
under the lava cliffs
    Wasco County
Washington State now on a long, dry slant down
  to the river
and this side opening out,
getting lighter, getting dryer,
the rain a little sparser.

Suddenly the grass is yellow
        We Can Handle It. The Dalles.
   Powerlines on the high bare hills.
   Blank wood walls.
The dam's open, Columbia roars out, white breakers
  in reverse,
a mist of water.
Washington lies in dim dun-gold levels in the rain.

It's sagebrush now and rabbitgrass,
the lava breaking through in buttresses,
pinnacles, organpipes, paws of iron-dark enormous

lions.
Washington is sphinxes' feet.

    Sherman County
under rimrock by the big grey flood.
        Breakfast at Biggs Junction
        at the Riviera Café
        by the Nu-Vu Motel
        Greyhound and Trailways
        calling their passengers
        from the bacon-haunted restrooms.

    Morrow County
Cross the John Day River wide and flat
and the castles vanish:
    FLAT.
Sagebrush at its intervals.
Power poles at their intervals.
Raindrops at their intervals.
        Somewhere behind this
        Coyote is hiding.
    Umatilla County
    Fred's Melons.
    High Water.
Grey sage, grey black-stemmed willows in the reedy
    sloughs.
    Umatilla.
    Night Crawlers at the Western Auto,
    a gloomy wooden cowboy twenty feet tall at
      the Key Buy Store.
Gulls in the rain over irrigation arcs
in the desert of Irrigon, Oregon.
        ENTERING WASHINGTON
    across the rainy river
    foaming from McNary Dam.
Pale colors, pale browns of plowland, fading off
                and off
                and off

Palouse.
Treeless.

No trees.
    Pasco: lines of morbid poplars
    blue in a vast swale.
    Snake meets Columbia, and we cross Columbia
    for the last time this time.
And the ash begins.
    Roadcuttings whitish.
    Top of every rock at the roadside white.
    The roadshoulder greyish-white.
The dry snow of the eighteenth of May, 1980,
  thirteen months ago.

As we turn from Washington 397 onto US 90
  I remember the radio
that morning: Highway 90 is closed on account
  of DARKNESS.
Now the darkness
lies white on the roadsides.

    Spokane.
After the handsome city on its river the mountains
start to rise to the right hand,
westernmost Rockies,
forested, beclouded
        And IDAHO WELCOMES YOU!

A wet white horse runs in the rain
over Lake Coeur d'Alene on steep cloudy pastures.
    Coeur d'Alene National Forest
    pine fir spruce pine fir spruce
Fourth of July Summit three thousand and eighty-one
    feet yoopee! over the top!
And we level down into parklands, lower, to a marsh
    lonesome
    hills and clouds on every side
and a great grey heron flops slowly south
over the lonesome marshes of the River Coeur
  d'Alene.

    Shoshone County
        Shoshone, Shoshone, Shoshone

They didn't leave things
only names, only words
They owned very little
other than breath
a feather, a whisper
Shoshone

Smelterville.
A scruff of sheds and shacks and fences
under the steep hills;
high thin smokestacks of the mill, black,
and the black tip.
Kellogg.
Kellogg Memorial Park No Bottles in Park
but a helluva lotta litter.
Vangs Shoe Repair
on the despairing wall on which is written
WALLACE SUX

The Shoshone Humane Society
is a ten-by-twelve-foot building all alone on the
river bank
between the railroad and the highway
in the Rocky Mountains.
Heaven and Earth are not humane.

Osburn, three mines, Silverton,
and Welcome to Historic Wallace Silver Capital
of the World.
Somewhere in historic Wallace on the wall is written
KELLOGG SUX.
But the weary traveler benighted in the mountains
finds
a broasted chicken Sunday Dinner with slaw,
biscuits and honey, mashed potatoes, rainbow sherbet, beer and coffee, at Andersons
Hotel in the old, high dining room.

And all night in the motel in the silence of the
mountains
the raingutters drummed on barrels in the alley
Rocky Mountain music.

THE NEXT DAY

Six a.m. leave Wallace
in its high grey sodden solemn fir-dark cloud-encum-
    bered hills.
I-90 follows fast Gyro Creek past mines:
                Golconda District
                Compressor District
                Gold Creek
                tailings at Mullan
Lookout Pass, four thousand six hundred and eighty
    feet
            hello MONTANA!
        hello Rocky Mountain Time
        hello Lolo
We're doing 55 and so's the St. Regis River in the
    opposite direction
jade green on granite
    Food Phone Gas Lodging
    No Services
            Breakfast in Superior
            at the Big Sky Café
        eggs up and square hashbrowns
    Alberton
across the wide Clark Fork, way down
at night in Alberton you must hear the river rivering
and see the car lights way up on the highway passing
    Missoula County
    Granite County
    Bearmouth
    Chalet Bearmouth
The rocks are pink, tawny, tawny red, orange, violet,
blond, gold, brown, purple, layered, lined, folded,
striped like Roman stripe.
        Drummond
        under the snowy mountains
        cottonwoods, church tower, wooden walls.
        What do you do in Drummond?

            What you do in Drummond is climb up the
            tall bare hill above I-90 and paint your high-
            school class year on the granite cliffs near the

big white D for Drummond if you can find
any room left the highschool class years there
go back to 34 BC.

Country Village Store 24 Miles. Gas Soup
  Moccasins.
That's what it said: Gas Soup Moccasins.
    Phosphate. NO SERVICES. Where do you pee
      in Montana?
    Silver Bow County.
    Anaconda.
The huge dark rusty stack and flume under
  mountain shoulders,
rain coming fast from the west,
our rain, we're bringing it along,
traveling with our cloudy retinue from Oregon.
    Crackerville.
High sagebrush range, red caprock, pointed
  cedars scattered wide.
    Come to the IT Club in Rocker, Mont.
    Downtown Helena is FUN! NO SERVICES.
And after Butte under its terrific raped rich
  disemboweled mountain we go
                    UP.
Deerlodge Forest: sandstone pinnacles, I swear
  they are blanketed people
standing silent among the cedars
as the road goes winding fast and up
to the place where the rivers part.
              Continental Divide
          Homestake Pass, six thousand three
              hundred and ninety-three feet.
Seabottom sandstone, ice-split, foliated, leaved by the
  fingers of the cold,
dun and silver-grey, red and buff, big round worn
  shapes, seabottom
here at the top of the continent
at the place my heart divides.
    Farewell O rivers running to my sea.
    Jefferson County.
Down we go and it begins to level down

rolling in hills and sweeps
and valleys and ranges and vast lovely reaches of land,
sagebrush and high grass, cedar and cottonwood,
the colors of cattle, the colors of horses.

     Whitehall   stop stop stop we got to stop
                      it's a hundred miles
                      since breakfast—

In Whitehall at the gas station they won't let you
use the john unless you buy gas and they don't
have diesel O God but there's a semi-defunct self-
serve station and they don't give a damn they're in
there busy arguing toothlessly in low sullen voices
and the door of the john is propped open so it
won't lock so the builders working right outside
can use it if they need to and also they can see right
in and you can't shut the door but who cares, and
inside that door another traveler has written in
large letters:

     THANK GOD FOR THIS TOILET

Amen, amen, amen.

Three Forks: the Jefferson, Madison, Gallatin
   Rivers

   the rivers with galloping names.

Horses, horses in Montana,
     clump together in the great spaces of their
         life,
     have pony faces, clever faces, fat bellies,
     are Indian colors, colors of Rockies rocks:
       buckskin, grey, roan, appaloosa, sorrel,
         paint.

     Sweet Grass County.

The Yellowstone   goes shining off among
                     cottonwoods and meadows
                     toward lovely lines of rainy hills.

     Big Timber
          Frye's Charles M. Russell Motel.

I walked in the evening of Big Timber:
     a lot of trucks
     spits of rain
     far-off cobalt mountains streaked with white
     sweet grass of Sweet Grass County

quaking aspen whispering in side yards of
    little wooden houses
mountain ash in bloom in June
birds whistling and whispering
columbine: faint tawny pink and gold,
color of the rocks, the Rockies' own
    wildflower.
  I picked up a pink rock, granite, my piece of
    the action.

THE THIRD DAY ON THE ROAD

Under a bright and cloudy sky we go by
    Greycliff
    Stillwater
    Springtime
    Yellowstone
    Absarokee   That was what they called
              themselves,
             the ones we called the Crows.
    Here by the Yellowstone lightly poised stood
      tall cities,
    the city a circle, each house a circle,
    twenty-eight lodgepoles, the door open to the
      east, the circle open.
    Gone now. Empty.
    White ranges in white clouds
    above the river's green and empty valley:
      Absarokee.
  A broom of light, amazing, sweeps through bluish
      mists
        over cliffs in a huge perspective
        beyond the pewter river, the cottonwoods,
        the pastures of the ghosts of the buffalo.
  Big Horn County
      Bighorn River
        Little Bighorn River and Battlefield.
The battlefield. A middle-aged Crow Indian at the
Agency sent us to the detour, patient and polite. The Crow
were on Custer's side, a lot of good it did them. The stuff at
the building at the hilltop is all Custer, that vain and petty
man, and uniforms, and battle diagrams. One single postcard with the faces of the warchiefs of the Sioux and the

Cheyenne, heavy handsome fierce sad faces of old men,
but of Crazy Horse not even a postcard. He had no pictures taken. He didn't leave much behind. A name, a
breath, a feather in the wind.

> We walked down that long hill. Down from the
>   building
> a small invisible voice led us,
> a voice in the grass of the battlefield
> beside the path, always just a couple of steps ahead
>   çhirk
>   chirruk!
>   leading us on
> invisible, a bird, a voice, a sweet, indifferent
>   guide.

All around the battlefield
>   (which stank of rotting bodies for weeks so
>   that no sane man would go within a mile)

all around the battlefield between hilltop and river
larks trill and chirk in the long sweet grass and the
    sage,
the holy sage, that purifies.
Crickets. Cloudshadows.
Marble gravestones for the white men. Officers have
    their names carved in the marble. Enlisted men do
    not.
As for the others, they aren't there. The ones who
    won the battle and lost the war. No stones to weigh
    their feather spirits down.

>   Wild roses
>   prickly pear
>   a lily like the mariposa
>   bluebells
>   tall milkweed stars
>   and all the grass in bloom, long spiked or soft
>   or ruffled green
>   and here and there a small, pale-scarlet Indian
>   paintbrush
>   dipped in blood.

II
INDIANA AND POINTS EAST
****
III
THE DEEP AND SHALLOW SOUTHS

[. . .]

We started West from Russelville at five in the hot moist
dark just before daybreak. Rosyfingered dawn above the
Ozarks. Beside the road in the twilight of morning a little
yellow dog looked up at us: but no dog ever looked at
human eyes across so wide a gap.
>   A little god in Arkansas
>   O Coyote, you made my country.

At Indian Nations Turnpike we have left the South.
There's a dry wind blowing over the scrub oaks on the
long, low ridges; and things aren't even green and humid
blue, but other colors, dry, distinct.
>   Okfuskee County
>   Weleetka
>   Wetumka
>   Okemah
>   Shawnee
>   Wewoka
>   North Canadian River
>   Seminole
>   Pottawatomie
>   Kickapoo
>   Tecumseh
>   Choctaw
>   Anadarko
>   Caddo   These are the names, the true names,
>   Names of the world Coyote made.

At the Cherokee Trading Post there's lamps and cactus
jelly for sale, totem poles—Cherokee totem poles?—and
Perfumes of the Desert.

>   O Coyote you always got things all wrong
>   and then ran off with your tail between your legs
>   laughing

There: all the little black elegance of foot and ear and
   jackrabbit brain
is gone to a bit of bloated bloody ragged mud by the
   tire-side.
A million times a night on our ten thousand roads.
The trouble with us is, you know what the trouble
   with us is?
     we waste food.
               O Coyote get it right next time!
North Fork of the Red River
from this valley they say you are going, do not
   hasten to bid me adieu,
and there's sagebrush, yahoo sagebrush,
and we enter Texas at the Wheeler County Line.

                           ANOTHER DAY,
and here's a sunrise for you. In the Panhandle, dawn
among the thunderstorms. A gentle rain and lightning in
the dark, packing the car to leave Shamrock, Texas, and
the sky above I-40 mottled with black clouds and lighter
patches of sky holding one faint wet star. Thunder,
thunder near and far. From the dark, dark rain falls and
lightning flares in huge bright blurs northward, to the
right. And the earth is without form, and void. Slowly
light, slowly light slowly enlightens the soft fertile dark
world-cave, defines, separates Earth from Heaven.
     A fourlegged god with yellow eyes
     is making the world over.
And the roadside signs creep into being out of unbeing,
selling beds and goods and foods and Texas Souvenirs.

   At nine a.m. the road falls off the edge of things
      into the desert.
     Sagebrush ahead and mesas, far as the eye
      can see,
     under the sky of turquoise and white shell.
     NEW MEXICO. Names of New Mexico:
Tucumcari.
Santa Rosa.
       A heavy red river, the Gallina, like a red
        snake, crawls

past Santa Rosa through rock-strewn,
    brush-dotted, red-green hills.
Colonias.
Pecos River, red, braiding red mud
San Miguel
    A sweet dry air.
    Dark green juniper
    dark red dirt
    dark blue sky
    bright white clouds
    Flowers: white stars, gold pads,
        purple spikes & yucca
Tecolote turnoff
These names are far between,
miles apart
Bernal
Behind the dark purple northern mesa is a great
Source of Clouds: from it clouds rise and float and
feather out and fade in silver shell-ripples above
the deserts.
Glorieta
Mesa Glorieta
Villanueva, San Juan, San José, and on to
Santa Fé.

ANOTHER DAY

Oh, one more sunrise, this is the next to last,
leaving Cortez, Colorado.
To the right a distant mesa is on fire.
Behind the San Miguels and Mesa Verde, a citron sky
    streaked orange-pink
The lights of Cortez fade under the mountains,
    under grey-haired rainclouds;
and to the left, a full moon rides faint in veils of rose
    and blue,
over the long mountain called The Sleeping Ute.
The mesa on fire blazes up, and then a huge, soft
    raincloud
sits down on the sunrise and puts it out.
After a long time from the grey one shaft of pure
    light rises, white,

too white for the eye to bear, and Coyote wins again,
    and welcome
to Dove Creek, Colorado, pinto bean capital of the
    world!

IV

FAR WEST GOING WEST

WELCOME TO UTAH early in the morning.
The sunflowers are confused, haven't got turned
    sunwards yet, face every whichway.
Juniper. A good, strong, catspray smell of juniper in
    the high dry air.
Sagebrush, chamiso, the little yellow-flowered
    clover that's been along
our way from Oregon to Georgia and back. And
    crows.
Suddenly we descend from mountains into desert
where there are monsters.
A potbellied Mexican waterjug two hundred feet
    high
turns into a sphinx as you pass it.
A throne of red rock with no seat, a hundred feet
    high.
Red lumps and knobs and kneecaps and one-eyed
    skulls the size of a house.

The sunflowers now are all staring east like
    Parsees,
except a couple in the shadow of the roadcut, which
    haven't got the news
or received orders yet.
        There aren't a whole lot of names, in Utah,
        but here's one: Hole in the Rock:
            big white letters on a big red bluff with a
                hole in it, yessir,
            and also Paintings of Christ and
                Taxidermy.
A lone and conceivably insurgent but probably
    uninformed sunflower
stands in the shadow of a cliff, facing southwest, at

7:41 a.m.
Well the last time *I* saw the sun it was over *there* and
   how do I know where the damn thing's got to?

Arches National Monument, near Moab: Red stone
arches. Red stone lingams, copulating alligators, camels,
triceratops, keyholes, elephants, pillows, towers, leaves,
fins of the Ouroboros, lizard's heads. A woman of red
stone and a man of red stone, very tall, stand facing the
falconfaced god of the red stone. Many tall, strange stone
people standing on the red sand under the red cliffs; and
the sanddunes have turned to stone, and the Jurassic sea
that lapped on these red beaches dried and dried and
dried away and shrank to the Mormons' bitter lake. The
sky is as blue as fire. Northward, stone dunes in white
terraces and stairways pile up to the violet-red turrets and
buttresses of a most terrible city inhabited by the Wind. A
purple fortress stands before the gates, and in front of it,
four tall, shapeless kings of stone stand guard.

NEXT MORNING

Heading out of green and gentle Delta to the Nevada line,
early, to get across the desert in the cool.

> Jackrabbits flit
> on the moonlit salt pans
> to the left of the mountains of dawn.

> Jackrabbits dance
> in the moonlit sagebrush
> to the left of the mountains of dawn.

> Four pronghorns drift
> from the road into the sage
> in the twilight of morning
> to the left of the mountains of dawn.

Nevada
There are no names here.
> The rosepink shadowless mountains of dawn now
> are daylit.

deepshadowed, and the moon has lost her
    dominion.
    In this long first sunlight the desert is greyish-
        gold.
By the road as straight as an imaginary canal on
    Mars are flowers:
        Michaelmas daisies, Matilija poppies white as the
            moon up there,
        milkweed, blue chicory. The green lush South
            was flowerless.
There are
five fenceposts
    in the middle of the vast sagebrush flat of which
        the middle
    is everywhere and the circumference nowhere.
Five crows
one crow per post
soak up the morning sun.
        Only Crow's been with us all the way,
        north, middle, south, and west. Even the
            redwing blackbird
        gave out in Nevada, but Crow's here, Crow of the
            Six Directions.
Jackrabbits go lolloping off like wallabies
    with magnificent blacktipped ears.
Gabbs Luning. There's a name for you!
    At Gabbs Luning there's a Schneelite Mine.
    I don't believe anything in Nevada. This is pure
        Coyote country.
A vast lake that holds no water
is full to the brim of glittering light.
Far out, toward the center of the lake,
lie the bones of a wrecked ship
that struck on the reef of the mirage
and sank through heatwaves down and down
to lie now bleaching fathoms deep in blinding light,
all souls aboard her drowned in air.
Probably a potash mine. Who knows? We drive on
    west.

EAST TO THE WEST

May 2004. Homeward from teaching in New York State, I'm driving west from Chicago on Interstate 80, passing stubble fields, white farmhouses, little round-topped silos, and the mounded, freshly leafed-out crowns of hardwood forest between the farms. La Salle, Rock Island, the Mississippi River—no, it doesn't begin here—and into Iowa as a slight roll comes to the green land. There's a muddy stockyard full of cows near Iowa City, the prairie patched with fields and pastures, and fewer trees now—clumps, singles, strands along fencerows and small rivers, a few fresh limbs on the ground from yesterday's big wind. Toward Council Bluffs the land takes longer swells, and I'm crossing the Missouri—no, not here—under a lowering, gray-plate sky, storm warnings breaking into the radio talk show, new corn a few inches high in the moist fields.

In Nebraska the limit jumps to seventy-five, a sure sign of wester-ing. Near Lincoln the fields stretch out plainsier now, and closing in on Grand Island, in bright sun, the Midwestern roll is gone from the land and big-wheeled sprinklers shine in the fields, the first I've seen, ready to boost the summer rainfall that won't be enough. Here, maybe? But now I-80 falls in with the Platte River, its braided channels lush with forest. The *names* are Western now—Pioneer Village Motel, Stagecoach Restaurant—and three or four miles short of Kearney, the earth is dry enough for a scat-ter of pines, which don't like wet ground. Under the Great Platte River Archway Monument that spans the freeway—definitely not here—I'm cruising at eighty, a windmill spinning hard to my left, a tractor throwing up clouds of dust, neat-rolled hay bales spotting the sprawling fields. Irri-gation equipment is everywhere, for corn and hay. Black Angus graze the pastureland. I ride the Plains neck and neck with a Union Pacific freight train, off to my right—if we're not in the West we're mighty close—and then, a few miles past Gothenburg, under flat-bottomed cumuli in a vast-ness of sky, to the southwest there's a low, solitary ridge spotted with junipers.

Here.

There won't be another cornfield. There will be cattle in pastures and feedlots, the bumpy fringe of the Sand Hills to the north, ranch houses with windbreaks of tall poplars, exposed crops of volcanic rock, power line towers marching into distance, a few oil rigs bowing and rising like praying insects, homesteads and settlements of double-wides with sheds, old cars and trucks, and machinery. There will be tumbleweed, sagebrush, and just over the Wyoming border, the first undramatic glimpse of the Rocky Mountains—but by then, in my book, I've been in the West for two hundred miles.

The West began for me in 1966 when I was eighteen, driving Route 66 in a very loud Jeep across Oklahoma and the Texas panhandle into New Mexico. The flat expanses looked naked and glary to my East Coast eyes, but the land was wide open and so was my spirit. I passed the miles bellowing the lyrics of "Mr. Tambourine Man," trying to out-shout the Jeep. My brother, at George Air Force Base in the Mojave Desert, had taken a shine to that country of Joshua trees and creosote bush, but to me, then, it looked only parched and desolate. I was happier with the California coast—Big Sur, San Francisco, the misty redwoods, and finally western Oregon, where I would conduct my brief career as a college student. It rained all winter and stayed green all winter. The trees were enormous and so were the mountains, the seaside rocky and stormy and fine. Even the wet earth smelled sweet. I began to suspect I'd been born on the wrong coast.

For the forty-four years since, I've lived between the Columbia River and San Francisco Bay, a member of the long Pacific coastal region that curves from the glaciered, islanded wilds of Alaska down through British Columbia, the wet Northwest and the redwoods, and on south into the grassy, oak-strewn hills that line the west of California. It's a country of earthquakes and volcanoes, dramatic coastline, abridged versions of once profuse rainforests and salmon-thronged rivers, and a half-dozen of North America's great cities with their proliferating suburbs.

Theodore Roosevelt once observed that in California, seaward of the Sierra Nevada, he felt he wasn't in the West but west of the West. I agree. This sundown fringe of the continent is geographically, geologically, climatically, biotically, and culturally distinct from the broad, drier interior region it borders. It surprises many from the East to learn that the two-thirds of Oregon inland of the Cascade Range are not verdant with Douglas firs and mossy-rocked streams but more like Nevada—semiarid plateau with a baseline elevation of four thousand feet, a country of sagebrush and juniper expanses, buttes and cinder cones, clumps of conifered mountains.

It certainly surprised me, unpleasantly, when in my mid-twenties I moved to Klamath Falls for a railroad job, pursuing my dropout curriculum of drink, self-doubt, and confusion. But the open landscape grew on me. I liked the breathing room, the drama of visible distance, and I liked it that the land presented itself in particulars. Not the enveloping hardwood forest of the East, not western Oregon's thick stands of conifers, but *this* twisted juniper with a packrat nest at its base. This angling ponderosa pine, its orange bark scored with a lightning scar. This huddle of aspens around a spring in sagebrush barrens, and off in the distance a few small buttes alive with the slow-moving shadows of clouds.

I stayed ten years in that broad and lonesome country. I would have become a writer elsewhere, I suppose, but I didn't. I became the writer I am in a particular northwestern edge of the American West where a calming clarity seemed inherent in the land itself, where space and stillness helped me shed my quandaries over what I had and had not done, where the singularity of stone and tree and distant height awakened inklings of a singularity within, some secret that was mine to puzzle out and give voice to if I cared enough to try.

Since then I have lived west of the West, in the Bay Area, in Portland, and now in the central Oregon Coast Range, but my wife and I light out frequently for the territories. We leave our house amid tall Douglas firs, blackberry brambles, and wild hazelnuts, and we leave the gray weather that produces such botanic exuberance. We drive over the mountains to swap the wealth of green on our little piece of land for a wealth of sky and sun, and snow in winter, on the ranch where I first tried to write half a lifetime ago. We settle our eyes on green in its subtler shades, on an earth not swarmed with plant life but wearing it lightly. The West, for us, is four hours east. I love going there and I love coming back. I love the talkative patter of rain on my roof, I love the dry windy spaces, and I love each more for knowing the other.

I appreciate literature of many kinds, but I am drawn most to work that depicts human lives still involved—like it or not, for better or worse—with the primary given world our culture seems intent on divorcing. I don't mean "nature writing" alone, but also works of fiction, memoir, poetry, history, and journalism—writing that incorporates land, weather, and living creatures not merely as backdrop or scenic embellishment, not as objects of an aestheticized admiration of natural beauty, but as part of the imaginative matrix of the work itself, inseparable from the lives and longings of men and women in their various places.

The Northwest and the greater West it overlaps have many such writers, but we are not unique to a region. We sprout up anywhere—local variants, perhaps, of one species. Some of us were born to our places; some, like me, have transplanted ourselves. We have in common a wish to belong to the land we live in and to welcome its influence into our work, to become, as writers, the fullest shrub or tree that our particular place, region, climate, luck, and hard work will produce. We may be the writers Henry Thoreau imagined in his essay, "Walking," after he read that the skin of antelope gives off a delicious odor of grass and leaves: "I would have every man so much like a wild antelope, so much a part and parcel of Nature, that his very person should thus sweetly advertise our senses of his presence, and remind us of those parts of Nature which he most haunts."

Thoreau never journeyed west of Minnesota, and regretted traveling that far, but in his essay he imagined a West that I recognize. On days when he had no specific destination for a walk, he tended to settle on a westward or southwestward course, following an inclination of spirit more than a compass bearing. "I must walk toward Oregon," he wrote, "and not toward Europe." The West to him meant freedom, discovery, a transcendent sense of relation to all of nature through the particular portion of landscape he was traversing. "The West of which I speak is but another name for the Wild," he wrote, "and what I have been preparing to say is, that in Wildness is the preservation of the World."

Henry Thoreau lived and lives on in that West, the writers and readers of his ilk live there, and the hope that sustains us lives there too. Wilderness survives in tattered remnants, but wildness abides throughout our land—under the subdivisions and commercial misdevelopment, within the hard webwork of highways and freeways, in those endless crop fields doused with chemicals and in the bedrock beneath them, and in the roots of old trees silently buckling city sidewalks. Wildness can be stifled but never destroyed. It lives in the scalped hills and dammed rivers and cow-burnt rangeland of our Northwest as surely as it lives in the stands of ancient trees, the meadows of native grasses, and the stretches of free-running waters that remain.

Despite the damage done, by all of us, we cannot live here and not be hopeful. If an old-growth Douglas fir or ponderosa pine can rise through time to become the entire battered wholeness that it is, if it can so eloquently bespeak its rightful place and being, then surely we can do our best to bespeak ours. And if a dying chinook salmon, after three or four years in the North Pacific, can return to the Columbia River and swim eight hundred miles over eight tall dams to the small stream of its birth in the Sawtooth Mountains of Idaho, then surely we can ask of ourselves— we *must* ask—at least some measure of that tenacity, that heart, that ferocity for home.

David Guterson | THREE POEMS

CLOSED MILL

Some of those trees are gone now and some remain.
The mill, evaporating, has left behind moss.
There's a skein of cable amid the blackberry
By the river—in the interstices of thorns,
Seized chokers, a seized engine.
Even the sawdust mountain's blown to weeds
Where there's no evading nettles any longer.
I remember the morning the cook
Quit, leaving his crumpled apron
Beneath warming lamps while slabs of french toast
Smoked on the griddle. I made enough enemies
To color the future. I didn't do anything to
Get off the wheel. My friend wanted
Jack Daniel's in the hospital and got it.
Someone tried to hit me with a hammer.
There was nowhere to go and we went
There together. Returning's no worse than
A bad dream, I think—but I'm remorseful,
Now, about that running mill.
All those trees pushed loudly through the saw
In the era when I was king.

NEIGHBORS

I'd like to move four stones and ten stumps
Out of the field today, but right now
Silence is enough, and fire, an answer
For dread, a forgotten dream's distress,
Guilt over solitude, the physics of stumps,
How to get a chain around one that won't slip off

Or offer grief while not deluding myself,
Stones, too, plus this regret at what I'm not doing
That might imply meaning, that odious filter,
And yet stones and stumps, their geometry and weight,
Retain a superior claim, as does rising for a dying fire
To feed it fir from two storms back, when the road
Was blocked by so many firs you couldn't progress,
Not without a saw and neighbors sharing your condition.
Who else is awake on our end of the island,
Wondering what to do before the sun rises?

WHITE FIRS

They didn't like wet feet is their epitaph—
Snag klatch of white firs across from the gate,
Down from the bull rock dumped by the stream,
Near where a neighbor re-starts his siphon
With a generator and pump in a van.
Gradually they came to ask against the sky,
Ivy refused them, sticks clashed and dried,
And sometimes I thought they looked like men—
Stolid, accusatory, questioning. They set themselves
Off with their leafless June fretwork, they fell in winter,
Cold with disregard. Those still remaining stood
Among the heaped like final pieces on a chessboard.
We called them piss firs for the stink they exhumed,
Struck with a maul, but they were no good for burning
And held whole ponds—so why were they dropping now?
Not even owls dignified their silhouettes.
They were freight cars on the ground, wrecked.

The last wretch fell in the road Monday morning,
And the UPS man, stopped, explained,
"This thing's in the way. Too heavy to move.
I've put in a call. They're bringing a saw.
They'll clean it up and we'll get through.
All of us have things we have to do."

Craig Lesley | CELILO FALLS

For over five thousand years, Native Americans had gathered at Celilo Falls, the greatest salmon and steelhead fishery on the North American continent. At Celilo, located just thirteen miles east of The Dalles, the Columbia narrowed down to a series of chutes and falls only three hundred yards wide.

As the salmon moved upriver to spawn every spring and fall, the people caught them in hooped, long-handled dipnets when the fish were in the basalt chutes or attempting to leap the tiers of the Falls. Shaky wooden platforms extended over the churning waters. The fishermen stood on the platforms, holding the long dipnets steady by bracing them against their chests and shoulders. Some wore rubber boots and rain gear to keep from getting soaked by the mists rising above the water, and they smoked their pipes upside down to keep the mists from putting out the tobacco.

The returning salmon rose out of the water like silver ribbons as they leaped the tiers of the Falls. When the fish swam into the hoop-shaped nets, the Indians hauled them out and brought them to the waiting women who clubbed the salmon as they flopped against the twine webs. Later, they ate the plentiful salmon, sold some to tourists, dried many to eat during the long winters. A good fisherman would catch around two thousand pounds of fish each day.

But the gathering involved more than fishing. Warm Springs, Umatilla, Walla Walla, Nez Perce, Yakama and many other tribes traveled to Celilo to gamble, gossip, feast, and brag of hunting exploits. Fishing and gathering to celebrate the salmon's return defined their way of life.

Celilo Falls was a frequent stop on my grandfather's Sunday drives around The Dalles. He worked for the local newspaper, the *Dalles Chronicle* and knew most of the Indians at Celilo Village, even the venerable Chief Tommy Thompson, who treated me to salmon jerky and hard candies.

My grandparents took in roomers, young men who worked on construction of The Dalles Dam, a 1950s project by the Army Corps of Engineers designed to control flooding, provide cheap electricity, and help irrigation. My grandfather took me to the dam site but showed little enthusiasm for its progress. He knew what I didn't, that the dam and the Falls were on a collision course.

As a young boy who had seen the amazing power of the Falls, I had no idea that the dam would eventually destroy them when the floodgates closed. Like many of the Celilos themselves, I thought nothing could stop the astonishing Falls. Some of the people, like Tommy Thompson, never cashed their checks from the federal government, believing that if they didn't take the money, everything would be okay.

But when the engineers closed the floodgates on the dam, Celilo Falls drowned, and the mighty roaring river became a hushed lake. In the process, a way of life was destroyed. The Indians felt the most pain, but everybody lost when Celilo fell.

The years passed and knowledge of Celilo faded into memory, then altogether out. Finally, one night in Portland, I mentioned Celilo to a class of creative writing students. They returned blank stares; no one knew what I was talking about.

Astonished and frustrated, I vowed that I would write about Celilo Falls and make its destruction a central theme in my first novel, *Winterkill*. One of the writer's duties, it seems to me, is to preserve the history of a place—to let future generations learn what happened. Another duty, one more political perhaps, is to prevent tragedies like Celilo Falls from happening again. I wanted to be a part of protecting this Oregon country from ever undergoing a similar disaster.

Now in Oregon, five dams along the Rogue River have been removed or are scheduled for removal, making three hundred more miles of spawning grounds available to the salmon. And the talk about the Columbia River focuses on removing three dams, including The Dalles, to help promote and restore salmon runs. Today, only seventy thousand wild salmon enter the river compared with two million before the dams. Also, a number of the tribes are installing fish hatcheries to ensure an increase in the salmon population.

My grandfather took me out to Celilo the day they closed the dam's floodgates. For a few hours it didn't seem to make much difference. The whitewater came rushing down the chutes, roaring and crashing over the Falls. But down below I could see the water hit the dam and start rolling back against itself, like wild horses driven into a blind canyon cutting back on their trail. By the middle of the afternoon, I could tell the water was rising. A large pool stretched across the river, but the Falls kept on roaring as if nothing could stop them.

Finally, the lake reached the base of the first Falls, so the engineers in their hard hats and the politicians in their ties lined up for pictures, the last pictures of the Falls. Then I heard a high wail. It was even louder than the roar of the Falls. All the old Celilos had turned their backs to the rising water and were lined up facing the canyon wall. Their arms were crossed and they were chanting the death chant.

The lake rose against the Falls as the water kept pouring over them, but the more it crashed into the lake, the higher it rose, choking them back. I closed my eyes, praying it would stop. My grandfather put his hand on my shoulder. Then I opened my eyes and stared. One after another, the Falls drowned themselves, until the roaring stopped, and I couldn't hear anything but the sucking of the dark, eddying lake as it grew larger and larger, filling up the canyon.

As the noise from the Falls died, the wailing grew louder, like a shriek. One of the reservation chiefs, who had been standing with the engineers and politicians, walked away from them and joined the old Celilos with their backs turned to the dark water. He was crying when he passed us and he said, "We sold our Mother and now they have drowned her."

It grew dark and some people built fires. The chanting Celilos cast long shadows against the canyon walls. Some of the young people started up their new cars and pickups. The headlights shone over the smooth black lake as they drove down the hill and into The Dalles to go drinking or see a movie.

The old Celilos still stood facing the canyon wall, refusing to look at the lake that had drowned the Falls. They had stopped wailing by then, but the silence was worse.

I remember my grandfather stayed very quiet as we drove back to The Dalles. Later, he told me Tommy Thompson was in a nursing home the day they flooded the falls. All the Celilos said he could feel the cold water rising and he kept crying out for more blankets.

A DARK LIGHT IN THE WEST:
RACISM AND RECONCILIATION

As it happened I went West twice. When I was three, in 1948, my mother and father and my younger brother and I moved from Mamaroneck, New York—on Long Island Sound in Westchester County, outside New York City—to Reseda, California, a town in the San Fernando Valley northwest of Los Angeles. In the late forties and early fifties, the western and northern sections of this valley represented one of the most productive agricultural regions in the United States; twelve years later, agriculture had become almost vestigial there, pushed out by ambitious suburban development. The orchards and citrus groves were largely gone, and most of the irrigated hay and grain fields had been converted to blocks of tract housing. The last undeveloped, unirrigated stretch of this once semiarid expanse, the area around Chatsworth in the valley's northwest corner, was by then no longer unsettled enough to serve as a backdrop for the TV and motion picture Westerns Hollywood was used to making there.

My first California home, on the northern outskirts of Reseda, was too isolated to have a neighborhood of its own, but close enough to the town of Encino for me to begin attending a Catholic grade school there in 1950. Reflecting on it today, I can't recall any Latino or Asian students having been in my classes—though I am relying here solely on memory—and I am aware now that the valley back then was home to few African Americans. The social world I inhabited at the time, as a middle-class, suburban white boy, was predominantly, if not thoroughly, white.

My mother began teaching in public schools in the valley two years after we arrived, first at a junior high school in the city of San Fernando and then at Northridge Junior High. She became at these schools the confidante of young students marginalized by their social class or ethnic culture, and through her, in the early 1950s, I became acquainted with several Mexican families. These were households in which the fathers worked, typically, in the valley's orange groves or perhaps at commercial nurseries or alongside braceros in the fields. My mother's interest in and rapport with young people living outside mainstream American culture became part of the pattern of her teaching life, and this pattern remained unchanged until the end of her career.

My parents divorced shortly after our move from New York; in 1955, Mother remarried, and the following year we moved back East to Manhattan, where my stepfather lived. She started teaching again in 1960, this time at P.S. 155 in East Harlem, a predominantly black, coeducational school on East 117th Street.

It was obvious to me the first time I visited P.S. 155 that my mother's new students, mostly young black women, were comfortable in open-ended conversation with her and not self-conscious in her presence. I am relying on memory again, but starting with those early years in California, I am unable to recall any moment of tension in my mother's dealings with people culturally or racially different from herself—not until my stepfather came into the picture. An immigrant to America from Asturias, the "county of kings" in northern Spain, he was born into a hidalgo family in Southampton, England, during the years his father was Spain's First Secretary to the Court of St. James's. My stepfather was a man suspiciously alert to issues of class and race.

My mother grew up on a large farm in eastern Alabama in the 1920s. Yearning for something very different, she moved into a nearby residential college, Montevallo, in 1930. Shortly after she graduated, she married—and then divorced—a Catholic immigrant from Czechoslovakia, an artist and aeronautical engineer. A few years later she got married again, this time to my father, a first-generation Irish Catholic advertising executive from New York, whom she also later divorced. The divorces—and the men—caused her family to distance themselves from her. The circumstances she was born into in the Deep South, of course, gave aspiring women little latitude for personal expression; and it was not until later in my own life, after having seen how young, marginalized female students were attracted to her, that I recognized the parallel: her life, too, had been shaped by narrow and unreasonable judgments. These young women sensed in her, I think, a kind of empathy they found difficult to locate in other white people.

My stepfather, whose surname I was given when he married my mother, was openly prejudiced, especially toward African Americans, Jews, and gay men. His indignant pronouncements rarely emerged—within my hearing—in his business dealings, but they were apparent around the house and came more fully to the fore in conversations with other men in his private social environs—at the Essex County Country Club in northern New Jersey, for instance, and at the New York Athletic Club in the city. After my mother died in 1976, he told me—a non sequitur out of the blue one day—that he believed Mother had "had some Negro blood in her." This was relatively common, he reassured me, even among well-born Southern women.

I was uncomprehending.

"Yeah," he continued, "you could see it in her face, in the bone structure."

What compelled such relentless racism in a person?

As a teenager in New York I was made point-edly aware of racial and ethnic divisions that earlier, in suburban California, had had no real shape or emphasis to them. Such distinctions were routinely made there, certainly—I knew firsthand how socially constrained the lives of braceros could be; and whenever we went to the Farmers Market in Hollywood, I saw the unconcealed looks of contempt certain white men shot at the Japanese truck farmers there; but living in New York, a polyglot city where ethnic and racial divides in the borough neighborhoods were part of people's everyday orientation, and living with a stepfather who frequently felt it necessary to remark on these arrange-ments, I experienced racial and ethnic distinctions in a different way. In the agricultural and then suburban setting of my California boyhood, living in a family where my mother didn't discuss racial and ethnic dif-ferences in a disparaging tone, I never felt called on to take a stand. In New York, my stepfather and some of my parents' friends encouraged me, instead, to mark these distinctions and to take them into account when dealing with people. My stepfather, for example, impressed upon me the need, especially as a young man with a Spanish surname, to dis-tinguish between people who emigrated to the United States from Spain and Spanish-speaking people who had arrived in New York from places like Puerto Rico.

At this point in my life I began to comprehend that an awareness of cul-tural and racial differences, and of the social divisions maintained to dif-ferentiate among several economic classes, partly determined the expres-sion and display of one's social manners. And further, however insensitive any stereotypic characterizations rooted in such perceptions might be, I saw that they helped people navigate in a multicultural, urban society without, they believed (or hoped), giving offense. Still I was puzzled ini-tially by the nuanced judgments my stepfather frequently felt compelled to offer concerning relative strangers—that, say, the building superinten-dent next door was in fact not "Italian" but a Sicilian, and that he took the train in every day from Borough Park, a Jewish neighborhood in Brook-lyn—and by his listing of the behavioral traits one might expect to observe in such individuals. Generally, I continued to feel only embarrassed or vaguely naive whenever the mention of anyone's religion or cultural origins or race automatically generated an assumption about them in everyday conversation.

When I was seventeen, my stepfather enthusiastically supported my interest in attending Notre Dame, his alma mater. He felt its white, middle-class, Catholic student body would provide me with an edifying environment in which to mature. As a student at Notre Dame in 1962, I didn't fully grasp how intellectually constraining the university's exclusionary racial and religious politics were, nor how severely this limited the opportunity to learn about people different from myself. These insights would not come until later; in the meantime, I tried to abide by my mother's dictums: pay attention to individual people, not categories; accept and honor obvious differences; and then begin to imagine, "Where do we go from here?"

After I graduated, knowing I would likely always remain blind to certain dimensions of my own racial and cultural prejudices (or preferences), I made a conscious effort to explore unfamiliar racial and cultural circumstances. I tried to be deliberate and thoughtful about this, with the intuition—and this I did get from a university education dominated by European thinking and history—that another sort of national and international politics was coming, one not shackled by assumptions of racial and cultural superiority, and that this politics would change everyone's ideas about privilege.

When I moved west a second time, in 1968, it was to enter graduate school at the University of Oregon in Eugene and to begin, as a newly married man, an independent adult life. I felt strongly attracted to the landscape's heavily forested and snow-capped mountains, to its lush emerald valleys and white-water rivers, and was immediately comfortable there. In some ways, moving to Oregon felt like coming back to California. I quickly became familiar, as any immigrant might, with the publicly traded narrative of Oregon's early settlement, but I discovered, too, the much more obscure chronicle of its history of racism and domineering cultural imposition, the fuller story of settlement that every state seeks to diminish or manipulate in presenting itself. In Oregon, this disconcerting history included the plundering of Indian lands; the rescinding, in 1868, of the state's 1866 ratification of the Fourteenth Amendment (guaranteeing citizenship and basic civil rights for African Americans); the formation of violent anti-Chinese leagues in Portland in the 1880s; and, later, the state's collusion in the development of a reckless system of commercial exploitation of the region's natural resources, especially timber. This uncomplimentary account tended to undermine the twentieth-century image of western Oregon as a modern American Eden, an idyll many young people invested in and believed would unfold there in the years following Woodstock and the Summer of Love.

When I arrived in Eugene, the deep wounds engendered by Manifest Destiny were still healing, especially on the Indian reservations. In southwestern Oregon, an area some historians believe drew a disproportionate number of immigrants from the American South after the Civil War, de facto sundown laws (no nonwhites present after sunset) were still in effect in many of the small towns. Also, a general shift in the state from small-scale agrarian and ranching life to a more corporate, industrialized economy had, by then, created obvious and extensive environmental damage. On the other hand, harsh criticism of commercial logging and of ranching and agricultural practices that had degraded Oregon's landscapes—an objection to the status quo especially strong in the late sixties among western Oregon college students, many of whom were attending the University of Oregon—spawned one of the earliest and best-organized environmental movements in the country. This movement's political activism—focused on contentious issues like logging and the pattern of urban growth—and such regulations as newly mandated bottle deposits, changed the state's political landscape during the governorship of Tom McCall. The popular backlash against these changes—against the implementation of land-use planning, the protection of roadless areas, and the passage of recycling laws—had a distinct "native Oregonian" component to it. Reactionaries, self-identifying as "real" Oregonians, regarded the state's young environmental leaders (many of them from California, Michigan, New England, and the mid-Atlantic states) as nothing more than carpetbaggers. The reactionary voice was anti-progressive, anti-environmental, and anti-government, a sometimes belligerent jingoism strongly supported by the timber industry and real estate developers.

In the national conversation, at least as I have listened to it over several decades, people often assume that the western states have had a history of settlement more or less in keeping with that of the eastern states; but this is untrue in a fundamental way. Most of the West lacks water; vast stretches of its lands are managed by the federal government; and many local economies have been shaped by mining, logging, and ranching, not manufacturing and industry. Further, the major events that influenced much of the molding of the American character—the Revolutionary War, the Civil War, the Industrial Revolution—hardly affected the West. The War of Independence occurred before there was an American West; the War between the States was contested a thousand and more miles away; and the Industrial Revolution, as defined by the textile mills of Massachusetts and the steel mills of Pennsylvania, never arrived. The West's principal contributions to the shaping of the American character, arguably, were its promotion of a folklore of self-reliance and independence; its championing of unlimited development, linked to a philosophy of endless financial opportunity and unrestrained personal freedom; and its support for the taming of all things wild—Indians and land in particular—as an unalloyed social good. Unacknowledged in this Western laissez-faire, entrepreneurial, and opportunistic promotion of the good life, however, was an ipso facto strain of racism.

Lane County, Oregon—Eugene is the county seat—was one of the whitest counties in the United States when I moved there in 1968. If you happened to see a young black man walking down the street in Eugene, you assumed he was an athlete at the university. In that same year my surname became the fourth Lopez listed in the telephone book for a county of 206,000. And when I attended Mass in the city for the first time, I was told I should be aware that Catholics were a distinct minority in western Oregon. The oddest thing to me about this cautionary remark, back then, was the assumption that I would need such information in order to get along.

Even a callow newcomer to Eugene might easily have discovered in those years that another, minority community lived on the social and geographical outskirts of the city—Indians, Asians, blacks, and Mexicans who either chose to keep their distance or who felt compelled to. This historical chasm between white and nonwhite cultures throughout Oregon has remained largely intact down to the present. According to legal historian Cheryl Brooks, the gap is so pronounced that many white Oregonians are able to regard themselves as racially tolerant today only because they so rarely encounter anyone who is not white.

Oregon, the only free state ever admitted to the Union with a black exclusion clause in its constitution, has a long, virulent, and occluded history of racism. Not until 1948, following a US Supreme Court decision, did the state revoke its Alien Land Law, making it possible for an Asian immigrant to purchase property. Marriage between whites and nonwhites was illegal until 1951. And the state legislature, in addition to withholding its reratification of the Fourteenth Amendment until 1973, did not ratify the Fifteenth, protecting African Americans' right to vote, until 1959.

During my first few years in Oregon I noticed not only how infrequently I encountered African Americans, even on the streets of Portland, but also how often I met Native Americans in the general population. This was a different mix of cultures from the ones I'd known in California and New York, and also from the one I'd become familiar with while visiting my mother's relatives in Alabama and Georgia.

Today, looking back at the racial situation I encountered in Oregon at the age of twenty-three, I can see that it was consequential in determining the direction of my life.

The most affecting teacher I had in graduate school at the University of Oregon in the late 1960s, Barre Toelken, was a white man from Massachusetts married to a Nisei Japanese (on her father's side) named Miiko (née Kubota). Toelken taught medieval English literature, American folklore, and what would later be called Native American literature. At that time, whatever was going on in the very small world of university blacks, Asians, and Native Americans in Eugene was news to be gleaned around the Toelkens' table. Several of us, mostly graduate students in the English department, were always glad to get an invitation to visit their home, where we might meet a black musician just in from Memphis, or a visitor from Japan. During those years, the Toelkens introduced the shifting group of us to traditional people from Eskimo communities in Alaska and to Native American artists and leaders from throughout the West. (Barre's second family, his first wife's relatives, were Navajos from the area around Blanding, Utah.) A few years after I left the university, when I was writing a book about wolves and looking for guidance, Barre sent me to the Bitterroot Valley in Montana to meet his close friend Joseph Epes Brown, a professor of comparative religion. Brown had lived with Black Elk during that Lakota elder's final years and had also written *The Sacred Pipe*, a definitive work on Lakota ceremony.

What Toelken taught, in and out of his classroom, was in effect comparative epistemology. As nearly as I can understand it at the distance of forty years, if my mother had brought me to the notion of amicable ease and common sense with people who were culturally different, Toelken brought me to an awareness of other people as ultimately unknowable. Because of the range of individuals the Toelkens invited to their home, however, I also began to grasp the intrinsic value behind a familiarity with different ways of knowing.

I was also fortunate in those same years to work as a writer alongside other people whom I came to admire for the breadth of their cultural views. One was Bob Stephenson, a large mammal biologist at the Alaska Department of Fish and Game in Fairbanks and one of the first American field biologists to suggest bringing the empirically based knowledge of native peoples into mainstream discussions about wildlife behavior and management. Later, I would become friends with Richard Nelson, an Alaskan anthropologist and another pioneer in elucidating how deeply informed indigenous oral natural histories could be. Even as my own circle of contacts and friends grew, however, I continued to reflect on Toelken's formative and unobtrusive guidance, on how he had helped me to frame my questions.

When I left the University of Oregon in the spring of 1970 I embarked, without really understanding what I was doing, on a lifelong course of being tutored—or instructed—by people different from myself on subjects I was eager to explore and about which they were knowledgeable and also curious. I learned about wolves from Nunamiut Eskimos in Alaska's Brooks Range (through Bob Stephenson's friendship with those people), and about narwhal behavior from Inuit on northern Baffin Island. I learned from Toelken's Navajo friends about shape-shifting and about fossil evidence for hominid evolution from Kamba men working with paleontologists in Kenya. From Warlpiri people in the Northern Territory in Australia, I learned how a small endangered marsupial, the rufous hare-wallaby, fit into the Dreaming of these Aboriginal people. My excitement at these encounters didn't derive entirely from being informed by individuals who knew what I didn't, nor from the fact that, frequently, the impressive and complex systematics and genealogy of their ideas were not ones formulated by Plato and Descartes. Rather, the encounters inflamed a passion in me for coming more fully to life. I felt that my enthusiasm for immersion in the mystery of everything surrounding us—myself and the informant—was shared, and that the unity of this pervasive mystery, in the end, was as unpredictable for the most adept of shamans as it was unfetchable for the most studious of cosmologists.

In those moments when I thought I understood what another person meant—someone of a different race, or from a different culture or with different spiritual beliefs, or someone who had lived long in a geography altogether different from my own—I also came to believe that racial or cultural exceptionalism was a deceiving way station, a comfortable place you finally had to leave if you hoped to get anywhere. What I learned from these exchanges, I think, was that racial or cultural superiority was, in the end, a refuge erected by the fearful.

An enigmatic but defining figure in Oregon's nineteenth-century racist history was an attorney named Matthew Deady. In 1859, with the arrival of statehood, Deady was appointed Oregon's first federal district judge. His special place in the judicial history of the American West derives, in part, from a series of opinions he wrote during the three decades he spent on that bench. His rulings reinforced principles of fair treatment and equal rights in a political climate that was strongly— even on occasion violently—critical of any sort of equality for nonwhites, especially the Chinese. During the years of his adjudication (1859–1893), while Oregon's legislature continued to pass laws to legitimize and protect white racism, Deady ruled in favor of Chinese plaintiffs who had been abused and penalized by discriminatory labor laws and by taxing and licensing ordinances. He was openly critical of a prominent strain of "nativist" hostility in Oregon's politics, an anti-Indian, anti-black, anti-Chinese, anti-Catholic position taken, Deady believed, by an uneducated "pisantry" (as he put it in a letter to his friend James Naismith). Prior to Deady's appointment to the federal bench, however, his publicly stated political views were often blatantly racist. Only after his federal appointment by President James Buchanan did he gradually begin to assume, from our modern perspective, a disinterested stance on racial issues—and to become an enigma to some of his longtime friends.

Deady's "conversion," according to Ralph Mooney, a legal historian and emeritus professor at the University of Oregon's law school, had no Rubicon moment; but his change in point of view is an important episode in a larger story of racism, one unique to the West: the harassment and sometimes deadly violence directed against Chinese immigrants, starting at the time of the California gold rush in 1849 and symbolically culminating in the passage of a series of federal Chinese Exclusion Acts in the 1880s.

Some social critics argue today that nations around the world will continue to reject any American critique of the ethnic repression that occurs within their borders until America, in an official public ceremony, acknowledges the role racial prejudice and genocide have played in its own development. Although such a ceremony, regrettably, is unlikely to take place, we have made some progress toward the goal of at least making more public the inventory of early unethical behavior.

The modern effort to achieve this kind of transparency in the record of American history, one might logically argue, begins with the civil rights movement of the 1950s and 1960s. With the publication of popular revisionist histories of the West such as Dee Brown's *Bury My Heart at Wounded Knee* (1971), and testimonies like James Baldwin's *Go Tell It on the Mountain* (1953), many, if not a majority of, American college students, including myself, became aware of the long history of intolerance and injustice that lay behind pivotal events in the country's social evolution— among them, the 1965 voter registration drive in Selma, Alabama, and the 1973 occupation of Wounded Knee, South Dakota. By now, more have looked into such things as the Christian religious fervor that drove an un-provoked military attack on Southern Cheyenne and Arapahoe families at Sand Creek, Colorado, in 1864 in which dozens of people were killed; or they have read extensively about the lethal psychopathology of the Middle Passage. Still, the gap in public awareness between what *actually* happened to Native Americans and to minorities in America and what is popularly *believed* to have happened to them remains sufficiently great to draw the continued attention of national and international social critics.

In the same way that many well-meaning Oregonians, unaware of how small the African-American population of the state is, came to believe that theirs was a "color-blind" society, so have most Americans overlooked, denied, forgotten, or "moved on" when it comes to questions about the nation's history of racial brutality. (Most of us, of course, having read school board-approved histories, were never exposed to this history to begin with.) The worst unprovoked massacre of Indian people in the West, for example, still remains a virtually unknown incident. This attack, on a Shoshone winter village by a restive group of California Third Infantry and Second Cavalry volunteers—whose offer of military service in the Civil War had been declined by Union officers—took place at Bear River, Idaho, on January 29, 1863. More than three hundred Indian men, women, and children were bludgeoned, raped, tortured, and shot to death by this cadre of white men spoiling for any sort of fight. Similarly, although many Americans might be aware that Chinese laborers played a role of some sort in building railroads in the West, and that they worked in Western mines and opened laundries and offered domestic services in many Western towns and cities, few among us today, even in the West, are aware of the number of wanton, racially driven mass murders that occurred. Twenty-eight Chinese coal miners were killed at Rock Springs, Wyoming, in 1885; five Chinese men were hanged by white vigilantes at Pierce, Idaho, in 1886; and thirty-one were robbed and murdered near Deep Creek, Oregon, in May 1887. An amateur historian of this last event, H. R. Findley, reports that one of the ringleaders of the massacre felt that he and his accomplices were simply "doing their country a favor" by ridding it of Asians who were, by the murderers' lights, "stealing" gold that belonged to local white people.

During the first few years I lived in Oregon, I read and heard stories of how native people had been driven off their lands, how these lands had been confiscated and parceled out to others, how some of the tribes had later been forced onto confederated reservations, and how articles in their treaties with the United States had been selectively and unilaterally annulled, effectively closing Indian people out of their traditional hunting and fishing grounds. This framework initially organized my thoughts about a history of racial prejudice in the state. Early on I had learned that southwestern Oregon was not a place where African Americans should ever travel alone (the region's largest town, Grants Pass, had been a nationally recognized Ku Klux Klan stronghold). And I had read about anti-Chinese rioting in Portland in the mid-1880s, when arsons had been committed and beatings administered by nativist xenophobes egged on by the city's mayor, Sylvester Pennoyer (soon to be elected the state's governor), and by such local publications as the *Catholic Sentinel*, whose editorials were written to appeal especially to working-class Irish. But for many years I remained largely unaware of what had actually been done to Chinese people in Oregon in the nineteenth century.

This lack of awareness became apparent to me in the spring of 1995 when I began researching a story near Astoria, the site of the fur-trading post John Jacob Astor had had built there in 1811 at the mouth of the Columbia River. I'd gotten to know a local ceramic artist, Richard Rowland, through Lillian Pitt, a Wasco artist from the Warm Springs reservation on the east side of the Cascade Range who regularly fired her ceramic masks and other work in a wood-burning kiln Richard had constructed at his home. A community of potters from Portland and northwestern Oregon had coalesced around this anagama-style kiln, which employed a sloped-tunnel technology developed in China about 1000 BC and later refined in Korea and Japan.

Richard's father was a white veteran of World War II, his mother a native Hawaiian. Richard was born and raised in the Coast Ranges south of Astoria, in the drainage of the Nestucca River on what was once Tillamook land, but he had spent most of his adult life near the mouth of the Columbia. In middle age he traveled to Tasmania to earn a Master of Fine Arts degree in ceramic art at the University of Tasmania at Launceston. When I asked him why he had traveled so far to get his degree, he told me that in a dream he had seen his grandmother standing up in the Hawaiian islands, one hand stretched out to him in Oregon, the other pointing to Tasmania.

Richard and I were cutting wood for his kiln one day when he said he had something he wanted me to see. We drove to a stretch of alder woods on the south side of Astoria, land that forms part of the north bank of the Youngs River. During the halcyon days of the Columbia River commercial salmon fishery, just after the turn of the nineteenth century, Chinese cannery workers built a settlement here. Given a choice, they preferred to live away from white domiciles; white people, for their part, preferred not to see the Chinese in public except at work in the canning factories or out on the tidal flats of the Youngs River, building dikes to create pasturage. Prevented from using Astoria's city dump, the Chinese set up one of their own.

The remains of the dump, now a kind of reliquary, lie in an open copse of red alder. The space between clumps of trees is overgrown with Himalayan blackberry vines and clusters of native salal and sword fern. The day I explored, the site was overcast, and the flat gray light encouraged feelings of melancholy as Richard and I pushed our way through the blackberry thickets. Here and there on the forest floor weak beams of sunlight picked up the sheen of something broken or discarded. Neither of us said much, but the objects we picked up to examine (and then replaced)—part of a child's toy, one shank from a pair of pliers, cracked medicine bottles— spoke poignantly of the complex sense of loss and disruption that is part of barrio life all over the world.

Not until that day with Richard did my imprecise and unorganized sense of Oregon's Chinese history begin to come into focus. The fragile quality of a child's sense of self still adhered to the derelict toys; and who knows what palliatives had once filled the empty medicine bottles? The undistinguished trash before me triggered an acute awareness of the tenuousness of human existence.

Chinese workers began arriving in Oregon in the 1850s, initially looking for mining opportunities and for work on the railroads. Many of them came up from San Francisco under the auspices of one or another "company," all of these, in effect, Chinese benevolent associations brought together in a consortium called the Chinese Six Companies. (Each company—there were, oddly, actually eight—represented a different geographical region in China.) Brokers for these companies made arrangements for Chinese laborers to work either independently or with Oregon employers. Occasionally company representatives traveled north with the workers to help them deal with the complicated web of exclusionary laws and discriminatory regulations that enforced white prejudice.

With late nineteenth-century fluctuations in the economy, including a nationwide depression in the 1870s, the periodic dismissal of railroad workers, without regard to race, became routine. When Chinese workers agreed to return to work at a lower wage, they fueled resentment among lower-class white railroad workers who refused to do so. In the worst cases of scapegoating the Chinese for the economic hardships every worker faced, Chinese laborers and their families throughout California and the

Northwest were intimidated and harassed until many of them moved away. Some, as happened in Tacoma in 1885, were forced to board passenger ships bound for elsewhere while their homes and belongings were put to the torch. Others were simply murdered.

The most outrageous episodes of violence—the shootings at Rock Springs and Deep Creek, a series of seventeen lynchings in Los Angeles in 1871, thirteen Chinese murdered over a three-month period in San Francisco in 1885—come to mind only hazily today for many who nevertheless identify themselves with the heritage of the American West. One presumes the majority of such people are at least aware of, and perhaps less indifferent to, the long catalog of horrors visited upon Native Americans west of the Mississippi, which includes the "virgin soil" epidemic of smallpox that came up the Missouri River in the summer of 1837, devastating thousands of Mandan, Arikara, Gros Ventre, Pawnee, Hidatsa, Assiniboine, Blackfeet, and Yankton and Santee Sioux; the burning of Comanche, Kiowa, and Cheyenne winter villages at Palo Duro Canyon, Texas, in 1874; and the relentless pursuit of fleeing non-treaty Nez Perce by cavalry troops in 1877.

Sensitized to the Chinese history of Oregon following that afternoon in the woods with Richard, I recalled, vaguely, having read some years before of an incident in the Wallowa Mountains in the northeastern corner of the state: a large group of Chinese men, placer mining for gold somewhere in the Hells Canyon reach of the Snake River, had been robbed and murdered. I first encountered the story, I later determined, in a historical novel by Craig Lesley called *River Song* (1989). Shortly after that day with Richard, I read a more detailed account of the massacre in the *Oregonian*, the Portland newspaper, by a reporter named Greg Nokes: thirty-one (perhaps as many as thirty-three) Chinese, he wrote, camped near the confluence of the Snake River with Oregon's Deep Creek, sixty-five miles upstream from Lewiston, Idaho, were shot to death by a local gang of small-time stock thieves and schoolboys, the youngest of whom was fifteen. Nokes references one chronicler who suspects the group robbed the men of about $5,000 in gold dust and nuggets, a fortune at the time. In 2009 Nokes published a book about the murders, *Massacred for Gold: The Chinese in Hells Canyon*. In the book Nokes is as much concerned with how his efforts to investigate the crime were thwarted by county officials as he is with what happened to the Chinese; he exposes, for example, the determination of some local residents to preserve, down to the present, a distorted version of their pioneer history, dismissing both the heinous nature of the crime and their ancestors' anemic efforts to arrest and charge the perpetrators.

Precisely what happened to these thirty-some Chinese miners at the mouth of Deep Creek in May 1887 is unlikely ever to be made clear. The names of only eleven of the victims are known, all immigrants from the Punju district of Guangzhou (Canton). The men were working under the aegis of the Sam Yup Company of San Francisco, whose inquiries into the crime and demands for justice were frustrated at every level of government, including the office of the secretary of state in Washington, DC. The killers were led by a twenty-one-year-old man named Tighty Canfield, already suspected of murder and robbery in Idaho, and by his older sidekick, thirty-two-year-old Blue Evans, a foundering rancher. The gang seemingly acted with impunity, if not indifference. They knew that if they were caught, strong, local, nativist prejudice against the Chinese would stand them in good stead. Three of the gang were arrested and then acquitted in a summary trial; the others, including Evans and Canfield, were never charged.

In deadly human encounters like this, one is tempted to try to make guilt and innocence elementary, but such an approach rarely serves any deeper truth. Researching these particular long-forgotten murders, we can never learn how premeditated the violence was, or whether some of the victims were also tortured, or who among the gang was actually present during the shootings, or whether all this took place on May 25 or over a period of several days. Neither can we ever know what constituted the sequence of thinking that culminated in the crime.

The insidiousness of racism, in circumstances such as these, resides in part with an illusion that somehow the slate can be wiped clean, the injustice purged, if the guilty are simply brought to a just trial. In the history of our country—of all the innocent men, women, and children who have suffered miserable deaths at the hands of mobs and duly appointed militias, or who were killed by bigots and psychopaths—it is hard to accept that the punishment of a culprit has ever properly made up for the crime. If any such deadly act can ever be redeemed, it will be through some kind of enlightenment that, for most of us, is still some ways off. Such an enlightenment would have to be rooted, I think, in a reexamination of ideas about exceptionalism and private property. In the end, redemption may lie only with the termination of efforts to purge one's own society of "the foreign" and of the closely aligned urge to take possession of what rightfully belongs to others.

At the start of World War II, at the same time the Imperial Japanese Navy was planning its strike at Pearl Harbor it was also planning a series of submarine attacks on the West Coast of the United States. The Japanese wanted to serve notice on their eastern flank that they would brook no interference from America—just then on the verge of entering the war in Europe—in their military quest southward, across the Indochinese peninsula, through the island chains of the western Pacific, and into the Philippines and New Guinea. Part of this plan—never fully implemented—called for Japanese submarines in the eastern Pacific to shell American installations, to torpedo West Coast shipping, and generally to disorient and scare the American civilian population, in part to encourage fears of invasion. The overall strategy included the launching of an armed floatplane, the Yokosuka E14Y-1, from massive submarines using a compressed air catapult. The mission of these small aircraft, broken down and stored for transport in a watertight extension of the submarine's conning tower, was to fly inland and drop incendiary bombs across the evergreen forests of the Coast Ranges. The hope was thereby to ignite vast, uncontrollable forest fires.

On the morning of September 9, 1942, a 356-foot Japanese I-class submarine, the I-25, surfaced in darkness some miles off the Oregon coast. The crew assembled and, at first light, launched its E14Y-1 aircraft. The pilot flew the single-engine plane east over the water, directly to a lighthouse marking a prominent headland, Oregon's Cape Blanco. He then turned south-southeast and flew about fifty-five miles to a spot near Mt. Emily (2,926 ft.) where he dropped two 170-pound thermite incendiary bombs in the forest, about ten miles east of the coastal town of Brookings. The morning was foggy and overcast, and the Douglas firs and redwoods on the mountainsides were damp from recent rain. One bomb apparently failed to start a fire; the other ignited a blaze that was quickly spotted and later in the day brought under control.

The pilot, Warrant Flying Officer Nobuo Fujita, took the E14Y-1 back out to sea after the bombing run and landed at a prearranged rendezvous site. The deck crew, quickly hoisting the seaplane aboard, broke it down and stored it. Just as the I-25 was disappearing below the surface, it was spotted by the flight crew of an American patrol plane, a Hudson A-29, which dropped several bombs but could not confirm a hit or locate the submarine again because of low cloud cover. The I-25, suffering only minor damage, moved undetected into a cove near Cape Blanco—the outer harbor, actually, of the town of Port Orford—where it sat on the bottom for most of the day while repairs were completed.

In the weeks following, the I-25 sank two oil tankers off the Oregon coast, the *Camden* and the *Larry Doheny*. On October 10, it sank a Russian submarine, the L-16, with an American liaison officer aboard, off the coast of Washington. Its seventeen torpedoes spent, the I-25 returned to its home port on Tokyo Bay. (Prior to all these attacks, on June 21,

1942, the *I-25* had surfaced at the mouth of the Columbia River. Having successfully followed the local fishing fleet, returning that afternoon on its secret safe course through a near-shore minefield, the *I-25* then sent seventeen 5.5-inch shells from its deck gun toward Fort Stevens, directly across Youngs Bay from Astoria.)

The *Larry Doheny* was the last American ship sunk by a Japanese submarine along the West Coast during the war; shortly afterward, the Imperial Japanese Navy moved all its submarine operations from the eastern to the western Pacific. A new plan, however—one also meant to alarm and confuse the American civilian population—was soon underway. It culminated in the launching of as many as ninety-three hundred bomb-laden paper balloons from several sites on the southeast coast of Honshu. Filled with hydrogen gas and about thirty-three feet in diameter, the free-floating balloons rose swiftly into eastward-flowing jet stream winds and crossed the North Pacific in a matter of a few days. The balloons were designed to descend and release incendiary bombs over America's Western forests; some also carried antipersonnel bombs.

Historians speculate that about one thousand of these balloons reached North America; for a variety of reasons, however, the apparatus proved almost completely ineffective. After part of a balloon was found on December 11, 1944, near Kalispell, Montana, the Office of War Information requested a voluntary news blackout to keep the Japanese from learning anything about the weapon's effectiveness. Between November 1944 and the end of the war, the remains of more than three hundred balloons were found, some as far north as Alaska and one as far east as Grand Rapids, Michigan.

Local rumor about the origin and purpose of the balloons was rife in Montana and across the Pacific Northwest during the winter of 1944–1945, but the news blackout kept speculations from traveling very far—until a tragedy occurred. Of the forty or so balloons known to have landed in Oregon (more than in any other state), one, armed with an antipersonnel weapon, came down near the small town of Bly, in the south-central part of the state. On May 5, 1945, the balloon's weapon-and-ballast carriage was discovered in underbrush on Gearhart Mountain and probed by five curious youngsters and a twenty-six-year-old woman embarked on a picnic. It detonated almost immediately, killing everyone. The six of them became the first, and only, American mainland casualties of World War II.

Three of the five children were buried at the Linkville Cemetery in Klamath Falls, Oregon, a graveyard where ten Japanese infants were also interred during the war, in an unmarked plot. They had died of natural causes at Tule Lake, California, just over the border, the site of a Japanese internment camp.

For many Americans these stories of injustice and harm—the persecution of the Chinese, the Japanese attacks—are unremembered or unfamiliar. The same is undoubtedly true of lesser-known episodes of the mistreatment of Native Americans: the massacre of almost two hundred unoffending Indians, mostly Yurok, by ranchers at the mouth of the Eel River in Northern California in 1860 (an incident that prompted Guenter Lewy, writing in the *Journal of Genocide Research* in 2007, to characterize volunteer militias and vigilante groups in California generally as sometimes displaying "a flagrantly exterminatory mentality" in murdering large numbers of Indians); and the relentless attacks on Captain Jack's recalcitrant Modoc band in 1873 in the lava beds around Mt. Lassen in Northern California. (The Rogue River Indian wars, waged in the 1850s between white miners drifting north from played-out gold fields in California and several tribes living in southwestern Oregon's Coast Ranges, were fought in the same country Nobuo Fujita would cross ninety years later en route to dropping his incendiary bombs in the drainage of the Winchuck River.)

The most widely circulated histories of wars are left not only to the victors to write, but also to the emissaries and enforcers of whatever economic order is put in place after the devastation. Such histories, of course, can be, and are, revamped by people with the patience and determination to upend these tendentious accounts; clarifying lessons from revisionist histories about the American West have recently been set out by historians like John Unruh, in *The Plains Across* (1979), and by novelists like Cormac McCarthy in *Blood Meridian* (1985). These reassessments of violent behavior in the West have, understandably, been ignored by some who have an investment in the same kind of distorted folklore that Greg Nokes encountered in Wallowa County when he was researching the Deep Creek massacre. Analogously, recent attempts to revise the general conception of how the West was "settled," such as Patricia Limerick's *The Legacy of Conquest* (1987) and Annette Kolodny's *The Lay of the Land* (1975), have raised the ire and earned the denunciation of influential Westerners in the same way that California agribusiness leaders were outraged by the publication of Steinbeck's *The Grapes of Wrath* (1939). The attempt to write with greater accuracy about what happened historically, however the effort might be characterized by people with something to lose, is arguably only an expression of the fundamental impulse in every civil society to continue to pursue justice.

Reflecting on all this, I find one of the lessons that has grown out of many late twentieth-century revisionist histories of the West—revisions that have taken into account the lives of native peoples and haven't overlooked the experience of braceros and Wobblies and Chinese laborers—is a lesson about a need for tolerance. And where tolerance has been forged, a further lesson can emerge about a need for reconciliation. To my thinking, what finally proves important in our attempting to reconcile with the past is not necessarily the making of amends but our offering silenced parties the opportunity to tell their own stories without interruption, according to their own sense of timing, and without fear of refutation. For those in power simply to let what others say stand as their truth, and to go on from there, is a critical part of the healing that might conceivably take place after racial and ethnic violence.

Whenever I am in Southern California and have a chance, I drive past the houses I grew up in. The neighborhoods have changed. They are not so white now. The school I attended accommodates African-American, Latino, and Asian students, along with students from mixed racial and ethnic backgrounds. I like to think that, as a boy back then, I got some direction from my mother about how to approach the trouble that has come to us now, decades later, in a time when international cooperation concerning global climate change, nuclear disarmament, and the conservation of ocean fisheries is imperative. A child of the Deep South in the 1920s, knowing that poor white sharecroppers and unenfranchised blacks eked out a living side-by-side on her father's 640 acres, my mother chose to search out and abide by another kind of ethics. And I like to think that Barre and Miiko Toelken opened another door for me into what the future would look like, when all those years ago people from different cultures traded stories around their dinner table about the mystery and profundity, the extremes of pleasure and pain, that come with trying to live out a full human life.

On the horizon for us in the West are failing supplies of fresh water; more acres of salt-saturated and collapsing farm land; more logging and mining enterprises, some of them still driven by anachronistic, wildcatting personalities; and the continued plummeting of salmon stocks. No one I've read or heard speak seems to have an answer to this ecological catastrophe, outside of a hope placed by some in a kind of nongovernmental, noncorporate, and still hard-to-define activism called "the movement toward civil society." This effort, virtually ignored by the mass media, is essentially leaderless, though it includes a number of charismatic personalities, among them Paul Hawken, who describes the movement in *Blessed Unrest* (2007). If I were asked to imagine exactly how human enclaves in the West are to cope effectively with what's coming, I would not consider first either state or municipal governments. I would point instead to the phenomenon of emergent "mestizo" spokespeople—men and women with cross-cultural or biracial backgrounds, nonaffiliated visionaries who have in recent years become bridges in their neighborhoods and communities between several ways of knowing, several ways of believing. They model now the profound courtesy that is required everywhere in the world today if our just treatment of one another, regardless of our racial and ethnic backgrounds, is to have any chance.

On May 28, 1962, six years before I moved to Oregon, the E14Y-1 pilot Nobuo Fujita stood up next to his wife at a banquet in Brookings, the invited guests of the local Junior Chamber of Commerce. Through his twenty-six-year-old son, Yasuyoshi, Fujita said, "I never dreamed that I would ever visit the United States again. But at this moment I am here. . . . This is the finest possible way of closing this story." The man who had dropped the bombs twenty years before then produced a *wakizashi* samurai sword, which had been in his family for four hundred years and which he had carried in the cockpit of his plane that day in 1942 and throughout the war. The diminutive aviator presented it, through his son, to the mayor of Brookings. He recounted the history of the sword and explained the proper way for it to be handled.

"It is in the finest samurai tradition," he said, "to pledge peace and friendship by presenting a sword to a former enemy."

Though repeatedly threatened with harm by anonymous local residents, Nobuo Fujita continued to visit Brookings until his death in 1997 at the age of eighty-six. He funded the development of a collection of books for young readers about different cultures, shelved today at the Chetco Community Library in Brookings, where the sword is also on display, and he underwrote the cost of bringing three local high school students to a science fair in Japan in 1985.

The year after Fujita died, his daughter, Yoriko Asakura, spread some of his ashes in the forest where his bomb had exploded—at a site he himself had visited several times. (Initially forgotten, the site had been located again in 1972.) In October 2008, just a few days after the long-awaited dedication of a historical exhibit erected there took place, hooligans defaced the placards, carving racist symbols and epithets into their wooden frames and into a meditation bench built nearby in front of a large redwood tree. The image of Nobuo Fujita on one of the placards, reproduced from a World War II photo of him as a pilot, was decapitated, and a crude caricature of a Japanese face was carved in its place.

I had considered Fujita's honorable actions to be singular until I learned of a gift made to the families of victims of the antipersonnel bomb that exploded near Bly in 1945. The gift was sent by a small group of elderly Japanese women who, as innocent schoolgirls, had participated in the construction of some of the paper balloons that had carried bombs across the Pacific. They did not learn until many years after the war that the balloons were designed for this purpose. Hearing that five children and a young woman had been killed, the women folded one thousand paper cranes and mailed them to the families. In 1996, one of these women was among a small group who came to Oregon for a ceremony of reconciliation at the bomb site. Later, another Japanese woman had four cherry trees planted there. In 1989, when the unmarked grave of the Japanese infants who had died at Tule Lake was finally honored with a headstone at the Linkville Cemetery in Klamath Falls, the families of the Gearhart Mountain victims accepted an invitation to be present.

These reconciliation efforts were all initiated and facilitated by John Takeshita, a retired professor of health education at the University of Michigan who, as a boy, had been interned at the Tule Lake Relocation Center.

The first time I visited the Fujita bomb site, I made some notes about the suite of plants growing on the heavily wooded slope at that altitude. The small clearing faces southeast in an isolated part of the forest, at the end of a trail eight-tenths of a mile long. Coral root and Oregon grape, along with sword, deer, and bracken fern, grow amid Douglas firs, nut-bearing chinquapins, and coastal redwoods. Evergreen huckleberry, manzanita, wild rhododendron, tiger lily, Solomon's seal, and clumps of bear grass border the winding trail. The day I was there the woods were still. Also silent.

On September 9, 1992, on the fiftieth anniversary of his incendiary bombing, Nobuo Fujita planted a redwood seedling there, saying, as he often did according to his Oregon hosts, that the war "was such a stupid idea." Seventeen years later, the seedling I beheld had, in my eyes, taken on the look of a tree.

The West is about dirt. Good dirt. Rich dirt. Thick dirt. Lots of dirt. Dirt defines me. I write dirty stories.

My people came from places where dirt was used up, the land was too crowded, or there wasn't enough. My grandfathers emigrated from rural Japan; they were second sons from small, struggling farms, and the property would not be passed on to them. So they searched for new dirt and found it in America's West.

My home lies in the fertile Central Valley of California, a vast ancient lakebed fifty miles wide and hundreds of miles long. We work a small, eighty-acre organic farm south of Fresno.

Once I drew a map for a friend, showing our farm resting in the middle of this valley, in the middle of this state. He laughed; my illustration made us look like a hub for the region, a center of life. For a dirt farmer and writer, perhaps that's true.

Native Americans traveled across this dirt, settling just south of our farm where a huge lake once provided ample fish and temperate climate. I often wondered if they wandered over my farm on their journey up to the Sierras, a pilgrimage to Yosemite to the east of us. I imagine their footprints on our farm. Like many even today, they didn't stop for long; they were just passing through, not even long enough for a story.

Later, thousands of settlers arrived to work the earth, create a valley of farms and a land of many emigrants from many nations. They brought their stories from distant homelands—Japanese, Armenians, German Mennonites, Swedes, Mexicans, Italian Swiss, and later Filipino, Asian Indians, Oaxacans, and Hmong. Because of this legacy, I can't help but farm and write in color.

Many had no intention of returning to their homelands. In our dirt they discovered inspiration and planted roots. This was dirt worth fighting for.

Growing up in our vineyards and orchards, I'd hear foreign words from farmworkers, never knowing the exact translation but sharing the stories of sweat, love, and poverty. I watched the old-timers with heavy accents and gestures, all speaking through a wave of arms, calloused hands and fingers, old tired eyes blinking. Their wrinkled, weathered faces knew both the hard life of laboring in the fields and also the gentle, contented smile of a harvest.

Some sang—almost like a chant that echoed over the vines or through the treetops. Working-class songs from those who knew the dirt too well, a type of blues that translates into stories of loss and hope. This was the earth where my stories were born.

My family came to the West from the west. For my grandparents, this land was not the end of a continent but the beginning. They brought the baggage of culture but shared with neighbors a sense of the land from the old country: these were families who knew dirt from centuries as peasant farmers.

The openness must have overwhelmed. The West meant space and that implied opportunity. Dare they dream?

But for foreigners this was also an unforgiving land. Most of it had not been tamed; they were the first to plow the earth only to discover hardpan, an evil rock that doesn't even have the status of rock—rather, it's a layer of mineralized clay with all the moisture and life sucked from it.

And many Japanese settlers discovered a hardpan attitude from others—prejudice and racism were part of this frontier landscape. The dirt didn't care if you were part of a community of color. The earth wasn't concerned if you did not believe in God and if you were a good Christian. But others did. My West was settled with stories of intolerance, accommodation, and sometimes acceptance.

In order to plant roots, farm families needed water. So they tried to control the rivers and streams and for a while, the liquid gold flowed. But we live with a constant fear of drought. This land cannot be easily settled.

The drama here is gradual, like an epic novel with meaning unfolding through generations—stories are often only understood in the context of history. As a writer, it has taken decades to learn the lay of the land and only after inheriting neighbors from my father.

But Western dirt is young—there always seem to be undiscovered places, land still untouched and virgin. Though we never planned to farm elsewhere, the potential of someplace else seemed to make life better. We had options, blinded at times by a false sense of hope—but hope nonetheless. Perhaps that's why I can't write truly dark stories. There always seems to be some light out in the West, even if only moonlight and starlight.

My dirt is a sandy loam. Light to touch, powdery when dry, like sifted flour. With water, create a thick roux. Plow and the aroma of turned earth fills your lungs.

Our soil drains well, unlike heavier clays that soak up and retain moisture. Some claim we lack the richness of deep, thick topsoil. I would not know—I know no other dirt. I don't feel comfortable in another land. I wouldn't know how to work it. It would take years, if not a lifetime, to get to know the character of another place and its dirt.

Once I got a tractor stuck in the mud on a friend's ranch—the clay sucked in the front tire and before I could stop, the large rear tire was trapped. I sank deeper and deeper and had to wait for weeks and drier weather to pull the tractor out. I learned my lesson—don't mess with someone else's dirt.

The earth tempers my stories, always present, never far, part of the character of a place and its people, woven into the fabric of words. Writing without dirt is like farming without soil.

While the land in other parts of the country has been worked for multiple generations, our fields feel wild. Wildflowers still bloom. I discover weeds that I have never seen before. Not all the rocks—hardpan—have been cleared. Nature still dictates what I can or can't do. I only borrow the earth for a season and have to return it each winter as the crops slip into dormancy.

It's no different from my writing: I borrow words and if I'm lucky, some root themselves and grow into a story. My narratives germinate from the authentic and real—that's why I write creative nonfiction. I tried fiction but lack the imagination—these lands pull me back to reality; I gravitate to a truth embedded in the earth.

Western dirt can break me. It humbles my work. I hate it, loathe it, love it, fear it, and depend on it.

My father understood this after working a lifetime in these fields. Perhaps that's why at the end of a long summer workday, driving a tractor up and down row after row, Dad allows the dust to collect on all parts of his body; he doesn't try to dust himself off while working. His shoulders and arms become dirt repositories, his back and pants deeply embedded with the fine, hoary particles.

One time, after Dad climbed down from the tractor, a small puff of dust hovered around his body. His eyelashes carried a thin veil of earth. I gently patted his body, knocking loose the dirt and creating small puffs. As I worked my way up from his legs to back and shoulders, he bowed, a genuflection. He paid homage—not to me but to the dust. He understood that without dirt, we were nothing, our story ungrounded in all ways.

I grew up in this valley of dirt with the Sierra Nevada on one side, the Coast Ranges on the other. Valley people—we're flatlanders and have a love/hate relationship with mountains.

As a youth, these mountains locked me in, trapped me on the farm, and prevented escape. I was always tempted with curiosity and the lure of what was on the other side of the mountains that ringed our valley. Later, after running away for college and living in Japan, I came home, back to the dirt. Now as I age, I find the same mountains comforting. They provide security, perhaps protecting me from larger forces.

I don't believe I can write without this isolation. I take refuge in my stories, content to be alone with words and the dirt.

I am a rooted writer. I cannot, nor do I want to, separate a geography of place from my stories. This land is in my blood—historically, socially, culturally, and economically. The dirt grounds me: a good place to call home.

But the West is becoming civilized. Cities are growing, our valley swelling. Though we live in the middle of farmland, just to the north is the city of Fresno—considered rural and part of the "other California" beyond San Francisco and Los Angeles—with a population of over five hundred thousand. Within fifty miles of our farm over a million people live. Not your sleepy countryside.

Farming has evolved into a big business that's less about growing and more about producing. Much of the food from these lands is not for eating and nourishing the body. Instead, it's manufactured in order to be consumed: products designed for feeding.

We live in a new culture of abundance, farmers growing too much food. And in the frantic pace of new technologies, a simple, heirloom peach becomes lost and insignificant, swallowed by the pace of change.

I fear my stories will too.

There's a danger of the dirt becoming just dirt. A product once used up becomes obsolete. Like writers who write about place and nature and the land?

Or could this be an opportunity to become lost? I'm at my best when I'm lost in my dirt. Writing in the West remains isolating and I find that comforting. I can begin stories without rejection.

Working in the West, I have a vision of an endless landscape, a vision of the possible. Even after years of farming and writing, I still find myself wonderfully naive. A year ends with the close of autumn and a time for recovery over the winter. The land fools me in the cold, dark months; it appears dead, static, and unchanging. Then, with the first warmth, it stirs with life. Spring begins anew, no matter how badly I acted or performed the year before. The dirt is forgiving.

Armed with optimism, my stories can start over. I believe as a writer I too am still becoming. Like the West. I may be able to add something to this history of the land. I have learned that even in death, the richness of decay adds microbial life to the soil. I too can leave behind my mark in the earth.

Western dirt breeds a land of dreamers. I hope people can continue to sense the land and feel the grit of the soil in my words. Taste the earth in the fruits from my farm—in my peaches and in my stories.

Gary Snyder | TWO POEMS

THE BLACK-TAILED HARE

A grizzled black-eyed jackrabbit showed me

irrigation ditches, open paved highway,
      white line
  to the hill . . .
  bell chill blue jewel sky
       banners,

banner clouds flying:
the mountains all gathered,
  juniper trees on their flanks,
       cone buds,
  snug bark scale
  in thin powder snow
over rock scrabble, pricklers, boulders,

pines and junipers
singing.

The mountains singing
to gather the sky and the mist
  to bring it down snow-breath
       ice-banners—
  and gather it water
sent from the peaks
  flanks and folds
down arroyos and ditches by highways the water

the people to use it, the
   mountains and juniper
do it for us

     said the rabbit.

COVERS THE GROUND

> *When California was wild, it was*
> *one sweet bee-garden . . .*
>
> JOHN MUIR

Down the Great Central Valley's
blossoming almond orchard acres
lines of tree trunks shoot a glance through
     as the rows flash by—

And the ground is covered with
cement culverts standing on end,
house-high & six feet wide
culvert after culvert far as you can see
     covered with
mobile homes, pint-size portable housing, johnny-on-the-spots,
concrete freeway, overpass, underpass,
     exit floreals, entrance curtsies, railroad bridge,
long straight miles of divider oleanders;
scrappy ratty grass and thistle, tumbled barn, another age,

yards of tractors, combines lined up—
new bright-painted units down at one end,
old stuff broke and smashed down at the other,
cypress tree spires, frizzy lonely palm tree,
steep and gleaming
fertilizer tank towers fine-line catwalk in the sky—

     covered with walnut orchard acreage
irrigated, pruned and trimmed;

with palleted stacks of cement bricks
 waiting for yellow fork trucks;

quarter-acre stacks of wornout car tires,
dust clouds blowing off the new plowed fields,
taut-strung vineyards trimmed out even on the top,

cubic blocks of fresh fruit loading boxes,
long aluminum automated chicken-feeder houses,
  spring furze of green weed
  comes on last fall's hard-baked ground,
    beyond "Blue Diamond Almonds"
come the rows of red-roofed houses
& the tower that holds catfood
with a red/white checkered sign

crows whuff over almond blossoms
beehives sit tight between fruit tree ranks
eucalyptus boughs shimmer in the wind—a pale blue hip-roof
house behind a weathered fence—
crows in the almonds
  trucks on the freeways,
    Kenworth, Peterbilt, Mack,
    rumble diesel depths,
like boulders bumping in an outwash glacial river

  drumming to a not-so-ancient text

  "The Great Central Plain of California
  was one smooth bed of honey-bloom
    400 miles, your foot would press
  a hundred flowers at every step
  it seemed one sheet of plant gold;

  all the ground was covered
  with radiant corollas ankle-deep:
  bahia, madia, madaria, burielia,
  chrysopsis, grindelia,
    wherever a bee might fly—"

us and our stuff just covering the ground.

Louis B. Jones

"IT'S LIKE THEY TILTED THE WHOLE COUNTRY EAST-TO-WEST. AND EVERYTHING THAT WASN'T TIED-DOWN SLID"

Here's another dilapidated antique mining town, sweet, peaceful, tumble-down, Victorian, burned-out, arsenic-soiled, where people now will be hosting film festivals. This one is called Nevada City, though it's in California. The whole county all around is beautiful, the economy might as well be 1940, there's only one stoplight, and it's out at the highway, we've got a clothesline and a kitchen garden and fruit trees and meadows, and a forest all around us where there are creatures a lot bigger and cagier than I, and a limitless supply of firewood. Last year, cross-country skiing with my son off Highway 20 in eight feet of snow, we'd been traveling for hours on the big ridge above the Yuba, seeing no colors but three—the blue of the sky, the green of conifers, and the white of the snow (*four* colors if you count tree trunks)—and when we stopped for lunch over a canyon, unwrapping our sandwiches in all those columns of silence, where the *creak* of our skis had ceased, I found myself telling him to look around. Because sixty years from now he could be sitting at this very spot, sipping his tea in the window of a Regional Mega-Starbucks among parking lots, trying to tell some other old man about how it was in the old days.

I picture California in 1820, 1830, 1840, before statehood, before gold, and I imagine the handful of original Old Californios down at sea level, with their peace and quiet, with their vastness, all in the pigments of the *plein air* painters who were considered "romantic" and "sublime" in the nineteenth century—with their haciendas, with their herds, with their vineyards—I picture John Reed the Irish adventurer who got himself a Spanish land-grant rancho in southern Marin County, where eventually he was running two thousand head of cattle and four hundred horses on what would be Mill Valley and Tiburon and Belvedere, and where he built an adobe house for his wife, Hilarita, daughter of the commandant at the Presidio—I picture him in the sunset under the great eaves with his goblet, a guitarist off to one side cross-hatched in purple shade, and probably houseguests (Reed's place was on the spot where, today, the 2AM Club faces the Mill Valley BMW dealership; it's a four-way stop on Miller Avenue; you might Google Earth the spot, but you won't see the hacienda anymore, nor any vestigial archeological print of its foundation), and while the guitarist plucks out little melodic garlands, and the lanterns are being lit for the evening, Reed is telling his guests, lifting a wineglass to swing it across the landscape, "You should have seen it. You should have seen it before *we* got here. The real West is gone."

The I-80 corridor, Eisenhower's big project, the whole thing from New York to here, has been a formative influence in my personal life. But there is a particular stretch I seem to be snagged on, in recent years especially, on and off its entrance ramps and exit ramps on various errands, in various kinds of vehicles in all seasons. It's on the west slope of the Sierra, the hundred-mile ascent from the Sacramento Valley, climbing through Gold Run and Dutch Flat and Blue Canyon and Emigrant Gap, climaxed by the mountain pass at seven thousand feet, Donner Pass, where, once upon a time, delirious cannibalism was the gateway to a vision of paradise. The Donner Party episode persists among us here, a century and a half later, and in my own mind has been rising to the stature of a "founding myth." (Or, that is, a "founding scandal," as so many civilizations seem to find their legend of origin in some seminal crime.) Where I'm from—Wilmette, Illinois—the founding myth was of a marriage, ringing the bell of husbandry over that flat land, the conjugal story of the French fur trader Antoine Ouilmette, who wedded the half-Potawatomi maiden Archange by the lake, and who, together with her, settled there on the shores of Lake Michigan, right at a spot where, today, the Michigan Shores Club stands, the limestone club with the imposing porte cochere, where my friends and I infested the swimming pool on cold winter days and charged BLTs and Cokes to my friends' parents' accounts. That was the Midwest. That's what I left. The marriage of Antoine and Archange, that original ceremony subduing the wilderness, was suffused in a radiance that just perfectly outshone the numinous miscegenation in Archange's being, herself, the daughter of an earlier French trader and a full-blooded Potawatomi woman, christened with that diaphanous French name of a Judaeo-Christian angel in the wilderness. The legend of "The Donner Party" out west, by contrast, seems to be the story of a series of unwise or even vicious indirections and misjudgments and bad luck. All pioneers move from failure to failure. That's their glory. Zigzagging from one disgraceful wreck to the next disgraceful wreck. Today's pioneers, too—say, in Silicon Valley or the movie biz—will have some ingredient of the crash-and-burn mentality. It's been the story of a lot of good writers' lives, always swinging for the fences and, so, mostly "failing," and failing big-time. This great unexplored, mostly unmapped province of failure out here, where indeed seldom is heard a discouraging word, is still open for all comers. On Interstate 80 on any day you can see the U-Hauls with Ohio or Indiana plates, they're headed west, men and women all destined for the mistakenness, the redeeming mistakenness. It's a story that needed a myth. Not only were the Donners impetuous and uncareful, there's an additional element to their story: on the mountain pass among those rock peaks, they paid a price in their greater deliverance, they committed a terrible enormity. Or so people like to hear it told. It seems true enough, and anyway it makes a good story. It provides a dark metaphor for every Californian in his verdant valley paradise, his suburban backyard with barbeque and spatula, his picture window overlooking the marina, his sparkling view of a long bay, his table at Chez Panisse: we're all immigrants, or come from emigrants, and somewhere back there somebody had to gnaw off something essential in order to free himself. Immigrants are immigrants for a reason. They're here. They're not back there.

What did I, personally, gnaw off? In my life I'm not interested in the question. Really, I'm not interested. You keep what you can use. What you can't use, you don't go on carrying around with you. I can say, however, that I'm grateful over the years to have changed shape, somewhat, in the kiln I envisioned as "the West." A convention of popular novels of the pulp Western genre is that the characterization, out in the frontier territories, is pretty much limited to "fools" and "scoundrels." That is, society is divided (with the exception of the "hero") into two types: the bushwhacked innocents and the predatory troublemakers. The point-of-view character, the hero, is the one who sorts them out. He's probably the sheriff. Or if he isn't he oughta be. In fact, I've come to know something of the law enforcement mentality, and I suppose any CHP officer, still today, expects to meet up with that same dichotomous division of human nature, whenever he dismounts his motorcycle and makes "that long walk" of his, to confront a driver he's pulled over: this will be either (a) a fool or (b) a scoundrel. A clueless civilian type or a potential perp: in his experience, that's who's out there. As for me, here I am today safe in my farmhouse in the mountains. If we survive and we're lucky over the years, *compassion* is the exalted, while quite practical, state we might achieve, and during my wanderings in California I'm grateful to have been both, fool and scoundrel, in plenty of incarnations; I'm just lucky there was still a little bit of frontier wilderness left, and that I survived it.

But that's only a metaphorical wilderness, you'll say; only a wilderness of the mind. You'll object that I didn't need "the West" for such a transfiguration: I might have been unwise and unguided anywhere. *That* particular wilderness is just as accessible in the streets of Chicago or New York or Poughkeepsie.

Well, but the special generosity of this place the West always lay in a particular—a singular, a unique—ecological circumstance. It was the *natural environment* that enabled such a triumph of liberty and democratic opportunity. I've known a number of feckless or guileless people to end up "rich" out here (if "rich" is considered a decent desideratum) in this fabulous *ecosystem* that has been so liberating. It wasn't the work of the legislators under their white domes. It wasn't our rational Keynesian and neoclassical "mixed" capitalism, it wasn't Yankee ingenuity or immigrant pluck or muscular Christianity or, necessarily, the principles framed in the Constitution. All this pursuit of happiness, yes, might have benefited under such enlightened political and cultural regimes, but more fundamentally it's been allowed to us by the land, all along, throughout the whole American country but latterly in the West, the deep mineral wealth, the petroleum, the swift, clear cobble-bottom rivers, the long beaches where you can find a dry place for your sleeping bag and no one bothers you, the fisheries in the Pacific and the great rivers, the natural ports and the consequent military-industrial wealth, the sunny lawlessness of population sparsity that was available to the early movie business entrepreneurs fleeing New York, the disposable income that, through all this abundance, winds up in the pockets of the middle class, the veritable mêlée of social class fluidity, unlike anything Back East (advantageous especially to a boy like me, who, in migrating, dropped suddenly low in the ranks of the mysterious American "class system," yet also liked the drop), the swaths of real estate to be sold to retirees, the mile-deep fertile soil in the Central Valley, the vast forests of timber: at the base of it all is an ecological gift, unprecedented in world history (at least since, maybe, the ecological gift of the Lower Nile's seasonal floods). After we'd either killed or married any Indians, we had easy access to unlimited resources, opulent possibilities for mistakenness, and, in consequence, a cultural wealth unmatched since the Athenians'—whose Classical eminence itself was, comparatively, somewhat tainted by the necessities of colonial empire. So far, we actually *haven't needed to speak of empire*. We've been able to keep our innocence. Call it innocence, call it virtue, call it our terrific innate resourcefulness or "know-how." Whatever you call it, we like to think we've got it. So we enjoyed comparing ourselves to those benighted, compromised Europeans in the Old World. All the while, in all these forests and canyons and beaches and fertile valleys, there's been a terrific quantity of *room* to spread our wreckage. They didn't have that in New York or Chicago, not on the same scale. Let alone Paris or Rome. Or Jerusalem or Baghdad.

Me, I'm hardly affluent; I long ago decided to settle for an "artistic" standard of income; but yet today actually I cut down for firewood trees that, back in Wilmette, would have been treasured and discussed and admired from lawn chairs and treated as heirlooms. The woolly old Romanticism is still going on out here, and the old mess is still being created, we've still got so many board-feet of lumber standing around. Back in the Mediterranean basin, cradle of Western capitalism and democracy, the principle building materials, for thousands of years, have been stone and cement and plaster and ceramic. Earthquakes or no earthquakes, masonry is the prevalent form. Wooden beams, back in Europe, may serve as a valuable structural element, but wood will seldom go to make an entire house. Once as I drove up I-80 into the Sierra with a woman who had been living mostly in Spain and Ecuador, she remarked on the passing homes, "What is it like living in a wooden house?"—as if they were fine cabinetry. She said it with some perplexity (*living in a wooden house*) as you might say, *What's it like pedaling a gingerbread bicycle?* The implication seemed to be, a wooden house might be hard to keep clean—harder than the tile floors and plastered masonry she was used to. But she remarked, also, that such a house might smell great.

I tried to describe how they need continual scraping and painting, or oil-staining, and occasional surgery for dry rot (as I know well, because at home, all too much of my own time is occupied by the scrape-and-paint business, the putty-glazing of windows, the rough carpentry), and how, like a guitar, a wooden house will respond to the atmosphere in various seasons. But all the while, through her eyes I could see my own passing neighborhood as a vanishing shire, already a little misty, like a museum diorama, of say the Carboniferous Period. These Western states have always been the territory of 8 × 8 beams, rail fences, redwood decks, bat-and-board siding, cedar shingles, clapboard. Only now, in this strange century, is stucco and vinyl coming to replace the old materials, along with aluminum, HardiPlank, Trex decking, all textured to look like "the real thing." Last year, when I was putting up a small building in a meadow behind the house, I couldn't evade the vigilant eye of the county building inspector (*his* new exaltedness! another sign, around here, of the end of an era). It turned out *the county wouldn't let me* use wood siding. It's the new code. It's a wildfire-abatement thing. So I settled on a Hardi-Plank product: never again dry rot, never again repainting, never again termites; also, HardiPlank worked out to be *one-quarter* the expense of Western red cedar, which is running at almost thirty dollars for one single eighteen-foot board. In any case, it was illegal to use now. I love wood and I resented the county requirement, but secretly I felt that maybe—for someone who's getting to be a little more provident in general, and a little more prudent in his time expenditures—a fake-wood building might be all right, especially in future years around this place.

Peter Fish   STAR STRUCK

In 1962 we moved to Southern California. We had come from colder places and my parents bought a house a half-block from the Pacific hoping to make up for years of snow tires, parkas, and bronchitis.

The town we moved to was Ventura. It was, and is, the seat of its namesake county and at the time was a city of about thirty-five thousand. It was a beach town, fronted by a long curving stretch of sand with a decent surf break. But it was not a beach town in the way Malibu, to the south, and Santa Barbara, to the north, were. Unlike Santa Barbara, it lacked a patina of strenuous old money, of Hobie Cat races and champagne brunches at the Coral Casino swim club. Unlike Malibu, it did not have a Barbie named after it.

It was a ranching town—ranching in the California sense of raising not cattle but crops that elsewhere might be said to grow on farms. Lima beans, walnuts, but especially citrus—oranges in the hotter inland valleys and, nearer the coast, lemons. It was an oil town, with a strong Texas-Oklahoma accent, cousin in many ways to hardscrabble inland oil towns like Bakersfield or even Taft. It's a testimony to Ventura's wobbly public image that the landmark most linked to it in the popular mind—Ventura Highway, from the drippy 1970s soft rock hit—does not exist. There is no Ventura Highway in Ventura: there is the Ventura Freeway, which people in Ventura don't call that (they refer to "the 101") and Ventura Avenue, known for its burrito joints, its Hell's Angels headquarters, and its oil field.

But for my parents, Ventura was a precinct of heaven. Later, Southern California became a synonym for dysfunction, for riots, celebrity murders, and Stage 3 smog alerts, but for them—for my parents' entire generation, really—it was paradise and the future all at once. Here, on the shore of the sundown sea, you could abandon the person you'd been in Midland or Des Moines and become someone more successful, more handsome, more fun. My parents were high school sweethearts from a tiny town in upstate New York, where for five months a year people holed up in their snowbound houses engaging in petty arguments with relatives and heavy drinking. It wasn't for them.

They were ambitious, they were lively, they were a little glamorous. My father had the good looks of a 1950s TV star—think John Forsythe or Guy Madison, with curly dark hair and slightly heavy-lidded eyes. My mother was petite and sporty, loving the ocean so much that my most vivid memory of her is her riding waves on a boogie board, floral bathing cap flashing like a lotus in the foaming surf.

In Santa Barbara or Malibu they might have struggled, but in Ventura we lived well. They bought the house near the ocean, they joined a country club, my father took up skin diving, they had beach barbeques with their new California friends, many of whom, the women at least, had exotic California names: Jinx, Boots. We exchanged the old Buick Century, suitable for snow, for a metallic lilac Thunderbird with burgundy leather interior and landau roof. When we drove back from somewhere and neared the Seaward Avenue off-ramp my father pressed a button and the driver's side window descended with a satisfying electric purr. "Feel that ocean breeze," he would say.

Their paradise, not mine. I didn't fit. I was fat and pale and ill at ease, a secret loudmouth who spent time formulating clever sarcastic remarks but was too shy to make any friends to tell them to. I found California kids with their tans and skills at skateboarding and skimboarding intimidating, and I found many of the adults odd. The alcoholic neighbor who mistakenly believed we had moved from Chicago, which we had never seen, and would confront me with "Chicago! Helluva town! Gotta love the Loop!" My piano teacher who, many years later I realized, must have suffered from Tourette syndrome and who interrupted my keyboard performances of "Born Free" with shouts of "What?" "Who said that?" and "Who's there?" As it turned out, I liked the ocean but didn't like being seen in a bathing suit, my white belly spilling over the elastic waistband, so I would run across the sand and plunge immediately into the waves, where I would bob until dangerously cold and tired because I didn't want to return to the beach until everyone else had left.

I was a docile child. When my parents made me take golf lessons and tennis lessons and tumbling lessons I acquiesced. But what I really liked to do was sit inside and watch TV. Spy shows, shows where people possessed secret magical powers, *Walt Disney's Wonderful World of Color* episodes, featuring kids tangled up in wacky adventures, kids like me but more handsome, thinner, and with friends. Each week I scanned *TV Guide* and circled in crayon the shows not to miss. *World of Color 7 p.m. Sammy the Way-Out Seal: In this hilarious comedy, two boys bring home a mischievous seal without telling their parents and soon they find that you can't keep a house-bound seal a secret for very long.*

Trying to find something to belong to, I joined the Boy Scouts. The scoutmaster was another oddity, a retired Army officer who filled his Boy Scouts of America-issue canteen with bourbon and who claimed that on the beachhead at Anzio he'd picked up valuable German radio reports of troop movements via the fillings in his teeth. Later he became obsessed with pyramidology and lectured us about it around the campfire. "The Great Pyramid of Giza! Its measurements reveal everything that will happen in the future. Reveals the date and year of the second coming of Christ."

I joined a boys choir. It was taught by a Mr. Cook, a short, capon-plump man who favored blue berets and made us all wear blue berets and called us the Blue Beret Boys Choir. We also wore pumpkin-orange velour sweatshirts. By now it was the late 1960s, which meant that you couldn't turn on a radio without hearing the Rolling Stones' "Let's Spend the Night Together" or the Doors' "Light My Fire," but Mr. Cook was immune to this musical and social tumult. Our song list featured "Wonderful Copenhagen" and "Hello, Dolly." For the latter, he dressed up one of the boys as Dolly, in Carol Channing Gay Nineties drag—blonde wig, eye shadow, feather boa—and made him sashay around the stage, twirling the boa while the rest of us wolf-whistled and hooted. We sang in shopping centers, we sang in senior citizens homes, we sang at the state mental hospital, where the Thorazined patients sat in folding chairs watching us, touching themselves. Our big closing number was sung to the tune of the Boer War anthem "Marching to Pretoria"—another indicator of Mr. Cook's cultural currency—but with lyrics of his own devising:

> We are singing in Ventura
> Ventura, Ventura,
> We are singing in Ventura
> Ventura is our home.

But for all of its peculiarities, its dowdiness, Ventura had an ace up its sleeve. Hollywood, manufacturer of dreams, was only an hour away. A large portion of Ventura County lies within what the film industry refers to as the "Thirty Mile Zone"—a thirty-mile circle centered on West Beverly and North La Cienega Boulevards in Los Angeles. Trade union and other rules make it less cumbersome and costly to film motion pictures and television shows within this circle. Even portions of the county beyond the circle were deemed scenic and convenient substitutions for more far-flung locales. Scenes from *Spartacus* were filmed in Ventura County and much of *It's a Mad, Mad, Mad, Mad World*. The rest of the nation watched *The Dukes of Hazzard* and saw Bo and Luke and Daisy taunting Boss Hogg in Hazzard County, Georgia, but I knew their 1969 Dodge Charger General Lee was in fact roaring around Ventura County's back roads. Burt Reynolds filmed his short-lived television show, *Dan August*, in the county, so that years later as a college student in Madrid I watched dubbed reruns on a small black-and-white television and told my host family, *Burt Reynolds conduce por mi escuela secundaria*.

We had celebrities, too. Not A-list celebrities, but celebrities in transition, in trouble, in retirement, on the skids. The 1940s movie star June Allyson married a Ventura dentist, although by the time she moved to the county she was best known for shilling adult diapers. For some years, Johnny Cash lived north of town in a ranch house on a hill where each December he set up loudspeakers and blared Christmas carols down on the people below, including the residents of his Johnny Cash Trailer Rancho mobile home park. It was not, I think, a happy time in his life. One of the expensive beachfront homes a block away from us was said to belong to the creators of *Lassie*, and for a time I walked the beach hoping to meet the heroic collie and have her become best friend to the family Labrador and me.

So you see it seemed possible to leap from Ventura to entertainment fame, even if, like me, you had shown no previous inclination, ability, or experience in singing or dancing or acting. You see, too, that in conflating television Lassies with actual dogs I conflated what occurred on television with what occurred in the real world. Somehow, I believed, I would appear on television—not as the star, I knew that was beyond me, but as a sidekick, smart-alecky but loyal. When that happened, my television life would shape my true life, filling it with adventures involving collies, race cars, and seals.

It happened. My teacher, Miss Rush, from Indiana with watery brown eyes magnified by rhinestone glasses, told me to report to the principal's office. I was not someone who got in trouble so was not afraid but puzzled. When I arrived I saw three other students, equally bemused.

"Who here," the principal asked, "has seen *Art Linkletter's House Party*?"

Better to ask who in the world hadn't seen it. *Art Linkletter's House Party* was among the longest-running shows on television, the first in the line-up of programs I watched when I returned home from school. Every weekday afternoon, Art—the only person in television history to have five network shows running at the same time—chatted with famous guests, then interviewed schoolchildren, prodding them to make embarrassing remarks. He would collect the remarks in best-selling books like *Kids Say the Darndest Things*, a copy of which sat in our home bookshelf. Somehow the Art Linkletter people had discovered our Ventura school. Somehow our principal had deemed the four of us worthy of conversing with Art. We would drive to Hollywood the next week to appear on the show.

By the time I walked home that afternoon, I felt as if I'd stepped into my own *Disney World of Color* episode. *In this rollicking comedy, an elementary school outcast appears on TV and saves the day!* I was excited, although uncertain why the principal had selected me and the other three students: in retrospect it seems clear it was because we were all bland children unlikely to say "fuck" on live television. My parents were pleased, too, although they saw the appearance as an excuse for an enjoyable field trip rather than the life-altering experience I knew it would be.

In the week before our appearance, excitement turned to worry. I wanted to wear clothes that would make me appear muscular and commanding. But we were advised my favorite plaid shirt would not photograph well on television. My mother put me in red BanLon—BanLon being an unfortunate offshoot of polyester—that gave me the look of a beefsteak tomato on little legs.

I worried, too, about what clever and amusing things I would say. The classic Art-child encounter went something like this:

Art: What does your sister look like?

Child: My mother.

Art: And who do you look like?

Child: The mailman.

Art: Really?

Child: That's what my dad is always telling the neighbors.

It was a problem. Successful *House Party* conversations often involved sex, which I knew nothing about, and siblings, of which I had none. Pets peeing on things was a possible topic, and parents falling into toilets.

We drove down to Hollywood, principal and four children in one car, four accompanying mothers in the other. This was, I think, my first trip into Los Angeles, and after Ventura it seemed intimidating, with the long, flat boulevards—La Cienega, Olympic, Wilshire—lined with spectral palms and a light much harsher than the sea-coast light I was used to. CBS Television City was a block-long complex of white buildings, each dominated by a large CBS eye.

It is a testimony to my complete self-absorption that I don't remember who the other three students with me were, although all were in my same grade in a rather small elementary school. We ate lunch at the studio commissary. We were daubed with cursory makeup, we were led through the wilderness of cables and cameras backstage to the greenroom, where we watched the start of *House Party* on a TV monitor in the corner. That day, Art's celebrity guest was the advice columnist Dear Abby. She told a story about one of her readers who had written in admitting she'd run out of liverwurst before a dinner party and served canned dog food on Ritz Crackers as an appetizer. The reader wanted to know if she should fess up. "I told her," Dear Abby said, both she and Art cackling, "never tell *anybody* what lucky *dogs* your dinner guests were."

Dear Abby left. At a commercial break the four of us were led on stage and directed to perch on four high stools. The commercial ended. The studio lights dimmed, the stage lights blazed, and here was Art again, with his wide white face and his natty sports coat, holding his big microphone.

I was on the first stool. Very fast he bore down on me with the microphone.

"You're a big boy," he said, big in this case clearly meaning "fat."

I giggled stupidly.

"And a happy one," Art said. Then he moved on.

That was it. He was gone. I felt, sitting beneath the bright lights on my tall stool, the way I did trapped in the ocean: cold, exhausted, but afraid to move for fear of being exposed to further ridicule. None of the other kids said anything interesting. Disappointments, we were led backstage to receive our complimentary prizes—coupons for Rice-A-Roni, a copy of the Art Linkletter-endorsed board game, The Game of Life, and a large Waring Blender. I mumbled something to the production assistant who had handed me the blender.

"Run," he said. "Run back on stage and tell that to Art."

I ran back on stage, cradling the blender as an Oscar recipient cradles his golden statuette. Art had been alerted to my return, and as I approached him, he held the microphone in my face again.

"Thank you for the blender," I said, surprised and delighted by the way my amplified voice filled the studio, "because my mom melted ours in the dishwasher."

The studio ignited with laughter. Art bent double, his wide face reddening. The audience roared.

"Is your mom here?" Art asked when he recovered himself.

"Yes," I said.

Art turned to the audience. "Mom, can you stand up?"

My mother rose. The audience laughed and applauded. Art grabbed my shoulder. I was, finally, where I wanted to be: on stage, in the spotlight, adulation warming me like the sun.

Back at home in Ventura, my parents were happy for me. I think they were pleased, too, that a portion of my celebrity had rubbed off on my mother, that the nation had seen her on television, an attractive woman receiving applause at the end of the show. But they were also concerned. They knew that I hoped—how? A producer calling? Art Linkletter calling? I was entirely ignorant of how show business worked—my television appearance would vault me into celebrity, and they knew that would not occur.

But it didn't matter. Or, rather, it mattered and then did not. It was an opening. At school, people began to approach me, began to say, You were on TV. Cool. For the first time I felt I might have a life here with the ocean and skim boarders, that Ventura and I might be suited to each other.

I received fan mail, by which I mean five letters, two from relatives back East and three from people with time on their hands to write benign notes to children seen on Art Linkletter. One letter was from an old woman in Missouri who shared my surname and thought we might be related. She enclosed a long, folded family tree, annotated in her spidery hand:

William D.—prominent lawyer in Springfield.

Cousin Roscoe—died age 8 from eating match heads.

What should I do with these, I asked my mother.

"They're letters," she said. "You answer them."

I sat down and wrote. "Thank you for your letter. It was fun being on TV. Art Linkletter is very nice. I hope to be on TV again soon."

I see myself at the dining room table, writing, and I understand now that I had learned three things that have stayed with me longer than I might have expected. That all attention is good, and that there is no harm in making a public spectacle of yourself. That on occasion loony desires are fulfilled. All three strike me as very Southern California lessons, as very Ventura lessons, not to be depended on in many situations. But they have their use.

Maxine Hong Kingston | DÍAS DE LOS MUERTOS

In my poem, "I Love a Broad Margin to My Life," I travel East, and of course arrive West. In China, I anticipate my burial in French Camp, California. Here, out of context, are lines 1,481–1,524 in the 5,226-line poem:

. . . Cry "Open Sesame!"
and enter the good earth. People walking
the wide, pathless ground, placing on the thresholds
flowers and red paper, wine and food,
incense. Ah, altars, doorsills of graves.
Ah, Ching Ming. All over China,
and places where Chinese are, populations
are on the move, going home. That home
where Mother and Father are buried. Doors
between heaven and earth open wide.
Our dead throng across the bourn,
come back to meet us, eat and drink with us,
receive our gifts, and give us gifts.
Listen for, and hear them; they're listening for
and hear us. Serve the ancestors come
to visit. Serve them real goods. If
no real goods, give symbols.
Enjoy, dear guests, enjoy life again.
Read the poems rising in smoke. Rituals
for the dead continue, though Communist Revolution,
Cultural Revolution, though diaspora. These hills
could be the Altamont Pass, and the Coast Range
and Sierras that bound the Central Valley. I
have arrived in China at the right time, to catch
the hills green. And where shall I be buried?
In the Chinese Cemetery on I-5?
Will they allow my White spouse? We integrate
the cemetery with our dead bodies? All my life,

it's my embarrassing task to integrate every
social function I attend. Can't even
rest at the end. Can't rest alongside
my father and mother. Cremate me then. Burn me
to ashes. Dig me into the peat dirt
of the San Joaquin Valley. Dig
some more of me into the 'aina of Hawai'i.
Leftovers into the sipapu
navel at the bottom of the Grand Canyon, and more
leftovers at the feet of oaks in Oakland
and redwoods in Muir Woods and eucalyptus
in the Berkeley grove, and around Shakespeare's
plants in Golden Gate Park. All my places.
Yosemite. The Sierras. All California (except LA) . . .

Harold Gilliam THE SAN FRANCISCO PSYCHE

Late on a cold winter afternoon, I was walking through a forest of Monterey pines in the Presidio of San Francisco when I emerged into an open area on a bluff top above the Golden Gate and my eyes were suddenly assaulted from the water below and the Pacific offshore.

The sun was low in the west, and congregations of cumulus clouds were throwing moving shadows on land and water. From where I stood on the cliff top, most of the land areas were in relative darkness. In the total chiaroscuro scene, even the great swinging steel span a quarter mile to my right was subordinated to the dazzling incandescence below and to the west.

Few buildings were readily visible, and my immediate impression was that I was experiencing a time warp. I was seeing this place much as it had appeared to the first explorers. Near this spot Juan Bautista de Anza stood in 1776, marveling at this five-mile-long strait that opened into San Francisco Bay. His chaplain, Father Pedro Font, wrote in his diary: "And there we saw a prodigy of nature it is not easy to describe . . . the port of San Francisco . . . might well be called the harbor of harbors . . . and I think if it could be well settled like Europe, there would not be anything more beautiful."

Thirty years later, a Russian explorer, Nicolai Petrovich Rezanov, sailing south from Russian outposts in Alaska, gazed in astonishment at this same sight and wrote in a report to his superior in St. Petersburg: "Even without any great sacrifice on the part of the treasury, all this country could be made a corporeal part of the Russian empire."

Neither the Spaniards nor the Russians were able to follow up fully on their visions of empire, but there were others who were. In 1846 the American explorer John C. Fremont arrived here and was so gripped with his own vision of empire that he gave this strait an inspired name: "I gave it the name 'Chrysopylae' or Golden Gate," he later wrote, "for the same reason that the harbor of Byzantium was called Chrysoceras or Golden Horn." Byzantium was the capital of the eastern Roman Empire, at the crossroads between Europe and Asia. Fremont envisioned a similar role for a world capital here, facing Asia across the Pacific.

The name was fortuitously appropriate in another way that he could not have anticipated. Two years after Fremont figuratively raised the American flag here, gold was discovered in the foothills of the Sierra Nevada, and this strait became a gateway to El Dorado. As I stood on this promontory, I could see in imagination, passing below, the veritable procession of vessels—clipper ships, square riggers, steamers—loaded with Argonauts from all over the world to join those who came overland in the greatest gold rush in history.

The sleepy bayside village of Yerba Buena soon boomed into a city of several thousand, renamed San Francisco. That explosive birth continues to shape the character of the city and its region. It was the origin of a persistent mind-set that might be called the San Francisco psyche.

Argonauts who had the urge to leave home and make the long tortuous land-or-sea journey for gold—many died en route—were by necessity men of a particular character. (Very few women arrived during the early years.) They were risk takers—bold, aggressive, energetic, venturesome, innovative, drawn by ambition, greed, the illusion of riches, and perhaps by the ancient impulse of westering, the millennial migrations from halfway around the world in search of a better life.

They came to a near-wilderness over a thousand miles from the nearest centers of population, a place that had no functioning government able to provide law and order, no traditions, no organization. They were forced to improvise as best they could (the Vigilante Committees, for example, were organized to bring some measure of rough frontier justice to curb inevitable criminality).

Like the first Europeans to settle on the East Coast, they felt they were moving into a New World, making a clean break with the past. They overlooked the fact that the New World was already the home of an indigenous population. In California, the native peoples had already been partly displaced by Spanish-Mexican colonists. But the territory was still sparsely settled, a loosely held colony largely ignored by the distant Mexican government. The colonists were quickly overwhelmed by the onrush of the ambitious Americans. In the early mining camps, all bets were off, and it was every man for himself. Some cooperative projects gradually evolved, and eventually nascent forms of government were set up, including police and jails.

In the long run, the greatest fortunes were made not by panning gold but by ingenious merchants selling supplies to the miners: picks and shovels, tent canvas, wood for cabins and sluices to channel the creeks for panning. Among the prosperous storekeepers in San Francisco or closer to the mining camps were future railroad tycoons Leland Stanford, Charles Crocker, Collis Huntington, and Mark Hopkins.

San Francisco became a burgeoning capital of commerce and manufacturing, with banks, newspapers, general stores, lumber mills, foundries, theaters, churches, and a shipping industry. Gold was only the beginning. The aggressive, innovative mind-set of the Gold Rush was reinforced by the prospect of developing the superabundant resources of the hinterland—the Central Valley's rich soils, the Sierra rivers as sources of water and power, the mountain forests for lumber. In the city, this activity required foundries, mills, machine shops, clothing factories, concrete plants, banks, and an educational infrastructure for technological research and to train engineers, lawyers, doctors, and teachers. Fewer than twenty years after the first forty-niners arrived, the University of California was chartered—at a time when the only passage west was still by ship or wagon train.

Out in the valley, groundbreaking landowners and farmers were devising new technologies that revolutionized many aspects of working the soil, such as the clamshell dredge and the steam combine harvester. The caterpillar tractor was invented to cope with the soft peat soils of the Sacramento River Delta, the fertile marshland where the Sierra rivers merged before flowing into San Francisco Bay. (The vehicle with tracks instead of wheels was later adapted into a formidable weapon, the military tank, which dominated the battlefields of Europe.)

Gold, then, and its accompanying mind-set, sparked chain reactions in many directions. Within ten years after the first Argonauts arrived, manufacturing and agriculture incomes each exceeded the value of all the glittering metal from the Mother Lode.

Not all the innovations were beneficent. Hydraulic mining was a prime example. One man with equipment like a fire hose with a special nozzle could turn a powerful jet of water on a gold-bearing mountainside and wash away great quantities of soil and gravel into creeks and rivers, causing floods, burying farmlands, and eventually silting up shipping channels in San Francisco Bay. Opposition to the practice was stymied for decades by the shrewd operators and their hired-gun lawyers until the devastation in the Sierra was finally halted by a court decision in 1884. Although the practice continued elsewhere on a smaller scale, that decision was a legal milestone, the first major halt to environmental destruction in the US. It established a precedent prohibiting uses of private property that cause damages elsewhere.

Another type of egregious destruction was reckless logging that leveled forests of some of the world's biggest trees—leaving eroded badlands—to supply the insatiable demand for lumber in the booming city and towns. The devastation incited mountaineer John Muir, farming at the time in the Bay Area at Martinez, to sound an alarm in national magazines, leading to the creation of Yosemite and Sequoia National Parks in 1890. Two years later, Muir and some UC Berkeley faculty members founded the Sierra Club, the beginning of the organized conservation movement.

Muir's innovative spirit reverberated down the years, into the 1960s when three Berkeley women became alarmed at the ongoing exploitation of San Francisco Bay. The bay was being filled for thousands of acres of garbage dumps, freeways, airports, and residential/industrial subdivisions. The three women launched the Save San Francisco Bay Association, aroused conservationist fervor, rallied public opinion, and lobbied relentlessly. The California legislature eventually crowned their efforts with the creation of a commission that halted most bay filling. This was the first regional organization to preserve a natural resource in an urban area. That precedent inspired activists elsewhere to follow suit, making similar efforts to protect Chesapeake Bay, the Hudson River, Puget Sound, Long Island Sound, bays in Galveston and Tampa, and Narragansett Bay in Rhode Island, among others. Under Executive Director David Lewis, Save the Bay has instigated a national alliance of these and other groups, to "Restore America's Estuaries."

The achievement of the three Berkeley women and their followers marked a historic turning point—the expansion of the conservation movement, devoted to protecting wildlands, into environmentalism, devoted to saving urban resources and ultimately the planet itself.

The same mind-set had resulted in major innovations in San Francisco itself. Gold Rush magnates, along with others enriched by Nevada's Comstock Lode silver, coveted some of the civic amenities of other world-class cities, including parks. Frederick Law Olmsted, the designer of New York's Central Park, came to San Francisco in the 1860s and concluded that it would be impossible to site a park where it was contemplated in the western tracts of the city, which were mostly sand dunes swept by ocean winds. Undeterred, the city fathers gave the job to a young engineer named William Hammond Hall who, starting with daunting wasteland, laid out the thousand-acre Golden Gate Park.

An even more doubtful venture was the Golden Gate Bridge. The notion of spanning the mile-wide narrows of that five mile-long strait had been left to stargazers, including the popular zany dreamer who called himself "Emperor" Norton. Ideas like the emperor's had been good for laughs after a few drinks. But until the early twentieth century, there had been no serious proposals. No single span that long had ever been built anywhere. It would cross a wild stretch of water where currents many times the volume of the continent's largest rivers charged through in opposite directions twice a day. That mighty flow over the eons carved out a channel more than three hundred-feet deep. The water was usually accompanied by winds, often bringing fogs that reduced visibility to zero.

In 1918, Chicago engineer Joseph B. Strauss presented the city with a bridge proposal—which was opposed by a battery of engineers who said it wasn't feasible, naval officials and shippers who feared it could block the harbor, bankers who claimed it could never be financed, and skeptics who maintained that the dangerous strait could never be bridged. But Strauss pushed his vision with eloquence and tireless campaigning, gaining supporters along the way. In a 1930 bond election, voters passed the measure with a thumbs-up, three-to-one majority.

However, the Depression had begun, and bankers cold-shouldered the voter-approved bonds; the bridge was too speculative. So Strauss went to a maverick financier, A. P. Gianinni, founder of the Bank of America. He agreed to take the risk, and the project was on. The actual construction was headed by Strauss's assistant, Clifford Paine. The bridge was completed on schedule after four years of extremely hazardous work, including major setbacks, and in 1937 was "dedicated" by two hundred thousand celebrants.

The lithe swinging span across the turbulent waters was another culmination of the "dare to do it" spirit born in the Gold Rush.

Yet any history of the region should point out that pioneers and their descendants took outsized risks and turned conventional wisdom upside-down more in pursuit of power and wealth than for uplifting and humanitarian purposes. Civic corruption, ruthless politics, and grinding social conditions all cast a pall over San Francisco. The dark side of the region's history has been amply probed by investigative writers and journalists, most notably Upton Sinclair, Lincoln Steffens, and Carey McWilliams in the early twentieth century and Gray Brechin (*Imperial San Francisco*) in the early twenty-first.

But the innovative temperament continues and has veritably exploded in a new Gold Rush in Silicon Valley, where a similar sense of freedom, risk-taking, exuberance, and experimentation is having a global impact. Among the valley's start-ups known worldwide are Google, Apple, Yahoo, HP, Fairchild, and Twitter. Historian Kevin Starr has noted that "millisecond by millisecond, millions were being navigated through the swirling galaxies of the Internet by companies that hadn't even existed a few short years earlier . . . ." Perhaps the valley's most ambitious venture capitalists are those devising sustainable technologies to cope with the threat of global climate change.

The San Francisco psyche has always embraced the unusual, the bizarre, and the defiance of convention. It is no accident that the city in the 1950s and 60s hosted the primary expressions of the counterculture: the beatniks and later the flower children who congregated on "hippie hill" in Golden Gate Park and in the nearby Haight-Ashbury neighborhood, where neo-hippies and tourists still search out the vibes of the time. The city's free-thinking mind-set also accounts for the militant but fun-loving gay-lesbian community in the Castro district, led in its early stages by the charismatic city supervisor, Harvey Milk. The taste for the unconventional even shows up in some religious expressions. In the century-old congregation Sherith Israel, a stained-glass window depicts Moses receiving the Ten Commandments not on Mount Sinai but in Yosemite Valley.

The Gold Rush and its consequences have not been the only cause of the city's special mind-set. Another probable influence is the relatively stable weather. In the summer the cool winds off the Pacific offer a climate far more physically and mentally stimulating than is the oppressive heat in most other parts of the country. In winter the moderate temperatures here seem more congenial to creative thought than the frigid snowbound weather of the Midwest and the East Coast.

The region's diverse topography also contributes to widening of thought. The bay's blue expanse and the hills around it afford constantly changing panoramas to lift one's focus from routine trivia to farsighted views of how puzzle pieces fit together. It is difficult to stand on Twin Peaks, for example, and gaze at the vast congeries of cities, bay, and mountains without an exhilarating sense of awe, wonder, and mental expansiveness.

The region's diverse landscapes are matched by its ethnic diversity. From the beginning, when "The World Rushed In" (the very apt title of J. S. Holliday's account of the Gold Rush), San Francisco has been a magnet for peoples from nearly all continents. Probably both the spectacular topography and the cosmopolitan ethnicity influenced President Franklin D. Roosevelt's choice of San Francisco as the birthplace of the United Nations in 1945. As he was concluding the Yalta Conference with Churchill and Stalin, Eleanor Roosevelt wrote him: "I think having the first UN meeting in San Francisco is a stroke of genius."

These various sources of creative energy, along with the city's position at the edge of the continent, have encouraged the concept of San Francisco as an "imperial city," a symbol conjured by explorers like Fremont and later by ebullient journalists and some historians, most notably in the multivolume works of Hubert Howe Bancroft.

In the twentieth century, however, the city's imperial aspirations evolved into more enlightened views of the westward movement, as expressed most dramatically in the Golden Gate International Exposition on the bay at Treasure Island in 1939–1940. The central theme of the fair was not empire in the traditional sense but the future meeting and creative blending of Pacific cultures. The dominant motif was embodied in the colossal statue, *Pacifica*, the figure of a woman with her hands raised in peace. Bas-relief murals portrayed figures representing East and West coming together in prolific encounters. It seemed that the Golden Gate was symbolically opening westward to a New World in the Old World.

In the shadow of World War II, the fair's theme was far ahead of its time and was quickly replaced by wartime concerns. However, in the second half of the century some of the fair's cultural anticipations seemed to be confirmed here in the growing interest and participation in aspects of Buddhism, particularly Zen, including such practices as meditation. In the early twenty-first century it has also become common here to see in city parks groups going through the deliberate exercises of yoga and tai chi.

Bay Area educational systems sponsor Asian studies, including Japanese-American schools and preschools as well as Chinese-immersion curricula. There are Asian motifs in theaters, museums, restaurants, entertainment centers, and residential architecture, as well as in ashrams, facilities for Asian spiritual activities. Young people of various ancestries often meet to enjoy Westernized versions of karaoke, the Japanese songfest.

On the far side of the cultural interchange, Asian youths are engrossed with American popular music, from rock to African-American dance to hip-hop, and American youth attire, including oversized battered blue jeans and imprinted T-shirts. Many older Asians attend concerts of Western symphonic and operatic music, with ardently applauding audiences for Asian tours of such celebrities as violinist Isaac Stern and tenor Luciano Pavarotti (now both deceased).

Are we seeing in these signs on both sides of the Pacific the beginnings of a fulfillment of the vision of the Treasure Island fair? If so, it is notable that the meeting of cultures parallels growing concern about the prospects of increasing trade with the burgeoning economies of China and India, as well as the emergent regions of Southeast Asia.

As I stood on that cliff top at the Golden Gate with the light welling up from the ocean, I began to wish that my time warp could be reversed so that I would be seeing in my mind's eye not the past two hundred years but the next. Would I be watching a clash of civilizations as some historians predict, or a harmonious blending of cultures in the spirit of that prophetic exposition on Treasure Island? Or some degree of both?

I imagined that the continued spread of worldwide electronic communication would facilitate cultural merging, but the issue of trade would doubtless be more problematic. To judge from the current multiplication of goods we find labeled "Made in China" or "Made in South Korea" or "Made in Vietnam," the US manufacturing base is losing out to low-wage competition overseas. Americans are buying from abroad more than we are selling, an unsustainable situation. There are other ominous clouds on the horizon: nuclear proliferation, unlimited population growth, disastrous climate change. Will we—the global *we*—curtail our personal consumption habits enough to avoid climate catastrophe?

My reverse time warp was growing dim. I could only hope that the innovative mind-set—like that born in the Gold Rush—might create ways to cope with these dilemmas as unimaginable now as the electronic revolution was a century ago. Perhaps, I speculated, our best hope might lie not only in technology but also in unforeseeable developments and discoveries in the arts and humanities. Possibly poets would be as vital to our future as technologists.

Standing there at the edge of the continent, watching the cumulus clouds throwing moving patterns of light and shade on this passage to the Pacific, I thought again of this place as the climax of the long westward migrations, and there came to mind some lines from Walt Whitman:

Facing west from California's shores
Inquiring, tireless, seeking what is
yet unfound,
I, a child, very old, over waves,
towards the house of maternity,
the land of migrations, look afar,
Look off the shores of my Western
sea, the circle almost circled . . .
Long having wandered since, round
the earth having wandered,
Now I face home again, very pleased
and joyous,
(But where is what I started for so
long ago? And why is it yet
unfound?)

Jane Hirshfield | THREE POEMS

THE SUPPLE DEER

The quiet opening
between fence strands
perhaps eighteen inches.

Antlers to hind hooves,
four feet off the ground,
the deer poured through.

No tuft of the coarse white belly hair left behind.

I don't know how a stag turns
into a stream, an arc of water.
I have never felt such accurate envy.

Not of the deer:

To be that porous, to have such largeness pass through me.

BUILDING AND EARTHQUAKE

How easy it is for a dream to construct
both building and earthquake.
Also the nine flights of wooden stairs in the dark,
and the trembling horse, its hard breathing
loud in the sudden after-silence and starlight.
This time the dream allows the building to stand.
Something it takes the dreamer a long time to notice,
who thought that the fear was the meaning
when being able to feel the fear was the meaning.

THE DARK HOUR

The dark hour came
in the night and purred by my ear.
Outside, in rain,
the plush of the mosses stood higher.
Hour without end, without measure.
It opens the window and calls its own name in.

MARIA EVANGELISTE

Her name was Maria, which was what the priest at St. Rose Church called all the Indian girls, even this girl Maria Evangeliste, who ironed his vestments and each Sunday played the violin so beautifully as the communicants marched to the altar to receive the sacraments that Jesus was said to smile down from the rafters at the dispensation of his body and blood. That was why on a Friday when she hadn't returned by nightfall, and still no sign of her at mass on Sunday, the priest worried as much as her family, and after mass notified the sheriff. The flatbed wagon that she had been driving was found by an apple farmer outside his stable, as if the pale gray old gelding was waiting to be unhitched and led to a stall inside. The two cherrywood chairs she'd purchased on the priest's behalf stood upright, still on the wagon bed, wedged between bales of straw. The priest had contracted the chairs for his rectory from a carpenter in Bodega, and Maria, needing any small amount of compensation, offered to drive the old gelding nearly a ten-mile trip west and then back. Still, she should have returned before nightfall for she left at dawn, the priest's money for the carpenter secure in her coat pocket.

A number of things could've happened to her. The horse might've spooked, jerking the wagon so that if she wasn't paying close attention she would've been tossed to the ground—she might be lying on the roadside someplace, knocked unconscious, a broken back, God forbid a broken neck. She could've been raped, left in the brush somewhere even. At the time, in 1903, American Indians had not yet been granted US citizenship and therefore had no recourse in a US court. A lone Coast Miwok girl in Sonoma County was easy prey for marauding American men and boys who roamed the back roads, as the old Indians used to say, like packs of dogs.

But wouldn't they have hesitated, considering the possibility that Maria Evangeliste was a US citizen of Mexican descent, a guise many Indians used? Surely, approaching the wagon they would have seen the wooden cross hanging from her neck. If that didn't stop them, she had the ultimate defense, an embroidered crimson sash the priest wore at mass and had given her that morning as proof of protection from the church, which she'd kept folded in her other pocket, ready in the event someone should assault her, even if only to search her pockets to steal the priest's money for the carpenter. But none of these things happened.

As she rounded a hilly curve on the dirt road, which is now paved and called Occidental Road, she spotted two women. They were Indian women in long nineteenth-century dresses, scarves covering their heads and tied under the chin, and Maria Evangeliste recognized them immediately. They were twin sisters, childless elderly southern Pomo women from the outskirts of Sebastopol just a couple miles up the road. They did not resemble one another, one twin short and stout, the other taller, much darker, the color of oak bark. But, at that moment, hardly would Maria Evangeliste have remarked at their appearance, or the fact that, side by side, they stood in the middle of the road halting her passage, or even that she was in the vicinity of the rumored secret cave old people talked about in revered whispers. She understood what was happening without thinking, knew all at once. So when the taller of the two women commanded her off the wagon with only a nod of the chin, she knew she had no choice but to get down and follow them. And, it is told, that was how it started, how the twin sisters took Maria Evangeliste to train her as a Human Bear.

Why Maria Evangeliste was traveling on Occidental Road is a mystery. The usual route from Santa Rosa to the coastal town of Bodega was, and still is, the road west across the lagoon to the town of Sebastopol and then more or less straight to the coast. Returning from Bodega, she would have had to venture north along one of two or three narrow roads, wide paths really, to reach what is now Occidental Road—which would have been a longer, circuitous way to go, not to mention more dangerous given that she would be more isolated in the event she was assaulted. There was also greater risk of the old horse stumbling, some kind of accident with the wagon, on an unreliable road. Did she not want to pass through the town of Sebastopol because it was Friday, late in the day, and gangs of men off work from the sawmill and nearby orchards would already be gathered around the pubs, men who were drinking and might catch sight of her alone? There was an encampment of Indians where Occidental Road emptied onto the Santa Rosa plain— had she a friend she wanted to visit? Winter rain flooded, and still floods, the lagoon—was she traveling at a time when the water was high, when she needed to cross the northern bridge over the lagoon rather than the bridge in Sebastopol?

Following an ancient story of how the Human Bear cult started, where a lone boy picking blackberries was kidnapped by grizzly bears and afforded their secrets and indomitable physical prowess, it is said that most initiates to the cult were likewise kidnapped. Human Bears might watch a young person carefully for some time, months or even years, regarding the young person's suitability for induction. Stories are told of Human Bears traveling far distances to study a potential initiate, often in the guise of wanting only to see an old friend or to trade. They might even warn chosen individuals of their impending abduction, reminding them that they had no choice henceforth but to acquiesce and keep silent. Had Maria Evangeliste made arrangements beforehand, driven the priest's wagon north to fulfill her obligation?

Four days later, on a Tuesday morning, she returned. She lived with her family and a changing assembly of relatives forever in search of work in a clapboard house west of town. The small house, said to be owned by a dairy rancher for whom her father worked, sat above Santa Rosa creek. Behind the house, lining the creek, was a stand of willow trees. My grandmother's sister's daughter, who first told me the story, said Maria Evangeliste appeared from behind the trees. Later, another older relative pointed to a bald hillside while we were driving on Occidental Road and mentioned the story, claiming that Maria Evangeliste was first discovered standing in front of her house, not behind in the willows, and that in the faint morning light she was still as stone. Both versions posit that she was unharmed, returned as she had left, groomed, unsullied.

She could not tell where she had been. Did she lie, perhaps say that she lost control of the wagon after the horse spooked? Did she say as much in order to lead others to believe she'd run off with a young man? What was the sheriff told? The priest? However the case was resolved in the minds of the sheriff and the priest—whether from whatever story the girl might've relayed or from whatever either of them surmised themselves about what happened—the Indians were not so easily satisfied. For the Indians, enough of them to pass on a story anyway, the girl's answers were suspect and pointed only to one possible outcome: the two old twins in Sebastopol had found a successor.

I visited the bald hillside a couple of weeks ago, parked my car on Occidental Road, then crawled under a barbed wire fence and hiked through brush and looming redwood trees, dark shade. Where would the secret cave be—this side of the hill, below the steep face of naked rock, or around the backside? Would such a cave exist still? Might not loggers or farmers have destroyed it long ago? Unable to see past a thicket of blackberry bramble, I could no longer look back and see the road. The outcropping of rock, exposed above the curtain of treetops, was a face with crater formations and crevices, as if the hill, like an enormous and uninhibited animal, was observing my approach. I became agitated. The story filled me. Oh, these are modern times, I told myself. What's a story these days? If anything, I should be worrying about trespassing on private property. Nonetheless, I stopped. Looking over the blackberry bramble to the trees, I attempted to regain my bearings, again trying to gauge my distance from the road.

In 1903, when the twin sisters abducted Maria Evangeliste, loggers had leveled the trees a second time—or were about to. The magnificent original redwoods, reaching down from the Oregon border to present-day Monterey County, were for the most part cleared between 1830 and 1870. The trees before me, a third growth of redwoods, were about a hundred years old, and a hundred feet tall. In 1903, the gigantic original trees that once sheltered the grizzly bears were gone, and, whether or not the second stand of trees still stood, the grizzly was extinct in the region, killed decades before by Mexican vaqueros and American settlers. The Human Bear cult, like the grizzly bear, was dependent on the trees and on an open landscape, unencumbered by fences and ranchers protective of livestock. Stories abound—even among local non-Indians—of ranchers felling a bear only to find when they went to retrieve the carcass an empty hide. The twin sisters, how did they instruct their last recruit? Did they show Maria Evangeliste a route that was still safe to travel under a moonless nighttime sky? Did they have only memories to offer, power songs unsung outside the old cave?

Secret societies, such as the Human Bear cult, both perpetuated and reflected Pomo and Coast Miwok worldview, where every human, just as every aspect of the landscape, possessed special—and secret—powers. Cult members with their special power and connection with the living world played an integral role in the well-being of the village. Human Bears, assuming the grizzly's strength and extraordinary sense of smell, could locate and retrieve food from far distances. They possessed "protection," often songs, that caused illness, sometimes death, to anyone who might attempt to harm them—or some feature of the landscape they might use, such as a cave. You would thus think twice about harming anyone. Same with a bird, a tree, any tiny stone. Respect becomes the only guarantee of survival. This respect is predicated on remembering that, even with unique power, you are not alone, absolute. As renowned late Pomo Indian doctor Mabel McKay told me, "Be careful when someone [or something] catches your attention. You don't know what spirit it is. Be thoughtful." The Kashaya Pomo elders refer to Europeans as *pala-cha*, miracles: instead of being punished for killing people and animals, chopping down trees, damming and dredging the waterways, the Europeans kept coming.

There were numerous secret cults. Many were associated with animals, bobcat, grizzly bear, even birds and snakes. Others were associated with a particular place, a meadow, a canyon, an underwater cave where the spirit of the place empowered its respective cult members. Cults were often gender based: women's Bear cults were considered among the most powerful. In all cases, cult initiates endured long periods of training, not only learning about the essentials of their animal powers for instance, but simultaneously of the larger environment as well.

Sonoma County, about an hour north of San Francisco, was at the time of European contact one of the most geographically complex and biologically diverse places on earth. Below arid hills, covered with only bunchgrass and the occasional copse of oak and bay laurel, were rich wetlands, inland bays, lakes, a meandering lagoon, a substantial river, and numerous creeks where hundreds of species of waterfowl flew up so thick as to obliterate the sun for hours at a time. Immense herds of elk, pronghorn, and black-tailed deer grazed along these waterways on any number of clovers and sedges. West, lining the coastal hills, were redwoods so thick that several yards into a forest all was dark as night. The shifting shoreline, steep cliffs dropping to the water then to broad sandy beaches, was rich too, rife with edible sea kelps, dozens of species of clams, mussels, abalone, and fish, salmon the most prized. Despite these distinct environments—arid hills, lush plains and wetlands, redwood forest—the landscape was usually inconsistent, tricky even. Amidst the arid hills below Sonoma Mountain were numerous lakes and spring-fed marshes. Meadows, prairie-like, appeared unexpectedly in the otherwise dense and dark redwood forests. A narrow creek might empty into a wide and deep perch-filled pond just on the other side of a small, barren-looking knoll. Traveling through an expanse of marshy plain you might discover, stepping from waist-high sedges, a carpet of rock a mile wide and several miles long, habitat for snakes and lizards that would otherwise be found in the drier foothills. Nothing appeared quite what it seemed. The landscape, complex in design and texture, demanded reflection, study. The culture that grew out of a ten-thousand-year relationship with the place became like it, not just in thought but in deed. Pomo and Coast Miwok art—the most complicated and intricate basketry found among indigenous people anywhere—tells the story.

Human Bears learned the details of the landscape: where a fish-ripe lake hid behind a bend, where a thicket of blackberries loaded with fruit sat tucked below a hillside. At the same time, regardless of their unique ability to travel great distances and seek out food sources for the village, they could not disrespect the hidden lake or thicket of berries, needing always to know the requirements for taking the fish or fruit. The lake had a special—and potentially dangerous—spirit, just as the Human Bear, so too the blackberry thicket. Developing a heightened sense of the Human Bear's unique power necessitated a heightened sense of the land. Ultimately, the Human Bear cult didn't only play an integral role in the well-being of the village, but more precisely in the well-being of the village with the larger world.

By 1903 most of the landscape was transformed. Gone were the vast wetlands. The water table throughout the region had dropped an average of two hundred feet: creeks went dry in summer. The big trees were gone. Many of the great animals were extinct in the region, not just the grizzly bears, but the herds of elk and pronghorn, and the mighty condors gliding the thermals with their fourteen-foot wingspans. Regarding these remarkable ancestral birds, *Tsupu*, my great-great-great-grandmother, sitting atop a wagon toward the end of the nineteenth century, gazed up at the empty sky and asked, "How are the people going to dance without feathers?" If there was a route safe for Maria Evangeliste to travel as a Human Bear in 1903, would there still exist a familiar bountiful blackberry thicket? An ocean cove where she might collect a hundred pounds of clams?

Just as the landscape was transformed, increasingly so too the eons-old way of thinking about it. Catholic missionaries put in the minds of Coast Miwok and Pomo villagers the notion of an eternal and spiritual life that was elsewhere, that could not be derived and experienced from the land. The God of an elsewhere kingdom overruled, in fact, deemed as evil, anything on the earth that might be considered equally powerful, worthy of reverence and awe. While Christianity was forced upon the Natives, usually under conditions of duress and enslavement, the new religion might have made sense. After European contact, Coast Miwok and Pomo no doubt looked upon the transformed landscape and found that they recognized the place less and less, that, in essence, they were no longer home. Indeed miraculous, the new people could kill animals, level a hill, without retribution. Couldn't their one almighty God from another world stop a Human Bear? Yes—seen once as necessary to life and land, a protector of the village, the Human Bear—anyone who would participate in such things—was now more and more an enemy of our well-being, dangerous at best, evil.

Did Maria Evangeliste know what stories people told about her? If, secretly, she left a cache of ripe fruit or clams outside her home as Human

Bears once did in the villages, might she not implicate herself, reveal her secret life in a world hostile to that life? Wouldn't relatives deem the food devil's work and toss it out? She was the last Human Bear, they say. When did she stop visiting the cave? When was it over?

The morning she returned she said that she had lost control of the wagon. Or she said she visited a friend and hadn't tied the old gelding well enough. Or she said she met a man. In any event, she went that afternoon with the priest and retrieved the wagon with its still upright rectory chairs from the apple farmer. And that was how, before sunset, she came back to town, driving the wagon as if nothing was unusual, four days had not passed at all. She continued to play violin in the church. She was still entrusted with work for the priest. Sometime later she married a Mexican immigrant. They had eleven children, all of whom lived to adulthood. A great-granddaughter sat next to me in catechism class. The last time I saw her, Maria Evangeliste that is, was sometime in the early 1970s, about ten years before she died at the age of ninety. I was at a funeral in St. Rose Church. She was in the crowd of mourners, a small Indian woman in a dark dress. She wore a veil, respectfully.

I left town sometime then and did not return for thirty years, until only recently. I visited, seeing family. And for the past eighteen years, I have served as chairman of my tribe, which brought me back to Sonoma County at least once a month. But I wasn't really back—I wasn't home—which I hadn't realized, much less understood for some time. I wrote about Sonoma County—stories, essays, plays—from memory. In fact, I'd hardly written about anyplace else. But what was I remembering? What did I understand?

Sonoma County had changed dramatically. From the center of once small-town Santa Rosa, strip malls and housing developments spread over the vast plain, covering irrigated clover and vetch pastures, fruit orchards and strawberry fields. Gone, the black-and-white spotted Holstein cows. Gone, rows of prune and pear trees; the apple orchards north and east of Sebastopol, almost each and every one routed by grapes, pinot noir, cabernet. The arid foothills are now also covered in grapes: gone, the copses of oak and bay laurel there. Visiting, I noticed these changes; coming home for good, I saw how thorough they were, how far-reaching. Where was my home?

I bought a house on Sonoma Mountain. Bay laurel trees, live oaks, and white oaks surround the house, and, past the trees, there is an expansive view west over vineyard-covered hills and the urban sprawl below, to the

Pacific Ocean, which is where at night the web of streetlights stops—and where on a very clear night the full moon lights the sea. That light—that path of moon on the water—was how the dead found their way to the next world, or so our ancestors said. And those same ancestors gathered pepper nuts from the six-hundred-year-old bay tree outside my gate. But I was like that—suspended between the old bay tree and the far horizon—as I negotiated what it meant to be home. I hadn't lived on the mountain before. I grew up below, in Santa Rosa.

Then the place remembered me. Stories beckoned. The dead rose, collected with the living, so that more and more the landscape became a meeting hall of raucous voices. I knew the faces. Not merely my tribal members, as if I was convening a tribal meeting, but the land itself—mountain and plain, oak trees and city lights, birds and animals, Indians and non-Indians, Mexicans, Italians, Blacks, Filipinos, Jews—whomever and whatever I'd known, whomever and whatever I knew, was before me, beckoning. Yes, the dead and the living—how could anything die this way? History, it's no less tangible, palpable than that grandmother under whose care you found yourself. In a kitchen you have known all your life with its familiar smells and colors, this grandmother sets a plate of warm tortillas on the table with a bowl of chicken soup and says eat.

Driving here and there, to the university, to the Laundromat, the market, here and there with no worry of catching an airplane, seeing this relative or that friend before I left again, I had time, the idleness that accompanies routine, and the old lady with the tortillas and soup was able to catch my attention. Driving over a bridge west of town—west of Santa Rosa—I glance down and see the riverbank and willows: a bonfire lights a moonless night and Filipino men are gathered around the fire there, and my grandmother, a seventeen-year-old Coast Miwok girl, eyes my grandfather for the first time, a *pinoy* dandy in his pin-striped suit, the big gold watch chain dangling from his breast pocket reflecting firelight, and the bloodletting fighting cocks clashing midair, their tiny silhouettes jumping in his watch glass like a pair of enchanted dancers performing a wild tango my grandmother already wants to learn. From behind the townhouses on Coffey Lane, Holstein cows emerge one by one, full udders swaying, and collect in front of the 7-11, where Mrs. Andreoli, forty and soon to be a widow, opens the wooden gate to her milk barn. And Old Undle, old Pomo medicine man—"don't say his real name"—he's on a bench uptown in Courthouse Square, suspenders and Stetson hat, or he's in his garden behind the fairgrounds where two hours ago he built a fire below the tall corn stalks and thick gourd vines, witnesses as he holds now an ember in the palm of his hand and sees and hears in the orange-red ash "all manner of things": people and animals, songs, old earth rules. Isn't this how some folks saw Maria Evangeliste when she returned on foot after four days to her parents' house? And years later, when they found themselves next to her, scooping rice in the market or picking prunes in the heat dusty orchards, didn't they still think and remember?

Here I am not a stranger. Looking back, I see how I'd been a stranger, a newcomer at best, wherever else I had lived. I drove back and forth to the university, to the market, in Los Angeles. I did errands in Manhattan. But it wasn't the same. No stories. No old earth rules. Or, put it this way, I had to learn the stories, listen to the rules as a newcomer, and, like that, as mindful as I could be, make a home. Still, Fifth Avenue midday remained less busy for me than a remote redwood grove in Sonoma County. I could be alone in Yellowstone. Or the Grand Canyon. These latter places in particular, beautiful yes. And solitude. But then what is solitude, however blissful? Can it be experienced except by disengagement from the land's stories, spirits? Wilderness. The old people said the land became wild after we became separated from it, when there was no longer enough of us to hear its demands and tend to it accordingly. Could Thoreau and Muir experience the landscape as pristine and know solitude in it as such, if they knew its stories? If that old woman was there, tortillas and chicken soup in hand, would the land be silent?

Two weeks ago last Saturday at a tribal General Council meeting, I saw Maria Evangeliste's great-granddaughter, the same girl I knew in catechism class. Approaching sixty, a heavyset woman now with a shock of dyed black hair, she sat amidst the sea of faces listening to questions and answers regarding the status of our casino. She looked disgruntled, arms crossed over her chest, face puckered in a scowl, and walked out before the meeting was over, leaving me wondering if she was mad at me or someone else on the Council or life in general. Her life, from what I'd heard, hadn't been easy. Five children. Two were in prison. One was dead. Ten grandchildren, five of whom she was raising. Where was the soft-faced, flat-limbed teenager who listened with me as Sister Agnes Claire attempted to explain the Holy Ghost? Some tribal members say I've been away too long, that I've gotten "too white." Did she feel that way about me, that I didn't know my people well enough any longer? Her husband, the father of her five children, was a Mexican immigrant. Did she know that her great-grandfather was a Mexican immigrant also? Had she heard the stories about Maria Evangeliste? Did she care? Perhaps I write for no other reason than to leave a record for her or anyone besides me who might care, a set of tracks, however faint, down the mountain into the plain and back, connecting to those infinite other pathways that take us and keep us in the land and its life here. But this is what I'm thinking now, as I consider what it means to be a writer here. It wasn't what I was thinking during the meeting, seeing Maria Evangeliste's great-granddaughter.

I went to the cave. Driving on Occidental Road, I was quite certain of the spot my cousin had pointed to years before—the bald hillside—if for no other reason than that a hippie commune was there at the time, a settlement of teepees past the redwoods, which I mentioned, prompting from my cousin her story of Maria Evangeliste.

The road curved under a canopy of oak trees and tall pines; four o'clock in the afternoon, autumn, the land was already in shadow, the road lead gray like the occasional patch of sky above. Human Bears traveled only at night in the pitch black; they did not set out from their villages in human form for their caves until late at night either. Secrecy was the initiate's first rule. Mabel McKay once told me of a father up in Lake County who, curious about his daughter's whereabouts at night, unwittingly followed her to a Human Bear cave, whereupon her cult sisters gruesomely murdered him right before her eyes. "Ain't supposed to be seeing them things," Mabel said. "Respect." With this story in mind and a darkening landscape, it's no wonder that past the barbed wire fence and into the trees, I was agitated, so much so that when I looked back and couldn't see the road, I stopped. Respect? Was I disrespecting? These are modern times, I kept telling myself. What's a story these days? Wasn't I curious just to see the cave as a landmark, an outpost of memory? Yes, nothing more. I would leave something, a dollar bill, my handkerchief, out of respect. A lone jay shrieked from somewhere on the other side of the blackberry bramble. I looked up, above the line of trees, to the outcropping of rock, enormous and still watchful, then I left.

It was enough, I told myself. Enough. But I kept thinking of Maria Evangeliste. In the car, driving back to town, my excitement only grew. Past the overreaching branches and thick brush on either side of the road, I saw how a uniform gray light enveloped the land, a color such that everything I could see seemed made from it. I had never seen the light in such a way at that time of day, and, I thought that though Maria Evangeliste, after her first four nights with the twin sisters, emerged and came back to town at dawn, the light and land must have looked this way, new, as she had never seen it before. Then I rounded a curve, and, coming down the hill, I saw the broad plain clear to the mountain. City lights shown like tiny flags in the gathering darkness. I pulled over, stopped the car. No, I thought then. After Maria Evangeliste first came out of the cave, it was like this: stories, places—an entire land—that she knew day or night, light or no light, not as if for the first time, but better.

Author's note: Evangeliste was not the actual name.

My father was hopeful he knew the spot—as in the *exact* spot.

It was right next to a tall, winter-aged ponderosa pine on the Nevada side of Lake Tahoe, with the backdrop of the blue water and the perpetual snow cross on the face of Mt. Tallac over on the opposite shore (rising 9,739 feet out of the Desolation Wilderness with a fine view of Pyramid, a slightly higher, sheer tooth of granite, from the summit of which on a very, very clear morning, you can at least think you can see with your naked eye all the way west to the Golden Gate).

It was beside this pine tree on the eastern side of the lake that he'd come with ritual devotion every summer—and it was crucial to him to have the location as exact as possible. He was still a minister then, and in matters of religion, especially a private religion, you don't mess around.

Once in position, standing proudly—like a member of John Fremont's expedition party, with Kit Carson as their guide (the first white men to see the lake in 1844, long before the Golden Gate Bridge had been dreamed of)—he'd begin to sing—or rather to hum extremely loudly. He had a rich strong baritone voice . . . but what came out of his mouth wasn't exactly a hymn or a spiritual—not even one of his John Henry/hobo folksongs. No, from some unknown zone within him would come a passionate childlike rendition of the theme song to *Bonanza*.

Yep.

The place I speak of is the presumed spot where Lorne Greene in the character of Ben Cartwright would smile back beneficently from the saddle of his palomino at the beginning of each show, while the infectious theme music played, the map of the Ponderosa ranch would catch fire, and Ben's costarring sons would appear on their respective trademark television horses.

I wasn't sure back in those days and I'm less sure now whether my father's ceremonial fascination was heroic, pathetic, or simply comical— but I remember as a kid I sang along lustily with him. I loved that guitar twang break. *Dang-dang-dum, dang-dang-dum . . . donh ta donh ta donh . . .*

Still, I knew the old man was always plagued by the possibility that he wasn't quite right in his assignment of the sacred spot. I think the towering rough bark pine never looked perfect enough to him. The angle to the mountain across the lake and the other site referents always seemed just slightly askew—mobile, fluid, illusory. Doubt gnawed at him, even as he hummed louder.

To this day something of my father's nagging uncertainty sums up my sense of the American West.

We seek out the West, we actually stand right in it, hitting our mark as an actor would, only to find that when we do—much to our surprise—we feel like actors, only pretending. We aren't really all the way there. What we took to be our goal was/is an ideal, an illusion, show business, some dream we bought into. Or the biggest, strangest dream and theme park of all—history—an imagined, managed past we can never fully inhabit, reclaim, or even really know.

Conceived in Hawaii, America's most western point, born and raised in California, with a childhood spent traveling the eleven Western states, idealizing the West came as easily to me as putting on cowboy pyjamas (and like many boys my age I actually went to school for two whole years dressed in full cowboy regalia, including chaps).

Colorful costumes were in fact all the rage then in Berkeley, where we lived. Young people from across America and around the world were flocking into town wearing crazy clothes. It looked like a book of fairy tales had come to life (a phenomenon heightened by the fact that a lot of them were high out of their minds). They came to the Promised Land from Ohio and Arkansas to transplant and reinvent themselves—all of them looking for that one backdrop, that special scene/spot/moment/ happening when they'd know they'd arrived. An awful lot of them ended up muttering to themselves with vacant eyes and panhandling on Telegraph Avenue or Haight Street—sitting on the dock of the bay. My old stomping ground? City of the Lost Tribes.

"The west is the best," Jim Morrison said. "Just get here and we'll do the rest."

Maybe. Ever since the 1840s, when in what were then the "Western" towns of Kansas, where a cast-iron skillet cost an arm and a leg and thousands of white people waited on the edge of the prairie for the spring thaw and the grass to grow tall enough to feed their oxen and horses, the waves of migration have washed over this part of America. But what too often the new arrivals have found is not the glint of gold, the wild surmise of booming surf, or a part in the movies, but what Jack Kerouac called that "end of land sadness," or what Jack London termed "work hard enough to break any heart."

Worried about the economy and consumer confidence today? Just check out the price of an ordinary shovel in 1849 San Francisco or Sacramento. Concerned about your escalating utility bills? Think of burning scavenged corncobs around an oilskin tent like the Okies on the banks of Merle Haggard's "mighty Kern River." All you have to do is walk down Hollywood Boulevard to see the spittle on the Stars right now.

If you've ever picked raspberries for money or moved irrigation pipes in Steinbeck's Salinas lettuce fields, you have a different perspective yet again on the "bounty" of the West. And what a thing it is to be celebrating your hourly wage as a white seventeen-year-old with an Ivy League future ahead of you, when right beside you on precisely ten cents less per hour is a Mexican man of forty-five with four children to feed and a plywood hut to do it in—out behind the tractor sheds where the evening fogs loom thick and cold.

Therein lies the riddle of the West. The continuous discrepancy between the noble, majestic images you inherit—the grandeur of the geology and natural history, the commercial vitality—contrasted with the human realities. Frailties. Tragedies.

There's the no-small-issue of millions of bison carcasses that were left rotting in the sun, the diminution and displacement, if not outright slaughter, of some of the world's finest ecologists, and the economic enslavement of enough Chinese for not only every railway tie in the West, but for every damn iron spike to carry a name that very few white people can read.

The illegal immigration crisis today? Where I grew up, half the names of everything were Spanish (and Thomas Jefferson no less argued that all Americans should learn Spanish). We tend to conveniently forget that Mexican laborers were originally "recruited" to harvest America's food in that same genteel way that "kanakas" from the Pacific islands were warmly encouraged at the end of a bullwhip to cut the cane in Queensland, Australia, in 100-degree heat and 100 percent humidity. Hell, someone has to do that ass-sweating work.

And for all those who would like to think that the West has offered a reprieve from slavery and institutionalized racism, a casual glance at the banking practices and civic ordinances of the 1950s in the so-called liberal Bay Area will show rather definitively why there are some African Americans who are a little pissed off and fairly well-armed in East Oakland this very minute.

No, I think the only way to live in the American West is to idealize it. You have to make it up or you'll never really find it—or what you do find you may very well not like.

In one of his best songs, Tom Waits turns the old shaving cream Burma-

Shave, famous for its advertising billboards, into a mythic place two fugi-
tive strangers are trying to reach before the sun comes up, only to die in a
car crash just before they arrive. *They say that dreams are growing wild,
just this side of Burma-Shave.* Only the American West could give rise to
such a mirage. Here mythologies and legends grow wild. It's always been
a haunted region. Spirits. Ghosts. Dreams. Schemes.

There's forever that tantalizing hint of promise and potential. If the
dark republic can roll out just a bit farther, there's something waiting
for you over the next ridge. A second chance. A fresh start. That, to me,
is what the West truly signifies: the hope of youth, or at least imagined
youth regained—that sense that it's not over yet. No other country in the
world has given humans such a compelling embodiment of this idea—no
matter how fragile and even bitterly disappointing it may ultimately be.

The West, and Going West turn out to be as portable and adaptable
concepts as they are elusive. I saw this very clearly when I ran out of
personal West in my twenties and so headed farther west still—to Australia. That was how I thought of it then, and I think I was exactly right. I
didn't leave America. I didn't settle in Australia. Not really. I headed West.
That's how I framed it in my mind. Many Australians intuitively understand this notion—whether they head out to Western Australia literally,
or to the United Kingdom, or wherever.

I've seen the same affinity all over the globe. Whether people have ever
been to the American West or not, they have an idea of what it means and
that it means something important and aspirational. Yes, of course it conjures up certain images (as it did for my father), but what people really connect with is the idea of freedom and newness—the ability to make one's
own rules or at least to try. To try to take back some control over one's
destiny.

Now I'm on the move again. Further. Farther. But always West.

Maybe I'll go north—disappear into the dense mist forests of Papua
New Guinea or watch the monsoon rain fill my teacup in Vietnam.
Maybe I'll make a beachhead on the fishnet golden sand of southern Thai-
land. I'll still be heading West.

America has given the world some of its most inspiring and dangerous
dreams. The West is surely one of the most seductive and elastic fantasies
of all. There may be eleven Western states, but the real West is somewhere
you never actually get to, it's always where you're going.

Years ago, I was on a Greyhound bus, riding from the Port Authority in
Times Square to downtown wino LA, snorting bourbon, smoking joints. I
got off to stretch my legs in the near-ghost town of Hydro, Oklahoma, at
straight-up noon, not a shadow on the ground, and I chanced to witness

a bloodred dust devil whirling outside the Dairy Queen that would set in motion a complex personal mythology and plant the seed for my eventual career as a novelist.

I ended up swapping cigarettes and stories with a young teenage boy who reminded me of myself—or what I might've been like if I'd grown up in that wishbone-on-the-window-ledge, boarded-up, dime store hamlet.

He took a shine to me—I was somewhat more interesting than his mangy dog chewing its fleas or the fat man on the tractor with the face as red as the dirt. The kid followed me back to the bus and his words ring down the Route 66 road and years of my memory still. *"Hey mister* (the first time anyone had ever called me that) . . . *where ya headed?"*

"West," I said. But in that desolate water tank town with a worn-out cotton field breeze gusting . . . and the diesel motor of the Hound Dog rumbling . . . it sounded like *"Yes."*

I'm still saying that, all these years later.

We idealize the American West because we can't help it. The West we're really seeking is a place inside ourselves where there are things still to be discovered. We always end up heading west whenever we need to find more life to keep us living.

I want to say a few words on behalf of all of us poor saps who don't know who we are, where we are, where we came from, or where we properly belong. Or at least think we don't. My father, who had a good deal to say on the subject of being Western, liked to distinguish between those who had a clear sense of their geophysical "place" on the planet and those, like my grandfather, who were "as footloose as a tumbleweed in a windstorm." Pop admired the stickers and was uneasy with the boomers. Himself born on wheels (as he liked to put it), he spent his youth "envying people who had lived all their lives in the houses they were born in, and had attics full of proof that they *had* lived." His own narrative, by contrast, was defined by motion and by a father who was forever in search of that elusive mountain where the bluebird sings to the lemonade springs.

Curious how history tends to repeat itself. Looking back at my own youth, by the time I was thirteen and my father, at age forty-one, finally applied the brakes to the family's perambulations, we had lived in eight different houses in five different states, and I had never gone to the same school two years in a row until I was in the eighth grade, which I missed, actually, because I had my sorry ass dragged around the world for seven months while Pop was being engaged as a kind of literary ambassador by the Rockefeller Foundation.

World travel is of course its own form of education. I learned to forage for myself in an interchangeable sequence of seedy hotel dining halls, where a weary and equally interchangeable old gentleman in a shiny black tux (sans cummerbund) slaughtered a medley of Strauss waltzes on his violin, and I ingested yet another breaded cutlet, cold boiled potato, with a wadding of Brussels sprouts. While my parents were being wined and dined by the literati of Europe, Africa, and Asia major/minor, I read Modern Library classics in cold, drafty rooms under none-too-clean feather comforters and, during the day, poked around devastated neighborhoods in every bombed-out city from London to Nagasaki. During this sojourn, my father, unlike his father, was not searching for a pot of gold at the end of the rainbow, but the perpetual motion required by his job had something of the same migratory feeling that characterized much of the life that preceded it.

In 1950, the Stegner family finally settled down in the house in Los Altos Hills, California that my parents, then in their early forties, built and would inhabit for the rest of their lives. I wish I could report that this habitat would at last feel like home. I wish I could properly reminisce on the musky smell of damp oat grass in the fields surrounding the house and the pungent odor of bay and eucalyptus along the driveway that wound a mile up from the country road that led to town, the pale luminosity of San Francisco some fifty miles to the north against the night sky, the abrasive sawing of crickets and the trill of tree frogs filling the background as me and Huey Frame push my old man's Frazer out of the garage and down the long drive to where we hot-wire the sonofabitch with a bobby pin, pop the clutch, and sneak away to joyride around Woodside and Portola Valley, drinking sloe gin and 7-Up and tossing the cans at the stop signs.

I'd like to just kick back and put my feet up and recollect those hot summer afternoons stringing barbed wire along the line between us and the Sterlings' property, and how me and Johnny Sterling would sneak off down into the creek bottom under the live oaks where it would be cool and quiet and we'd find a place to stretch out for a while where the horses hadn't gotten and left us a pile of road apples. Or those winter storms in January, February, March, when the wind whipping in off the Pacific would drive a cold rain nearly horizontal over the Coast Range mountains and great tendrils of dark cloud would snag in the ridge tops, and my old man would send me out to the woodpile for another armload of wet logs for the fire.

I wish I could do justice to that kind of wistful nostalgia, but I put a lot of that kind of stuff into my first two novels, and while there is no question that place was as important in those two books as character and story, it was about moral tumbleweeds that I was writing, not roots and rhizomes, and none of my working habitats had cellars or attics.

I mean, how do you capture the heart and soul of a place, not to mention *your own place* in that place, when it transforms itself every couple of years and becomes somewhere else? That kind of revolution defines coastal California from about the middle of the twentieth century on and does not qualify as revelation. The San Francisco mid-peninsula of my late childhood and teenaged years is utterly unrecognizable today; it has, in fact, been serially unrecognizable for over fifty years. When my family moved to Palo Alto in 1945 they had 20,000 neighbors; there are nearly 70,000 today. And another 30,000 in Menlo Park to the north and 138,000 in Sunnyvale to the south. And everything from the Stanford campus south to San Jose and all the way to Gilroy has been filled in and paved over by the malevolent sprawl of Silicon Valley, where industrial parks, malls, shopping centers, crisscrossing freeways with metered on-ramps and empty carpool lanes, cookie-cutter McRanchos comically character-ized as Manor Estates and Executive Villas have replaced the once mag-nificent open fields and rich patchwork of cherry and apricot orchards.

Stanford University, where I spent nearly seven years as an undergradu-ate and graduate student, has been similarly (and serially) mutated. If it were not for Hoover Tower, also known as Herbert's last erection, I could not find my way from Memorial Auditorium to the library (and just which library were you looking for, sir?) or to the English Department, where for four years I shared an office with Denis "Mugger" Moran and the inscru-table N. Scott Momaday, or to the Student Union, which, come to think of it, didn't exist in my day.

I suppose all I'm really demonstrating here is that I've become an old fart. It's true, I am disrupted by change. But the point is not that my home-town went and aw shucks changed on me (whose hasn't?), but that it did it so fast and so often that it never provided any kind of useful conti-nuity to me as a fiction writer. Which is probably why I got out of that racket after three novels and spent the rest of my career writing nonfic-tion, albeit most of it focused on the West and matters pertaining to the Western experience.

Because whether I like it or not, I am a Westerner, and not just by birth but by temperament. Some years back in the introduction to a book of essays entitled *Outposts of Eden*, I recalled the first time this notion really struck me, the first time I realized that I had a strong regional bias, and that it wasn't so much a *place* that defined me as it was space. This epiphany occurred, naturally enough, on wheels, while I was headed for the left coast after three years working in Washington DC and Latin America. I was not finding much in the rearview mirror to like about Ohio, Indiana, Illinois, or Missouri, but eventually, somewhere well past Oklahoma City I stopped the car to stretch the legs and, as I wrote in my journal, "looked off in every direction at . . . nothing. Blessed nothing. The horizon. I felt as if someone had lifted a pack off my back and pulled the cotton out of my nose. Space. Boundless, limitless, endless, infinite, shoreless, trackless, pathless space. I felt I was home."

So that's it. "Give me land, lots of land under starry skies above / Don't fence me in." Space. Oh sure, there are other Western things like the smell of sage, and the sound wind makes whipping through chamiso, and how many variations on the color of dun can you find in this picture. There are jackrabbits and antelope and grizzlies, and the clatter of a solitary cow pissing on a flat rock. There are magpies and meadowlarks. There's air so dry that nose pickers have been known to bleed out before they reached help.

There is no such thing as *the* West, of course, only a vast array of sub-Wests. You've got your prairie, your high plains, three kinds of deserts, slickrock plateaus, canyon lands, alkali basins and alluvial ranges, two vast mountain chains, California's central valley, and thirteen hundred miles of seacoast—all of this as culturally unlike as cowboys and Indians and as topographically unrelated as Seattle and Socorro.

The West is a lot of things, but except for pockets of oasis civilization, it is still a lot of mostly dry, mostly empty, spirit-lifting space. And thanks be to a merciful God (or global warming) world-class eyesores like Phoenix, Denver, Salt Lake, Albuquerque, and Las Vegas are running out of water, and there is reason to hope that their metastasization may soon grind to a halt. California is not only in the tank financially, but its southland is living on borrowed Colorado River water. What happens when it has to make do with its own allocation?

Who knows what is in store for the twenty-first-century West, but one thing for sure is that water (or the lack of it) is going to continue to play its major role in the socioeconomic structure of every subregion except a few parts of Washington, Oregon, Idaho, and Montana. But until someone finally figures out how to finance the diversion of northwestern rivers into the Colorado drainage, we'll probably be okay out here in our land of little rain. Growth and progress may even cease to be synonymous in the twenty-first-century Western mind. The developer may go the way of the trapper and the cowboy. The lights might go out on the Strip, though probably not. Nevertheless, I'm betting that in the not-too-distant future human habitat is going to get seriously reorganized in a lot of subregions of the West. When the taps in Tucson start blowing dust, I'd say, look out, Missoula.

But if things start to get too crowded back in town, you can still climb on your tumbleweed and ride. Which brings me around to my original point, and my epiphanic Oklahoma moment. It is possible, after all, to find out much about yourself even though you have no taproot and no attic to prove you ever lived. That sense of comfort that comes with open country and great distances, that need for elbow room, and the exaltation that comes with a hundred-mile view—these things alone will tell you a great deal, after all, about the stuff you're made of and the fact that you are not from Boston. In Boston there are no magpies, and the meadowlark is never heard.

BIOGRAPHIES

DAN AADLAND was raised primarily in the Dakotas and, since the third grade, in south-central Montana. The son of a Lutheran minister, he escaped town life whenever possible to hunt, fish, straddle a horse, and hire out as a ranch hand. He earned a BA in English and history at Rocky Mountain College, and later, after service in Vietnam as a Marine officer, an MA and a PhD in English and American Studies at the University of Utah. Returning to Montana in 1973, Aadland taught English at several Montana high schools and began ranching on land that had been in his wife Emily's family since the late 1800s. He has written many articles for outdoor and equine magazines, as well as eight books, including *Women and Warriors of the Plains; Sketches from the Ranch: A Montana Memoir; The Best of All Seasons: Fifty Years as a Montana Hunter;* and *In Trace of TR: A Montana Hunter's Journey.* Dan and Emily reside on their ranch south of Absarokee, Montana. Their three sons are David, an economics professor; Jon, a Boeing engineer; and Steve, an operatic tenor.

JONIS AGEE is the author of eleven books, including five collections of short stories, five novels, and a book of poetry. Three of her books, *Bend This Heart, Sweet Eyes,* and *Strange Angels,* were named *New York Times* Notable Book of the Year. Her most recent novel, *The River Wife,* won the John Gardner Fiction Prize. She has also received the Mark Twain Award for contribution to Midwestern literature, the AWP George Garrett Award for contribution to literature, a National Endowment for the Arts Fellowship in fiction. She has a long-standing love of open spaces and spends her free time driving the back roads in her jacked up 4 × 4 in search of the perfect place to plant her dreams and keep her horses. Agee is currently at work on the third book of her Sandhills trilogy, exploring the lives of people who ranch in Nebraska and who live just across the border on the Rosebud reservation in South Dakota.

JIM BARNES grew up in the hill country of eastern Oklahoma, a place called Summerfield, near what was once called the Texas Crossing on the Fourche Maline River. As a young man, Barnes migrated to Oregon, worked in the tall timber for a decade, then returned to Oklahoma to take a BA at Southeastern State University and subsequently a PhD at the University of Arkansas. He is former Distinguished Professor of English at Brigham Young University. His poetry, short stories, translations, and essays have appeared in over four hundred anthologies and magazines. Among his notable books are *On Native Ground* (2nd ed., autobiography, University of Oklahoma Press, 2009), *Visiting Picasso* (poems, University of Illinois Press, 2007), *Paris* (poems, University of Illinois Press, 1997), *The Sawdust War* (poems, University of Illinois Press, 1992), and *The American Book of the Dead* (poems, University of Illinois Press, 1982). His work has been awarded both the Oklahoma Book Award and the American Book Award. He has held two Rockefeller Bellagio fellowships and two Camargo Foundation fellowships. In 1993–1994 he was Senior Fulbright Fellow to Switzerland. In 1978, before his first book was published, he was awarded a National Endowment for the Arts Fellowship for poetry.

KIM BARNES was raised in the logging camps of the Clearwater National Forest of Idaho. She is the author of two memoirs and two novels, most recently *A Country Called Home*, which received the 2009 PEN Center USA Literary Award in fiction and was named a best book of 2008 by the *Washington Post*, the *Kansas City Star*, and the *Oregonian* (Northwest). She is the recipient of the PEN/Jerard Fund Award for an emerging woman writer of nonfiction, and her first memoir, *In the Wilderness*, was nominated for the Pulitzer Prize. Her work has appeared in a number of publications, including the *New York Times*; MORE; O, *the Oprah Magazine*; *Fourth Genre*; *Georgia Review*; *Shenandoah*; and the Pushcart Prize anthology. Her novel, *American Mecca*, an exploration of Americans living in 1960s Saudi Arabia, will be published by Knopf in 2011. Barnes, a former Idaho writer-in-residence, teaches writing at the University of Idaho and lives with her husband, the poet Robert Wrigley, on Moscow Mountain.

RICK BASS is the author of twenty-five books of fiction and nonfiction, including, most recently, a novel, *Nashville Chrome*. A memoir, *Why I Came West*, was a finalist for a National Book Critics Circle Award, and his short stories have been collected in anthologies such as *Best American Short Stories*, *Pushcart Prize*, and *O. Henry Prize Stories*. A collection, *The Lives of Rocks*, was a finalist for the Story Prize, and he has received fellowships from the National Endowment for the Arts and the Guggenheim Foundation. Bass was born in Fort Worth, Texas, grew up in Houston, studied wildlife science and geology at Utah State University, worked as a geologist in Alabama and Mississippi, then moved to the Yaak Valley of northwestern Montana in 1987. He and his family live in the Yaak and in Missoula, Montana. Bass is a member of the Yaak Valley Forest Council (www.yaakvalley.org), where he has long been active in efforts to help protect as wilderness the last roadless lands in the Yaak Valley.

JUDY BLUNT spent more than thirty years on wheat and cattle ranches in northeastern Montana before leaving that life to attend the University of Montana. Her book of poems, *Not Quite Stone*, won the Merriam-Frontier Award and was published in 1991. Her best-selling memoir, *Breaking Clean*, was published by Knopf in 2002. Recognition of Blunt's work includes a PEN/Jerard Fund Award for nonfiction, the Whiting Writers' Award, Mountains and Plains Booksellers Award, Willa Award for Nonfiction Book of the Year, and a National Endowment for the Arts writer's fellowship. Blunt received a Guggenheim Fellowship in 2005. She's an associate professor of English, teaching creative nonfiction at the University of Montana, Missoula.

CHARLES BOWDEN has lived in the Southwest since childhood. A former newspaper reporter, he now writes for magazines and squanders his meager earnings scribbling books. His most recent effort is a trilogy— *Inferno*, *Exodus*, *Trinity*—on the land, people, and violence of the region. He likes red meat, red wine, bird watching, and recording how the lights are going out in the Sunbelt.

C. J. BOX is the author of twelve novels, including the Joe Pickett series. He has won the Edgar Award, the Anthony Award, Prix Calibre 38 (France), the Macavity Award, the Gumshoe Award, and the Barry Award. His short stories have been featured in *America's Best Mystery Stories* of 2006. The 2008 novel *Blood Trail* was nominated for the International IMPAC Dublin (Ireland) Literary Award. The novels have been best sellers and have been translated into twenty-three languages. Box is a Wyoming native and has worked as a ranch hand, surveyor, fishing guide, small town newspaper reporter and editor, and he co-owns an international tourism marketing firm with his wife, Laurie. In 2008, Box was awarded the BIG WYO Award from the state tourism industry. An avid outdoorsman, Box has hunted, fished, hiked, ridden, and skied throughout Wyoming and the Mountain West. He served on the board of directors for the Cheyenne Frontier Days Rodeo. Box and his wife have three daughters. He lives in Wyoming.

RON CARLSON is the author of ten books of fiction, most recently, the novel *The Signal*. His short fiction has appeared in *Esquire*, *Harper's*, the *New Yorker*, *Gentlemen's Quarterly*, and other journals, as well as *The Best American Short Stories*, *The O'Henry Prize Series*, *The Pushcart Prize Anthology*, *The Norton Anthology of Short Fiction*, and other anthologies. A graduate of the University of Utah, Mr. Carlson is director of the Graduate Program in Fiction at the University of California, Irvine. Graywolf Press published his book on the process of writing, *Ron Carlson Writes a Story*. Among his awards are a National Endowment for the Arts Fellowship in fiction, and the Cohen Prize at *Ploughshares*, the McGinnis Award at the *Iowa Review*, and the Aspen Foundation Literary Award.

DENISE CHÁVEZ is a novelist, playwright, teacher, and performance writer based in Las Cruces and Mesilla, New Mexico. She has roots in far West Texas with her mother's family and in Las Cruces, New Mexico, with her father's family. A true child of La Frontera, Chávez is the author of the memoir, *A Taco Testimony: Meditations on Family, Food and Culture*, as well as *Loving Pedro Infante*, *Face of An Angel*, and *The Last of the Menu Girls*. She has published a children's book, *La Mujer Que Sabía El Idioma de Los Animales/The Woman Who Knew the Language of the Animals*. Chávez performs her one-woman shows, "Women in the State of Grace" and "El Muro/The Wall: A Chorus of Immigrant Women's Voices," throughout the United States. Currently, Chávez is working on a novel, *The King and Queen of Comezón*, a border mystery/love story; a collection of stories, *El Inglés Tan Bonito/Beautiful English*; and a book, *Río Grande Family*, about her Sephardic Jewish roots in Chihuahua and Delicias, México. Chávez is the director of the Border Book Festival, a national and regional book festival based at the Cultural Center de Mesilla, a multicultural bookstore that has recently opened an art gallery, Galería Tepín.

JOHN CLAYTON is the author of *The Cowboy Girl* (University of Nebraska Press, 2007, a finalist for the High Plains Book Award) and the forthcoming *The Last Good Dam*. Raised in Massachusetts, he has lived in a small town in central Montana since 1990. Parts of this essay originally appeared, in shorter and very different form, in *High Country News* and several regional newspapers subscribing to the HCN Writers on the Range syndicate, in the spring of 2004.

JOHN DANIEL was born in South Carolina, raised in the Maryland suburbs of Washington, DC, and immigrated to the Northwest in 1966. After briefly attending Reed College, he worked as a logger, railroad inspector, hod carrier, rock climbing instructor, and poet in the schools. He began to write poetry and prose while living on a ranch in south-central

Oregon and has gone on to author eight books—most recently, *The Far Corner*—and edit one. *Rogue River Journal* won a 2006 Pacific Northwest Booksellers Award, and two books, *The Trail Home* and *Looking After*, have received the Oregon Book Award in literary nonfiction. His work has also been honored with a Pushcart Prize, the John Burroughs Nature Essay Award, a Wallace Stegner Fellowship at Stanford University, and a Creative Writing Fellowship from the National Endowment for the Arts. Daniel has taught widely in writer-in-residence positions at colleges and universities around the country. These days he travels extensively in Oregon. He lives with his wife, Marilyn Daniel, plus a dog, two cats, and usually a packrat, in the Coast Range foothills near Noti, where he is working on a novel.

SALLY DENTON is the author of *The Pink Lady, Passion and Principle, Faith and Betrayal, American Massacre, The Bluegrass Conspiracy*, and, with Roger Morris, *The Money and the Power*. She has been the recipient of a Guggenheim Fellowship, two Western Heritage awards, a Lannan Literary Grant, and the Nevada Silver Pen Award. She has been a Hoover Media fellow, a Woodrow Wilson Center scholar, and has been inducted into the Nevada Writers Hall of Fame. Her award-winning investigative reporting has appeared in the *New York Times, Los Angeles Times, Washington Post, American Heritage, Wild West*, and *Daily Beast*. She lives with her three sons in Santa Fe, New Mexico.

GRETEL EHRLICH was born on a horse ranch in California and was educated at Bennington College and UCLA film school. She is the author of thirteen books, including three collections of narrative essays, a novel, a memoir, three books of poetry, a biography, a book of ethnology/travel, and a children's book, among others. They are *The Solace of Open Spaces; Heart Mountain; Islands, The Universe, Home; A Match to the Heart; Questions of Heaven; A Blizzard Year; John Muir, a Biography; This Cold Heaven;* and *The Future of Ice*. She has published in *Harper's, Atlantic, New York Times Magazine, Time, Life, National Geographic Magazine, National Geographic Adventure, National Geographic Traveler, Aperture, Architectural Digest, Orion, Shambhala Sun, Tricycle, Antaeus*, and *Outside*, among many others.

LOUISE ERDRICH was born in 1954 and grew up in Wahpeton, North Dakota. She has published novels, nonfiction, poetry, children's books, and a short story collection. She received a National Book Critics Circle Award, the Heartland Prize, the O. Henry Prize, and was twice a National

Book Award Finalist, as well as a finalist for the Pulitzer Prize. Her books are published in sixteen languages. At present, she lives in Minnesota and owns Birchbark Books (birchbarkbooks.com). Louise is a member of the Turtle Mountain Band of Chippewa in North Dakota.

GARY FERGUSON has written for a variety of national publications, including *Vanity Fair* and *Los Angeles Times*, and is the author of sixteen books on nature and science. *Hawks Rest: A Season in the Remote Heart of Yellowstone* (National Geographic Adventure Press) was the first nonfiction work in history to win both the Pacific Northwest Booksellers Award and the Mountains and Plains Booksellers Award. *Decade of the Wolf* (Lyons Press) was chosen as the Montana Book of the Year, while *The Great Divide* (W. W. Norton) was an Audubon Magazine Editor's Choice selection. Ferguson was the 2002 Seigle Scholar at Washington University, St. Louis; he also served as the William Kittredge Distinguished Visiting Writer at the University of Montana and was a Distinguished Visiting Writer at the University of Idaho. He is currently on the faculty of the Rainier Writing Workshop at Pacific Lutheran University and is a member of the National Geographic Speakers Bureau. Growing up in the corn and rust of northern Indiana, Gary, at age nine, announced to his parents that he was moving West, to the Rockies. Which is where he's been for the past thirty-two years, mostly in southern Montana, at the edge of the Greater Yellowstone ecosystem.

PETER FISH grew up in Ventura, California. He received a BA in American History from Yale University. He was a Mirrielees Fellow in creative writing at Stanford University and a Hoyns Fellow in fiction at the University of Virginia. He has written and edited for *Sunset Magazine* for many years and is currently *Sunset's* editor-at-large. He has also written for *Health Magazine*, where his work earned a Western Publishers Association Maggie Award. His anthology of California literature, *California's Best: Two Centuries of Great Writing about the Golden State*, was published in 2009. He lives in San Francisco with his wife, Nancy, and son, Joseph.

HAROLD GILLIAM is the former environmental columnist for the *San Francisco Chronicle* and author or coauthor of fourteen books on the environment of Northern California, most recently *Weather of the San Francisco Bay Region* (University of California Press, 2002). In 1962–1963, he worked in Washington DC as assistant to Secretary of the Interior Stewart Udall and later as environmental consultant to the Army Corps of Engineers. He is currently writing a book on the uses of history. His chief recreation is hiking—in Golden Gate Park, at the Presidio of San Francisco, on Mount Tamalpais, and sometimes in the High Sierra, huffing and puffing.

DAVID GUTERSON was born in Seattle in 1956 and spent his childhood and college years there. After college, he taught high school English in the Seattle area and began writing for *Harper's*, where he eventually became a contributing editor. His nonfiction work has appeared in, among other publications, the *New York Times*, *Los Angeles Times*, and *Washington Post*. In 2002, Guterson co-founded Field's End, an organization for writers in the Pacific Northwest. He also mentors writers from the University of Washington's creative writing program. Guterson's books include a collection of short stories, *The Country Ahead of Us, the Country Behind* (1989), and a book of essays called *Family Matters: Why Homeschooling Makes Sense* (1992). He is the author of the novel *Snow Falling on Cedars* (1994), which won the PEN/Faulkner Award for fiction, and his subsequent novels are *East of the Mountains* (1998), *Our Lady of the Forest* (2003), and *The Other* (2008). Of late, his poetry has appeared in *Narrative*, *Poetry Northwest*, *Ploughshares*, and other periodicals. He currently lives on Bainbridge Island, Washington, where he is at work on a new novel and more poetry.

DEBRA GWARTNEY'S 2009 memoir, *Live Through This*, was a finalist for the National Book Critics Circle Award, as well as a finalist for the Books for a Better Life Award. The book was also shortlisted by the Pacific Northwest Booksellers Association and the Oregon Book Award and named one of the *Oregonian*'s top ten books of the year. Debra is co-editor with her husband Barry Lopez of *Home Ground: Language for an American Landscape*. She has deep family roots in Idaho—born in Salmon, Idaho, and raised in the state. She and Barry Lopez currently live on the McKenzie River in Oregon, and Debra teaches in the MFA program at Portland State University.

ALYSON HAGY was raised on a farm in the Blue Ridge Mountains of Virginia. She is the author of six books, including the novel *Snow, Ashes* (Graywolf Press, 2007) and the story collection *Ghosts of Wyoming* (Graywolf Press, 2010). Her work has been published in a number of journals and magazines, including *Ploughshares*, *Shenandoah*, *Virginia Quarterly Review*, and *New York Times Magazine*. Her fiction has also been recorded for National Public Radio. Hagy has received fellowships from the National Endowment for the Arts and the Christopher Isherwood Foundation. Her short stories have been awarded a Nelson Algren Prize and a

Pushcart Prize and have been included in the *Best American Short Stories* series. Hagy currently lives in Laramie, Wyoming, and teaches at the University of Wyoming.

RON HANSEN was born and raised in Omaha, Nebraska. He attended Creighton University, the University of Iowa Writers Workshop, and Stanford University, where he held a Wallace E. Stegner Creative Writing Fellowship. His Western novels include *Desperadoes*, *The Assassination of Jesse James by the Coward Robert Ford*, *Atticus*, and the screwball comedy, *Isn't It Romantic?* He teaches fiction writing and film at Santa Clara University in California.

JIM HARRISON is the author of over thirty books of poetry, nonfiction, and fiction, including *Legends of the Fall*, *The Road Home*, *Dalva*, and his recent novella, *The Farmer's Daughter*. A member of the American Academy of Arts and Letters and winner of a Guggenheim Fellowship, he has had work published in twenty-seven languages. Harrison lived most of his life in Michigan but now divides his time between Montana and Arizona.

ALLISON ADELLE HEDGE COKE holds the Distinguished Paul W. Reynolds and Clarice Kingston Reynolds Endowed Chair of Poetry and Writing at the University of Nebraska, Kearney, and is a Great Plains Fellow at the Center for Great Plains Studies, University of Nebraska at Lincoln. Her five authored books include: the American Book Award-winning poetry volume, *Dog Road Woman*, and the labor poetry volume, *Off-Season City Pipe*, both from Coffee House Press; *Rock Ghost, Willow, Deer*, an AIROS Book-of-the-Month memoir from the University of Nebraska Press; and *Blood Run*, a verse-play from Salt Publications. She has published fiction in *Best American Fiction*, *Black Renaissance Noire*, *Indian Country Noir* (Akashic), and *Bombay Gin*. Hedge Coke has edited eight additional collections, including *Ahani* from Oregon State University, *Effigies* from Salt Publications, and *Sing* from the University of Arizona. A legal resident of South Dakota, born in the Texas panhandle, fostered into Colorado, Kansas, and Oklahoma, and otherwise raised in North Carolina and Canada, she came of age working fields, waters, horses, and in factories.

JIM HEPWORTH grew up in southern Idaho and eastern Washington. He lives now in Lewiston, Idaho, where he is the publisher of Confluence Press, a professor of Humanities at Lewis-Clark State College, and special projects coordinator for the college's Center for Arts and History. Books under his imprint have won a Small Press Book Award, two Idaho Book Awards, two Pacific Northwest Booksellers Awards, and four Western States Book Awards. He is the author of a collection of poems, *Silence as a Method of Birth Control*, and a book of interviews with Wallace Stegner, *Stealing Glances*. He is also the co-editor of *Resist Much, Obey Little: Some Notes on Edward Abbey* (with Greg McNamee) and *The Stories that Shape Us* (with Teresa Jordan). Hepworth's essays, articles, and interviews have appeared in a variety of anthologies and periodicals, including *Outside Magazine*, the *Oregonian*, and *Bloomsbury Review*, where he is a contributing editor.

JANE HIRSHFIELD is the author of six books of poetry, most recently *After* (HarperCollins, 2006), named a "best book of 2006" by the *Washington Post, San Francisco Chronicle*, and England's *Financial Times*. Her fifth collection, *Given Sugar, Given Salt*, was a finalist for the National Book Critics Circle Award. Other books include a now-classic collection of essays, *Nine Gates: Entering the Mind of Poetry* (HarperCollins, 1997), and three books collecting the work of women poets from the past. Other honors include fellowships from the Guggenheim and Rockefeller Foundations, the National Endowment for the Arts, and the Academy of American Poets. Her work appears in the *New Yorker, Atlantic, Times Literary Supplement, New Republic, Poetry, Orion, McSweeney's*, and five editions of *The Best American Poems*. Hirshfield has taught at UC Berkeley, Bennington College, and the University of San Francisco and has been a visiting writer at universities and literary festivals throughout America and abroad. Born in New York City and educated at Princeton University, she arrived West in 1974 in a red van with tie-dyed curtains. She has lived in Northern California since that time; from 1984, on the hem of Mount Tamalpais in the San Francisco Bay Area.

A sixth-generation Utahn and longtime wilderness advocate with the Southern Utah Wilderness Alliance, AMY IRVINE lives with her family in southwest Colorado, where she writes and keeps goats. Her second book, *Trespass: Living at the Edge of the Promised Land*, won the 2008 Orion Book Award and the 2008 Colorado Book Award.

LOUIS B. JONES is the author of the novels *Ordinary Money, Particles and Luck*, and *California's Over*.

STEPHEN GRAHAM JONES is the author of six novels and one story collection and teaches in the MFA program at CU Boulder. Born in Midland, Texas, he grew up all over West Texas and lived as far south as Austin and as far east as Tallahassee before finally getting to Colorado. And, though he claims not to write essays, this is his third or so non-essay to get published. Before this, the only time he'd written on "The West" was a few of his definitions for *Home Ground*—and all of his novels and stories, none of which take place anywhere else.

Raised as part of the fourth (and last) generation on an isolated cattle ranch in Wyoming, **TERESA JORDAN** has written or edited seven books about Western rural life and culture, including the memoir *Riding the White Horse Home* and the classic study of women on ranches and in the rodeo, *Cowgirls: Women of the American West*. With her husband, Hal Cannon, she created *The Open Road*, a series of documentary features about the outback West, for *The Savvy Traveler* on Public Radio International. Recipient of the Western Heritage Award from the Cowboy Hall of Fame for scriptwriting and a literary fellowship from the National Endowment for the Arts as well as other literary awards, she lives in Salt Lake City, Utah, where she is also a visual artist. Most recently, she has started working with the Salt Lake City Public Library to create a community-focused, interactive website.

ED KEMMICK was born in Mahtomedi, Minnesota, in 1955 and, except for four years spent back in the Twin Cities, has resided in Montana since 1973. He has lived in Bozeman, Missoula, Anaconda, and Butte, and since 1989 has called Billings home. He has worked as a reporter and editor for thirty years and is now a reporter and columnist for the *Billings Gazette*. He and his wife, Lisa, have three grown daughters.

MAXINE HONG KINGSTON was born on October 27, 1940, in Stockton, California, and now lives in Oakland, California, with Earll Kingston, a fourth-generation resident of Oakland. She graduated from UC Berkeley and taught there, as well as in schools in Hawai'i and Oakland. Her books are *The Woman Warrior*, *China Men*, *Tripmaster Monkey*, *Hawai'i One Summer*, *The Fifth Book of Peace*, and *To Be the Poet*. She's edited two anthologies: *The Literature of California: Native American Beginnings to 1945* and *Veterans of War Veterans of Peace*. Her most recent book, *I Love a Broad Margin to My Life*, is a poem of 5,226 lines.

WALTER KIRN is a fiction writer and essayist living in Livingston, Montana. His books include *Up in the Air*, the novel that served as the basis for the feature film; *Lost in the Meritocracy*, a memoir about his troubled undergraduate years at Princeton University; and *Thumbsucker*, another novel that was made into a movie. His book reviews, essays, and reported pieces regularly appear in the *New York Times, Atlantic, Rolling Stone,* and numerous other publications. He has two children, Maisie and Charlie.

WILLIAM KITTREDGE grew up on the MC Ranch, a horseback cow outfit in the Great Basin country of southeastern Oregon. After a decade of running the farm operations on the ranch, some eight thousand acres, his family sold out in 1967, and he went on to the Iowa Writers' Workshop and lucked into a teaching job in the MFA program at the University of Montana in Missoula. He still lives there, except in the winter when he goes south seeking warmth, someplace where "they've heard about snow but they've never seen any." Kittredge worked with Richard Hugo and hung out with James Welch and Jim Crumley and the like and taught for twenty-nine years, until he retired in 1997. Over the years, he has helped edit anthologies such as *The Last Best Place* and the *Portable Western Reader;* published a memoir, *Hole in the Sky,* dozens of stories, essays, and a novel, *The Willow Field.* He's presently at work on another novel.

MELISSA KWASNY is the author of four books of poetry: *The Nine Senses* (Milkweed Editions), *Reading Novalis in Montana* (Milkweed, 2009), *Thistle* (Lost Horse Press, 2006), and *The Archival Birds* (Bear Star Press, 2000). She is also the editor of *Toward the Open Field: Poets on the Art of Poetry 1800–1950* (Wesleyan University Press, 2004) and co-editor with M. L. Smoker of *I Go to the Ruined Place: Contemporary Poems in Defense of Global Human Rights* (Lost Horse Press, 2009). She was born in LaPorte, Indiana, and has lived in Montana, but for a few years in San Francisco, since 1974.

PAGE LAMBERT leads creative outdoor adventures, often working in partnership with organizations such as the Women's Wilderness Institute, the Grand Canyon Field Institute, and the Aspen Writers' Foundation. Her River Writing Journeys for Women were hailed by *O, the Oprah Magazine* as "one of six great all-girl getaways of 2006." Born in Colorado, she calls the Rockies west of Denver, the Black Hills of northeast Wyoming, the high desert of Santa Fe, and the rivers and canyons of Utah, home. Winner of the 2009 Orlando Nonfiction Award from AROHO, she is the author of the memoir *In Search of Kinship* (a Rocky Mountain best seller) and the novel *Shifting Stars* (finalist for the Mountains and Plains Book Award). Recipient of two literary fellowships from the Wyoming Arts Council and a fellow at Jentel, her work has appeared in, among other publications, the *Writer*; *Sojourns* (journal of the Peaks, Plateaus and Canyon Association); *Christian Science Monitor*; *Homeland: Ranching and a West that Works*; *Ranching West of the 100th Meridian*; *Deep West: A Literary Tour of Wyoming*; *Writing Down the River: Into the Heart of Grand Canyon*; *Parabola: Magazine of Myth and Tradition*; *Heart Shots: Women Write about Hunting*; and *The Stories that Shape Us: Contemporary Women Write about the West.*

DAVID LEE, reared in the skillet-flat Texas panhandle, is the author of seventeen books, including *A Legacy of Shadows: Selected Poems* and *So Quietly the Earth*. He received the Western States Book Award, Mountain and Plains States Booksellers Award, Utah Book Award, and a Critics Choice Award. He has been nominated for the Pulitzer Prize and National Book Award. He received multiple fellowships from the National Endowment for the Arts and the National Endowment for the Humanities. He served as Utah's first poet laureate from 1997–2003. After thirty-two years of service, he retired from Southern Utah University in 2003. He won every teaching award given by the university, including being named Professor of the Year on three occasions. He presently lives very quietly on his huge four-acre ranch outside Bandera, Texas, where he scribbles and wanders local roads and trails, all at about the same rate and pace.

URSULA K. LE GUIN has published twenty-one novels, eleven volumes of short stories, three collections of essays, twelve books for children, six volumes of poetry, and four of translation. Her best-known fantasy works, the six Books of Earthsea, have sold millions of copies in America and England and have been translated into sixteen languages. Her first major work of science fiction, *The Left Hand of Darkness*, is considered epoch-making in the field for its radical investigation of gender roles and its moral and literary complexity. Le Guin has received many awards, including multiple Hugos and Nebulas, a Pushcart Prize, a National Book Award, and a PEN/Malamud Award. Her most recent publications include a volume of poetry, *Incredible Good Fortune*; the novel *Lavinia*; and an essay collection, *Cheek by Jowl*. She lives in Portland, Oregon.

CRAIG LESLEY is the author of four novels, a memoir, and two anthologies. His work has earned awards from the Pacific Northwest Booksellers Association. He is the recipient of two National Endowment for the Humanities grants, a National Endowment for the Arts fellowship, and a Bread Loaf fellowship. *Winterkill* won the Western Writers of America best novel of the year. He is currently the Senior Writer-in-Residence at Portland State University.

PATRICIA NELSON LIMERICK is the faculty director and chair of the board of the Center of the American West at CU Boulder, where she is also a professor of history. Limerick has dedicated her career to bridging the gap between academics and the general public and to demonstrating the benefits of applying historical perspective to contemporary dilemmas and conflicts. Limerick has received a number of awards and honors recognizing the impact of her scholarship and her commitment to teaching, including the MacArthur Fellowship and the Hazel Barnes Prize, CU's highest award for teaching and research. She has served as president of several professional organizations, advised documentary and film projects, and served two tours as a Pulitzer nonfiction jurist. She regularly engages the public on the op-ed pages of local and national newspapers and in the summer of 2005, she served as a guest columnist for the *New York Times*. Limerick has authored, co-authored, or edited more than a dozen books and reports as well as a multitude of articles. Her books include *The Legacy of Conquest: The Unbroken Past of the American West* (1987) and *Something in the Soil: Legacies and Reckonings in the New West* (2000).

KENNETH LINCOLN grew up in the northwest of Nebraska, south of Wounded Knee, and has taught Contemporary and Native American Literatures for forty-one years at UCLA. Beginning with *Native American Renaissance* (California 1983), *The Good Red Road* (Harper & Row 1987), and *Ind'n Humor* (Oxford 1993), he has published many books in American Indian Studies and written novels, poetry, and original essays about Western Americana. His latest books are *White Boy Blues* (Fulcrum, 2007), *Speak Like Singing: Classics of Native American Literature* (University of New Mexico Press, 2007), and *Cormac McCarthy: American Canticles* (Palgrave/Macmillan, 2008). He lives in Santa Fe, New Mexico, and is presently writing *A Man's Word: Meditations on Masculine Literacy*.

BETH LOFFREDA grew up in Audubon, Pennsylvania, and later attended the University of Virginia and Rutgers University. In 1998, she moved west to Laramie for a position at the University of Wyoming, where she is now an associate professor of English. She currently directs the university's MFA Program in Creative Writing and teaches courses in nonfiction writing and contemporary fiction. Her book, *Losing Matt Shepard: Life and Politics in the Aftermath of Anti-Gay Murder*, was published in 2000 by Columbia University Press.

BARRY LOPEZ is the author of thirteen works of fiction and nonfiction, including *Arctic Dreams* for which he received the National Book

Award. His writing takes him regularly to remote and densely populated parts of the world and he collaborates frequently with a variety of artists on a diverse range of projects. He is a recipient of the Award in Literature from the American Academy of Arts and Letters, the John Burroughs and John Hay medals, and fellowships from the Lannan and Guggenheim Foundations. His essays and short stories appear often in American and foreign magazines and are in dozens of anthologies, including *Best American Essays*, *Best Spiritual Writing*, and the "best" collections from *National Geographic*, *Georgia Review*, *Paris Review*, *Orion*, *Witness*, *Outside*, and other periodicals.

LARRY MCMURTRY is a novelist, screenwriter, and bookseller. He currently divides his time between Tucson and his bookstores in Archer City, Texas, where the stock of his bookshops fills five buildings.

DAVID MAS MASUMOTO is an organic farmer and the author of five books, including *Wisdom of the Last Farmer*, *Heirlooms*, *Letters to the Valley*, *Four Seasons in Five Senses*, *Harvest Son*, and *Epitaph for a Peach*. A third-generation farmer, Masumoto grows peaches, nectarines, grapes, and raisins on an organic eighty-acre farm south of Fresno, California. Masumoto is currently a columnist for the *Fresno Bee*. He was a 2006–2008 Kellogg Foundation Food and Society Policy Fellow. His writing awards include Commonwealth Club Silver medal, Julia Child Cookbook award, the James Clavell Literacy Award, and he was a finalist in the James Beard Foundation awards. *Wisdom of the Last Farmer* was honored as "Best Environmental Writing in 2009" by National Resources Defense Council. Masumoto received the "Award of Distinction" from UC Davis in 2003 and the California Central Valley "Excellence in Business" Award in 2007. He is currently a board member of the James Irvine Foundation and the Public Policy Institute of California. He has served as chair of the California Council for the Humanities. Masumoto is married to Marcy Masumoto, Ed.d., and they have a daughter, Nikiko, and a son, Korio.

Originally from the corn-and-soybean country of southern Minnesota, **KENT MEYERS** moved west of the Missouri River to Spearfish, South Dakota, in 1980. He is the author of the novels *The River Warren* (Hungry Mind/Harcourt, 1998), *The Work Of Wolves* (Harcourt, 2004), and *Twisted Tree* (Houghton-Mifflin-Harcourt, 2009), the collection of short stories, *Light in the Crossing* (St. Martin's, 1999), and a collection of essays, *The Witness Of Combines* (University of Minnesota Press, 1998). *The River Warren* and *Light in the Crossing* were listed as Notable Books by the

New York Times. The Work of Wolves was named to the *Christian Science Monitor*'s list of best books and also won the Mountains and Plains Booksellers Association Award and the American Library Association's Alex Award. Meyers's fiction and essays have appeared in the *Georgia Review, Southern Review, Sonora Review,* and elsewhere, and his stories have been anthologized in both *The Best of the West* and *Best American Mystery Stories.* Meyers is writer-in-residence at Black Hills State University, where he teaches Literature of the American West and creative writing.

TOM MILLER writes about the American Southwest and Latin America. His ten books include *Revenge of the Saguaro, The Panama Hat Trail,* and *Trading With the Enemy: A Yankee Travels Through Castro's Cuba.* He has written for *Smithsonian,* the *New York Times, Natural History,* and *Life,* among other publications, and his papers have been archived at the University of Arizona library. In 2008, Miller was proclaimed a Huésped Ilustre de Quito (Illustrious Guest of Quito) for his literary contribution to Ecuador. He owns some eighty versions of the song "La Bamba."

GARY NABHAN was one of the dozen Westerners who helped forge the rancher-environmentalist manifesto Finding the Radical Center. His twenty-some books of prose and poetry bridge nature writing with food writing, and natural science with Franciscan spirituality. He tends an orchard of heritage fruits in Patagonia, Arizona.

ANTONYA NELSON is the author of four novels, including *Bound* (Bloomsbury, 2010), and six short story collections, including *Nothing Right* (Bloomsbury, 2009). She is the recipient of the USA Artists Simon Award in 2009, the 2003 Rea Award for Short Fiction, as well as National Endowment for the Arts and Guggenheim Fellowships. She teaches in the Warren Wilson MFA Program, as well as in the University of Houston's Creative Writing Program. She lives in Telluride, Colorado; Las Cruces, New Mexico; and Houston, Texas. She has also "lived" in Bonanza, Colorado, in a 1965 Airstream trailer, and in the summer of 2010, from that trailer, she listened to her husband cut plumbing into the 140-year-old post office that they are transforming into a dwelling. They own, as well, a defunct mine and the cemetery.

DAN O'BRIEN is the author of a short story collection, five novels, three memoirs, and the text for a photography book on the Great Plains. He was born and raised in Ohio, but came to the plains of South Dakota in 1970 where he worked with several conservation groups to help restore peregrine falcons to their historic range. He lives with Chef Jill Maguire between the Black Hills and Badlands National Park in western South Dakota. They operate a buffalo ranch and promote Great Plains restoration through the sale of grass-fed and field-harvested buffalo meat. Their company is Wild Idea Buffalo Company, located in Rapid City, South Dakota. He is currently working on a young adult novel.

LAURA PRITCHETT is the author/editor of five books. Her fiction includes the novels *Sky Bridge* and *Hell's Bottom, Colorado;* her three anthologies include *Pulse of the River*, *Home Land*, and *Going Green: True Tales from Gleaners, Scavengers, and Dumpster Divers*. Pritchett has also published over one hundred essays and short stories in numerous magazines, including *The Sun*, *Orion*, *High Country News*, and *High Desert Journal*. Her work has received numerous awards, including the PEN USA Award, the Colorado Book Award, and the Milkweed National Fiction Prize. Pritchett received her BA and MA in English at Colorado State University and her PhD in Contemporary American Literature/Creative Writing at Purdue University. She teaches writing around the country and is a member of the faculty at Denver's Lighthouse Writers Workshop. She lives in northern Colorado, near the ranch where she was raised.

LEE ANN RORIPAUGH'S third volume of poetry, *On the Cusp of a Dangerous Year*, was published by Southern Illinois University Press in 2009. A second volume, *Year of the Snake*, also published by Southern Illinois University Press, was named winner of the Association of Asian American Studies Book Award in Poetry/Prose for 2004. Her first book, *Beyond Heart Mountain* (Penguin Books, 1999), was a 1998 winner of the National Poetry Series. The recipient of a 2003 Archibald Bush Foundation Individual Artist Fellowship, she was also named the 2004 winner of the *Prairie Schooner* Strousse Award, the 2001 winner of the Frederick Manfred Award for Best Creative Writing awarded by the Western Literature Association, and the 1995 winner of the Randall Jarrell International Poetry Prize. Roripaugh was born and raised in Laramie, Wyoming, and is currently an associate professor of English at the University of South Dakota in Vermillion, South Dakota.

RUSSELL ROWLAND was born to a rodeo clown and a teacher, creating an immediate dilemma about the relative seriousness of life. He returned to his home state of Montana in 2007 after living in thirteen different states in twenty years. He has worked as a lounge singer, a ranch hand, a college professor, and a fortune cookie writer. His first novel, *In Open Spaces* (Harpercollins, 2002), made the *San Francisco Chronicle*'s best-seller list and was named among the "Best of the West" by the *Salt Lake City Tribune*. The sequel, *The Watershed Years* (Riverbend, 2007) was a finalist for the High Plains Book Award for fiction. He has an MA in Creative Writing from Boston University, and is fiction editor of *New West Magazine*.

KRIS SAKNUSSEMM is the author of the novels *Zanesville* and *Private Midnight*. His shorter work has appeared in a wide range of literary journals, including the *Boston Review*, *Hudson Review*, *Antioch Review*, *Prairie Schooner*, *Zyzzyva*, and *Chelsea*. A native of the San Francisco Bay Area, he traveled widely in the American West as a child before moving farther west, to Australia and the Pacific Islands, where he has lived for many years.

GREG SARRIS was born and raised in Santa Rosa, California, and, after nearly thirty years away, he has returned, teaching American Literature and Creative Writing at Sonoma State University, where he holds the Graton Endowed Chair in Native American Literature and Humanities. He received his PhD in Modern Thought and Literature from Stanford University, where he was awarded the Walter Gore Award for Excellence in Teaching. He has published several books, including the widely anthologized collection of essays, *Keeping Slug Woman Alive: A Holistic Approach to American Indian Texts*; a novel, *Watermelon Nights*; and an award-winning collection of short stories, *Grand Avenue*, which he adapted for an HBO miniseries of the same name and co-executive produced with Robert Redford. He has written several plays and pilot scripts for Showtime and HBO. Before returning to Sonoma County, he lived in Los Angeles, where he was first a full professor of English at UCLA and then the Fletcher Jones Professor of Creative Writing and Literature at Loyola Marymount University. He has completed a cycle of children's stories, *How a Mountain Was Made*, and is currently finishing a novel. An enrolled member of the Federated Indians of Graton Rancheria, he is serving his eighth consecutive elected term as the tribe's chairman.

ANNICK SMITH is the author of the memoir *Homestead*, a collection of essays, *In This We Are Native*, and a history of the tallgrass prairies, *Big Bluestem*. She was coeditor with William Kittredge of the Montana anthology, *The Last Best Place*, and coeditor with Susan O'Connor of *The Wide Open—Prose, Poems and Photographs of the Prairie*. Her short stories and essays have appeared in many magazines and journals including *Story, Outside, Orion, Audubon, Travel & Leisure*, and the *NY Times Traveler*. She was executive producer of the feature, *Heartland*, and co-producer of *A River Runs Through It*. Her documentary credits include a public television series about seven tribes in the Inland Northwest, *The Real People*, as well as a portrait of poet Richard Hugo, *Kicking the Loose Gravel Home*. Smith has taught creative writing at the University of Montana, as well as numerous writing workshops and conferences. She is currently completing a dog/memoir/travel book, *Crossing the Plains with Vruno*. She was born in Paris and raised in Chicago, but has lived in Montana's Blackfoot Valley for many years.

GARY SNYDER grew up in the Pacific Northwest where he worked on the family farm and seasonally in the woods. He graduated from Reed College in Portland in 1951 and went on to study linguistics at Indiana University and East Asian languages at UC Berkeley. At the same time he managed to be part of the Beat writers scene in San Francisco with Kerouac, Ginsberg, Whalen, and others. In 1956 he moved to Kyoto to study Zen Buddhism and East Asian culture. In 1969 he returned to Turtle Island and for the last twenty-nine years he has been living in the Yuba river country of the northern Sierra Nevada. Snyder has also traveled widely, lecturing and giving poetry readings, teaching Buddhist thought and practice, and "exploring the mythopoetic interface of society, ecology, and language." On his home ground he works with the Yuba Watershed Institute focusing on sustainable forestry issues and community interactions with public land. He formerly taught at UC Davis in creative writing and the innovative cross-disciplinary Nature and Culture program. These days he's back to writing and doing local chores.

SUSANNA SONNENBERG is the author of the memoir *Her Last Death*. Her essays have appeared in *O, the Oprah Magazine, Elle*, and *San Francisco Chronicle*, among other publications, and her work is included in the anthologies *About What Was Lost, Behind the Bedroom Door*, and *The Secret Currency of Love*. Raised in New York City, she has lived in Missoula, Montana, since 1993.

LYNN STEGNER spent the best part of her early years in the stern of a twenty-six-foot skiff, trolling for salmon in Puget Sound and the San Juan Archipelago. She has written three novels, *Undertow, Fata Morgana*, and *Because a Fire Was in My Head*, which won the 2007 Faulkner Award for Best Novel, was a Literary Ventures Selection, a Book Sense Pick, and a

New York Times Editors' Choice. Her novella triptych, *Pipers at the Gates of Dawn*, was awarded the Faulkner Society's Gold Medal for best novella of 1997. She has also written short stories, poems, and essays, including a critical introduction to her father-in-law's short fiction, *Collected Stories of Wallace Stegner*, as well as editing a Penguin edition entitled *Wallace Stegner: On Teaching and Writing Fiction*. Ms. Stegner has taught at the University of California, Santa Cruz; University of Vermont; National University of Ireland, Galway; College of Santa Fe; and currently for Stanford University's Continuing Studies Program. Among other honors, she has been the recipient of a Western States Arts Council Fellowship, a National Endowment for the Arts fellowship, a Fulbright scholarship to Ireland, the Bridport Prize, and a Raymond Carver Short Story Award. At work on a volume of stories called *The Anarchic Hand*, she divides her time between a mud house on a dirt road in New Mexico and a log cabin in northern Vermont, with her husband, the writer Page Stegner, and their daughter, Allison, a newly minted paleoecologist.

PAGE STEGNER was born in Salt Lake City, Utah, in 1937. He attended Stanford University, where he received his BA in History in 1959 and his PhD in American Literature in 1964. From 1965 to 1995, he was professor of American Literature and director of the Creative Writing Program at the University of California, Santa Cruz, retiring in 1995 to devote full time to writing. He currently lives with his wife, novelist Lynn Stegner, and his daughter, Allison, in Santa Fe, New Mexico, and Greensboro, Vermont. He has been the recipient of a National Endowment for the Arts Fellowship (1979–1980), a National Endowment for the Humanities Fellowship (1980–1981), and a Guggenheim Fellowship (1981–1982). Page is the author of three novels, two works of literary criticism, three collections of essays on the American West, a natural history of the Grand Canyon, a history of the opening of the American West, and he has been a frequent contributor over the past thirty-five years to numerous publications, including *Harper's, Atlantic, Esquire, Audubon, Outside, Sierra, New York Review of Books, New West, Los Angeles Times, Arizona Highways, National Parks, Geo, McCalls, Mademoiselle*, and many others.

STEPHEN TRIMBLE has received a broad range of awards for his photography, his nonfiction, and his fiction, including: the Sierra Club's Ansel Adams Award for photography and conservation; the National Cowboy Museum's Western Heritage "Wrangler" Award; a Wallace Stegner Centennial Fellowship at the University of Utah Tanner Humanities Center; and a Doctor of Humane Letters from his alma mater, Colorado College, honoring his efforts to increase our understanding of Western landscapes and peoples. As writer, editor, and photographer, Trimble has published twenty-two books, including *Bargaining for Eden: The Fight for the Last Open Spaces in America; Lasting Light: 125 Years of Grand Canyon Photography; The Geography of Childhood: Why Children Need Wild Places* (with Gary Paul Nabhan); *The Sagebrush Ocean: A Natural History of the Great Basin; The People: Indians of the American Southwest;* and *Talking With the Clay: The Art of Pueblo Pottery in the 21st Century.* Trimble teaches writing in the University of Utah Honors College and makes his home in Salt Lake City and in the redrock country of Torrey, Utah.

DOUGLAS UNGER was born in Moscow, Idaho, and is the author of four novels, including *Leaving the Land*, a finalist for the Pulitzer and Robert F. Kennedy awards, and *Voices from Silence*, a year's end selection of the *Washington Post Book World*. His most recent book is *Looking for War and Other Stories*. Douglas Unger is the co-founder of the MFA in Creative Writing International program and Schaeffer PhD with Creative Dissertation at the University of Nevada, Las Vegas. He serves on the executive boards of *Words Without Borders*, Point of Contact/Punto de Contacto, and on the editorial advisory board of The Americas Series (formerly TALI) with Texas Tech University Press. He worked for five years as grants and acquisitions director for the International Institute of Modern Letters, and he travels extensively in support of literary activism around the world.

LARRY WATSON was born in Rugby, North Dakota, where both his father and paternal grandfather were sheriffs. His maternal grandfather was a cowboy in Montana in the early 1900s before homesteading in North Dakota. Larry attended public schools in Bismarck, North Dakota, and received his BA and MA from the University of North Dakota and his PhD in creative writing from the University of Utah. He and his wife Susan live in Milwaukee, Wisconsin, where Larry is a visiting professor at Marquette University. Larry is the author of the Montana trilogy, *Montana 1948*, *Justice*, and *White Crosses*, and other novels. He has published stories and poems in *Gettysburg Review*, *New England Review*, *North American Review*, and other journals and quarterlies. His book reviews have appeared in the *Los Angeles Times*, *Chicago Sun-Times*, *Washington Post*, and elsewhere. His work has been anthologized in *Essays for Contemporary Culture*, *Imagining Home*, *Off the Beaten Path: Stories from the Nature Conservancies*, *Baseball and the Game of Life*, *The Most Wonderful Books*, *These United States*, and *Writing America*. He has received two fiction writing fellowships from the National Endowment for the Arts. Watson's latest novel is *American Boy*.

TERRY TEMPEST WILLIAMS is a writer and a lifelong Westerner who migrates between the Colorado Plateau and the Greater Yellowstone ecosystem, where her work and words are rooted. Her books include *Refuge—An Unnatural History of Place*; *Leap*; *Red—Patience and Passion in the Desert*; *The Open Space of Democracy*; and most recently, *Finding Beauty in a Broken World*. She is a monthly columnist for the *Progressive* magazine, and her essays have been published in newspapers and anthologies worldwide. A recipient of a John Simon Guggenheim Fellowship and a Lannan Literary Fellowship in creative nonfiction, she has received the Bob Marshall Award from the Wilderness Society, their highest honor given to an American citizen. She also received the Distinguished Achievement Award from the Western American Literature Association and the Wallace Stegner Award given by the Center for the American West. In 2009, Terry Tempest Williams was featured in Ken Burns's PBS series on the National Parks. She is the Annie Clark Tanner Scholar in Environmental Humanities at the University of Utah.

LARRY WOIWODE'S fiction has appeared in the *Atlantic*, *GQ*, *Harper's*, *Paris Review*, *Partisan Review*, and elsewhere, including two dozen stories in the *New Yorker*, and has been chosen for four volumes of *The Best American Short Stories*. His novels include *What I'm Going To Do, I Think*, winner of the William Faulkner Foundation Award; *Beyond the Bedroom Wall*, finalist for the National Book Award and Book Critics Circle Award; *Born Brothers*; and *Indian Affairs*. His stories are collected in *The Neumiller Stories* and *Silent Passengers*. In 1995, he received the Award of Merit from the American Academy of Arts and Letters for "distinction in the art of the short story." His memoir, *What I Think I Did*, was his sixth book to be named "notable book" of the year by the *New York Times Book Review*. He is a Guggenheim and a Lannan Fellow, has conducted writing seminars and workshops in the U.S. and Europe, and for three years, he directed the creative writing program at SUNY-Binghamton. He lives in southwestern North Dakota where he and his wife Carole raise registered quarterhorses, dividing his time between there and Jamestown College, where he is writer in residence.

Born and raised in southern Illinois, **ROBERT WRIGLEY** took a graduate degree at the University of Montana and has lived since 1977 in Idaho. His eighth book of poems, *Beautiful Country*, was published by Penguin

Books in 2010. He is also the author of *Earthly Meditations: New and Selected Poems* (Penguin, 2006); *Lives of the Animals* (Penguin, 2003), winner of the 2005 Poets Prize; and *Reign of Snakes* (Penguin, 1999), winner of the 2000 Kingsley Tufts Award in Poetry. *In the Bank of Beautiful Sins* (Penguin, 1995) won the San Francisco Poetry Center Book Award. His poems have appeared in the *New Yorker*, *Atlantic*, and *Poetry*, among many other magazines, and his work has been twice reprinted in the *Best American Poetry* anthology and six times in the Pushcart Prize collections. Recipient of fellowships from the Guggenheim Foundation, the Rockefeller Foundation, as well as two from the National Endowment for the Arts, Wrigley is professor of English and teaches in the MFA Program in Writing at the University of Idaho.

WILLARD WYMAN was born in China in 1930, the son of a career Army officer, and spent his childhood on cavalry posts in the West. He did not begin writing until he retired from an academic career, his childhood with horses providing ample material. During World War II—with his father in combat and his mother in a psychiatric ward—he was shipped to Montana to the Spear-O Ranch, an experience that led to a lifelong devotion to packing into the mountains of the West. After teaching and coaching high school football, he began graduate work at Stanford. After taking his PhD, he taught English and served as a dean of students. He went on to serve on the faculty at Colby College before becoming headmaster of the Thacher School, where horses remain a central part of the curriculum. The Western Writers of America named his novel, *High Country*, which draws upon his packing experiences, "Best First Novel." More importantly, they named it "Best Novel of the West." He has also published in *Epoch*. His second novel will be published in 2011.